MW00835136

في ذكرى

مارك لينز

INTERFAITH SERIES

Series Editor
Joshua Ralston

OTHER BOOKS BY MOUCHIR BASILE AOUN

Philosophy

La polis heideggerienne, lieu de réconciliation de l'être et du politique

Frédéric Gentz: De la paix perpétuelle

Philosophie et religion. Études sur l'athéisme contemporain

*Herméneutique philosophique. Histoire occidentale
des théories de l'interprétation*

Heidegger et la pensée arabe

*Une pensée arabe humaniste contemporaine. Paul Khoury
et les promesses de l'incomplétude humaine*

*Ces Libanais! Essai sur les symptômes de pathologie
structurelle de la personnalité libanaise*

Anthropologies croisées. Essai sur l'interculturalité arabe

Pensée philosophique contemporaine au Liban (ed.)

Pensée philosophique contemporaine en Syrie (co-ed.)

Pensée philosophique contemporaine en Tunisie (co-ed.)

Précis de philosophie française (ed.), 10 vols, vols I–IV

*La révolution qui s'annonce. La philosophie engagée
en faveur du soulèvement libanais*

Pour un nouveau pacte au Liban. Lectures critiques et prospectives (co-ed.)

Métaphysique. Questions fondamentales

L'homme sous les auspices de l'être. Heidegger en arabe

Science of religions

The Arab Christ

Towards an Arab Christian theology of conviviality

Mouchir Basile Aoun

Translated from the French by Sarah Patey

First English edition published in 2022 by
Gingko
4 Molasses Row
London SW11 3UX

First published in French by Les Éditions du Cerf in 2016
Copyright © Les Éditions du Cerf 2016
The English language translation Copyright © Sarah Patey 2022

Mouchir Basile Aoun has asserted his rights under the Copyright, Designs and Patent Act 1988 to be identified as the author of this work.

A CIP catalogue record for this book is available from the British Library.

All rights reserved. Except for brief quotations in a review, no part of this book may be reproduced in any form or by any electronic or mechanical means, including information storage and retrieval systems, without written permission from the publisher.

ISBN 978-1-914983-02-3
e-ISBN 978-1-914983-03-0

Typeset in Times by MacGuru Ltd
Printed in the United Kingdom by Clays Ltd, Elcograf S.p.A.

www.gingko.org.uk
@GingkoLibrary

Contents

The painful advent of the Arab Christ

Sociopolitical and sociocultural conditions are evolving and changing in the West, giving rise to a slow yet profound mutation in both the patterns and ways of thinking. Nothing of the kind has happened in the Arab Middle East. Conditions may undergo radical change from one decade to another, but philosophical, theological and political discourse remains more or less the same, with rigid concepts expressed in sclerotic pronouncements.

The reflections in the French edition of my book *Le Christ arabe*, which I wrote around twenty years ago, were formulated well before its publication by Cerf in 2016, against a geopolitical and sociocultural background that was very different from the present situation in the Arab world. Arab countries are sinking irretrievably into chaos; political ideologies that previously held undisputed sway are being fractured and undermined by loss of trust and social cohesion; social structures imposed by ideological despotism are being blown apart, leaving Arab men and women in torment and despair.

The numbers of Christians in the societies of the Arab world are falling irrecoverably, with the result that their presence is increasingly becoming symbolic, particularly in those countries where they have formerly had demographically significant representation, especially in Iraq and Syria. Even in Lebanon, which has been battered by its structural contradictions and confessional tensions, there is a dramatic fall in the Christian population. At a deep level, this is due to the widespread state of mind among Christians. It finds expression in a feeling of existential disillusionment and national bitterness. Young Lebanese, especially among the Christian communities, no longer believe the country has any political future and are no longer keen to marry and have children; above all, they are leaving the country for good in large numbers. Any prospect of a Christian presence in Lebanon is clearly permanently compromised by this haemorrhaging of the population, which undermines any desire to bear witness to the faith.

This gloomy picture is sadly reflected across the Arab world, which offers little real hope in the third decade of the twenty-first century. Arab societies are disintegrating, in the Mashriq and the Maghreb, and there is little prospect of anything better. At the most, one can expect some kind of grim end to the political and economic crises that are crushing these profoundly destabilised countries – the same societies that once upon a time were hoping to welcome all that the end of the Cold War promised, including economic, scientific, technical and cultural globalisation. When the despotic Arab regimes collapsed, a deep abyss was created in the collective Arab unconscious that was not yet sufficiently mature or rigorously trained to rise with dignity to the challenges of the changes experienced by the population.

Cue another monster, Islamism – with all its divisions, and the variety of its groupings and of their claims – to enter and join the general dance of events. From pure and hard Islam to moderate Islam, only one voice rang out: Islam is the only regime that conforms to the Law of God as written in the Koran and called to rule all human life from now on. Arab Christians thus found themselves trapped in the mechanism of a humiliating, agonising choice: either submit to Islamic rule, or surrender to the dictatorship of Arab tribalism claiming to be humanist, socialist and secular. The so-called liberal spirit of the countries in the Arabian–Persian Gulf is still plagued by structural incoherence. On the one hand, it aims to adapt to the requirements of technical modernity conveyed through globalisation; on the other hand, it still tolerates attitudes and practices that betray its literalist and conservative adherence to legal Koranic traditions. There have been some attempts at modernisation in social and political life, but religious conservatism is still the dominant influence that deeply imbues the way people think.

The monarchies and principalities in the Arabian–Persian Gulf are indeed, for now, the only Arab countries that still enjoy some degree of political stability and are continuing to experience a reasonable level of economic prosperity. Large numbers of intellectuals have emigrated to these countries, drawn by attractive financial conditions and the seductive mirage of stability. But there is an inevitable price to pay as these regimes fight on three fronts: they want to protect their societies from invading Islamism, to guarantee the hereditary succession of the ruling families and to stand up to the ideological expansionism of neighbouring Iran, which is shamelessly offering unconditional support to a wide range of Arab Shiite minorities in their efforts to assert their identity. Beyond these three strategic and existential priorities, they are prepared to tolerate much else that does not stray outside reasonable Arab traditions.

As to the Arab–Israeli or Israeli–Palestinian conflict, it is disintegrating into fratricidal conflicts between Palestinian communities, and lethal tensions between Sunni and Shiite Arab groups. The emphasis is no longer on proclaiming the rights of nations, but instead on how the best practical and sensible way to share out the resources and energy available, especially in terms of groundwater and deposits of oil and gas. The effect of realpolitik among major international powers is to impose irrational compromise and forced agreements.

In the midst of this extremely complicated and clearly ephemeral context, the deeply suffering Christian communities, mercilessly tested and decimated, are struggling to survive in the four countries where traditionally a significant Christian presence goes back to the birth of the Church, in a form that has been decisively enriched by its cultural context: Lebanon, Syria, Iraq and Egypt. It seems to me that the Christians in these four countries have for the most part lost all hope that Arab reason, mentality and truth might ever recover and reform. They prefer either to keep a low profile and survive in the shadows on the basis that they are tolerated as individuals, or to emigrate to Western countries where they might be able to find a more positive permanent future for themselves and their children.

The inevitable corollary of this situation is that Arab Christian witness will be affected by the shrinking and degradation of the community. We need to remember that contemporary Arab Christian theological discourse has experienced three gestation periods. The first, inspired by the theology of the second Vatican Council, during the 1960s and 1970s, was characterised by a spirit of optimism and universalism. The second, during the 1980s and 1990s, experienced the trauma of nationalist and ideological Arab wars, and was marked by cautious realism. The third has taken place during the first three decades of the twenty-first century and has been deeply affected by the dissolution of Arab societies; it has been a time of deep suspicion, in which the only refuge seems to be an eloquent silence born of a bitter sense of impotence.

No Arabic-language Christian Church now feels able to initiate any process to raise awareness or instigate activity. Any shared energy they might have had has been shattered by ideological disillusionment and political setbacks. It is only at a private level that some feel able to express their witnessing. Small individual efforts on a modest scale are carried out in various social services organisations. And anyone expressing their Christian faith in their everyday Arab life now only ever does so in a discreet way, conscious that contemporary Arab Christian theology can only be shaped in the light of the ambiguous criteria determining how it is received and contextualised, and aware that in a broken and traumatised Arab world the sociopolitical and sociocultural realities need to be redefined.

Intellectual investment in the Christian faith is decreasing in phases as the Christian population declines and consequently there is a diminishing enthusiasm for witnessing and commitment. What is emerging is a theology for surviving, not for living, driven by a sense of urgency rather than long-term security. Laudable projects are being attempted in various places and particular circumstances, in the hope of reviving painfully suppressed enthusiasm, or a role that has been suffering in silence.[1]

Absent a modern, humanist, pluralist and open Arab society, it is impossible to contemplate that an authentic Christian presence, or an appropriate contextual Christian theology, might be able to flourish. In the current circumstances experienced by Arab Christianity, any thoughtful and faithful Christians can only hope for a regional cataclysm, a kind of general revolution – and its theoretical conditions are not yet in place – that might restore dignity and self-worth to the Arab people; that is to say, an eschatological event, a kind of cosmic shock that might show the full subversive power of the truth of the Kingdom, and promote the redemption of the whole of humanity. The atrocities happening in Eastern Europe between Russia and Ukraine at the time of writing foreshadow the advent of an impotent democratic world, deeply marked by the decline of its own values. Beyond these two possibilities, a mute theology, involuntarily apophatic, might reveal on an individual and collective basis a dull, disfigured Christian life, one that has lost its fundamental characteristic: its joy in witnessing through daily life to the urgent need for the salvation, here and now, of the Kingdom of God.

I therefore believe that contemporary Arab Christian theological discourse is above all homiletic. Patriarchs and bishops compete in eloquently exhorting their flocks to stay the course and resist the temptation to emigrate. They remind their hearers of the key principles of the Universal Declaration of Human Rights, though without daring to denounce the structural deficiencies that hinder

---

1 I should mention here the study carried out by a group of Christian, Lebanese and Arab theologians who are aiming to reassess the sociopolitical and sociocultural situation in the contemporary societies of the Arab world. Their work has yielded a document that is recently published and distributed under the title *Nous choisissons la vie* (We choose life). It synthesises the problems and challenges facing men and women in the Arab world. It includes heartfelt expressions of hope in the form of wishes. However, it is merely intended to be a preliminary task. It lacks as yet any development in terms of systematic theology, or at least any specifically theological angle. So far, it announces the intended course of study of the group; there are no details that might be described as an *aggiornamento* theological introduction or as contextualisation. It does however include an authentic exhortation to have the courage to engage in this kind of theological commitment to the cause of contemporary Arab humanity, and therein lies its value.

the workings of democratisation and justice. If the 'Arab Christ', however, is to become incarnate in the historical reality of the modern Arab world, there must be a bold new formulation of *kerygma*. Three rational processes will enable this kind of contextual Arab theology to develop: a relevant description of the true state of affairs, a critical and prophetic denunciation of injustice, and the development of a new theological interpretation of the message of the Gospel that might correct the theoretical lacunae in the ways that contemporary Arab humanity practices liberation.

The first of these processes involves asking how we might best diagnose the paralysis affecting contemporary Arab theology.[2] Should we first blame the lack of a bold and prophetic theological vision? Or would it be fairer to blame the general loss of focus and the absence of any desire to truly engage with faith and a life of witness? The last aetiology could be to condemn the sad situation of those Christian communities planted in a volatile region in which the fate of the general run of human beings has been ruthless exploitation and death.

These three potential explanations are indeed relevant, but beyond that the general situation is still extremely worrying: Christians managing to survive in the societies of the Arab world are constantly reminded of the disastrous heritage of their history. Even in the midst of what is called the Arab Spring, and for the length of a brief eschatological spark, they believed the time had come for their martyred humanity to experience a worldwide resurrection. Disillusion, however, soon set in. It is widely agreed that the Arab Spring failed. As to why it did, there are different explanations for the underlying reasons.

Some blame the archaic structures in the Arab state, inherited from despotic ideological regimes. Others prefer to blame Islamism, which seized the revolutionary energy and subjugated it for its own hegemonic purposes. And yet others revive the ancient conspiracy theories and turn on the colonising West. Personally, I can still see serious ideological impediments in the anthropological vision of the Koran, which imprisons humans in a viceregent role that is obedient to the divine will and subjected to a relationship of voluntary dependence and servility. This viceregent status forbids any thinking subject from exercising individual autonomy or acting in any of the ways modelled elsewhere in Western modernity.[3]

Arab Christians have nevertheless always been tempted to espouse the cause of

---

2 Translator's note: throughout this book, any mention of 'Arab theology' refers to Arab Christian theology. If Arab Islamic theology is meant, that will be clarified in the context.
3 See my book on comparative anthropology, *Fils et vicaire. Pour une anthropologie islamo-chrétienne comparée*, Paris, L'Harmattan, 2015.

the Arab Spring. Some have even thought it highly beneficial to outline the *Line-amenta* of a Christian theology of the Arab Spring. But I have seen no evidence that this pious wish has taken shape as a serious and coherent exercise. In some few cases, there have been hopes that the Arab revolution would win out, but no clear theological foundation has been described, nor any description of how it would work in practice.

We should remember here that Arab Christians were keen, logically, to espouse the revolutionary movement. Mindful, however, of the cataclysmic and murderous history of the Arab world, in both modern and long past times, Christian institutions preached moderation and advised their flocks to maintain a low profile. The traumatic catastrophes of their past history caused them to suspect possible collusion between the intransigence of Islamism and the Machiavellian machinations of Western powers; as a result, the collective Christian mindset shape-shifted to defeatist fear and stifling neutrality.

In spite of their cautious attitude, Arab Christians are well aware that the West, the home of the Enlightenment, is clearly favourable to the cause of the Arab Spring, where it saw hope of possible salvation for Arab people, Arab societies, and, by extension, Arab Christians. The problem, however, lies elsewhere. The foreign policies of Western countries towards the developing world in general and the Arab world in particular have in reality persistently neglected the democratic and spiritual values of their own modernity. They focus instead on their strategic and economic interests.

A contextual theology for the Arab Spring must therefore boldly make a proper and fair evaluation of the four grounds listed above for the failure of the whole revolutionary enterprise. Might it nevertheless be possible to summon up the essential resources needed and the required categorical structures to enable the formulation of a theology of clear-sighted protest and decisive commitment to the rehabilitation of Arab humanity? There is no clear answer, especially given that an anxious and traumatised Christian minority is having to face up to its own structural weakness.

In the light of this nuanced approach, I would like to add a clarification related to the prospects for the future that I identified in the final chapter of *Le Christ arabe*. I deliberately stand by the crucial calls for reform that are an essential part of that chapter, but I would now like to add a note of realism arising from bitter observations of impotence and paralysis. For in the end, when a person is in physical danger, the most important thing is no longer to bear witness to their personal convictions, but rather to ensure that they can have a human life worthy of being chosen and lived.

A number of contemporary Lebanese Christian theologians and thinkers, as their lives drew to a close, eventually and with some bitterness came to share this view. I shall not name them individually, but in private conversations some of these writers confirmed to me that their disappointment was a bitter pill to swallow. Specifically, they were experiencing overwhelming existential tension. On the one hand, these theologians wanted to remain true to the demands and the hope of their Christian faith; on the other hand, they deplored the structural deadlock of the Arab world, and were experiencing a growing quiet despair that was making them question their own theological daring.

Sadly, I too share their quiet pessimism, while still working to find signs of hope in the attitudes, the behaviour and the thinking among the Arab elite who want to cast aside, once and for all, a Koranic theology that is still viscerally rooted in a bygone cultural, temporal and spatial context. In some Arab countries, political and economic stability are enabling modernisation and thus ensuring regional balance and interest from the international community, but in the short or medium term, the sociopolitical situation in the Arab world as a whole does not inspire hope or justify enthusiasm.

Mouchir Basile Aoun
Bikfaya (Lebanon), 28 February 2022

Introduction

It may seem paradoxical to take an interest in the theology of conviviality (that is, social and communal harmony and dialogue) in an Arab context that is consumed by material concerns and uncertainty about the future. Yet the topic is of more interest than it has ever been, and quite clearly it is increasingly both urgent and acute. The Christian communities of the Arab world are seeking to spread the message of Christian faith through openness to the Muslim Other, through a life of conviviality and fraternal solidarity.[1] To this end, they are working to develop a new contextual theology[2] that aims to ensure that the life they share with their Arab partner communities is rooted in their Christian faith and calling.

A theology of conviviality thus offers a focus for a number of community-level efforts and individual activities that serve as Christian witness to the value of difference and of sharing. The theme of conviviality frames an extensive Arab theological reflection seeking to witness to the reality of Christian faith within the multifaceted, protean context of Arab societies. This theological reflection, in order to guarantee not only the physical survival of the Christian communities but also the relevance and richness of their life-giving message, must address a threefold hermeneutical task. The first is accurately to describe the sociopolitical and sociocultural reality of the historical integration of these Christian communities in and across the Arab world. The second is to reinterpret the Christ event

---

1 One of the classic works on the subject is still, unarguably, J. Corbon's *L'Église des Arabes*, which first appeared in 1977 and was revised thirty years later (Paris, Cerf, 2007). His courageous and pioneering approach was characterised by a mystic perspective, which provides the context for his explorations and analyses. G. Hachem's Introduction shows the relevance of this method, in the context of the general anxiety that afflicts the mindset of Arab Christians.

2 A. Fleyfel's doctoral thesis, published with Harmattan, addresses the issues and the challenges of a contextual Arab theology (A. Fleyfel, *La théologie contextuelle arabe. Modèle libanais*, Paris, L'Harmattan, 2011). It is a first attempt at this kind of analysis and aims to revisit recent Lebanese theology in the light of contextual demands.

in line with the various challenges presented by Muslim otherness in its various social, economic and political dimensions. And the third suggests a journey of conversion, a kind of evangelical praxis that aims to foster the bonds of fraternal solidarity, of a collective spiritual quest, and of political and moral engagement among all those living in the Arab world.

This hermeneutical task points Arab Christian theology towards a new field of inquiry: a reinterpretation of kerygmatic faith, an explanatory process calling for both a new epistemological paradigm and a new structure for Arab theological discourse. The language used here may seem ambiguous, but in their theological scrutiny these communities must courageously challenge the archaic means of expression that persist in the official discourse of the Eastern Churches. It should not be a surprise, therefore, to observe that recent Arab theology has clearly evolved in the face of these demands.

Those who are working on this theology have agreed to call for the introduction of a paradigm of otherness as a cultural framework within which to challenge the conscience of Arab Christianity. Arab theology will need to adapt its approach in the light of this paradigm. An appreciation of the Other, in this case of the Muslim individual with whom conviviality is shared, needs to start from that person's own identity and experience, their own Islamic *Weltanschauung*, rather than from a place of Christian identity and experience. From this changed perspective, a remodelled Arab theological discourse will be dictated not only by the imperative to bear witness and draw people in, but also by the need for openness and integration.

The framework for this book follows more or less the line of thinking required for new theology. It is presented in two parts that bring together the chapters focusing on each of two contiguous areas of inquiry. Part 1 tackles the dual task of describing the realities of human daily life and laying the foundations for Christian witness. We shall examine Lebanese reality as a tapestry of confessionally diverse communities each with their own preferences. The investigation therefore needs to establish the sociopolitical features and cultural identities in Lebanese society. It will also study the local theological mindset, which is found both in university research centres and in theology faculties. Part 1 concludes with a foundational study that seeks to establish the integrity of a new contextual Arab theology. It seeks to identify the viability of such a theology, and in particular, to emphasise the dialectical relationship between the real experience of Arab life and the challenges of the Christian faith: how to bring to life the *kerygma* of the Christ event within the complex picture of human experience characteristic of the modern Arab world.

Following these preliminary investigations, Part 2 offers an analysis of some models of an Arab theology of conviviality. Each of these models seeks specifically to ground conviviality in the Christian faith and the resources it offers in the face of the challenges currently experienced by Arab Christians. It therefore examines the work of a number of Middle Eastern theologians and thinkers committed to the delicate task of exploring the meaning of their life and witness within the Arab world. Despite differences in their backgrounds and affiliations, they have all focused especially on the question of contemporary Christian witness in the Arab world. The various Middle Eastern Christian communities within the Arab world, thanks to their eventful and tenuous history, have frequently been the subject of fruitful theological and philosophical examination. At every key turning point, the vicissitudes of regional and world history have forced a new approach and vocabulary, but existential anxiety has been a constant. In fact, throughout the last century, despite differences of opinion, contemporary Arab Christian theologians – be they Orthodox, Catholic, Lebanese, Egyptian, Syrian, Palestinian, or Iraqi – have had to contend with three key problems: Islamic ideology as a global system for the organisation of Arab societies; Arabism as bearer and transmitter of Arab cultural expression; and modernity as the overall Western model shaping human life in the age of globalisation.

A study of these particular theological models, however, clearly shows the immense contribution Islam has made to the social, political and cultural configuration of Arab Christianity. Just as, for a time, secularism served as the defining horizon for Western Christianity, for now, Islamic ideology serves as the defining horizon for Arab Christianity. Current Arab Christian theology therefore crucially needs to adopt an interactive and multidisciplinary approach. This is an extremely delicate task: the truth of Christian faith must be revealed to the Arab world not only on its own terms, but also through its encounter with Islam. The approach adopted by Lebanese theologians and scholars can be explained by the recent experience, within the atypical social context of Lebanese society, of the socio-political institutionalisation of Muslim–Christian conviviality. This could lead to a suspicion that, within the scope of this book, Lebanese theologians are only of interest because they provide a justification for the notion of conviviality. This is certainly not the intention here: other models of theology could also be explored, from Egypt or Palestine, for example, though Arab Christian theology has fared differently in those two societies. Part 2 concludes with a personal reflection on the role that any such theology of conviviality should play in the context of the modern Arab world.

Pioneering thinkers inevitably tend initially to over-optimism, perhaps then to abandon their position if they come up against mundane reality. The discourse of contemporary Arab Christian theology, however, remains entirely apposite to the urgency of the Kingdom. Thanks to their efforts to date, a challenging opportunity is opening up for Arab Christianity, and opening ever wider. Arab Christians must face the urgency of the work of conversion, and an imminent encounter with reality – a reality that will chime with their sense of self within the Arab world. Their contribution to reconfiguring Arab conviviality will depend crucially on their commitment and their testimony to their faith. This book will have achieved its object if it can help prepare for that reconfiguration.

Mouchir Basile Aoun
Baabdat (Lebanon), June 2011

Part One

SETTING AND UNDERLYING ASSUMPTIONS FOR A THEOLOGY OF CONVIVIALITY

1

The Problem of Context

Arab Christianity has never developed in a pure form, without influence from the Arab world in which it exists and to which it bears witness of its faith. Although Churches in the Arab world[1] have never officially called themselves 'Arab Churches', they bear the marks of the sociopolitical and sociocultural realities around them. The behaviour of Christians at both the individual and community level is inevitably dictated by regional imperatives which, for better or worse, also strongly influence the sociological forces that will determine the communities' survival or disintegration.

It is therefore important to analyse the sociopolitical reactions and theological attitudes of these Churches, and this will be informed by a knowledge of their history, both recent and more distant,[2] of the social and political challenges they

---

1 'Ces Églises sont toujours vivantes dans la continuité historique d'un même territoire. Alors quel est le lieu actuel des Églises issues d'Antioche? Si l'on tient compte honnêtement des données paradoxales de la réalité, il faut répondre : cette terre de l'Orient arabe. Seule cette région que nous avons assignée comme limite à notre question offre la réponse adéquate : d'une part, les Églises actuelles autrefois nettement locales en font toujours partie et, d'autre part, leurs frontières d'aujourd'hui sont coextensives aux frontières de la région. L'Église présente en cette région s'identifie donc comme Église locale en tant qu'Église des Arabes.' ['These Churches are still living in the historical continuity of the same territory. So where do the churches descended from Antioch belong? If we honestly and fairly take into account the paradoxical facts of reality, we must answer: this land, the Arab Middle East. Only this region, from which we have defined our question, offers an adequate response: on the one hand, the current churches, which were always local to the region, still belong here; on the other hand, their present-day borders match the regional borders. The Church in this region thus sees itself as the local church, the Church of the Arabs.' – trans.] (J. Corbon, L'Église des Arabes, op. cit., pp. 31–32.)
2 Cf. J.-M. Billioud, Histoire des chrétiens d'Orient, Paris, L'Harmattan, 1995.

have faced,[3] and of their cultural affiliations[4] and theological sensitivities. Some studies have sought to highlight various aspects of their identity,[5] and they indicate a general consensus that three major factors have determined the course of their history: their ethno-cultural grouping (Syriac, Chaldean, Coptic, Arab, Armenian, etc.); their ecclesial and theological observance (pre-Chalcedonian Orthodox, Chalcedonian Orthodox, Catholic, or Protestant); and their recent sociopolitical integration (Lebanese, Syrian, Palestinian, Egyptian, Iraqi, etc.). Taken together, these are the defining criteria that can begin to elucidate the complexity of life and the struggle faced by all Christian communities in the Arab world.

These initial remarks clearly fit well with one particular aspect of current theological thinking: the cultural imperative that requires all theological discourse not only to take account of the prevailing sociocultural and sociopolitical context, but also to take as its starting point the demands and obligations experienced by Christians in such a context. An important initial observation is the terminological confusion that arises whenever one attempts to pin down the identity of these Churches. The terms used oscillate between Churches and communities. However, given the impact of the Arab tribe[6] and the Muslim *ummah* (nation), usage tends to privilege the notion of community over that of the Church, and this can have serious theological implications, one of which is the evident structural reluctance that prevents the majority of local Churches from investing themselves body and soul in the fabric of the Arab world.

---

3 Cf. L. et A. Chabry, *Politique et minorités au Proche-Orient. Les raisons d'une explosion*, Paris, Maisonneuve et Larose, 1984. See also A. Picini (ed.), 'Les communautés chrétiennes dans le monde musulman arabe. Le défi de l'avenir', in *Proche-Orient Chrétien*, Sainte-Anne de Jérusalem and Institut Supérieur des Sciences Religieuses de l'Université Saint-Joseph de Beyrouth, Vol. 47, 1997 ; Y. Courbage et P. Fargues, *Chrétiens et juifs dans l'islam arabe et turc*, Paris, 1992 (trans. J. Mabro, *Christians and Jews Under Islam,* London and New York, I.G. Tauris, 1997).

4 Cf. J. Hajjar (ed.), *Les chrétiens du monde arabe. Problématique actuelle et perspectives*, Paris, Maisonneuve et Larose, 1989. See also R. Khawam, *L'univers culturel des chrétiens d'Orient*, Paris, Le Cerf, 1987.

5 On Christians in the Middle East in general, cf. A. J. Arberry, *Religion in the Middle East*, Cambridge, 1969; R. B. Betts, *Christians in the Arab East: A Political Study*, London, 1979; A. Fattal, *Le statut legal des non musulmans en pays d'islam*, Beirut, 1958; Ch. Frazee, *Catholics and Sultans. The Church and the Ottoman Empire 1453–1923*, Cambridge, 1983; A. Hourani, *Minorities in the Arab World*, London, 1947; R. Haddad, *Syrian Christians in Muslim Society*, Princeton, 1970. See also 'Chrétiens dans l'Orient arabe', in issue 78 of the history of religion journal *Notre histoire* (May 1991), which focuses on Christians in the Arab world.

6 On this, see the study by T. Touma, *Paysans et institutions féodales chez les Druzes et les Maronites du Liban*, Beirut, Éditions de l'Université Libanaise, 1986.

The overall context remains that of the Arab world, but different Arab countries have evolved different patterns of social integration and interaction. It is therefore perhaps better to think in terms of a plurality of local contexts within the general Arab context.[7] Nevertheless, opinion remains divided; the principle of contextual unity is easier to engage with than the notion of plurality. In any event, it is generally clear that there is diversity both in circumstances and in levels of integration, and this suggests three ways of describing the lives of Christian Arabs.

First, a symbolic existence, without historic roots, evolved on the fringes of sociopolitical and sociocultural realities (in the Arab countries of North Africa, and the Arab countries of the Gulf and the Arabian Peninsula). Second, a minority existence, that has deep historic roots, plays only a limited part in sociopolitical and sociocultural life, and bears a more or less public and authorised Christian witness (in Syria, Egypt, Iraq, Palestine, Jordan, and Sudan). And third – and this concerns only one country, Lebanon – a Christian existence that is more strongly associated with national and political life than elsewhere, and where Christian communities have always assumed a vital role in shaping the country's sociopolitical and sociocultural identity.[8]

This book will focus its analysis on the realities in Lebanon and its unique characteristics. The book and its agenda are set against the realities of the whole Arab world, but its detailed consideration will centre on this third descriptive model. The task presents many challenges. The classification suggested here arguably fails to respect the complexity of the Arab world, and any observations on sociopolitical integration are unlikely to be reliable across the diverse range of Churches.[9] In order to establish facts and to reach more general conclusions,

---

7 Recent studies of Middle Eastern Arab Christianity highlight as a determining factor either Islam (Cl. Lorieux, *Chrétiens d'Orient en terre d'islam*, Perrin, 2001; B. Heyberger, *Chrétiens du monde arabe: un archipel en terre d'islam*, Paris, Autrement, col. Mémoires, 2003; A. Brissaud, *Islam et chrétienté. Treize siècles de cohabitation*, Paris, Robert Laffont, 1991; Bat Ye'or, *Les chrétientés d'Orient entre jihad et dhimmitude*, Paris, Cerf, 1991), or the Arab ideology of power, or the imbalances created by orientalism and colonialism, which in turn gave rise to the involvement between Israel and the United States (G. Corm, *Histoire du Moyen-Orient*, Paris, La Découverte, 2007; *Ibid, Le Proche-Orient éclaté 1965–2007*, Paris, Gallimard; R. Grousset, *L'empire du Levant. Histoire de la question d'Orient*, Paris, Payot, 1992).

8 In order to understand the sociopolitical structure of Lebanese society, we shall need to refer to the Ottoman system (see E. Akarli, *The long peace. Ottoman Lebanon 1861–1920*, Berkeley, University of California Press, 1993).

9 For an insight into the historical background to this complex picture, see J. Hajjar, 'L'Église au Proche-Orient (1715–1848)', in *Nouvelle Histoire de l'Église*, Paris, 1966, vol. 4, pp. 234–262, 469–492; *Ibid, L'Europe et les destinées du Proche-Orient (1815–1848)*, Paris, coll.

however, we need to concentrate on just one of these models, and in this case, it will be Lebanon.

Our starting point is a belief – and lack of space here forbids a full justification – that Lebanon both reflects and sharply focuses key aspects of the challenges experienced by Christians within the Arab world. The life of Arab Christian communities in Lebanon crystallises the experience of all Arab Christians: their apprehension, their disillusionment, their hopes and expectations, as they seek to give meaning to their present lives within their historic context. The diversity of Lebanese Christianity, moreover, accurately reflects that found throughout different societies in the Arab world.[10] An analysis of the Lebanese experience can thus provide an invaluable hermeneutic key with which to understand other models of minority Christian existence. We shall therefore address this analysis in two stages. First, we shall describe the realities of Lebanese human existence and their sociopolitical implications, and this will help to define more clearly Lebanese social and political realities and demonstrate their fragilities and inconsistencies. Second, we shall briefly present the religious profiles of the different Christian communities in Lebanon and highlight the distinctive traits that characterise the identity mission of each one.

Lebanese human realities and their sociopolitical implications

Lebanon has always been a land of refuge – a site of confrontation, but also one of Islamic-Christian conviviality and a melting-pot of intercultural encounter. It has been described as 'the Switzerland of the Middle East', not only for its natural beauty and its financial prosperity, due mainly to its many thriving banks, but also and especially because it has been home to some fifteen Christian and Muslim denominations that have sought to live peaceably in spite of religious, ethnic, cultural and social differences.

Given its particular geopolitical situation,[11] Lebanon should be able to take on the unusually difficult challenge of different communities needing harmoniously to share living space. Three major elements seem to suggest that European-style

---

Bibliothèque de l'histoire de l'Église, 1970. See also I. Dick, *Qu'est-ce que l'Orient chrétien?*, Tournai, in the series 'Église vivante', 1965. J. Assflag and P. Krügger, *Petit dictionnaire de l'Orient chrétien*, Maredsous, Turnhout, 1991.
10 Cf. G. Corm, *Le Liban contemporain. Histoire et société*, Paris, La Découverte, 2005.
11 See D. Chevallier, *La société du Mont-Liban à l'époque de la révolution industrielle en Europe*, Paris, Geuthner, 1971.

diversity, as found in Switzerland, should work well. First, there is a shared commitment to Christian faith, as understood in the light of its basic precepts. Second, there is a common affiliation to European culture, expressed in all its various local settings and practices. And third, integration in a European sociopolitical environment that for sixty years has been guided by humanist thinking, and which is centred largely on the Declaration of Human Rights and the legal consequences of a democratic vision of society. These three factors, glaringly absent from the Arab context, could have saved Lebanon from chaos and violence.[12]

The coexistence of Islam and Christianity is the main challenge facing Lebanon; it might well eventually be one shared by all of Europe and, most probably, the whole world.[13] And yet the issue of Lebanese conviviality is not the only difficulty faced by the Lebanese state. The nation's collective conscience faces three types of problem. First, the problems that come from being a nation made up of communities, in which each religious group in Lebanese society seeks to express its identity and achieve its aims.[14] Second, the problems inherent to managing not only the nation's resources and its means of production, but also its internal administration.[15] And third, the problems presented by the regional context and, in particular, the plight of the Palestinian people.[16]

Much to the detriment of the country's best interests, many people in Lebanon continue to conflate these three sets of problems. They speak of theological differences between Islam and Christianity[17] when what is lacking is the courage to reform administrative structures. They lay the blame for all their woes on their Syrian neighbours[18] or on the Palestinians to whom they have offered refuge,

---

12 It is worth emphasising here that Arab Christian intellectuals promoting the cultural Arab *Nahda* (renaissance) have repeatedly claimed it as humanist. On this, see J. Nasrallah, 'Les chrétiens et le nationalisme arabe', *Le Lien*, 43, 1978, pp. 49–57.
13 See the historic context of relations between Islam and Christianity as described by A. Brissaud in: *Islam et chrétienté. Treize siècles de cohabitation*, Paris, Robert Laffont, 1991.
14 The behaviour typical of the Lebanese can be described in general terms. In order to validate their identity as a person, a Lebanese person feels a subconscious need to act with violent defensiveness towards others (see M. Gislenan, 'Domination as social practice. Patrimonialism in North Lebanon: arbitrary power, desecration, and the aesthetics of violence', *Critique of Anthropology*, 6 (1), 1986).
15 On the social issues in Lebanon, see Cl. Dubar and S. Nasr, *Les classes sociales au Liban*, Paris, Fondation nationale des sciences politiques, 1976.
16 See G. Corm, *L'Europe et l'Orient. De la balkanisation à la libanisation. Histoire d'une modernité inaccomplie*, Paris, La Découverte, 2002.
17 See B. Beyberger, *Chrétiens du monde arabe. Un archipel en terre d'islam*, Paris, Autrement, 2003.
18 On Lebanon's policies vis-à-vis Syria, see C. Kaminski et S. Kruk, *La Syrie: politiques et*

whereas they should have the courage critically to self-examine the conflicts between their own tribal and community groups, which more often than not lead to inappropriate alliances and unhelpful loyalties. Instead of standing firmly against outside interference and surreptitious alliances that undermine the integrity of the Lebanese nation, they can be almost destructively self-critical about the naivety of the nation's desired identity and the fragility of their ambition for interconfessional coexistence. As long as the Lebanese people fail either to identify these problems or to recognise their seriousness, and thus to better understand and resolve them, their country risks interminable and meandering artificial tensions and an asphyxiating inertia of false solutions.

The origins of incoherence in Lebanon

Lebanon is suffering increasingly frequent political crises, and this clearly suggests that the Lebanese are no longer capable of managing a life of coexistence. The profound damage to their sense of patriotism undermines any thought that, as a nation, they might be able to withstand any challenge. The reasons for outside interference in the nation's life are well known, but the factors behind the frailties of the Lebanese state are becoming increasingly elusive. The political realities in Lebanon are under such strain from its multiple structural ambiguities and human complications[19] that they cannot simply be dismissed as secondary problems.[20] This chronic constitutional impasse shows that no structure within the Lebanese state is above criticism. The shortcomings evident in the way political power is allocated (based on the proportion of the population adhering to different confessional groups) and exercised render it unfit for purpose. Foreign observers and analysts frequently comment on the impossible complexity of Lebanese political organisation, but the Lebanese themselves fail to address their inherent weakness. Tragically, they are drifting further and further into the depths of mutual disagreement.

Any mention of inherent weakness is a reminder that the Lebanon shaped by the 1989 Taif Agreement has failed to leverage its history, its values and its

---

stratégies de 1966 à nos jours, Paris, PUF, coll. 'Politique d'aujourd'hui', 1987. See also A. Laurent et A. Basbous, Guerres secrètes au Liban, Paris, Gallimard, 1987; Ibid, 'Le Liban et son voisinage', doctoral thesis, Université Paris-II, Paris, 1986.
19 On the ambiguity of religious identity in Lebanon, see the religious history journal Notre histoire, 2 (June 1984), a special issue entitled 'L'imbroglio religieux du Liban'.
20 Cf. A. Beydoun, Identité confessionnelle et temps social chez les historiens libanais contemporains, Beirut, Publications de l'Université Libanaise, 1984.

mission in order to bring together the communities that form the fabric of its diversity, yet whose sociocultural backgrounds are distinct. The symbolic representations of national identity are the topic of constant heated discussion. There are widely varying interpretations of the key values of Lebanese patriotism, and the ways in which the Other is perceived by each community group can diverge in disastrous ways. Add in the scandal of Lebanon's scattered allegiances, and a disheartening picture becomes even worse. Most of Lebanon's political parties are under the influence of regional or Western powers. And tragically, the voices of ambassadors and consuls carry more weight and have a greater impact among the communities of Lebanon than does the wisdom of those few elite Lebanese politicians who are anxious to protect the uniqueness of the Lebanese model.

The idea that the nation might be intrinsically fragile is not the first or indeed the dominant notion when one considers Lebanon. Arab ways of thought make it impossible to the people of Lebanon to acknowledge their diversity, for the very concept of diversity evokes in the Arab mind a pathological resistance to secularity. Arab culture generally associates the idea of plurality with division, weakness and shame. A persistent optimism surrounds idea of the Lebanese nation – its unity and its psyche – crowning an imagined autonomous and sovereign Lebanon with a hazy utopian halo.[21] In fact, there are divisions among the Lebanese on all fronts. Various lines of division have given rise to irreconcilable and antagonistic dualities.[22] The first are confessional divisions. In the Middle Eastern context, this kind of division is at the root of all other rifts.[23] The second are social divisions. Widely diverging economic fortunes have given rise to a partitioning of social classes in Lebanon, who experience widely disparate lives and conditions. The third and final line of division is ideological in nature. It is clearly linked to the other two, but it gives rise to particular harm, since it rehearses and recycles the other two types of divisions.

---

21 On the origin and nature of the political constitution of Lebanon, see E. Rabbath, *La formation historique du Liban politique et constitutionnel*, Beirut, Publications de l'Université Libanaise, 1986.

22 On this, see A. Messarra, 'Le système politique libanais : évaluation en termes de droits de l'homme et perspectives d'avenir', in *Le droit à la différence. Pour plus de justice et de liberté*, Paris, CEROC, 1985.

23 A useful source on this is the work of one of the best scholars researching the true nature of religious life in the Middle East: G. Corm, *Histoire du pluralisme religieux dans le bassin méditérranéen*, Paris, Geuthner, 1998 (which links to his research *Contribution à l'étude des sociétés multiconfessionnelles. Effets socio-juridiques et politiques du pluralisme religieux*, Paris, LGDJ, 1971).

How religion and politics entwine in Lebanon

For it is this third and most serious type of division that most dramatically dis-
torts the relationships between religion and politics among the communities of
Lebanon. Monumental unfounded misappropriations of hostile politico-religious
ideologies weaken any attempt to bring healing to everyday Lebanese experience. Politico-religious ideology should effectively be understood here as a sort
of hidden bond that forms between the legitimate demands of a religious faith and
the unbridled ambitions of a political movement.[24] Clarity and determination are
missing; this compounds a toxic situation still further and undermines the witness
of the majority of religious leaders, who have refused to be critical of any such
misappropriations or manipulative moves. The religious authorities in the country
might not recognise this analysis, but there is a perception among many Lebanese
people that both powers – religious and political – sometimes knowingly, sometimes unknowingly, use and exploit each other mercilessly so as to increase their
stranglehold over Lebanon's entire existence.

This point is worth stressing, since those who wilfully ignore it are responsible
for the most damaging and persistent misunderstandings. The complicity between
politics and religion is a serious problem, and the Lebanese people would have
much to gain by denouncing the behaviour of the political class which continues,
for example, to defend the Lebanese confessional system. Yet leading experts
admit that this system, as amended under the Taif Agreement, deprives Lebanese
political life of any centre of gravity since it lacks an ultimate decision-making
authority.

This constitutional lacuna is compounded by the last amendment to the Lebanese constitution, which sanctions the distribution of political power (the presi-
dencies of the republic, of the legislative and of the executive branches), among
confessional groups, thus giving permanent justification to Lebanese confessionalism. It admittedly also discreetly stipulates and plans for the abolition of
confessionalism in two stages: the accession of a non-confessional Lebanese par-
liament and, simultaneously, the creation of a senate of experts representative of
Lebanon's main communities. The ideological backdrop of these amendments,
however, remains steeped in a confessional perception of politics – even though
this confessionalism is the source of all its ills. Some may consider that the Arab
Middle East is intrinsically religious, and that the Lebanese people should do better
than to paper over insoluble problems; it is important, however, to remember that

---

24 The following article by G. Salamé is illuminating here: 'En mal d'identité : conflits et
passions au Liban', *Maghreb-Machrek*, 110 (October-December 1985), pp. 5–22.

the negative effects of Lebanese confessionalism are so extensive and so harmful that even maintaining the status quo risks bringing about the permanent dissolution of the Lebanese nation. Certain regional forces, in collusion with most of the Lebanese political class, shamelessly exploit these rifts and subjugate the factions within Lebanon for strategic ends that ultimately threaten the national interest.

The symptoms and harmful consequences of Lebanese Confessionalism

Confessionalism, the primary cause of the fragility from which Lebanon suffers,[25] now requires sustained remediation, a radical transformation of both structures and mindset. A close examination of the symptoms may help point the way towards a cure. Confessionalism may present some small advantages, given the context of fragmentation in the Middle East along both ethnic and community lines,[26] but it dramatically undermines the credibility of the Lebanese model precisely because of the harmful consequences of the many ideological manipulations conducted by Lebanon's religious leaders. It is therefore insufficient to claim that confessionalism must be maintained because the reality is that Semitic Arab life in the Middle East can only be religious. Any examination of the disastrous consequences of the current situation makes it immediately clear that the confessional system cannot be allowed to persist.

One of the fundamental pathologies inherent in Lebanon's confessional system is the way in which Lebanese citizens are deprived of individual identity. The Lebanese political system recognises the citizenship of an individual only in terms of the religious community to which they belong, not by virtue of their life in civil society. The rights of communities are protected, and in consequence so are those of the individual members of the faith community, but the protection of individuals is only secondary and, worryingly, is less clearly established. The rights of individuals are substantially less well defended than those of the community. Lebanese citizens enjoy the rights to which they are entitled within their respective communities, but only insofar as they accept and practise the official doctrines imposed by the community's leaders. Paradoxically, they therefore fully enjoy their rights only by surrendering their individual freedom. As a result, people accept confessionalism in order to gain the limited rights that enable them

---

25 On the confessional nature of Lebanese society, see L.-H. de Bar, *Les communautés confessionnelles du Liban*, in the series 'Recherche sur les civilisations', Paris, 1983.
26 See G. Corm, *L'Europe et l'Orient : de la balkanisation à la libanisation. Histoire d'une modernité inaccomplie*, Paris, La Découverte, 2003. See also L. and A. Chabry, *Politique et minorités au Proche-Orient. Les raisons d'une explosion*, Paris, Maisonneuve et Larose, 1984.

to survive. The description here may have slightly exaggerated some aspects for the sake of clarity, but the repression of individuality in the Lebanese confessional system is thus clearly at the root of the many problems within Lebanese society.

Alongside the lack of rights, there is a second reason for the sense of alienation that undermines any sense of belonging to the nation. Given the nature of confessionalism, the nation exists only as an informal collection of communities living alongside each other.[27] The first allegiance Lebanese citizens owe is to their community, which thus defines their identity. An intermediary entity deprives them of any instinctive sense they might have of enjoying a direct relationship with the larger entity, the nation, thus creating a distorting lens: religious sentiment obscures national sentiment. And contrary to the claims made by those who defend the confessional system, the forced interposition of the community prevents Lebanese individuals from meeting one another on the neutral, welcoming ground that Lebanese national identity could have offered. Arguably, Lebanese communities constitute a cluster of small nations within a large nation, and thus each serves to promote the community's demands and ambitions by adapting them to the requirements and values of Lebanese diversity. However, the absence of democratic processes within these communities disenfranchises the members and effectively centralises power within an all-powerful, oligarchic circle. Lebanese society, as a result, suffers from dislocation and disintegration. The deliberate dispersion of communities within Lebanon thus sabotages any sense of national solidarity and security.

In a highly confessionalised country such as Lebanon, apparent unity can be compromised by any outside interference. Extraterritorial religious allegiances and ancient community identities can aggravate internal tensions and provoke lethal disputes. Anyone promoting a tendentious political message to promote the interests and survival of a small national group can claim affinity with a regional or Western power. The principles and values specific to Lebanese national identity, if interpreted differently in different confessional groups, can suffer distortions capable of being used to justify appalling aberrations. The transformation of religious differences into national disputes can lay the ground, in both intellectual and political terms, for community despotism and foreign imperialism; every local party involved then looks to recruit the sympathy of external forces to its own cause, thus exacerbating discord and provoking ever more lethal conflict.

We should also bear in mind that confessionalism tragically accentuates

---

27 On this, see A. Messarra, *Théorie générale du système politique libanais*, Paris-Cariscript, Beirut-Librairie Orientale, 1994, 406 p.

legitimate differences between systems and conceptions of the world that each hold a rightful place within the Lebanese region. There is a sense of rivalry between confessional communities that on the one hand is purely political and reinforces their loyalty and creativity, but on the other hand also exacerbates an esprit de corps in which unbridled sentimentality overcomes rationality. The slightest difference in opinion risks deteriorating into armed struggle once it takes the form of a confrontation between two religious worldviews. Yet, in most cases, the problems that haunt Lebanese society are of a more technical and practical nature, and amount simply to the management of resources within society. There is no need to invoke religion, unless it is to be enlisted for the benefit of an oligarchic coalition intent on strengthening its grip on the country's political future. It is precisely this ideological mystification that prevents the Lebanese people from having a true appreciation of their difficulties.

Indeed, the social ills of the nation as a whole have never been associated with any particular religious affiliation. Leaving aside some specifically religious values connected with the moral and spiritual life of citizens, the organisation of wider Lebanese society does not require a specialised religious authority. The social sciences can provide all that is needed in terms of tools to manage society. And, as we have seen, it is the ideological mystification which afflicts Lebanese politics that offers foreign powers their most powerful justification for repeated interventions.

On a final note, confessionalism ensnares Lebanese society in a sprawling intellectual tyranny. A monolithic understanding of 'truth' exacts a high price for security in daily life. The repression of intellectual freedom sets a seal on the state of inertia that crushes any local initiative. Instead of defending the right to free individual thought, Lebanese communities connive to use mutually destructive and toxic means to protect themselves from any form of innovation. As an instinctive form of silently agreed self-defence, they zealously censure and oust any free thinker, whatever their home community. Paradoxically, any threat of free thinking provokes an outbreak of solidarity between the various communities. In other words, the maintenance of the status quo seems to be the one point of agreement that is capable, however indirectly and artificially, of bringing the Lebanese communities together.

The fruitless anti-confessional struggle and the future of the Lebanese state

Lebanese confessionalism is haunted by what it perceives as powerful calls for freedom, so it aims to stave off the threat of free thinking by demonising any

attempts at innovation in a virulent reaction that will sooner or later lead to suffo-
cation and fossilisation. The longing for individual freedom, once suppressed, can
sour to potential violence and become a latent threat to the survival of Lebanon.
Repressed, disfigured violence will sooner or later resurface in the disputatious
relationships that set communities in Lebanon against each other. Paradoxically,
therefore, the slow asphyxiation of individuality can kindle a desire for vengeance that spills out. Even the most robust transconfessional alliances can fail to
contain the violent intercommunal confrontations that afflict the Lebanese political arena. Nothing seems able to stem these quarrels: not aristocratic links across
community boundaries, nor ideological sympathies that bridge confessional rifts,
nor even strategic deals made secretly, under the radar. Lebanese has endured
many kinds of violence, but it is confessional violence alone that undermines any
prospect of a peaceful and fruitful Lebanese coexistence.[28]

This brief, simplified overview clearly shows how obsolete and impractical
the Lebanese confessional system has become. The sociologists and political
commentators who still claim that confessionalism is theoretically a valid system
rarely bear in mind that a cultural ideal may be valid theoretically, but requires
confirmation by a credible historical example. These same commentators and
sociologists consistently place the blame not on their theoretical model, but on
the historical entanglement of Lebanon's corrupting compromise. The Lebanese
nation now has the experience of two centuries of coexistence, during which it has
experienced frequent and major structural crises. It is clear that idealised theoretical constructions are simply a utopia, and there is an urgent need to denounce the
theory of confessionalism as intrinsically destructive in the Lebanese context.

Inevitably, this calls into question the future of Lebanon as a nation. There are
two competing responses to this question. The first argues for the continuation of
the confessional system and calls for cosmetic repairs to remedy its faults and the
damages it has brought in its wake. The second, on the other hand, advocates a
thorough overhaul of the whole of Lebanon's society, and the setting up instead
of a moderate secularist system. My own inclination is of course to the second,
while acknowledging the magnitude of the task and the level of resistance it would
encounter. Lebanese society, afflicted by long-ingrained misoneism (opposition
to innovation), will stubbornly resist the introduction of any such system of

---

28 Cf. G. Assaf, 'Système communautariste et déconfessionnalisation. La problématique de la
maturation du système politique libanais', *Travaux et jours*, no. 64 (Autumn 1999), pp. 45–73.
See also J. Sleiman, 'Le Liban pluriconfessionnel', doctoral thesis, Université René Descartes,
Sorbonne, Paris, 1983.

organisation and management. Nevertheless, I no longer see any other plausible solution, whatever the inherent aversion to it in the Arab psyche.

In brief, moderate secularism can be achieved by clear separation of key areas of expertise, and a balanced approach to the key principles of human life. In other words, religious and political interests, as key areas of expertise, should be clearly separate, since they organise two different areas of need and two distinct aspects of human life. As to the fundamental values of life, both politics and religion should draw inspiration from a shared set of guiding principles that give meaning to the whole of human existence. Consensual hermeneutics on major principles of common life, such as freedom, justice, peace, solidarity, are therefore the only solution available to pluralistic societies such as Lebanon.

Quite clearly, consensual hermeneutics must be a part of moderate secularity,[29] since Lebanon encompasses a number of socioreligious and sociocultural population groups. In fact, it is because of consensual hermeneutics – which tends to promote debate and discussion around two types of restorative process – that I describe this notion of secularism as moderate. The first process is the emergence of an axiological semantics specific to the Lebanese context, and the second, the formulation of the best possible means of legal incorporation, established in a historically appropriate way. To guard against the dangers of corruption and attenuation, the Lebanese sociopolitical arena must be governed by the values that the three main spiritualities – Christian, Muslim, and secular – have in common. But it must also be defended from any directly religious influence. On a practical level, any regulations must be protected from any kind of confessional interference, and the affairs of Lebanese society must be managed independently and transparently, along purely administrative lines. Neither politics nor public administration are religious in character.[30]

My mention of the three main spiritualities is not intended to suggest any kind of syncretism, nor any potential tripartite restructuring of Lebanese social life. For the avoidance of ideological confusion, I am advocating that the Lebanese public

---

29 The Lebanese political commentator Antoine Messarra, although from a different perspective and with other motives, has offered a decisive contribution to the assessment of a consensual system in Lebanon: A. Messarra, *La gouvernance du système consensuel. Le Liban après les amendements constitutionnels de 1990*, Beirut, Librairie Orientale, 2003, 600 p. For a clearer explanation of the challenges of consociationalist democracy, see the special issue of *Revue Internationale de Politique Comparée*, 4 (3), December 1997. The article by É. Picard ('Le communautarisme politique et la question de la démocratie au Liban') is especially illuminating.
30 Here, an enlightening approach is to be found in the article by J.C. Eslin, 'Trois variantes de la séparation religion/politique', in *Esprit* (April-May 1986).

sphere should become a neutral space, but not devoid of any spiritual or cultural references. It is unthinkable, in fact, that any social system should be entirely free of cultural references.[31] The Lebanese social system has of course always been marked by religious references from both Christianity and Islam. The time has now come to introduce secular references, for the sake of secular Lebanese who claim no religious allegiance. A shared process, involving all three cultural elements, could thus collaborate in shaping a new Lebanese constitution that respects not only the plurality of its cultures but also the neutrality of its public sphere. And in terms of concrete legislation, all forms of discrimination between Lebanese people should be abolished, and civil legislation established that guarantees equality for all and fundamental liberties. An annexed protocol could include the charter of spiritual values that the Lebanese would like to subscribe to in adopting an agreed communal life.

My advocacy for moderate secularity in Lebanon is not due to any exotic fascination with it on my part, but rather to the acknowledged failure of the confessional system and the serious violations of personal liberty suffered by the Lebanese people. Those who object to this notion of secularity will seek ways to demonstrate its impracticability. The fact remains, however, that no solution yet proposed for reconciliation while preserving the prevailing confessionalism has been able to halt the appalling violence that is tearing through Lebanon: a vicious spiral of fear and vengeance, a terrible engine of brutality. Intellectual honesty demands that the Lebanese people give this alternative model a fair trial before declaring it useless or fruitless. And on balance, it seems to me, the current (2016) political situation might paradoxically favour a paradigmatic shift in the composition of Lebanon. Political life has come to a standstill, and efforts to rescue the situation have failed; the spiritual – maybe even physical – survival of Lebanon may depend on the attempt.

The impact of local geopolitics

The internal reasons for Lebanon's impasse, as described above, must be seen as part of a picture that includes larger regional problems. In order to understand the sociopolitical situation in Lebanon, we must take into account its full context. Many Lebanese citizens are currently unsure whether their country can still be described as one of the viable nations of the world. The question is

---

31 See B. El Hachem, 'Religion et intégration sociale et nationale', in Collectif, *Pour une théologie contemporaine du Moyen-Orient*, Jounieh, Éditions Saint-Paul, 1988, pp. 69–93.

justified, because chronic regional political tensions have a crucial impact on their country.[32]

These tensions focus on the interplay between outside interference in Lebanon and the allegiances of the Lebanese people. Members of the various Lebanese communities, because of their history and their religious beliefs, have been accustomed to observing extraterritorial religious practices. Real political power in Lebanon is shared by two major political blocs. One of these, the pro-Sunni and pro-American bloc, aligns itself unconditionally with the Sunni Arab regimes that promote a realistic and minimalist advocacy for peace. The pro-Shiite and pro-Iranian bloc, on the other hand, champions resistance in order to defend the Palestinian cause, inspired by a (utopian) idealism and a desire for major change. This bloc is driven by the large-scale strategic interests of Iran and Syria.

These two Lebanese blocs mirror faithfully the regional tensions that oppose pro-Iranians and pro-Americans. The Arab Sunni pro-American regimes, openly supported by the USA administration, are keen to do all they can to support Sunni power in Lebanon. The anti-American and pro-Iranian Arab regimes, on the other hand, give indirect support to the Lebanese Shiites who, for their part, demand that political power should be more fairly shared out (they have a blocking minority in the Lebanese Cabinet) – in other words, constitutional reform that would enable the Shiite community to defend its existence and its rights.

At the start of the modern Lebanese political state, Lebanese Christians, having lost the war in 1990, found that they were forced to align with one or other of these groupings. The Sunni grouping is working hard to maintain the prerogatives granted to their community by the most recent constitutional amendments. And beyond this internal strategy, it is working to ensure that Lebanon adopts Sunni Arab pro-American politics. The Shiite grouping, under the leadership of Hezbollah, is demanding a higher level (by which they mean 'more effective', a level that reflects the size of the Shiite community) of participation in the administration of the Lebanese state. There are fears of armed conflict, similar to the fighting in Iraq. During the Syrian occupation, disagreements and litigations arising from the Lebanese political system were dealt with directly, and despotically, from Damascus. The Lebanese were simply expected to obey. Now that the Syrians have left, there is a constitutional void: the Taif Agreement established an end date for the Lebanese war but made no provision for mechanisms explicitly designed to manage conflict between the Presidency (honorific power granted to a Maronite

---

32 For an overall analysis of the regional situation, see G. Corm *La méditerranée, espace de conflit, espace de rêve*, Paris, L'Harmattan, 2003.

Christian), the Chamber (legislative power granted to a Shiite Muslim) and the Cabinet (executive power granted to a Sunni Muslim).

In the background, there is still permanent tension between Palestinians and Israelis and, temporarily/at times less conspicuously, between the Israelis and Lebanese Hezbollah, which is supported by Iran. The international confrontation between Iran and the USA is now inimical to any interconfessional agreement, since there is a subconscious coalescing of positions around these two blocs. The American bloc appears to be demanding more democracy in the Middle East. In reality, it simply encourages Israel to humiliate the Palestinians, and exacerbates the situation in Iraq by increasing divisions between the Kurdish, Sunni and Shiite communities. The Iranian bloc claims that it wants to defend the causes of the Palestinians and other minorities persecuted in the Arab world, especially Shiite minorities. They, however, are deepening the rift within Arab societies between Sunni and Shiite, and risk instrumentalising Hezbollah in a suicidal armed conflict with Israel. The Iranian regime under the leadership of the religious jurist (*faqîh*) could damage society's democratic process, though universal suffrage and the bicameral system could limit the damage. The practices in some Arab regimes adhering to Sunni observance owe very little to the fundamental principles of Western democracy.[33] The Sunni *ulema* may not be directly involved in public administration, but these Sunni Arab societies seem to follow the same principle that political life is subject to religious control.

Together, these various factors show how little power Lebanese Christians – under threat, divided, disoriented – have over the course of events. They can no longer even appeal to the patriotic conscience of their Shiite and Sunni compatriots to work together on a peaceful solution to the situation, or to agree mutual concessions and reciprocal compromises that might preserve the special nature of Lebanese conviviality. The unfortunate Christians find themselves torn between the Shiite and Sunni blocs. For the moment, no significant Christian political movement would be able to gain any traction that might counter the negative effects of the worrying disintegration of the Christian political class in Lebanon.

Indeed, this has led many to think that Lebanon is currently facing one of the most dangerous political challenges in its history. It is in the eye of the global storm that confronts Islam and the West, and is suffering the disastrous consequences of the Israel-Palestine conflict, and the destabilising outcomes of the American invasion of Iraq and of the Western alliance against Iran. Thanks to its constitutional

---

33 The recent popular risings in various Arab countries demonstrate the strength of the desire for liberty, in spite of the relentless collusion between religious and political powers.

frailty, its integral diversity and the ethical irresponsibility displayed by most of its political leaders, Lebanon catastrophically lacks any form of self-protection.[34]

Lebanese leaders, rather than addressing these fundamental inadequacies, have instead concentrated on selfishly exploiting what resources the country still enjoys. No serious thought has been given to the future of the Lebanese constitution. Even electoral legislation in Lebanon is no longer fit for the aspirations of its people, who feel torn apart between confessional segmentation and the total disintegration of the nation state. Many Lebanese citizens now believe that electoral legislation needs a complete overhaul in order to enable the nation freely to express its choices and preferences. It is a challenge, however, to know how best to create appropriate electoral segmentation in order faithfully to reflect the demographic and sociopolitical changes that have affected Lebanese society. Any new electoral legislation will therefore first require a national consensus on the nature and mission of Lebanon in its Arab context. And this in turn will require a universally recognised legitimate, impartial mechanism to give the Lebanese people a voice and a channel through which they can voice their opinions. That said, it is also important to avoid what since Tocqueville has been called the 'tyranny of the demographic majority'. In Lebanon, that majority currently need to be educated in matters of public administration, including intercultural aspects.

Until this is remedied, I fear that Lebanon will continue to sink ever further into instability, chaos and, ultimately, armed conflict. For now, memories of the recent Lebanese war (1975–1990) continue to act as a deterrent. But when the day comes that Lebanese citizens feel that their identity is under extreme threat, it seems clear to me that the challenges of their present culture will make it almost impossible to defend their right to life, to peace, to prosperity, and especially to pluralist sensitivities.

At that point, I would argue, they will have to disregard their extraterritorial allegiances in order to reflect, in a peaceful and ordered way, on how to live in conviviality.[35] Once free of outside interference, they will be able to rediscover the joy of coexistence and of equitable distribution of power and responsibility. The Lebanese constitution will need a radically innovative revision if it is to enable Lebanese society to reach a place of peace and mutual reconciliation: it will need to be designed so that it preserves the communities' cultural characteristics and

---

34 See É. Picard, *Liban, État de discorde. Des fondations aux guerres fratricides*, Paris, Flammarion, 1988.
35 See Y. Moubarac, *La question libanaise dans les textes du patriarche Sfeir*, Paris, Cariscript, 1989.

the inalienable rights of all citizens. An ambivalent political system is called for, one that can assimilate the benefits of secularism and respect the need to safeguard community identities.

In my opinion, these measures will be essential if the political situation in Lebanon is to be retrieved. Absent an effort on the part not only of the international community but also of the various elements of Lebanese society, Lebanon's future will continue to be determined by the violent changes that have characterised recent Middle Eastern history.[36] Both the Lebanese and those who love Lebanon must therefore work together to highlight to the international community the very serious challenges that threaten the future of the Christian community in Lebanon.

Ultimately, the future of Arab Christian witness is heavily dependent on the future of the Christian communities in Lebanon and across the Arab world. This is not to argue that they should be granted a discriminatory status with special privileges and unconstitutional concessions. The future of conviviality could be seriously compromised, however, if the existence of Arab Christianity – in all its many physical, cultural and political forms – is persistently overlooked. The future of the Christian *Weltanschauung* in the Arab world is not necessarily bound up with the existence of any specific Christian community, since their message can reach Islamic Arab societies via other cultural media. But if their existence diminishes, Arab conviviality will suffer severely. An imagined confessional homogeneity could devastate the Arab experience of diversity.

The different elements of ecclesiastical life

An analysis of the life of Lebanese people clearly exposes the precariousness of Church life generally, and especially in the Arab Middle East.[37] It is only thanks

---

36 Some think that the problem is one that is intrinsic to the structures of society in the Arab world (cf. O. Carré, 'Réflexions sur les structures socioculturelles du Proche-Orient arabo-musulman', in Collectif, *Le mal de voir*, Paris, 1976, pp. 288–330; R. Cresswell, 'Le concept de structure au Proche-Orient', in *Travaux et jours*, August 1966, pp. 41–61).

37 'Pour découvrir l'Église en cette région du monde arabe, il fallait d'abord l'écouter à travers son histoire et entrer dans le silence de son mystère. Sur ce fond permanent de vie, nous pourrons mieux comprendre ce qui se passe aujourd'hui. Une évolution accélérée est en cours, qui concerne inséparablement le peuple arabe et son Église, ce peuple de Dieu et l'Église de Dieu. La question : quelle est cette Église? s'éclairera à la lumière d'une autre question : que signifie-t-elle pour ce peuple? Identité mais aussi signification. L'une et l'autre apparaîtront parfois en harmonie, souvent en conflit, toujours en défi d'émulation. L'Esprit et les événements ne cessent d'adresser leur appel aux Églises.' ['To discover the Church in this region of the Arab world, we had first to learn its history and to enter into the silence of its mystery. The longevity of their faithfulness helps to explain their present situation. It is now

to the sociocultural and sociopolitical context that it is able to survive and prosper. We must therefore examine how Lebanese people live, in the hope that this might focus the thinking of Lebanese Christians. This examination of ecclesiastical life, however, will not be a historical description, or a historical investigation laying out the historical facts about the Lebanese Christian communities. To achieve this would have required not only greater resources but also a larger canvas for fuller descriptions.

The key starting point is a clear understanding of the close correlation between ecclesiastical life and the life of the people. The Churches briefly presented here are socio-ethnic, sociocultural and sociopolitical entities.[38] These three dimensions are closely linked, and this further complicates the issue of identity. We shall examine them as living entities interacting with the Lebanese society within which they exist. These entities suffer from structural limitations and therefore face enormous challenges. Distressingly, their extremely difficult historic situation has affected both their life and their mindset. This has had tragic consequences for their Gospel witness and their theological discourse.[39] The sociopolitical difficulties present challenges equally to the two main groupings, Catholic and Orthodox.

Catholic Churches in the Middle East

Both legally and theologically, Middle Eastern Catholic Churches are seen as ecclesial entities that are mutually interdependent and in full communion with each other. Their shared sense of Catholic identity binds them together, and they are in communion with the Catholic Church represented by the See of Rome. Their identity and their vocation are both under constant threat from the vicissitudes of the political situation, the ontological fragility of their social structure, and their ambiguous status due to their dual allegiance both to the Middle East and to the West.

---

changing, ever faster, entwining its Arab members and their church, this people of God and the Church of God. We will receive a clearer answer to the question 'What is this Church?' if we also ask 'What does it mean for this people?' Identity and meaning go together. They sometimes agree, and often disagree, but they are unlike any other. The Spirit and events call constantly upon the Churches.' – *trans.*] (J. Corbon, *L'Église des Arabes, op. cit.*, p. 109.)
38 See one of the latest collected volumes on the subject: P. Blanc (ed.), *Chrétiens d'Orient*, Paris, L'Harmattan, 2008.
39 J.-P. Valognes (*Vie et mort des chrétiens d'Orient. Des origines à nos jours*, Paris, Fayard, 1994, 972 p.) gives an extremely realistic picture of the secular struggle by Middle Eastern Christianity, and lucidly identifies the principal challenges faced by Christian communities in the modern Arab world in terms of their physical, cultural and spiritual survival.

Most of these Churches have their root in the Antioch Patriarchate, and this affiliation makes conflicting calls on their ecclesiastical self-understanding. On the one hand, they all claim legitimate inheritance from the Church of Antioch. On the other, they bear the scars of the traumas and rifts that have devastated the Antioch Church's history.[40]

Because of the dignity of their apostolic heritage and their ambivalent status, these Churches have adopted a delicate position between two types of Church. They cannot realistically be seen in the same light as the national Catholic Churches of, say, France or Germany, or the Church in Africa, which are in the legal and administrative orbit of the Church in Rome; nor are they like the Autocephalous Orthodox Churches, whose relationship with the Western Catholic Church is one of fraternal neighbourliness and keen interest in engaging in theological dialogue and seeking potential doctrinal communion. And since they fit neither of these two models, it is not easy in the case of these Catholic Church communities to establish their clear identity, to promote their integration, or to infuse them with a sense of dynamic purpose. They claim heritage from the apostolic see of Antioch.[41] They claim an explicit vocation to ecumenism (the desire to enter into full communion with the Church of Rome), and their own particular national and cultural characteristics (their membership of the Arab world and their roots in the land of Lebanon). Each of the six Churches (Maronite, Melkite Greek Catholic, Syriac, Armenian, Chaldean, and Latin) has its own heritage, history, and liturgical and ritual sensitivities.

Before giving a brief description of the identity and current situation of each, it is important briefly to clarify their nomenclature. These are Middle Eastern Churches that attached themselves legally and administratively to the Roman Church as a result of missionary activity in the region by the Latin Church.[42] From the seventeenth century onwards, however, this unity was torn apart by

---

40 Cf. G. Hachem, 'Les Églises orientales catholiques : évaluation rétrospective et vision prospective', in Mgr. N. Edelby et G. Hachem, *Chrétiens arabes. Pont entre l'Orient et l'Occident*, Beirut, Cedrac, Publications de l'Université Saint-Joseph, 2007, pp. 33–57. In October 2010, a synod meeting was held in Rome on the subject of the identity, the condition and the vocation of Catholic churches in the Middle East: Benedictus XVI, *Ecclesia in Medio Oriente. Post-Synodal Apostolic Exhortation on the Church in the Middle East. Communion and Witness* (14 September 2012), sitography: vatican.va; We Choose Abundant Life Group (ed), *We Choose Abundant Life. Christians in the Middle East: Towards Renewed Theological, Social, and Political Choices*, Beirut, 2021.

41 See S. Gholam, 'Évolution et originalité de l'Église locale d'Antioche', in Collectif, *Église locale et Église universelle*, Chambésy, coll. Études théologiques 1, 1981, pp. 45–68.

42 Cf. J.-Cl. Roberti, *Les uniates*, Paris, Le Cerf, 1992.

an irresistible nostalgic longing for regional unity. Driven by the standardising ecclesiastical vison of the papacy, those who were campaigning at the time to re-establish the former unity of the Middle Eastern Churches were not to be satisfied by a simple sense of pious and cautious expectation. In a number of ways, there-fore, the creation of these Middle Eastern Churches attached to Rome (cf. the Uniatist movement[43]) was due to an erroneous ecclesiological understanding of Christian unity. Any return to the doctrinal communion that bound the Pentarchy together in ancient times would necessarily entail alignment to the Roman model and, ipso facto, subordination to papal authority.[44] Under the impetus of Vatican II, however, a new spirit of collegiality has been advocating for an ecclesiology of communion. The leaders of universal Catholicism have been suggesting that it should be based on the principle that all Churches are equal and on the urgent need for collegial cooperation in supporting the Pope, the faith, and charitable love.

An analysis of the ecclesiologies of each of these Churches will help to iden-tify the respective characteristics. They share a home in the land of Lebanon, the same Catholic faith, and the same ecclesiastical structures. They were not all involved in the crisis in Lebanon, but the reaction of each was determined by the sociopolitical situation that has prevailed for the past three decades. In numerical terms, Catholics represent 70 percent of Lebanese Christians. Christians, in turn, represent 40 percent of the four million who make up the population of Leba-non.[45] We can assume that the number of Palestinian refugees living in Lebanon is around 400,000, but it is difficult to be specific about other Arab population groups (Syrians, Egyptians, Iraqis etc.).

We can gain the clearest picture of Lebanese Catholicity from the Maronite

---

43 Cf. J. Hajjar, *Les chrétiens uniates du Proche-Orient*, Paris, 1962; *Ibid, L'Europe et les destinées du Proche-Orient (1815–1848)*, Paris, 1970. See also the collection of studies aimed at evaluating Uniatism in the wake of the Balamand declaration (Commission mixte catholique-orthodoxe, *Catholiques et orthodoxes: Les enjeux de l'uniatisme dans le sillage de Balamand*, Paris, Bayard-Fleurus Mame-Cerf, 2004).

44 On the part played by the Uniate Churches in resisting such a model, see C. Patelos, *Vatican I et les évêques uniates. Une étape éclairante de la politique romaine à l'égard des Orientaux* (1867–1870), Louvain, series 'Bibliothèque de la Revue d'histoire ecclésiastique', no. 65, 1981.

45 It is worth noting that there is a strong taboo in Lebanese society on the matter of gathering statistics, since they could expose strong feelings of inferiority and/or superiority that present a constant threat to any sense of Lebanese convivality. Objective and reliable sources are therefore rare. (cf. Y. Courbage, *La situation démographique au Liban*, Beirut, Publications de l'Université Libanaise, 1974).[Note also that the numbers here relate to 2011, when the original French edition was written – ed.]

Church and the Melkite Greek Catholic Church. The adherents of these two churches are not only more numerous than other Lebanese Christians, but also played a more significant part in the Christian contribution to creating both the past and the modern forms of the Lebanese state. Catholics who observe the Latin rite, both Lebanese and Western, also play an important part in the life of the Church and its cultural and spiritual energy, thanks to their schools, universities, and humanitarian institutions. The following descriptions deliberately omit any historical account, and aim simply to present the ways in which these three Churches are involved in the realities of social, political and religious life, and how this reveals the specific nature of Lebanese existence.

The Maronite Church

The Maronite Church and its statutes were established at the time when its complete and definitive communion with the Church of Rome was confirmed;[46] at the same time, the faithful retreated into the Lebanese mountains.[47] The Maronite Church, especially among its Syriac adherents, draws inspiration from its roots in the spirituality and theology of Antioch; yet it also clearly shows how to achieve full communion based on recognition of the primacy of Roman doctrine, while remaining faithful to its own liturgical and cultural autonomy.[48] Sheltered from schisms and heresies, it has stayed scrupulously faithful to Rome while maintaining a constant dialogue with the East.[49] Thanks to its established position in the

---

46 One of the places that facilitated the establishment of communion was the Maronite College in Rome, founded in 1584 to provide training for Maronite clergy based on the model of Latin Catholic theology (see N. Gemayel, *Les échanges culturels entre les Maronites et l'Europe. Du Collège Maronite de Rome (1584) au Collège de 'Ayn Warqa (1789)*, Beirut, 1984; see also the study by P. Rouhana, 'Histoire du synode libanais de 1736. Du patriarcat de Jacques Aouad à la célébration solennelle du synode', *Parole de l'Orient*, vol. 13, 1986, pp. 111–159).
47 See P. Dib, *Histoire de l'Église maronite*, Beirut, Éditions La Sagesse, 1962; *Ibid, L'Église maronite*, Beirut, 1973.
48 On the tradition, liturgy, and cultural characteristics of the Maronite Church, see the monumental 5-part work by Abbé Youakim Moubarac (*Pentalogie antiochienne. Domaine maronite*, 7 vol., Beirut, Cénacle Libanais, 1984). On the subject of Maronite adherence to the Church of Rome, it is important to stress that Maronite canon law reflects the dual aspect of the Church's allegiance (see J. Feghali, *Histoire du droit de l'Église maronite*, Paris, Letouzey & Ané, 1962; E. S. Saïd, *Les Églises orientales et leurs droits*, Paris, Cariscript, 1989).
49 The doctoral research of P. Rouhana presents a useful reassessment of the hermeneutic diversity in Maronite history ('La vision des origines religieuses des Maronites entre le XVe et le XVIIIe siècle'). His research is presented in an illuminating and concise way in P. Rouhana, 'Les versions des origines religieuses des maronites entre le xv et le xviii siècle', in Ch.

Lebanese mountains, it has remained involved in Lebanese political life, and has maintained its Lebanese national identity, which if anything has been strengthened by Lebanon's tumultuous history. The President of Lebanon, its army commanders, and, until recently, the key appointments in the executive, are all drawn from the Maronite community. The Maronite Church has thus been openly drawn into the successive political crises that have afflicted the country.

The challenges presented by the Lebanese war that broke out in 1975 were such that the Maronite community was split into several warring factions. The Maronite clergy were drawn into the conflict between the Christian – and indeed mainly Maronite – political parties and were caught in the crossfire of ideological battles and diametrically opposed political positions. The Patriarch and his bishops were deeply concerned by the threat to the future life of their congregations, and called on them to prepare for a Maronite synod that would seek to engage in peaceful and impartial reflection on the identity and mission of the Maronite Church in Lebanon and in its diaspora. Some Maronite theologians, including Youakim Moubarac, expressed the opinion that a Special Assembly of the Synod of Bishops for Lebanon, convened in Rome in 1991, should not detract from the theological importance and the pastoral significance of a local synod. A key challenge faced by the Maronite Church is to make the most of the inevitable complications that result from their involvement in two parallel synodical processes. The major anxieties that have such a hold on the Maronite mindset[50] should if anything encourage a fundamental reflection on the implications of their dual commitment.

On a positive note, the problems that are specific to the Maronite Church are challenges for which they can take responsibility. First, the community as a whole needs to redefine its role in Lebanese politics. This is a twofold task: first, a renunciation, and second, a denunciation. In assuming their political responsibilities, the Maronite faithful must be encouraged to do so not as Maronites but as Lebanese citizens, and renounce making self-interested decisions misleadingly presented as benefiting the Maronite community, and then also take up the cause of human dignity in Lebanon, denouncing these wrongs as a token of their renunciation pledge. Second, the Maronite community needs to commit to its ecumenical role in the Middle East as a Church not only proud of its Antioch heritage but

---

Chartouni (éd.), *Histoire, sociétés et pouvoir aux Proche- et Moyen-Orients*, vol. 1 : *Histoire sociale*, Paris, Geuthner, 2001, pp. 191–211.

50 See Y. Samya, *Maronites au présent. Libres approches d'un aggiornamento*, Paris, Cariscript, 1991.

also affiliated to the Roman Catholic Church. There is no 'Orthodox' Maronite Church, which means that the Maronites are spared guilt for historical mistakes, but it also implies great responsibility: the Maronite Church can bear witness to Church life in full communion with Rome while yet respecting pluralism. Third, it is the responsibility of Maronite congregations to strengthen their Gospel witness to politically divided secular Maronites in their own community. The Maronite Church must work at evangelising the political class in their own community in order to draw them in and foster wiser choices. They need to exhibit serious commitment to defending the rights of secular Lebanese citizens, and this in turn will enable the community to make a positive contribution to cleaning up both Maronite and Lebanese political life. The Maronite Church faces other difficulties, ones that are shared by all Lebanese Christians, and these will therefore be described elsewhere.

The Melkite Greek Catholic Church

This Church, administratively and legally, came into being at the time of the rise of Uniatism,[51] a Middle Eastern unionist movement at the start of the sixteenth century. It arose from a hierarchical and pyramidal concept of Christian unity. Of all the Uniatist Churches, both Eastern (Coptic, Armenian, Syriac etc.) and Western (Ruthenian, Greek Catholic, etc.) it was the Melkite Church that made the most significant contribution to the rapprochement between the Churches of East and West. And yet it paid a price, in terms of its own distinctive identity, by being the Church that most clearly demonstrated the ambiguity of a dual theological allegiance. For more than 250 years, the Church has suffered both physically and spiritually from division and from the tensions arising from a dedication to Christian unity heavily criticised by the Orthodox.

Taxed by its allegiance to both Antioch and Rome, the Church has made every effort to promote constructive dialogue between Byzantine theology and Latin theology. Its most important calling, fundamental to its identity, is to seek an ecclesiology of communion that is based on the principle of diversity in unity. The Melkite Church exercised this calling at Vatican I and Vatican II, serving as a bridge between two widely separate worlds; now both Latin and Byzantine scholars consider this mission obsolete and declare, even in Lebanon, that although the

---

51 Cf. I. Dick, *Sens et vicissitudes de l'uniatisme. L'écartèlement de la double fidélité*, Beirut, 1982. See also E. Lanne, 'La conception post-tridentine de la primauté et l'origine des Églises unies', *Irénikon*, 52 (1979), pp. 5–33.

presence of Uniatist Churches is tolerated, the understanding of unity that gave rise to Uniatism is a clear doctrinal error.

The Melkite Church was thus betrayed by its own cause, and torn between its Latin and Byzantine identities;[52] in Lebanon, in the Middle East and in diaspora, the Church is experiencing the worst crisis of its history.[53] Now only a minority community in Lebanon, keenly aware of its ambiguous identity, it continues to do what it can to exercise its political and social functions. It has been deeply involved in the challenges experienced by Lebanese Christians; eschewing all political ambition, and in spite of its dashed ecumenical hopes, it has served to bring together the different Christian communities in Lebanon and in the Middle East, and has made particular efforts to show the Islamic community that Arab Christianity can be apolitical and selfless.[54] Its political approach in Lebanon has often been determined by the pressing need to coordinate the witness of other minority Christian communities living among Arab Muslims in the Middle East.

Local synods have on two occasions called together both the clergy and laity of the Melkite Greek Catholic Church to address – with limited means and very specifically – the confusion surrounding the main characteristics of the identity and mission of the Greek Catholics. The outcome of these synods in the life of the dioceses, it appears, has in some cases been very different from the initial purposes of the synods to assess and heal.[55] The main problems affecting the life and witness of the Melkite Church, and which need urgent solutions in Lebanon, can be summed in three principal questions.

First, the Melkite Greek Catholic Church must examine keenly whether it is still able to take on the large theological and ecclesial challenge of going beyond the Uniate model and adopting, within the limits of its geographical reach and its numerical expansion, a new approach to unity – one based on a recognition of the sacramental mystery of the Church that is mutual and shared by each ecclesial

---

52 See É. Zoghby, *Uniatisme et œcuménisme*, Cairo, 1963; Id., *Tous schismatiques?*, Beirut, 1981.

53 Voir I. *Dick*, 'Les Grecs-Melkites catholiques: identité et mission', *Le Lien*, 50 (1985), no. 2, pp. 11–25; no. 3, pp. 41–49; no. 4–5, pp. 21–36. See also A. Raheb, 'Patriarcat grec-melkite catholique d'Antioche. Naissance, évolution et orientations actuelles', *Ekklesiastikos Pharos*, 52 (1970), n° 2–3, pp. 47–72.

54 The contribution Orthodox and Catholic Melkites have made to Arab culture is considerable (cf. J. Nasrallah, *Histoire du mouvement littéraire dans l'Église melchite*, t. I-IV, Louvain, Peeters, 1979).

55 Sur la conscience de la réforme dans l'Église grecque-catholique melchite, voir *Voix de l'Église en Orient. Voix de l'Église melchite. Choix de textes du patriarche Maximos IV et de l'épiscopat grec-catholique melchite*, Paris-Basle, 1962.

entity professing a Trinitarian faith and defending the fundamental hermeneutic status of Church tradition. Second, the Church should reflect long and hard on its current witness, and examine what its presence contributes within the context of Lebanese Christianity. The ambition of the Melkite Church is to promote a kenotic spirit of evangelical service to enable both Catholic and Orthodox Lebanese to show the best possible image of Christ to Lebanese Islam, and by extension to Arab Islam. Third and last, the Church must have the courage to engage in a process of critical self-assessment.[56] This should enable it humbly to acknowledge its weaknesses, and to prepare for a spiritual and pastoral regeneration of its official bodies and institutions, which have been badly affected by war in Lebanon and by the crisis in vocations that has affected both regular and secular clergy.

The Latin Church

This church enjoys a prominent position in Lebanese society, thanks to its cultural advantages and the intellectual contribution of its members, and it gives discreet and efficient support to the witness of Lebanese Christians.[57] Religious communities of the Latin rite and belonging to various Western institutions and congregations manage, lead and support key sectors in Lebanese life, including education, culture and hospitality. Their cultural competence in Lebanon has promoted many strong relationships and exchanges linking Lebanese Christians, especially Catholics, and various Western countries. Their pastoral contribution is self-effacing, but they have always played an important part in the theological and general education of Lebanese youth. They have therefore exercised an ever-increasing influence on the Lebanese Catholic Church. This has meant that, unlike Catholic communities in the West, this Latin community has displayed a keen loyalty to Rome in its defence of Catholic doctrine, and a remarkable spirit of discernment; as a result, religious theologians from this community have always been asked to give their opinion on certain delicate aspects of local theological discourse. The Latin approach to theology has always been one of vigilance, suspicion even, when faced with certain prophets of contemporary Lebanese theology. The Latin

---

56 This Church has regularly faced a succession of testing moments in its life (see, for example, R. Rouquette, 'Un malaise au sein de l'Église melkite catholique', *Études*, 91 (1958), pp. 391–394; see also P. Khairallah, 'L'Église melkite: être ou ne pas être', *Le Lien*, 39 (1974), n° 3, pp. 20–24).
57 On the history of the Latin Church in the Middle East, see J.-P. Valognes, 'Les latins d'Orient', in Id., *Vie et mort des chrétiens d'Orient des origines à nos jours, op. cit.*, pp. 502–524.

clergy in Lebanon, who are both technically and professionally competent, have carefully monitored and, if necessary, restrained local theological impulses. Their highly effective and salutary discernment in assessing popular Lebanese religiosity has, however, had the effect of deterring and hindering bold local theological innovations.

The Latin religious institutions were undoubtedly competent, but the historical circumstances under which they settled in the Middle East gave impetus to their thinking and boosted their moral influence. The Latin Church, having first arrived during the tumult of the Crusades, has worked hard – especially in Lebanon – to cast off its regrettable association with a historically erroneous and disrespectful proselytism. There is an increasingly urgent need for the Latin community in Lebanon to revisit its cultural references and re-examine its views and its actions in order to complete the process it has already begun of conversion to, and integration into, Lebanese and Middle Eastern Christianity. There is an increasing risk, however, that the serious drop in clerical and religious vocations in Europe may compromise the quality of spiritual and theological witness by Latin communities. The emergence of indigenous clergy is a positive and promising sign of enculturation, but it carries with it the risk of a damaging alignment with local clerical influences, which are often affected by theological immaturity and political tribalism.

In addition to these three Churches, three other Catholic Churches, albeit in very small numbers, have made their home in Lebanon. These are the Armenian Catholic Church, the Syriac Catholic Church, and the Chaldean Church. Their origins lie in Latin evangelisation, and they have come to Lebanon recently as a result of very complex processes of discrimination and marginalisation in a number of Arab countries. During its years of prosperity, Lebanon was seen as a haven of peace and freedom by these Christian groups. The present circumstances in Lebanon mean that they are in an increasingly precarious and ephemeral position. They are in transition, likely to move on elsewhere. They are unthreatening observers of Lebanese society, their political and ecclesiastical influence necessarily limited by the small size of their respective communities. They have maintained the use of their own liturgical languages, which necessarily limits their pastoral influence to their own congregations.

The Orthodox Churches

These represent about 30 percent of Lebanese Christians, and are divided into two principal groups. The first observes an Eastern pre-Chalcedonian rite (the

Syriac Orthodox, the Armenian Orthodox, and the Coptic Orthodox);[58] the second belongs to the Orthodox Church and recognises the Patriarch of Constantinople as the senior Orthodox Primate. The pre-Chalcedonian communities, who have few liturgical and cultural traditions, exercise limited direct theological and spiritual influence in Lebanon.[59] Their communities bear witness to their faith, but beyond that they do little apart from sustaining their internal pastoral and administrative duties. On a theological level, however, they are haunted by the injustices suffered by their religious communities in Turkey (the Armenians and Syriacs)[60] and in Egypt (the Copts).[61] Because of the uncertainties of life in Lebanon, they live with a perpetual sense of insecurity.

The Lebanese Orthodox, on the other hand, are prominent in both political and cultural life.[62] On a sociopolitical level, they have long enjoyed a cosmopolitan life in various cities and towns in the former Ottoman empire, and are therefore comfortable with secular, intercultural and transnational values.[63] Their excessive attachment to the Orthodox tradition of Antioch[64] can conflict with their tolerance and their humanist instincts. Their religious life inclines

---

58 Cf. J. Joseph, *The Nestorians and their Muslim Neighbors*, Princeton, 1981; Id., *Muslim Christian Relations and Inter-Christian Rivalries in the Middle East. The Case of Jacobites in a Age of Transition*, Albany (N. Y.), 1983; C. Chaillot, *The Syrian Orthodox Church of Antioch and all the East. A brief introduction to its life and spirituality*, Inter-Orthodox Dialogue, Geneva, 1998; C. Sélis, *Les Syriens orthodoxes et catholiques*, Maredsous, Brépols, 1988.
59 For a history of the situation of these Churches in the Middle East, see J.-P. Valognes, *Vie et mort des chrétiens d'Orient des origines à nos jours, op. cit.,* pp. 407–501.
60 See J. Yacoub, *Babylone chrétienne. Géopolitique de l'Église de Mésopotamie*, Paris, Desclée de Brouwer, 1996; J.-M. Fiey, *Jalons pour une histoire de l'Église en Irak*, Louvain, Corpus scriptorum christianorum orientalium, 1970; R. Le Coz S. de Courtois, *Le génocide oublié*, Paris, 2002.
61 On the situation and challenges of the Coptic Church in Egypt, see J.-P. Valognes, 'Les coptes', in Id., *Vie et mort des chrétiens d'Orient des origines à nos jours, op. cit.,* pp. 233–283. See also L. Barbulesco, *Les chrétiens égyptiens aujourd'hui. Éléments de discours*, Cairo, Dossiers du Cedej, 1985; P. Du Bourguet, *Les coptes*, Paris, PUF, 1988; Ch. Cannuyer, *Les coptes*, Maredsous, Brépols, 1990.
62 On the history and situation of the Greek Orthodox Church within the Antioch Patriarchate, see J.-P. Valognes, 'Les grecs', in Id., *Vie et mort des chrétiens d'Orient des origines à nos jours, op. cit.*, pp. 284–335.
63 Cf. I. Hazim, 'Le christianisme et la rencontre des religions et des cultures', *Contacts*, 1983, n° 123; G. Khodr, 'Christians in their Relationship with Islam. Spiritual Perspectives', *MECC Perspectives*, July 1985, n° 4–5.
64 According to one Catholic theological tendency, the Antioch Patriarchate has always been open to ecclesiastical diversity (cf. A. Raheb, *Conception de l'union dans le patriarcat orthodoxe d'Antioche*, Beirut, 1981). See the point of view of the Orthodox Patriarch in I. Hazim, 'Une vision antiochienne de l'unité de l'Église', *Episkepsis*, 1978, pp. 4–8.

to strict communitarian values that hark back to former Byzantine glories; in their national loyalties, however, their attitudes are more open and internationally minded, especially in regard to Arab federalism. A comparison with the Lebanese Maronites can highlight their particular characteristics: the Maronite community describes itself as open to renewal in its theological discourse and liturgical practice, whereas the Orthodox community displays extreme reluctance, bordering on rigid intolerance. When it comes to Lebanese patriotism and sociopolitical matters, however, the Maronite community is conservative and chauvinist, whereas the Orthodox community exhibits a liberalism and humanism that is open to the world.

Following a long period of intellectual lethargy among the Orthodox clergy, the Lebanese Orthodox community has experienced over the past thirty years a major spiritual and theological renewal, a key aspect of which is a desire for enculturation in the Arab world. They have been focusing especially on Muslim–Christian dialogue and on the sociocultural, but also sociopolitical, implications of taking their place within the modern Arab world. In any generalisation about the principal tendencies within the three large, active and influential communities in Lebanon, it is clear that their interests and focus vary according to their allegiances and sensitivities. In its involvement in Lebanese society, the Maronite Church concentrates its attention on pastoral and spiritual matters. The Orthodox Church expends much of its forces and its energy on a deeper relationship with the Arab world and on stimulating the dialogue between Arabs and Christians. The Melkite Greek Catholic Church, on the other hand, focuses on its witness to the value of ecumenism. Both Latin and Protestant Lebanese on occasion also play their part in the tripartite mission that these three Lebanese Churches, historically deeply implanted, exercise in modern Lebanon.

The Protestant Churches

Protestantism has been present in Lebanon since the first half of the nineteenth century. It started as a reform movement that sought to gain a foothold in the coastal towns and in some mountain regions. From intellectual beginnings, it took concrete form in what was originally called the Syrian Protestant College, a kernel of the subsequently prestigious American University of Beirut. Most Protestant denominations have become established in Lebanon. However, the numbers have remained small, and do not play a prominent part in Lebanese life. Their only theological contribution has been a keen commitment to ecumenism, and this has given rise to the creation of an ecumenical organisation called the Middle East

Council of Churches. Significantly, the Catholic Middle Eastern Churches were welcomed as full members.

The Protestant communities in Lebanon, in brief, witness in three areas crucial to the life of faith: promoting Christian unity, a keen focus on Bible study, and a commitment to theological debate on the subjects of ecclesiology, contextual theology, Mariology and feminist theology. Their dedication to ecumenism is worth noting, since most of these communities have not only raised enough money to fund the activities of the Middle East Council of Churches, but they have also taken on the role of catalysing and facilitating the development of relationships between the different Churches in the Arab world.

An uncomfortable diversity

In this necessarily brief presentation, I may have drawn a starker picture than the facts warrant, since the ecclesial landscape in Lebanon consists of nuances and contrasts, and its dividing lines are not necessarily coherent or clear. It is arguably a betrayal to leave out of this analysis the inherent ambiguities and uncertainties, so the reader must allow for a greater level of nuance than I have been able to convey. My principal object has been to bring to light the theological challenges faced by the Christian communities in Lebanon.

Any theological response, however, must also take account of the challenges presented by the sociopolitical context. Lebanon, as a country, is and has been severely traumatised. The consequences of the Lebanese war have undeniably been alarming.[65] The sociopolitical cohesion of the nation has been seriously undermined by various pathological signs, such as the fracturing of solidarities, the dislocation of the infrastructure, and increasingly extreme religious fanaticism. Lebanese Christians and Muslims have all but buckled under the appalling weight of atrocities mainly fomented by external interference. Christians, driven to the edge, increasingly feel the need to re-examine their political convictions and their Christian commitment. Christians may be able to counteract the devastating rates of emigration, the renewed indifference, and the exacerbation of pessimism, but only if they can honestly come to terms with their historical challenges as a community and their faith commitment.

The first problem is a political one, and it will be examined in detail in the next chapter. For now, a brief description of the context will suffice. Since Lebanon's

---

65 Cf. Kh. Abou Rjaïly and B. Labaky, *Bilan de treize années de guerre au Liban. Les pertes*, Beirut, 1987.

independence, the very delicate equilibrium wisely established between the different confessional groups of Lebanese society has been under constant threat from political shocks. In 1975, Lebanon was used by stealth as a theatre for the conflict between Arabs and Israelis. This upset the equilibrium, and the Lebanese lost their appetite for dialogue. The crisis in Lebanon was used as a vehicle for other regional political ambitions. Hostilities ceased two decades ago, but there has yet to be a renewal of any sense of peaceful openness between communities. In fact, among Christians and some Muslims, various inherited fears are being revived in different ways, including fear of being invaded or overwhelmed, fear that community identity might disintegrate, and fear that the community might finally lose heart.

The only secure hope for Christians – and by extension also for Muslims wanting to preserve their specifically Lebanese Islamic identity – would be a renewed reconciliation between communities in order to foster a neutral public sphere. A number of Lebanese analysts deplore the persistence of the Lebanese confessional system; with courage, the witness of the Christian communities could be to call into question the suffocating power of confessionalism. Secularism as an idea is radically inimical to Arab civilisation, and any minor changes to the Lebanese constitutional tradition could spill over into anarchy; it would be a brave and worthy move, nevertheless, to suggest a different model for conviviality. A radical re-evaluation of this nature would however involve deep changes in theological outlook.

Two issues will have to be thought through critically. On the one hand, Lebanese Christians must ensure their physical safety. On the other, they are called to proclaim true Gospel values. Some might suggest a form of extreme self-sacrifice, which would favour the Gospel mission over preserving physical safety. This could only be seen as reasonable and justified if the individual concerned were personally committed to it. If not, then such a gesture would run the risk of collective suicide. This is clearly and alarmingly demonstrated by the gradual disappearance of any Christian presence in Arab countries where there is no legal guarantee of constitutional equality between Muslims and Christians.

In other words, although Christ may not need military support for people in Lebanon and the Middle East to love and follow Him, the human community of Lebanese Christians will always need legal and constitutional protection for their physical safety in a region where people are recognised only in terms of their confessional adherence. Christians are in a minority in the Middle East, but in Lebanon they have legal status. They are well equipped to value the sensitivities of Lebanese Muslims; they must hope, however, that the Islamic communities will

not interpret Gospel values as the political opinions of the various 'Christian' political parties, nor see the legitimate anxieties of Lebanese Christians as an unnatural
desire to withdraw into isolation. Because conviviality in Lebanese society is, in
their experience, under serious threat, Lebanese Christians worry about becoming the guinea pigs in an experiment in fraternal living that seems doomed to fail.
The supposedly consensual tolerance of Lebanese democracy has, indefensibly,
failed to hold back the incursion of political and religious ideologies that do not
acknowledge Lebanon as an established and homogenous nation, and that favour
the gradual introduction of a religious regime that in some of its precepts conflicts
with the Declaration of Human Rights. Political changes of this nature will necessarily lead to the marginalisation and exclusion of Lebanese Christians.

As never before, Lebanese Christians are called upon to reflect in theological
terms on the magnitude of the political challenge they face. Unfortunately, the
theological position of the Churches in Lebanon has one particular vulnerability. They tend excessively to 'spiritualise' Christian political engagement. True
freedom, they proclaim, is freedom from the bondage of sin, and any other social
or political concerns arise from a wrong interpretation of the mystery of salvation. They claim, in other words, that any hope of salvation is of a spiritual nature,
regardless of any material considerations. If the power of the Spirit is alone able
to overcome human limitations, then the true freedom that comes through faith
is the forgiveness of individual sin, not the freeing of a whole community from
shared sin and injustice.

The experience of violence and terror has undermined the sense of national
identity in Lebanese communities. In Christian Lebanese communities the spirit
of resignation is reaching an existential low point. Those who have suffered political disappointment have sought refuge among the religious orders in the Lebanese
mountains. Having unwisely engaged in political matters, they have withdrawn
from the public eye in order to spare their Churches the embarrassment of their
wartime errors. A desire to protect religious authority from political authority, however, can lead to reckless condoning of random policies. The Lebanese
Churches, we must not forget, and especially the Maronite Church, have always
been called upon to play their part in politics. Their acute sense of community
identity has always imperilled the political activity of Churches. At the end of
the war, Lebanese Christians lost their political privilege, and many among the
Christian political class suffered persecution, which led them to seek the protection of their religious leaders. The move may have arisen from a deep-seated and
long-standing sense of threat to their identity, but to the Churches it conveyed a
reassuring sense of agency.

This complex situation puts the Lebanese Churches in a delicate position. On the one hand, they would like to maintain their influence over the mindset of Christians; on the other hand, some would prefer to depoliticise their witness and social commitment. This has given rise to a grumbling antagonism between Christian political leaders and religious leaders.[66] Political leaders complain that the religious leaders are wanting to interfere in the complicated and compromising affairs of Lebanese and regional politics. The religious leaders, for their part, complain that the political leaders are attempting to drag the Lebanese Christian communities into highly dangerous political alliances. Neither party, in reality, is behaving in a way that respects secular neutrality. Their mutual exploitation, sometimes in subversive connivance, sometimes in blatant conflict, does great damage to the lives and witness of Christians.

Another significant problem, in political terms, is the confusion around two levels of engagement. Many Lebanese Christians seem unaware of a fundamental and key distinction between an undesirable politicisation of a Church and the legitimate political commitment to advocate for human rights. A Church can be assimilated into a political entity, and Lebanese Christians have often succumbed to this particular temptation; but this is not the same as when the Church in Lebanon engages in defending political and religious freedom. The Church must learn to renounce political power, but it must also use its determination zealously to denounce the surreptitious collusion of the dual powers and to defend human rights in Lebanon. A clear-eyed political theology is called for, one that can discern where true political engagement is needed. The Christian communities must urgently, for example, address this running sore: should armed resistance be made legitimate? Many Lebanese Christians long to explore in the light of their Christian faith whether violence in the face of planned foreign aggression can be justified.

In terms of theology, three major problems nag at the Lebanese Christian conscience: the matter of Christian ecumenical understanding, the nature of their evangelical mission within the realities of their Lebanese and Arab context, and their witness to individual and community spiritual renewal. The first of these is crucial in the context of their existence as Christian minorities. The Lebanese war and the different alliances, planned or accidental, that emerged between Christian confessional groups clearly demonstrated that ritual and doctrinal differences

---

66 A study of the Lebanese feudal system can cast light on the origins of this complicity (see Ilya F. Harik, 'The Iqtâ' system in Lebanon : a comparative political view', *The Middle East Journal*, 1965).

between Churches only rarely dictate the political, social or moral choices of Lebanese Christians. In fact, these same Christians have been embarrassed to acknowledge that their Churches, which are minorities within the Islamic Arab Middle East, have until now refused jointly to proclaim the truth of their Christian faith to their Islamic fellow Lebanese citizens.[67] These shameful divisions, especially in Lebanon, have led to a serious erosion of Christian commitment. The Churches must therefore now switch their ecumenical focus away from theological concerns, since local and regional ecumenical activities have brought nothing but deep disappointment. Christians long instead for authentic theological and pastoral collaboration between the different Lebanese religious institutions.

The Churches in Lebanon have yet to take the courageous step of promoting a local ecumenical movement to echo international theological discourse; having faced up to the realities of the existing divisions, it should take prophetic steps to nurture reconciliation, not to hasten apparent unity, but rather to foster an economy of salvation befitting the realities in Lebanon. The Middle East Council of Churches is the only ecumenical institution recognised by the four Christian families (Orthodox, Catholic, pre-Chalcedonian Eastern Orthodox, Protestant), but it is presently suffering from structural failures and deep inconsistencies. On an international level, ecumenism is at something of a standstill, especially among Catholics and Orthodox, and this is undermining the commitment of local Christian communities in Lebanon and in the Arab world. Some Middle Eastern Churches are digging into dogmatic positions, and sapping the energy and dynamism of those working for reconciliation.

The need for ecumenism, however, is both urgent and clear, and the Churches must all make every effort to unbend and open themselves up to genuine exchange and agreement. One task is especially pressing: Christian communities must establish an ecumenical pastoral body mindful of the full range of diversity among Christians, and willing to encourage solidarity between them, not only in Lebanon but throughout the Arab world. Catholics, Orthodox and Protestants must together engage in a large-scale local theological consultation, leading to imaginative and

---

67 Georges Khodr, Greek Orthodox Metropolitan of Mount Lebanon, and a leading figure in contextual Arab theology, suggests the need for a humble offer of solidarity with Arab people: 'The Christian Middle East is a spiritual and doctrinal vessel, not simply a collection of ancient rites and communities fiercely defending their history; there is therefore a radical need to foster a meeting between brothers on a road that links that which was "given to the saints" to the suffering features of the Arab' (G. Khodr, 'Renouveau interne, œcuménisme et dialogue', in Collectif, *Les chrétiens du monde arabe*, Paris, Maisonneuve & Larose, 1989, p. 30).

energetic joint pastoral action, so that they can prepare in a spirited way for full communion. The world is facing huge challenges and disintegrations; Christians in the Arab world need to unite in a community of faith and commit to evangelical witness and to encouraging respect for all Arabs.

Rigid exacerbation of confessional identities increasingly hampers any such evangelisation, but it must remain the key concern of Lebanese and Arab Christians. There is now very little that Lebanese Christians can do, beyond the witness of their daily lives, to appeal to secular and Islamic Arabs. Their difficulties are in large part due to the perceived antagonism, fostered by Christians, between Christian truth and the realities of Arab culture. Many Lebanese Christians sincerely believe that Arab culture is impervious to the Good News.[68] This incompatibility is principally due to the paradox of the Incarnation. Arab mentality, it is argued, is incapable of conceiving that two opposing orders, the divine and the human, could coexist in the same being. The key theological truth at the heart of the Christian faith is therefore unthinkable in terms of Arab or Islamic religious reality. Arabs, in the light of their own culture, might also be resistant to, or even scandalised by, other spiritual and ethical aspects of the Christian faith. A completely alien concept in terms of Arab ethics and spirituality is kenosis, for example: its focus on humility and self-emptying cannot sit comfortably with the emphasis in Arab theology on divine transcendence and power.

This fundamental incompatibility remains a stumbling block for Christian evangelism in the Arab world, and tackling it will require theological diligence. Christian truth, however, is called to live in every culture. There is no one culture that has a monopoly on Christ – save of course Christian culture. The message was originally received in Greek culture, so there may well be scope for a creative theological formulation that would speak to Arab culture. Medieval Arab Christian theologians were able to frame workable formulations. Epistemologically and psychologically, however, a deep cultural rift has developed in the centuries since then. Few Middle Eastern Arab Christians have any sense of affinity with the medieval culture of their region. They remain, however, deeply influenced by the medieval culture that bestowed on them their liturgical heritage: Syriac, Greek, Copt or Armenian.[69]

---

68 Research by S. Kh. Samir argues for a structural and semantic collaboration between Arab culture and the essence of Christian kerygma (see S. Kh. Samir, 'Le patrimoine de langue arabe', in Collectif, Pour une théologie contemporaine du Moyen-Orient, op. cit., pp. 231–254).

69 J. Corbon highlights the universal dimension (catholicity) of a spiritual communion to which Christians should invite their partners in the Arab world, whatever their religious

The third and last theological problem relates to the spiritual renewal of Christian witness, characterised by evangelical authenticity. The task is demanding, but it must be tackled if the credibility of a growing Christian presence is to be preserved. The Christian believer engaging in this work of evangelism must above all be fully confident in his belief in Christ. So we are talking about restoring an evangelical authenticity marked by repentance and conversion. Lebanese Christians, and above all their clergy, must be willing to engage sincerely in ontological conversion, and to welcome God into the mundanity of daily life. In other words, to reveal the love of God that is offered to every human being, regardless of their cultural background or religious convictions. Christians who take on this task – even those who are burdened, hesitant, resistant, or secretly selfish – are called to carry the Word of God into the different patterns of daily human life in Lebanese society.

Very sadly, the Churches in Lebanon are crippled by a spirit of indifference and resignation. In some ways, they cannot yet be said to offer a true vision of Christ. The spirit of conversion must as a start reach and stir up the Lebanese clergy. I hesitate to set myself up as an infallible judge of the behaviour of Lebanese clerics, but I do think that a true return to Gospel values would shake the clergy out of an apparent lethargy and encourage a more credible form of ministry. A realistic approach can temper the emotional demands of what is required here; but we must not forget that the Gospel makes radical demands on all the baptised, whoever they are. In Lebanon, the task falls more heavily on the clergy, since they continue to exert extraordinary power to control and make decisions. Ultimately, Lebanese society needs a new impulse towards evangelical authenticity. Christian presence in Lebanon and in the Arab world will only bear fruit, in the present and in the future, if it is clearly authentic.

---

allegiances and ideological differences: 'All the questions that have arisen at each stage as we have come to know Arab Churches all come back to this communion of catholicity. We are familiar with the spirit of reconciliation in the disagreement between Peter and Paul at Antioch. There, both the question and the solution referred to catholicity. At the time, people wondered if the Greeks had to convert to Judaism to become Christian. Today, we ask: do Arabs need to become Maronites, Syriacs, or Byzantines to become Christian? The Judeo-Christians were not required to disappear. And today, we do not make any such request in our Churches. The Spirit invites them to communion, regardless of their particular nature. Whether we look at the varied course of historical events or at the challenges of the modern world, the Arab Church always bears the characteristics of catholicity. Rather than describe those events and challenges in detail, We invite readers to consider a global perspective of catholicity: The Arab Church is the only place where God meets with all the people in this region of the Arab world, which encapsulates the singularity of this pluralist church.' (J. Corbon, *L'Église des Arabes, op. cit.*, p. 208. [*trans.*])

Lebanese Christians must accept that a clear but critical eye need not over-whelm hope, and develop a fresh vision, a serving ear, and a keen eagerness for conversion. The Christian communities in Lebanon will face challenges, fears, resistance, objection, but will also experience fruitful and mutually enriching relationships, as together they follow their calling and engage in a positive way to address specific situations with carefully considered responses. There will be moments of weakness and lack of faith, but there are good grounds for hope if Christians, driven by a deep sense of urgency, will give of themselves and respond in a positive spirit of cooperative solidarity and loving thoughtfulness.[70] Good resolutions will bear fruit if those who take up the challenge of facing the realities of Lebanon, with its stark contrasts, firmly refuse to allow themselves to be weighed down by their history and instead, with clarity of vision, take on the challenge of spreading the subversive truths of the Gospel.

*

The analyses presented in this first chapter have aimed to show how the sociopo-litical and socioreligious context has shaped the development of a modern theol-ogy, one that responds to the challenges of the present. Not a simple task, in the light of the deep complexities of the Lebanese state. I have sought to draw out two factors in particular: the sociopolitical issues (which are integral to daily human living) and the unique intricacy of religious life (which we examined under the headings devoted to ecclesial life). Other possible factors could have included social divisions, economic life, the problems of education, and so on, and these could be the subject of further research. The initial intention here has been to propose a theological contextual approach, an approach that will be explored more fully in the following three chapters. This context provides a framework for a better appreciation and understanding of the calling for an Arab theology focused on conviviality.

---

70 From the time of the Arab renaissance (*Nahda*) until the last few decades of the twentieth century, Christians were fully engaged both sociopolitically and socioculturally in the societies of the Arab world. They give us grounds to hope that despite the numerical threat they are under, the Christian populations in the modern Arab world may once again bear fruit, and regain both focus and vigour (see the thorough historical overview presented by B. Labaki, 'L'engagement des chrétiens dans les luttes sociales et politiques', in Collectif, *Pour une théologie contemporaine du Moyen-Orient, op. cit.*, pp. 265–291).

2

The challenges of a problematic political theology

Political reality has a clear impact, as a study of Lebanon reveals. It would not be possible to develop a contextual theology of conviviality without radically calling into question the situation in Lebanon in all its complexity. In Lebanon, politics is experienced as exhausting, overwhelming even: everything is either explicitly or implicitly political – all things are subjugated to national power structures. We must therefore examine Lebanese political life in the light of the demands of the Christian faith. Specifically, we shall reflect on it under two critical headings. First, a descriptive reflection will examine Lebanese democratic practice and identify the fundamental principles underlying the political engagement of Lebanese Christians. Second, a forward-looking reflection will offer proposals for stabilising Lebanese political life, and present solutions to achieve improved synergies between the demands of Christian faith and existing political constraints in Lebanon.

There is a persistent fundamental issue: will it be possible for Lebanon to adopt the Universal Declaration of Human Rights as a sociocultural standard? If so, how will this happen and what would be required? Could a historical change be made to institute democratic government? In other words, in this second chapter we shall examine only the ways in which the Christian communities in Lebanon have been forced to manage the overlapping and conflicting demands of their Christian faith and their various political roles. Our investigation covers only some aspects of Lebanese politics, so it is necessarily limited in scope. We shall confine ourselves to an overview of the political activity of the Christian communities in Lebanon, and leave aside the many nuances arising from the diversity of the many confessional groups. First, we shall analyse the concept of democracy, as it finds expression in the specific sociopolitical context of Lebanese society. We shall also establish how the Churches' political discourse is unobtrusively informed by the Christian faith; it enables them to defend their political commitment at the national level to promote human rights and democracy, which they do in the face of the challenges to restore and reshape Lebanon following the war. Second, we shall dive deeper into a theological critique of Lebanese political life, and suggest ways in which the inconsistencies and imperfections of Lebanese political praxis might respond to the call for reform of the Christian faith and its subversive power to convert and redeem human life.

The political struggles of the Christian faith: causes and challenges

Describing the problem of Lebanese democracy

The long history of the Middle East has given rise to a variety of religious communities, both Christian and Muslim. The natural contours of Lebanon, with its magnificent mountain ranges, have made it a natural haven for those seeking refuge, and the prosperous coastline has exerted a magnetic appeal. In both ancient and medieval times, religious minorities (Maronites, Shiites, Druze) have found refuge in the land of cedars; the coastal regions, meanwhile, were occupied by the Sunni, who shared the religious affiliation of the Grand Caliph and the Ottoman Sultan, and by Eastern Orthodox Christians who accepted the discriminatory laws imposed by the Islamic political authorities (Umayyad, Abbasid, Ottoman).[1] Indeed, over the centuries, the Maronite Christian minority suffered not only from persecution by the various Islamic regimes in power but also from ill treatment by the Byzantine powers in Constantinople, inflicted because of their Semitic cultural origins and their marked affinity with the theological position of the Syriac Church. The Syriac theology of the Christian mysteries differed somewhat from the Greek and Byzantine. The Maronite Church adopted an openness to Western religion and culture as a way of seeking freedom from the influence of the two dominant political forces in the region. The six major religious communities of Lebanon (Maronites, Orthodox, Greek Catholic, Sunni, Shiites, Druze) have thus remained deeply marked by their religious affiliations, sociocultural affinities, and political preferences.

The theocratic Islamic understanding of social life has had a profound impact

---

1 A. Beydoun, *Identité confessionnelle et temps social chez les historiens libanais contemporains*, Beirut, Publications de l'Université Libanaise, 1984.

on the mindset and the structures of Arab societies,[2] and this is as true of Lebanon as of other nations. Two major concepts govern the political theology of Arab Islam: in any form of legislation and jurisprudence, an explicitly divine frame of reference, and in society, a patriarchal tribalism in which the individual is recognised only in terms of their membership of a community. Despite some isolated attempts (since Bonaparte's Egypt campaign in the late eighteenth century), the Enlightenment has never really touched the Arab world. Modern Lebanese society has suffered from this lack. Lebanese Christians, under the influence of their Ottoman political heritage, have since the nineteenth century accepted that communitarian confessionalism was the system that would most safely ensure their survival. Religious communities became entities that were not only social but also political and legal, with authority to regulate and decide on any individual's fate. Given the confessional diversity, the European mandatory powers, and in particular France, were happy to endorse the distribution of political power among the twelve other religious communities that were recognised as an integral part of the Lebanese nation. Each religious community was to have, according to the number of its faithful, a pro-rata number of representatives in the different political bodies governing Lebanon.[3]

The first identifiable characteristic of Lebanese democracy is therefore described as 'communitarian democracy'. Lebanese citizens are not free individuals with their own legal identity, but are only legally and politically recognised by virtue of their compulsory membership of a community. Lebanese democracy is therefore exercised only indirectly, by virtue of a person's community membership. And in turn, each community sets the norms for the ways in which it mediates its members' democratic power in the light of its own religious convictions. Access to representation is subject to the internal tribal mechanisms that regulate the exercise of power within the community.

This form of 'communitarian democracy' has been subject to much criticism in modern Lebanon, and it soon metamorphosed into 'consensual democracy' (or 'consociational democracy'),[4] in which all attempts at innovation and modernisation are likely to be quashed if they do not gain consensual approval from

---

2 J. Piscatori (ed.), *Islam in the political process*, London, Cambridge University Press, 1983.
3 Ed. Rabbath, *La formation historique du Liban politique et constitutionnel. Essai de synthèse*, Beirut, Publications de l'Université Libanaise, 1986.
4 A. Messarra, *Le modèle politique libanais et sa survie. Essai sur la classification et l'aménagement d'un système consociatif*, Beirut, Publications de l'Université Libanaise, 1983; A. Lijphart, *Democracy in plural societies*, New Haven, Yale University Press, 1977; A. Lijphart, 'Consociational Democracy', *World Politics*, 21, 2 (1969), pp. 207–225.

the majority of Lebanese communities. This second characteristic means that constraints of intercommunity consensus take precedence over the exercise of democracy. Seeking out the best consensus could ensure that Lebanese society lives in peace and concord, but in practice the consensus principle can be invoked to close down any corrections, adjustments and changes. 'Consensual democracy' damages the freedom of individuals by preserving the particular sociopolitical prerogatives of each community. Each community confers its own exclusive rights on its individual members who, anonymously merged into the whole, must learn to be content with the security and satisfaction this grants them.

At the end of an appalling civil war that afflicted Lebanon for fifteen years (1975–1990)[5] – strongly motivated by an unacknowledged desire to wipe out the Palestinian armed resistance that was very active in the south of Lebanon – 'communitarian' and 'consensual' Lebanese democracy became 'schizophrenic' and arbitrarily 'selective'. The Palestinian armed resistance – a permanent threat to the state of Israel – became lethally involved in the fratricidal struggles within Lebanon.[6] In order to defeat the Palestinian resistance, Americans and Israelis gave indirect encouragement to Palestinians within Lebanon in order to destabilise the Lebanese central government, which was in majority Christian hands.[7] Syria may not have shared these cynical objectives, but it drew intelligent advantage from the situation by giving support in turn to the Christians and to the Muslims; its purpose was to increase its hegemony over Lebanon and to reinforce its political position in the Arab–Israeli conflict by defending Arab interests in any political peace agreement that might be agreed and implemented in the Middle East. Thanks to its collusion with the USA, Syria helped bring about an end to the Lebanese war and to promote peace and impose conditions which to a certain extent ensured that the people of Lebanon were spared the worst of any intercommunity violence that might have ensued. Syrian influence, however, has been experienced in Lebanon as a limitation of democratic freedom. The Syrian government is aware of Lebanon's traditional 'democracy', but only as a part of an overall regional project to ensure political stability in the countries that surround the state of Israel. Lebanese politics feature arbitrary taboos that require the population to behave 'democratically' in some areas of political life; they must then, however,

---

5 S. Kassir, *La guerre du Liban. De la dissension nationale au conflit régional*, Paris, éd. Karthala-Cermoc, 1994; A. Laurent et A. Basbous, *Guerres secrètes au Liban*, Paris, Gallimard, 1987.

6 R. Brynen, *Sanctuary and survival. The PLO in Lebanon*, Boulder, Westview Press, 1990; G. Chailand, *La résistance palestinienne*, Paris, Seuil, 1970.

7 R. Rose, *Les Palestiniens. D'une guerre à l'autre*, Paris, La Découverte et Le Monde, 1984.

accept without question the requirements of the Syrian dictatorship in aspects of politics that are more sensitive, and that might compromise the exercise of power, given the vagaries of the country's complex constitution.

The *pax syriana* imposed on Lebanon and agreed by its Arab neighbours imposed considerable limitations on the freedoms available under the Lebanese 'communitarian' and 'consensual' democracy. Using a mixture of force and political dissuasion, Syria was able to 'tame' freedom of thought and freedom of choice in the various influential political milieux in Lebanon. Anxious to preserve the delicate balance between communities, Syria in fact perpetuated the divisions between Lebanese communities and robbed the Lebanese political system of any autonomous power. Major decisions shaping Lebanese political life as a whole, and those on foreign policy, are literally dictated by Syria. Syria has deliberately not involved itself in local financial management and in harmless political rivalry between local authorities and trades unions, since none of these have a major influence on the daily lives of the Lebanese people. This third and last characteristic of Lebanese democracy suggests in the minds of many Lebanese that the preservation of their country's unity, its stability, and its duty to resist the Israeli enemy, are at the cost of Lebanon losing its soul and its distinct identity. Because of the confessionalisation and consequent extreme fragility of Lebanese society, the elite among the political class are seriously torn between the 'disadvantages' of the *pax syriana* and their fears that the loss of an authentically Lebanese desire to share a common life, a lasting peace, and an imaginative approach to the government of Lebanese diversity would seriously jeopardise Lebanese national cohesion.[8]

Lebanon's democracy suffers from these three mutilations ('communitarian', 'consensual', 'selective') precisely because Lebanon has never really fulfilled the hopes invested in the nation. The inflexible Middle Eastern political landscape is determined by a multitude of negative factors: their obscurantist Ottoman heritage;[9] the mercantile instincts of the Western mandate powers;[10] the consequences of eurocentrism in the modern era; the gaping wound of the Palestinian tragedy; the intolerable arrogance of the Zionist worldview; the unpardonable

---

8 R. Avi-Ran, *The Syrian involvement in Lebanon since 1975*, Boulder, Westview Press, 1991.
9 C. E. Dawn, *From Ottomanism to Arabism. Essays on the origins of Arab nationalism*, Urbana, University of Illinois Press, 1973; M. J. Esman and I. Rabinovich (ed.), *Ethnicity, Pluralism and the State in the Middle East*, Ithaca, Cornell University Press, 1988.
10 D. Fromkin, *A Peace to End all Peace. The Fall of the Ottoman Empire and the Creation of the Modern Middle East*, New York, Avon Books, 1989; A. B. Gaunson, *The Anglo-French clash in Lebanon and Syria 1940–1945*, London, Macmillan Press Ltd., 1987.

fantasies of Arab despotism;[11] the appalling cynicism of US governments;[12] and the sclerosis of Arab societies under sublimated theocratic regimes.[13] Lebanon could have become a haven of mutual understanding between religious communities and a crucible for intercultural creativity, but instead, these destructive forces have transformed a vulnerable land into an arena for deadly confrontations.[14] It is difficult to see what the solution might be. The Lebanese people are finding it hard to agree on a shared vision of their communal life that would foster a period of true political sovereignty, real peace, and individual self-fulfilment, in which intercultural life might flourish.

The Western model of democracy is in fact much criticised among reformist thinkers and movements in Lebanese Islam. The Lebanese Christian intelligentsia, however, offer the most vocal criticism of the model of Islamic sharia. Other forms of 'adapted democracy' advocated by Arab regimes have proved to be incoherent and even disastrous. To date, no Arab society has been able to develop a form of democracy capable both of embodying the spirit of Islamic Arab culture and of responding to the deepest human aspirations. Given that such a form of democracy does not yet exist, Lebanese democracy, in its triply mutilated state, is sadly still the only government model for Muslim–Christian coexistence in Lebanon.[15] A threefold process of rehabilitation is the only way to bring hope for Lebanon, and indeed for the whole Arab world. First, a realistic and fair solution must be found to the Arab–Israeli conflict. Second, Arab regimes that are monarchical or semi-monarchical (whose leaders claim to govern as enlightened despots) must be replaced by political regimes that value not only Islamic Arab culture but also the positive benefits of worldwide modernity. And third, the Arab world and the Western world must find ways to establish peaceful relations that are both egalitarian and honest, and foster cooperation and solidarity. Both American political culture and Arab political culture will need to experience a conversion process if these three aims are to be achieved. In spite of the reservations of the Islamic

11 S. Khalil, *Republic of fear. The inside story of Saddam's Iraq*, New York, Pantheon Books, 1989; E. Kienle, *Ba'th vs Ba'th. The conflict between Syria and Iraq*, London, I. B. Tauris, 1990.

12 W. B. Quandt, *Decade of decisions. American policy toward the Arab-Israeli conflict*, Berkeley, University of California Press, 1977.

13 B. Maddy-Weitzman, *The crystallisation of the Arab state system*, Syracuse, Syracuse University Press, 1993.

14 Th. Hanf, *Coexistence in wartime Lebanon. Decline of the state and rise of a nation*, London, The Centre of Lebanese Studies and I. B. Tauris, 1993.

15 R. H. Dekmejian, 'Consociational democracy in crisis. The case of Lebanon', *Comparative Politics*, 10, 2 (1978), pp. 251–265.

world, and of any American inclination to exploit the situation, these conversion processes will both need to draw inspiration from the Universal Declaration of Human Rights.

The challenges of an emancipatory faith

Because of their unique status and history, when Lebanese Christians have drawn on their faith to inspire their political thinking, they have always championed three major political causes: preserving Lebanon as a haven for Muslim–Christian coexistence; respecting and implementing the Universal Declaration of Human Rights; and promoting the best possible social, cultural and spiritual outcomes for the people and society of Lebanon. Lebanese Christian intellectuals and spiritual leaders are drawn from and represent a variety of different Middle Eastern Arab Churches; they defend these three causes in different ways, and their commitment to them is prompted by a keen awareness of the demands that are fundamental to the Gospel message. Following a long process of synodical reflection and self-examination (during the Special Assembly for Lebanon in 1995), the Church of Lebanon, and especially its Catholic elements, declared:

> Strengthened by our hope in the risen Jesus Christ, here present in our Church, and renewed by his Spirit, we are now determined that, bearing witness to his love, we can rebuild our Lebanon anew, and we wish to share with you by means of this synodical message our faith and our hope.[16]

The Church of Lebanon is now called upon to live out in practice its professed faith in the evolving history of Lebanon and in Lebanese society.

The major problem faced by the political theology advocated by the Churches in Lebanon is one of credibility. The Lebanese bishops of all the Churches are well intentioned, but their words are hobbled by a double handicap. On the one hand, the behaviour of the Lebanese clergy is hampered by their evangelical inauthenticity, and on the other, they display a woeful lack of intelligence in their assessment of local and regional issues. Officially, their political theology appears to project a Christian concern to protect the distinctiveness of life in Lebanon. However, a

---

16 Assemblée Spéciale pour le Liban (Synode des Évêques), Le Christ est notre espérance: renouvelés par son esprit, solidaires, nous témoignons de son amour, [Special Assembly for Lebanon (Synod of Bishops), 'Christ is our hope: Renewed by his Spirit, in solidarity we bear witness to his love'] Publications de la Commission Épiscopale pour les Moyens de Communication Sociale, Centre Catholique d'Information, Beirut, 1995, § 2, p. 4.

key feature of any political thinking that claims to be distinct from official Church policy is that it must be capable of exercising free judgement, and of openly denouncing the unavowed collusion between the sectarian tensions among Leba-nese clergy and the sectarian manipulations of the Christian political class. But despite the ambiguity inherent in Lebanese political theology, some prophetic Christian voices have broken through, defending with an authentic voice the three fundamental causes of Lebanese life. So now, before suggesting a radical theolog-ical reform in Lebanese politics, we must first cast light on the distinctive nature of this theological voice.

The first political cause of the Christian faith: coexistence

To identify a theological defence we need to show that the notion of Muslim–Christian conviviality is clearly grounded in the requirements of the Gospel. Georges Khodr, an eminent Lebanese Orthodox theologian, highlights the ethical demands arising from the Incarnation:

> Since the time of His incarnation and ascension, Christ is firmly situated in history until the end of time, when he will have gathered up all of humanity and returned them to the Father. In His travels through the centuries, Christ meets Arabs as much as He does other peoples, He talks to them, He walks alongside them, and will continue to do so until human time flows into eternal time.[17]

The mystery of the Incarnation, he is telling us, invites Christians to take the risk of communion:

> Christians are a community of love, not a confessional community. For us who follow Christ, the only thing that binds us together is his promise to remain among us, and that has nothing to do with the tyranny of time. A testament of love is our binding force, and it is our only chance to help Muslims to taste fully the beauty of being human. We are the ones called to wash feet.[18]

---

17 G. Khodr, 'Le christianisme, l'islam et l'arabité', in *Contacts*, XXX, 110, 1980, p. 100.
18 G. Khodr, *L'espérance en temps de guerre*, Beirut, Éditions An-Nahar, 1987, p. 244.

When we celebrate the mystery of the Incarnation, we are committed to want, and therefore to seek, that it should become a political reality for Muslim–Christian coexistence, not only in Lebanon but also in other societies in the Arab world. Should communion flourish and become an unconditionally open attitude to the Other, it would inevitably blossom in concrete politics as a freely agreed and cooperative approach to governing cultural, social, political and religious plurality. With such a vision before them, Christians must resist any form of ghettoisation[19] or protective gated community. For the Christian faith is in its very heart an attitude of openness.

The Synod for Lebanon (November–December 1995) throws further light on the nature of the concrete politics Khodr mentions. Its reflections call for a pluralistic vision of Lebanese social space:

> Any religion, because it is incarnate, is expressed in cultural form; our
> religious adherence, whether Christian or Muslim, therefore necessarily
> has a sociological and communitarian dimension, and it gives shape to our
> family, social and spiritual life. [...] And it is this intercommunity structure
> that makes it possible for our Muslim–Christian conviviality to flourish
> in an atmosphere of liberty, of equality before the law, and of sincere
> collaboration; conviviality that, as John Paul II has put it, has made Lebanon
> more than just a country, but a message and a model for the Middle East and
> for the West.[20]

The Synod, by establishing this link between the intercommunity structure and the promotion of the democratic values of liberty, equality and fraternity, gave a stronger sense of coherence to the Christian vision for life in Lebanon. The Maronite patriarch Nasrallah Sfeir echoed this vision when he situated the Lebanese experience in the context of Eastern secular pluralism:

> There are two religions in Lebanon: Christianity and Islam. Each one has its
> own value system and its specific understanding of humans and of the world.
> We can therefore state that there are two cultures in Lebanon, one turned to
> the West and one to the East. These two cultures intermingle and coexist in
> Lebanon, as do the Christians and the Muslims. This does not prevent us from

---

19 G. Khodr, 'Sion et les temples', *An-Nahar*, 15 April 1984.
20 Assemblée Spéciale pour le Liban (Synode des Évêques), Le Christ est notre espérance…, *op. cit.*, § 19, p. 11.

living together under the same heaven, in a shared native country, and with a shared history and heritage.[21]

These words from the Maronite patriarch appear to endorse the theory of intercultural pluralism, a theory viewed with suspicion and disapproval by some Lebanese because of its potential separatist implications.[22] Most Lebanese theologians, however, tend to share his view and its respectful acknowledgement of the mosaic of Lebanese life. Metropolitan G. Khodr praises Lebanese cultural diversity, which he sees as an opportunity for liberty and for creativity. He willingly speaks of 'our inevitably pluralistic society, which may not be homogenous, but it is united.'[23] Lebanese theologians, realising that in a globalised world the uncertainties of Lebanese conviviality might serve to provide a focus for validation and interrogation, are rediscovering the eminently theological significance of religious and cultural pluralism.

Before the war, Lebanese Christians were unwilling to test the validity of such a model, thus missing out on the opportunity to benefit from illuminating critique and rehabilitation. Anxious to preserve their fragile Lebanese way of life, they sought only to extol the positive aspects of their lived coexistence, while silencing the demands that a true recognition of their pluralism might require. They are now revisiting this approach in the light of the war they endured, but they have no desire to weaken or reject it. One of the principal Christian theological voices locally, Mgr Grégoire Haddad, proclaims openly that

We are not thinking of a Christian Lebanon, but of Lebanon itself, a place where we live with others and work together as individuals, groups and institutional Churches, assuming responsibility in the light of Christian faith in Jesus Christ for the development [of Lebanon].[24]

---

21 Interview in the Lebanese daily An-Nahar, cited C. H. Dagher, *Les défis du Liban d'après-guerre: faites tomber les murs*, in the series 'Comprendre le Moyen-Orient', Paris, L'Harmattan, 2002, p. 42.

22 According to A. Saad, Patriarch Sfeir's vison for Lebanese identity evolved and matured. His early experience of Lebanese independence led him to see the principle of homogeneity as making mutual recognition necessary but also generous; as time went on he developed a more rigid and anxious view of religious and cultural plurality in Lebanon (cf. A. Saad, *Le soixante-seizième patriarche: Mar Nasrallah Boutros Sfeir*, ed. Jabalna, n.p., n.d., p. 83)

23 'Diversité culturelle et unité politique', Lecture given in Beirut, 18 May 1993, and cited in C. H. Dagher, *Les défis du Liban d'après-guerre…*, *op. cit.*, p. 95.

24 G. Haddad, 'Le Mouvement Social au Liban: un témoignage vécu', in Centre d'Études et

Having in the past taken a minimalist view of Lebanese coexistence, Lebanese Christians have now adopted a maximalist view, in the sense that they are aiming to unpack the theoretical and practical implications – social, political, legal, and ethical – of the concept of 'Lebanese plurality'.

They are now working to promote the notions of deconfessionalisation, decentralisation, regionalisation and even federation, while preserving the principle of national unity. Their principal concern is to open up communication and interaction between the identity-based communities and social entities. The Middle East Council of Churches has highlighted the possibility of an enriching and distinctly Lebanese theological synthesis:

> In the Middle East, and especially in Lebanon, the values of Western humanist secularism, which focus entirely on mankind, are in competition with theocratic values, which focus entirely on God. As a result, people are inclined to see God and mankind as mutually exclusive. We see Lebanon as offering a forum in which God and mankind are reconciled, thus ending the efforts to kill God in the name of mankind, or of killing people in the name of God.[25]

The suggestions from the Council of Churches take a wider view of religious coexistence in Lebanon and confer on it a noble cultural mission.

The views here arise from a variety of differing theological positions, but most agree that there is an urgent need to preserve the distinctiveness of Christian presence within the framework of Lebanese conviviality. Some propose confessionalism (the Catholic institutions, and especially the Maronite patriarchate), others propose secularism (Mgr Grégoire Haddad), and yet others a neutral shared public sphere (Mgr Georges Khodr, the Middle East Council of Churches). In all cases, however, they seek to promote Christian faith and Gospel values. Differences in perception can nevertheless provoke genuine theological conflict between Christians. The second part of this inquiry will explore the theological diversity that characterises Christian approaches in Lebanon. They might in some cases suggest diametrically opposed paths, but they share the same motivation: to take ownership of Lebanese plurality and to deepen mutual religious and cultural conviviality.

---

de Recherches sur l'Orient Chrétien (Ceroc), *La crise socio-économique et la doctrine de l'Église*, Beirut, Ceroc, 1988, p. 211.
25 Middle East Council of Churches, Lebanon on the MECC Agenda, 15–21 November 1994, p. 27.

The second political cause of the Christian faith: democracy and human rights

When Cyrille Bustros, an eminent Lebanese theologian in the Melkite Greek Catholic Church, gave his opening address at the interdisciplinary conference at Harissa (Lebanon), he boldly threw down the following gauntlet: 'If this God of whom we speak is truly God, then our words must be effective and make a difference in the world.'[26] In their daily lives, and apparently because of their faith, Christians behave in ways that demonstrate their political commitment to human rights. Georges Khodr confirms this tendency by saying that Arab Christians express their faith through their dedication to a 'political battle' and their 'cultural conscience'.[27] The political battle is related to the fundamental rights of humans. Lebanon is bruised by apocalyptic violence and appalling atrocities, which appeal to the religious conscience of Christians and call them to action:

> If we are to regain peace, it will be when all human rights are fully respected.
> We therefore urgently appeal to the state to stop all arbitrary arrests, abolish
> torture, set political prisoners free, explain the fate of the 'disappeared',
> permit those who have been deported from Lebanon without a judicial
> sentence to be free to return home and live in safety, and that equality of all
> before the law be restored. It is the disregard for human rights that unjustly
> causes Lebanese citizens to leave their country.[28]

The Lebanese Assembly of Bishops clearly states that it is only when human rights are respected in Lebanon that its people will be sure of enjoying understanding and peace. It is therefore essential to have agreement over the different articles, clauses and stipulations in the Universal Declaration of Human Rights. Multiconfessional and multicultural societies tend to defend differing legal and political interpretations of the fundamental values underlying the drafting and application of the Declaration. Is it possible, in a pluralistic society such as Lebanon's, to achieve an equitable distribution of power both within communities and across the nation? This is the kind of question that focuses the sharp differences of opinion that undermine the internal cohesion of Lebanese society.

Nevertheless, because of the composition of Lebanese society, measures to restore coexistence and to consolidate Muslim–Christian understanding are

---

26 S. Bustros, 'Conférence inaugurale', in Collectif, *Pour une théologie contemporaine du Moyen-Orient*, Jounieh, Éditions Saint-Paul, 1988, p. 20.
27 G. Khodr, 'Le christianisme, l'islam et l'arabité', in *Contacts*, XXX, 110, 1980, p. 101.
28 Assemblée Spéciale pour le Liban (Synode des Évêques), Le Christ est notre espérance , *op. cit.*, § 19, pp. 24–25.

arguably the only way to counteract the many discrepancies and errors that might sabotage the Lebanese understanding of human rights. Not long before the end of the Lebanese war, the Middle East Council of Churches shrewdly and bravely declared:

> In our view, saving Lebanon means that we also save the privileged and unique site of living ecumenism; without it, any dialogue between Christians and between religions would remain merely speculative and would lose its impact on history. [...] We remain hopeful of mutual respect and equality, thanks either to a creative form of conviviality, or to a viable model for Muslim–Christian society. [...] Dialogue among the Lebanese must be the vehicle that creates the state they aspire to, in order to preserve their life of diverse communities, but based on an equal distribution of power, and on a desire for unity and for national sovereignty.

> This implies a system that is non-confessional, but also not theocratic, not autocratic, and not oligarchic. Our Council is committed to a tireless search for an ethical and social order that would ensure that all Lebanese, throughout the country, and independently of their affiliations and allegiances, should enjoy freedom of thought and expression, equal opportunities, personal dignity, justice and peace.[29]

The ethical and social order earnestly sought by the Council should be seen as a shared goal, focusing all the aspirations and actions attempting to restore credibility and viability to the Lebanese way of life. For this to work, the Lebanese will need to rework the criteria and the norms that will enable them to distinguish what is acceptable from what is not as they seek to respond to the demands of conviviality. They will then be able to identify the options and commitments that are congruent with the values shared between Islamic and Christian traditions, and also with the universal benefits of human rights.

In order to present a conviviality model capable of appealing to voters and responding to the deepest aspirations of their fellow citizens, members of the Lebanese Catholic Church, for example, energetically defend the major principles of national identity and the overall values of Lebanese conviviality. Their arguments touch on three areas that have a profound effect on Lebanese political life:

---

29 Middle East Council of Churches, Lebanon on the MECC Agenda, 15–21 November 1994, p. 26–27.

freeing Lebanese territory of all foreign armed forces; removing the influence of confessionalisation from Lebanese conviviality; and democratising Lebanese political life.[30] Patriarch Sfeir asserts that if Lebanese society were deconfessionalised, it would be on the brink of secularism.[31] Many Muslim elements in Lebanese society are reluctant to agree to any such openness to secularism, but it could make a more modest contribution by repairing and rehabilitating the ethical and social order that will be essential to establishing a genuine and authentic political life in Lebanon. In this sense, secularism is synonymous with transparency, with mutuality in recognition and in relationships, and with openness and intercultural enrichment. The Christian understanding of this definition of secularism is highly unlikely to provoke a major drive in Lebanese society to question and reformulate Christian doctrine, as happened during the 1960s, when Lebanese Christians were untroubled by collective anxieties and identity-related tensions.[32] As the twenty-first century begins, the Church in Lebanon would claim to be ensuring the survival of the nation's Christian and Middle Eastern communities; however, it is not presently open to engaging in critical self-examination of whether its current perception is justified, or of the relevance of its theological discourse and its faith witness.

Above all, however, the first and principal aim that the Church must commit to is to defend the existence of Lebanon and its own distinctive vocation. So the most urgent task is to give wings to the political will of the people of Lebanon:

> All non-Lebanese armed forces must commit to leaving the national territory, and the Lebanese people must be able to choose the format that will regulate

---

30 A. Saad, *Le soixante-seizième patriarche...*, *op. cit.*, p. 84; see also C. H. Dagher, *Les défis du Liban d'après-guerre...*, *op. cit.*, p. 201.

31 'Patriarch Sfeir appears to wish to stray beyond the well-trodden paths of traditional Christian discourse, both on theology and on politics, in boldly advocating 'the establishment of a Lebanese constitution on the brink of secularism' (quoted by A. Saad, *Le soixante-seizième patriarche...*, *op. cit.*, p. 107).

32 It would be extremely informative, on a local theological level, to see a positive re-evaluation of the attempts at renewal, during the two decades preceding the war, led by two theological and pastoral initiatives, one centred around the association Église pour notre monde ('Church for our world', involving Grégoire Haddad, Élie Katra, Hector Douaïhy, Paul Féghaly, Salim Ghazal, Samir Mazloum), and the other following the movement led by the controversial Lebanese periodical *Afâk* (involving Paul Khoury, Grégoire Haddad, Jérôme Chahine). See *Notre Église en question, Un dossier de l'Orient Culturel*, Beirut, Éditions de l'Orient, 1969.

their shared life, faithful to their history, and to carrying forward their pluralist cultural and religious heritage.[33]

It is the duty of the Church to support all those politicians, both men and women, who sincerely wish to work towards realising this objective, since 'nothing is more demoralising for the people of Lebanon than to sense that they are no longer masters of their own fate. [...] As a Church, we must now highlight religious and human values, call on politicians boldly to assume the responsibilities they have to their conscience, to the nation and to history, and to accept any sacrifice necessary to preserve the independence of Lebanon and its ability to act freely in making both national and international decisions.'[34] This is a firm and irrevocable commitment, because the fate of Lebanese conviviality – a distinctive, yet ambiguous form of Muslim–Christian coexistence – is immediately dependent not only on the physical existence of an independent, free, sovereign Lebanon, free to be creative and innovative, but also on its cultural and spiritual influence.

A Christian view of Lebanese politics would grant undisputed precedence to conviviality over all other Arab political causes. The majority of Lebanese Christians accordingly believe that since they attach a higher importance to Muslim–Christian conviviality than to any human rights or secularist imperatives, Lebanese Muslims should also attach the same level of importance to it, above the demands of any Arab political causes (chiefly, the issue of the Palestinians, Arab unity, and the cause of Islam). If and when the requirements of the Universal Declaration of Human Rights are properly implemented across the Arab world, neither Christian nor Muslim Lebanese will need to refer to such mutual concessions. The first priority for now, in any case, is to promote a genuine commitment to democratisation throughout the whole of Lebanese society. If this does not happen, Lebanon is at risk of sinking into a deadly mire of lethargy.[35]

The Christian discourse on human rights, it seems, cannot avoid the issue of secularism in Lebanon. The political options for the Christian communities have

---

33 Assemblée Spéciale pour le Liban (Synode des Évêques), Le Christ est notre espérance , op. cit., § 51, p. 24.
34 Assemblée Spéciale pour le Liban (Synode des Évêques), Le Christ est notre espérance , op. cit., § 19, pp. 24–25.
35 'If the processes of democracy in Lebanon are undermined, then frustration, fear, and hegemony will lead to a new war, a lose-lose situation that will also stir up the country's Arab neighbours.' (A. Messarra, 'Projet de l'observatoire pour la démocratie au Liban', lecture given on 10 December 1997 and quoted in C. H. Dagher, Les défis du Liban d'après-guerre..., op. cit., p. 194).

therefore acquired a characteristic self-defence strategy. When Muslims demand
that political confessionalism should be abolished, Lebanese Christians suggest
going even further and introducing secularism into Lebanese sociocultural,
juridical and political systems. If the abolition of confessionalism were to grant
Muslims access to the chief judiciary (a powerful position currently reserved –
symbolically – to Christians), then universal secularism would grant to Christians
equality before the law. But while Muslims reject the secularist model, Christians
feel obliged to preserve the confessional system, as it is the only way to guarantee
their political survival in Lebanon. The impasse is structural. These fears, driven
by identitarian concerns, prevent all sides from granting any concessions. Christians, for their part, will remain captive in their entrenched position for as long as
they cling to the need for their existence to be politically visible. Their ability to
protect their rights is determined by the political and legal sophistication (or otherwise) of the Arab world. Since Lebanese Muslim communities define themselves
in terms of the Arab world, which they see as their principal point of reference
and inspiration, then the only way they will be able to flourish in sociocultural
and sociopolitical terms in their own country will be if Arabs embrace political
democracy.

The third political cause of the Christian faith: fostering humanity

The Lebanese Church often adopts a discourse that promotes commitment to the
person: every person, and the whole person; to the person who lives their daily
struggle within Lebanon and the societies of the Arab world. In the context of the
Arab world, a Christian political perspective that views Muslims favourably operates to some extent as a form of mediation. By its very nature, it gives not only
shape and validity, but also expression to Christian faith, feeding and building it.
This is a view held by several leading contemporary Arab Christian theologians.
Grégoire Haddad openly declares that: 'As a Christian, I believe that […] one of
the names of human love in our day is self-development.'[36] In a display of remarkably lucid theological thinking, he paints a bold picture of Christian practice in
Lebanon:

A Lebanese Christian who has faith in Christ, in Lebanon and in mankind as
the end of all things must act in the short, medium and long term. In the short
term, he must seek to serve all those in need in the best possible way and by

---

36 G. Haddad, 'Le Mouvement Social au Liban: un témoignage vécu', op. cit., p. 204.

whatever means; in the medium term, he must seek to coordinate the means he uses; and in the long term, he must aim to help establish secularism in ways that affect all socioeconomic aspects of life, action and service, omitting no one. This will result in a sovereign, united and democratic Lebanon. Christ will be liberated from the abuse he currently suffers from being instrumentalised, used and alienated. Each and every person will be honoured for who they are, and enabled truly to grow and flourish. [37]

Faithful to the spirit of the Gospel, each Christian must always carry a concern for humanity. The Gospel does not shy away from the notion of fostering human-ity; Christians are bound to serve the society within which they live to the best of their available time and energy. Given the multiconfessional and multicultural nature of Lebanese society, the service of evangelical solidarity is only possible in a neutral, open, generous and supra-confessional context. Human suffering does not present with a confessional identity, and nor should fraternal service be restricted to a confessional identity.

Christian witness, because it is given in the context of the Arab world, must necessarily be stripped of any attempts at proselytism or 'saving'. To serve human-ity is to reject, sincerely and completely, any kind of self-glorification: 'Christians, and Arab Christians in particular, do not seek forms of privilege that can only offer a false security. They seek only the privilege of serving every individual and the whole of society.' [38] Christians in Lebanon deliberately refuse simply to play the part of influential elites able to exercise influence over social services and educa-tion. Their attitude is not dictated by the political allegiances of those to whom they offer their Christian service, since they offer it, without any discrimination, to the whole of Lebanese society.

Discretion and restraint are especially called for when offering support to the wounded, the destitute, the oppressed, the persecuted, the crucified and the mar-tyred. The leaders of the different Christian communities in Lebanon declare that the suffering individual should be the first concern of Christian mission:

We wish our ecclesial and national union to be the servant of all, and most

---

37 G. Haddad, 'Le Mouvement Social au Liban: un témoignage vécu', op. cit., p. 207.
38 Council of Catholic Patriarchs of the East, 'Ensemble devant Dieu pour le bien de la personne et de la société. La coexistence entre musulmans et chrétiens dans le monde arabe' ['Together before God for the good of the individual and of society. Muslim–Christian coexistence in the Arab world'], Pastoral Letter no. 3, Christmas 1994, Bkerké (Lebanon), § 47, p. 74.

especially of those suffering in any way, whether it be from lack of hope, of liberty, of love, of security, or of the basic necessities for decent life.[39]

It is this unconditional openness to human suffering that sets the stamp of truth on the Christian faith. There is nothing religious, political or cultural that could undermine the strength of the web linking truth and service in the Christian community. According to Georges Khodr,[40] Christians should build relationships 'with non-Christians through love, not looking to political gain, for the Church is not a nation among other nations,' but its ultimate aim is 'the development of the whole Middle Eastern population.' The theology of service necessarily affects the way Christian truth is perceived in Lebanon, because 'it is impossible to live together in truth and not to live together in the service of others.'[41] It therefore falls to Christians to focus their faith on the delicate task of transforming Lebanese society so that its people experience solidarity and fraternity and are able to flourish.

If Christians are able to allow the orthopraxis of their Christian political commitment to take precedence over the orthodoxy of Christian truth, their witness will be open to tackling the many challenges of our times, in Lebanon and in the Arab world. The spirit of the Gospel contains and confers an energy for conversion and transformation that can inspire the orthopraxis of Christian charity to bring liberty to individuals and open them up to the welcome of the divine Spirit:

Arab Christians do not find Islam difficult, but they are concerned about under-development, the loss of Arab identity, and human suffering. The Gospel thus takes up the cause of oppressed Arabs. [...] When Christians place too much emphasis on what they say on liberty, it betrays that they have not realised that Muslims too are deprived of liberty, because of poverty and ignorance. If Christians, instead of defending their own liberty, were to take up the cause of liberty for all, then every person, the whole person, would become a potential host for Christ.[42]

---

39 Assemblée Spéciale pour le Liban (Synode des Évêques), Le Christ est notre espérance , *op. cit.*, § 24, p. 13.
40 Words cited from J.-P. Valognes, *Vie et mort des chrétiens d'Orient. Des origines à nos jours*, Paris, Fayard, 1994, p. 211.
41 *Ibid.*
42 G. Khodr, *L'espérance en temps de guerre* (in Arabic), Beirut, Éditions An-Nahar, 1987, p. 244. In the same vein, another leading contemporary Arab Christian thinker, Youakim Moubarac, invites Christians to transform their vision of the world into one in which there is a

All humans share the same longing for liberty; if this longing were to become ingrained in the sociocultural reality of Lebanese society and across the Arab world, this could lead to radical changes in their understanding of liberty and all that it entails. There may be different perceptions of liberty among Christians on the one hand and Muslims on the other; Christians nevertheless have a duty to claim ownership of their human aspiration towards liberty and dignity and they owe it to their Islamic fellow citizens to share it with them. Once they all enjoy liberty, both Christians and Muslims will be able freely to choose ways to develop and realise the organisational structures that will best safeguard their fraternal entente. The establishment, development and flourishing of a community of free citizens will offer the best way to foster this entente. Truthfulness will emerge in this community as the fruit of a sense of solidarity of purpose and authenticity of conduct, of creativity in acknowledging and responding to difference, of a sense of embracing the risk in ethical commitment, and of a sense of willingness to engage with confrontation and to show generosity in seeking collaborative consensus.

Lebanese political life as a forum for theological rehabilitation

Ambiguities and paradoxes

Political life in Lebanon is, in my view, irredeemably ambiguous.[43] All Lebanese,

---

better witness to the Gospel in the Arab world. 'Rather than simply, as in the past, setting a life pattern, the spiritual path we have inherited from our teachers should prompt us to commit ourselves afresh to our own times; and if possible, to halt the slow process that has over the centuries asphyxiated Christianity in the Middle East because it has relied too strongly on the force of arms for its survival, and when in trouble looked only to the eschaton. Christianity will be more likely to last and develop in the Middle East when the fight there is no longer for Christians against Islam, but instead for humanity – for each human, and the whole human; that fight must set its own rules, shared and agreed by all sides, whatever differences there may be in the energies that drive them.' (Youakim Moubarac, *La chambre nuptiale du coeur. Approches spirituelles et questionnements de l'Orient Syriani*, coll. 'Libanica', Paris, Cariscript, 1993, p. 98)

43 I would like first to establish a clear distinction between Lebanese politics and the Lebanese political context. By Lebanese politics I mean the general political activity of the communities in Lebanon and its political institutions; by Lebanese political context I mean only the underlying cultural background that underpins and influences political activity in Lebanon. Under the radar, however, there is in Lebanese society a collusion between politics and religion, so that I shall also use the idea of the Lebanese political context to refer to the hidden intersection between the political, religious and social aspects of Lebanese culture.

whether Christian, Muslim or secular, bear joint responsibility, if not for induc-
ing and creating this ambiguity, then at least for perpetuating and exacerbating
it. Given the Christian context for the present volume, it will focus its critical
examination on the position of the Christian communities. In order to present this
ambiguity in a way that is both objective and accessible, I have chosen to use the
notion of paradox.

Anyone interested in understanding the very particular nature of Lebanese life
cannot help noticing that it reveals a secular ambiguity between the Christian
approach to theology and the Arab/Semitic approach to politics. This ambiguity
has repeatedly frustrated attempts by Christians to identify a theological rationale
for Lebanese political reality; there is therefore an urgent need for any contextual
religious thinking to establish the root causes of this ambiguity if there is ever to
be any hope for progress.

I therefore firmly believe that the way in which this ambiguity is addressed
will have a crucial bearing on any prospect that Christians might live a life of
political liberty in Lebanon. Deeply engraved in the core of this ambiguity is the
triple paradox that characterises the Lebanese political context. Lebanese Christians feel racked by two opposing forces, one that makes legitimate demands on
them and one that offers a dubious compromise. Confessionalism appears to offer
security and affirmation, yet at the same time it confines them in suffocating social
fragmentation. Resistance of different kinds may appear to be the best and most
effective self-defence in order to preserve dignity, but where it leads to violence it
compromises their nature and vocation as baptised people. By exercising ingenuity, they may avoid the worst aspects of their precarious historical situation and
indeed gain respect in the Arab world, but any whiff of corruption can undermine
their competence and seriously endanger their credibility.[44]

This depiction of the paradoxical reality at the heart of the Lebanese political landscape not only debilitates but also exacerbates the pathological tension
that affects the spirits of Lebanese Christians. Tragically, it reflects the fragility
that pervades Lebanese society. It is the crucifying tension between confessionalism and isolation that characterises the paradox of survival. The paradox that

---

44 There is a highly relevant analysis of sociopolitics in Lebanon in G. Corm, Le *Liban
contemporain. Histoire et société*, Paris, La Découverte, 2003; G. Corm, *Géopolitique du
conflit libanais*, Paris, La Découverte/FMA, 1986; G. Corm, *Le Proche-Orient éclaté* II:
1990–1996. Mirage de paix et blocages identitaires, Paris, La Découverte, 1997. The cultural
causes of the war in Lebanon (1975–1977) have been critically analysed in P. Khoury, *La crise
libanaise dans le processus de mutation socioculturelle de l'Orient arabe*, Montreal, 1976
(unpublished).

characterises the protection of identity is embodied in a tragic indecision that moves from recognition of the principle of legitimate self-defence to a somewhat off-guard justification of violence. When all is said and done, the paradox of needing to maintain practical daily life is unsettling to the conscience of Christians, and they vacillate between the need for ingenuity and the seduction of corruption.

There is therefore an urgent need to examine this triple paradox and its effect on the spirit of Lebanese Christians. Theologians may not unanimously acknowledge the relevance of theological rehabilitation in politics,[45] but personally I believe that a therapeutic process of self-examination is a *sine qua non* for structural reform in society.

We are now in a position to examine the two problems addressed in the second part of this chapter. First, we shall present a reasoned account of the endless drift that hinders the Lebanese Christian community from addressing the necessary critical theological reflection on the mindset and political practice of its congregations. And second, we shall seek to identify how a Christian political theology in Lebanon might open up possible remediations, and hope to engage the Christian community in a form of political life that lives up to its vocation and its mission in the Arab world.

The current political landscape in Lebanon

Lebanese Christianity has of course never been able to observe strict political neutrality. Because politics and religion are fatally intertwined in Arab culture, the Churches in Lebanon, which in principle exert a purely spiritual influence, have over time come to occupy a privileged political position thanks to the power devolved to them in the arenas of social praxis and local politics. The need for Christians in the Arab world to prioritise physical survival has been the main justification for the powers granted to them.

From the start, therefore, it is important to point out that one of the major difficulties faced by any Lebanese political theology of Christian inspiration is the

---

45 R. Spaemann, a dedicated advocate of the thesis of secularism, is clear that theology is historically justified only as a way of getting beyond society. 'Theologians can help to awaken goodwill and love. They may even add that at the present time love may have a political dimension. But when they take on the political dimension, then they must be challenged, as they were in the seventeenth century, with "Silete theologi in muneri alieno!"' (R. Spaemann, 'Theologie, Prophetie, Politik. Zur Kritik der politischen Theologie', in Wort und Wahrheit, 1969, 24, p. 491). We therefore don't yet know if practical political maxims useful for the management of human society can teach us axiomatic theological principles for faith.

need to define the underlying political context. Clearly, the underlying political context is a discrete issue; it is arguably, however, extremely hard to discern as it is obscured by the paraphernalia of civil societies, education, science, commerce, family and much else. So is it then possible to draw a distinction between the Church, a mystical body and spiritual entity, and the purely political sphere?

There are two crucial aspects of Lebanon that support the notion that theology and politics are indisputably complementary. On the one hand, the theology of the last few decades has constantly shown that ecclesiology can only avoid losing itself in abstractions if it takes a holistic view of human society. On the other hand, the religious nature of Semitic daily life in the Middle East favours a close connection between the sacred and the profane. Political Islam appears to offer the best example of this.

As a result, there are two competing conceptions of political theology in the collective conscience of Lebanese Christians and in their discourse. The first of these argues for distinct levels, placing politics as a matter for the state and not the Church, the concern of the laity and not the clergy. The second maintains that this distinction is out of tune with the principle that nature and grace are integral, something that is moreover clear from the subversive character of the call to conversion in the Kingdom preached by Jesus.

In the Arab world and in Lebanon itself, the conjunction of the sociocultural and the sociopolitical makes it difficult to distinguish neatly between the two spheres, the sacred and the profane, and we must therefore seek to identify the theoretical conditions in which the relationship between the two spheres can be readjusted. The objective of the exercise would be to enable the theological imperative of the Christian message[46] to rehabilitate the political perception and practice of Lebanese Christians.

A salutary Christian influence could, if it were permitted, penetrate and transform social and political life in Lebanon. I am not intending here to address at length the nature of the theological Christian influence currently acting on Lebanese society. Objectively, however, it is clear to me that the extent of this influence is affected by the fundamental problems suffered by Lebanese society, and in particular by the Christian communities in Lebanon as a whole.

---

46 There is a topical development of the idea that the theological imperative might be a factor contributing to the correction and remediation of political reality in the work of J.-B. Metz (*Glaube in Geschichte und Gesellschaft*, Mainz, 1977). See also M. Xhaufflaire, *La théologie politique. Introduction à la théologie politique de J.-B. Metz*, Paris, 1972.

The limits of a theological critique in the context of Lebanon

We are aiming here to build a theological argument that might contribute to decontaminating the political practices within Lebanese society. These political practices, however, could have an impact on the shape of the decontamination, flexing it towards becoming a Lebanese compromise that would be hard to reconcile with a vision of the Kingdom and with the exacting demands of the Gospel. This is a real and potentially lasting risk, as demonstrated by the many vacillations of Christian political practice during the Lebanese war.[47]

It is after all well known that the behaviour of Lebanese Christian resistance fighters throughout the war, together with the involvement of the principal Christian factions in the fratricidal conflicts in the latter years of the war, not only discredited the theological message of Lebanese Christianity and any notion of the authority of the Church in the political domain, but also promoted secular society as the safest alternative to corrupt, totalitarian confessionalism, and thus thoroughly devalued any sense that there could be a political Lebanese Christianity. A large section of the Lebanese Christian community thus lost any interest in politics and a new theory of political indifference emerged.

A further structural defect has exacerbated the consequences of these political failings. In the terms of Carl Schmitt's isomorphism theory linking the social structure of a period in history with its metaphysical understanding of the world, it appears that in Lebanon this isomorphism suffers from a persistent weakness: the political instinct and behaviour of Christians have never been a faithful reflection either of their belief in universal redemption, or of the Gospel ethic of sacrificial love. There is a dilemma for Christians wishing to address this ambiguity: should they change their approach and their behaviour, or should they change their belief system, their theology – or even their religious affiliation?[48]

The four levels of Christian political discourse

We therefore need to distinguish four levels of affiliation in Christian theological political discourse. At the first level, Christians living ordinary lives are completely taken up by the needs of the present moment: material survival, preserving the dignity and honour of the Christian community and safeguarding its future.

---

47 A. Beydoun gives a useful global description of the Lebanese civil war in *Le Liban.
Itinéraires dans une guerre incivile*, Paris, Karthala/Cermoc, 1993.
48 See C. Schmitt, *Politische Theologie. Vier Kapitel zur Lehre der Souvernaität*, Munich, 1935; *Politische Theologie* II. *Die Legende von der Erledigung jeder politischen Theologie*, Berlin, 1970.

At the second level, we find the political structures and personalities supporting Lebanese Christians. Their political priorities and current concerns vary according to their ideological position and active alliances. There is one particular common cause – albeit in various interpretations – that links all political bodies in Lebanon: the need to use the Lebanese model to maintain and promote the visibility of Christian politics in the Arab world.

At the third level, we find the official hierarchy of the Churches of Lebanon. The official theological discourse of the Christian Churches appears to prioritise the importance of Christian unity, of the durability of the Lebanese political system, of Muslim–Christian conviviality, of consociational or consensual democracy, and of the intercultural vocation of Lebanon. Regrettably, the effectiveness of the official discourse is undermined by the fact that its universal principles are disseminated without any supporting definition of their practical application or content.

At the fourth and final level, we find an explicitly critical approach adopted by an intellectual Christian elite that takes inspiration from modern Western theology, philosophy and politics. In their discourse, members of this elite are keen to denounce the contradictions and weaknesses inherent in Lebanese Christian politics, and to emphasise the fundamental incompatibility between the structural injustices that result from the confessional regime and the clear demands for a democratic praxis in spirit of the Universal Declaration of Human Rights.

The three aberrations in the Lebanese political landscape

Beyond this somewhat simplistic schema, it is important to point out that the persistence of the democratic deficit is in large part explained by the notion of exceptionalism (borrowed from Hobbes[49]). Lebanese Christians see themselves as living through an emergency that calls for exceptional measures, both in their thinking and in practical terms. The severity of the stress affecting the minds of Lebanese Christians is such that their political and theological discourse oscillates between the four levels described above. Christian populations have been so much marginalised in most societies in the Arab world, and Christians have left the region in such large numbers, that those remaining hold out only frail hopes of their future capacity to witness to the Middle East.

The survival challenges faced by Christianity in the Middle East are exacerbated

---

49 Th. Hobbes, *Le citoyen ou les fondements de la politique*, Paris, Flammarion, 1982; C. Y. Zarka, *Hobbes et la pensée politique moderne*, Paris, PUF, 1995.

when taken together with the aberrations in the ways in which Christians conduct politics in Lebanon. The sociopolitical context of Lebanese Christianity includes three major threats that cannot be sidestepped by Christian political theology. In practical terms, there are three potentially tempting distractions for Christian political thinking.

The first temptation is *tribal confessionalism*, which appeals to the collective desire to double down in the face of strangers whose threats could extend to the physical annihilation of the Christian community.[50] Survival is the first absolute existential priority, and it jeopardises any self-examination that their Christian faith might require of Lebanese Christians in their life and witness. And of course the desperate fight for survival depends on the confessional system, which hobbles any hope that individuals and citizens might enjoy any inalienable rights.

The second temptation, *justifiable violence*, arises from a subconscious desire to use force as the preferred way to eliminate the threatening Other, however much this might undermine the rational and patient management of difference and inequality.[51] The second absolute priority is protection of the community's dignity, and yet this subverts authentically evangelical Christian spirituality, and weakens any witness by Christians to ethical Christian values of gentleness and sacrificial love.

The third and last temptation is *institutionalised corruption*; it is linked to the anomaly that lies buried deep within the social instincts of the Lebanese. Unconditional material success offers justification in that it immunises the family and community group from harm, guaranteeing shelter and effective protection from the precariousness of life in Lebanon; as a result, material success is seen as the third absolute priority, yet it sabotages any sense that those managing the lives of their fellow citizens might be transparent, honest and upright. In a confessional

---

50 A. Beydon describes the genesis of this aberration by invoking the traumatising historical experiences of the Lebanese. See his *Identité confessionnelle et temps social chez les historiens libanais contemporains*, Beirut, Publications de l'Université Libanaise, 1984.
51 The modern interpretation of justice attempts seriously to engage with the complexity of the very nature of ways in which conflict between humans gives rise to injustice, and of its subconscious or even hidden motivations. Cf. J. Rawls, *A Theory of Justice*, Cambridge (Mass.), 1971; Cl. Bruaire, *La raison politique*, Paris, 1974. Ricœur seeks, on the other hand, to define the formal conditions for justice by allying it to the necessary requirements for coexistence: 'It seems reasonable to assume that the wish to live together is universal. But as soon as we qualify this by expressing the desire for just institutions, we inextricably link the universal with the contextual. We immediately have to ask: what is a just institution? And, as a necessary corollary, we then have to ask who we want to live with and under what rules.' (P. Ricœur, *Le juste*, II, Paris, Éditions Esprit, 2001, p. 270).

society that resists any critical examination, the corruption of ingenuity seems to have become the only safety exit for Lebanese Christians, not only in the way they think about politics but also in their opportunistic political behaviour.

The seriousness of these three political aberrations should incite Christian political thinkers to raise the alarm in Lebanon about the fatal risk of being led into political behaviours dictated entirely by this triple anomaly. In order to help Lebanese Christians to resist this triple temptation, it should be possible to contextualise the Christian faith, in other words to adapt it for the current historical conditions in which they are living – within the context of the Arab world – in order to identify patterns of rehabilitation that local Christian communities might sanction and bring into being within relevant legal and political structures. The second part of this chapter is given over to exploring approaches to these patterns of rehabilitation.

Paths to conversion

Trinitarian openness, or confessional withdrawal?

The Christian faith operates in the context of interpersonal relationship; this speaks to the Lebanese confessional mindset in the sense that it uses the Trinitarian model as a form of individual yet collective expression.[52] The history of Lebanese Christianity has been marked by a defensive retreat into the mountains, but Christian faith calls for an open and bold attitude to human relationships.

The history of Lebanon has taught Lebanese Christian theology to see a somewhat unclear association between monotheism (one single God) and monarchy (one single political principle, one single confessional profile, one single guiding authority).[53] However, according to Y. Congar,[54] Christian political thinking has too often been in thrall to a form of paternalism or patriarchalism that has closed its eyes to the notion that God is a father only because he has a Son to whom he gives everything, and with whom he has a fraternal relationship.

In other words, if it is only through their bond of fraternal love, which we call the Spirit, that we can enter into relationship with the Father and with the Son, then it is that Spirit that preserves us from having the kind of purely paternal

---

52 Y. Congar, 'Le monothéisme politique et le Dieu Trinité', *Nouvelle Revue Théologique*, Louvain, 1981, 103, pp. 3–17.

53 Christianity does not see the power of the community as sacred; in its day, however, the understanding that the Roman empire (Pax Augustana) was unified granted providential advantage to the spread of the Gospel.

54 Y. Congar, *Jalons pour une théologie du laïcat*, Paris, 1954.

concept of royal authority that would exclude any notion of fraternity, of openness in relationship, and permanently infantilise the Kingdom's subjects. We might perhaps wonder whether the lack of a flourishing Trinitarian theology in Lebanon might not at least partially explain the crucial lack of the citizen status that could transcend the narrow limitations of communitarianism.

The paternalism discussed above[55] is naturally closely linked to the Pauline theology of the established order,[56] a theology dominated by the notion that the Second Coming is imminent. Such a theology need not be seen as essential in the Lebanese context. A contextual Trinitarian theology in Lebanon could, however, protect the Lebanese political sphere from the allure of confessional or community despotism. An understanding of the openness of relationship within Trinitarian life, seeing it as a free but necessary outpouring of self-revelation, removes the temptation for the Lebanese political powers, or for confessional groupings in an imperial fiat, subconsciously to imitate the divine power that can be exercised or withheld at will.[57] If Lebanese political forces could align themselves with the spontaneous Trinitarian outpouring of life, it could lead to the healthy development of a better forum for communication, interaction, and critical distancing within Lebanese society.

The effectiveness of gentleness, or the effectiveness of violence?

The Christian Lebanese political context seems to be the captive of a dialectic of verbal violence and unquenched revenge. Given this suppressed and expressed aggression, there is a need to choose one's words with care (Habermas's ideal speech situation) so that nothing can hinder free and open discussion and criticism of the more extreme injustices in Lebanon (Israeli aggression, Islamic fundamentalism, American cynicism, Arab obscurantism, the opportunism of Arab regimes, Lebanese tribalism). Christian Lebanese political theology must take it upon itself to demonstrate the crucial importance of healing through dialogue and mutual constructive criticism, over against the effect of the barbed verbal retort.[58]

---

55 E. Peterson, 'Der Monotheismus als politisches Problem', in *Theologische Traktate*, Munich, 1951, pp. 45–147.

56 J. Taubes, *Die politische Theologie des Paulus*, Munich, 1993.

57 M. Theunissen, *Negative Theologie der Zeit*, Frankfurt, 1991.

58 See J. W. Skillen and R. M. McCarthy (eds), *Political Order and the Plural Structure of Society*, Atlanta, 1991. See also these works by J. Habermas: *Théorie de l'agir communicationnel*, Paris, Fayard, 1981; *Morale et communication*, Paris, Cerf, 1986; *Droit et démocratie*, Paris, Gallimard, 1997.

The Christian faith is fundamentally based on an acknowledgement of the primacy of fraternal love.[59] Today, this love is above all conveyed through dialogue, through the welcome of the Other, and through a careful approach to difference. The right to be different is a key element in the Good News announced by Jesus Christ. Nowhere in the Gospel is it implied that you have to abandon your distinctiveness in order to enter the Kingdom of Heaven, or that you will be forced to conform. Nowhere in the Gospel is violence advocated as the solution to dysfunctional human relationships. Nowhere in the Gospel is vengeance seen as the way to restore peace between humans. Quite the opposite. The Christian faith, which is pure and radical, offers from its unending riches both gifts and forgiveness to all of humanity. The deep conversion of the human heart is the best guarantee of structural rehabilitation within human society.

The Gospel, in its gentleness,[60] could however compromise material survival. It is only if the seeds of evangelistic action are sown deeply that Christian witness will reliably bear spiritual fruit. Lebanese Christians must choose between two types of survival: either physically as a community, or spiritually in the form of their core evangelistic message. This is an agonising dilemma: a sincere adherence to living according to the Beatitudes has, historically speaking, rarely shown itself to be effective. Logic would suggest that in order to preserve their spiritual heritage, Lebanese Christians should work in favour of secularity,[61] which would be a guaranteed way to ensure a double survival, both physical and spiritual. If Lebanese society succeeds in establishing the rule of law while respecting the requirements of secularism, Lebanese Christians will benefit from a double advantage: the preservation of their identity, and fruitfulness for their faith.

The potential critical power of authenticity, or the corrupt fruits of ingenuity?

The scandal of Lebanese corruption also needs to be addressed by a programme of theological rehabilitation. The Christian faith does not prevent human creativity or the drive for self-fulfilment, and an ethical approach to evangelistic authenticity urges Lebanese Christians constantly to strive to transform themselves in the image of Christ in His exemplary integrity and pellucid perfection. The model that

---

59 B. Wannenwetsch, *Gottesdienst als Lebensform*, Stuttgart, 1997.
60 The word *douceur*, translated here as either *gentleness* or *mildness*, refers to the notion of 'the meek' or 'meekness', as in the third Beatitude (Matthew 5.5).
61 Cf. P. Manent, *La cité des hommes*, Paris, 1994; J. Milbank, *Theology and Social Theory. Beyond Secular Reason*, Oxford, 1990.

Christ set of a close relationship between his thinking, his words and his deeds offers huge inspiration to the actions of Lebanese Christians.

Self-confidence among members of Lebanese society is deeply scarred, and this owes much to Lebanese Christians having become accustomed to corrupt practices, to the extent that this has penetrated deeply into their character, and into the mindset of both individuals and communities. And yet, Christian faith frees individuals from the fears, both internal and external, that might lead them down the wayward path of corruption. But we can escape the false argument that this morbid money-driven logic is inevitable, if we can only acknowledge, in the light of God's superabundant grace, that we are both fragile and naked.

To counter the ingenuity of corruption, the spirit of evangelism highlights the value of a pure and healthy inner life, free from the influence of the oppressive concerns of Lebanese society. If and when Lebanese Christians can learn to value the evangelist at the core of their being, they will find strength to resist the morbid temptation vainly to seek success at the cost of their ethical values. Lebanese Christian communities must now urgently embark on an intense theological conversion in order to rekindle the virtues of personal integrity, rectitude and honesty. The stakes are high: their credibility, their witness and their Gospel message.

Towards a realistic political utopia

It is clear that the task is vast, in strong contrast to a contextual theology that bears itself with humility and discretion within the context of the Arab world. The reality of life in Lebanon is deeply integrated into Arab reality, and resistant, it seems, to any attempts to reform it. Many Lebanese Christians prefer, as a result, to focus their faith activities on other mission fields. They are instinctively aware that ideas alone will not be enough to change the Arab world. The current worldwide Islamic mindset is traditionalist, and presents a disappointing image of ineffectual sterility.

The disappointment is exacerbated by the weakness of the political landscape in Lebanon. A climate of ontological fear and paralysing uncertainty precludes any hope that Christians might harbour for liberty,[62] as defined in a global sense in the Universal Declaration of Human Rights.[63] The two predominant political

---

62 This claim, it seems to me, follows on from the theoretical attempts by Lebanese Christians in their political struggles to raise awareness and promote critical maturity (Collectif, *Le droit à la différence pour plus de justice et de liberté*, Centre d'Études et de Recherches sur l'Orient Chrétien, Beirut, 1987).

63 It is becoming ever more urgent to focus energies on promoting the adoption of the ethical

models in the region (*extra muros*, the injustice of Israel, and *intra muros*, Arab despotism) do not augur well for a democratic future. The collision of these two models has given rise to the Palestinian tragedy that has brought suffering to Lebanon also.

Many Lebanese feel torn between two kinds of commitment. A commitment to resist the hegemonic ambitions of the state of Israel, and a commitment to fight against the inconsistencies inherent to the very concept of Arab identity. No Lebanese would wish to endorse the injustice perpetrated against the Palestinian people. And in the same way, no Lebanese would choose to replicate the model of Arab identity as it exists in the majority of the Arab nations ruled by despots and opportunists.

In its political struggle, the Christian faith therefore aims to evoke in Lebanese society a heightened awareness of the tension experienced by Christians. The Lebanese Church is pleading in its political messages for a threefold recalibration towards rehabilitation. First, to rehabilitate Lebanese political life, it calls for the rejection of controlling interference by outside powers, and of institutionalised corruption. Lebanese society has suffered in silence from countless distortions and failures; it needs a clean break and a refreshed approach to the way politics is conducted.

Second, in order to heal the political landscape of the Arab world, Lebanese Christians, who feel a profound affiliation and solidarity with the Arab world and its peoples, especially the Palestinians, hope to promote a twofold relationship of solidarity. In support of the Palestinian people, they are urging the international community to influence the Israeli people towards a renewed approach to politics. In support of wider Arab populations, they are encouraging Arab societies to take urgent steps towards democratising the Arab world.

And third, they are engaged in fostering a healthy worldwide interculturalism. The Lebanese model, in spite of its weaknesses, its limitations and its challenges, is a precious forum in which Christianity and Islam are able to interact. Christians and Muslims share the same social, cultural, economic and political spheres on an equal footing in Lebanon. The war should have taught them to avoid two fatal temptations: to benefit outside powers because of disaffection in their political engagement, and to exclude the Other – an option that leads to national suicide. Most Lebanese are now well aware that a person, once humiliated, is open to

---

and legal principles of human rights in the Arab world (Collectif, *Vers une convention régionale des droits de l'homme au Moyen-Orient à partir du Liban et de l'Égypte*, Kaslik, Publications de l'Université Saint-Esprit de Kaslik, 1995.)

radicalisation. To counter the consequences of inspiring individuals to engage in murderous harm, as an alternative, they offer humanity an inspiration to act hospitably.

In the political struggle in which the Christian faith is engaged, however, there is no intention to offer a simplistic explanation for the complexity of the sociopolitical landscape either in Lebanon or in the wider Arab world. Nor is an ill-judged if comforting utopia on offer. Any attempt rapidly to skim over the contradictions and inescapable problems of Lebanese political life, and of the regional Arab context, runs the risk of seeming to sit lightly to the serious political, religious and cultural characteristics of the Middle East. But to abandon the fight is to underestimate the influence here and now of Christian faith on life in Lebanon, and to be content to settle it in a metahistorical eschatological shrine. If they are to live together and to convert political praxis in Lebanon, Lebanese Christians owe it to themselves and others to identify a realistic utopia that will achieve both individual and communitarian catharsis.

Whatever happens, faithful Christians in Lebanon are taking up the cause of human rights and democracy. So it is fair to say, without exaggeration, that the only Christian theology that is now relevant in Lebanon and able to challenge and mobilise the human potential of Lebanese society is one that is involved in politics and closely focused on liberty and interculturalism. Post-war Lebanese theology must aim to promote the importance of humanity and the rehabilitation of politics. A renewed approach to theology in Lebanon must work in tandem with a new approach to Muslim–Christian interculturality and to practising politics. Lebanese Christians must therefore ask themselves if they are able to seize all that this historic new opportunity offers in order to refresh their Christian witness, to make it existentially relevant and spiritually fruitful.

If they are willing to do this, they should take into consideration a theological approach to the Cross[64] that may be tremendously helpful in rehabilitating the Lebanese political landscape. According to the Lutheran theologian J. Moltmann, the scandal of the Cross could suggest that Christians should constantly criticise political regimes that are at risk of crucifying the righteous. A responsible Lebanese Christian theology should therefore have the courage to dissociate concern for communitarian survival from the theological calling to denounce the failings of the Lebanese political system and social structures. Instead of sanctifying the social order, for which the imminent Second Coming is not a necessary concern,

---

64 J. Moltmann, *Der gekreuzigte Gott. Das Kreuz Christi als Grund und Kritik christlicher Theologie*, Munich, 1973.

Christian discourse in Lebanon should aim to foster in their fellow citizens a sense of responsibility, and an adult attitude to the problems caused by their argumentative patterns of behaviour.

It remains to be seen whether the theological rehabilitation offered by the Christian faith might be welcomed by Lebanese Muslims. Whatever happens, the effect of conversion on Lebanese Christianity can only have a positive influence on good relationships within Lebanon, and foster a desire for reform and rehabilitation. If Saint Paul[65] and Saint Augustine[66] considered political power to be both a punishment for sin and a way of limiting the harm of sin, then true social and political justice in a multicultural society such as Lebanon's might perhaps demand obedience to the true God, an obedience that can take effect only through Christ.

Yet the conversion of Lebanese Christianity argues for the centrality of Christ. And the saving value of Christ's mediation is not acknowledged in the same manner in all the Lebanese Christian communities. Does this mean that any rehabilitation of the Lebanese political landscape will need to invoke a Muslim–Christian theological correction? A positive approach to this question requires agreement on the shared religious content of any such correction that might fit in with both Christian and Muslim theological worldviews, as well as being capable of offering rehabilitation for the threefold failures of Lebanese politics.[67] The secular element in Lebanese society is institutionally separate, yet it should also be able to contribute to the rehabilitation of the complex texture of the Lebanese political landscape.[68] Given the intricacies of Lebanese life, the most fruitful

65 J. Murphy-O'Connor, *L'existence chrétienne selon saint Paul*, Paris, 1974; S. Westerholm, *Israel's Law and the Church's Faith. Paul and His Recent Interpreters*, Grand Rapids (Mich.), 1988.

66 Augustin, *La cité de Dieu*, Paris, Garnier, 1957; *La foi chrétienne*, Paris, Desclée de Brouwer, 1982; É. Gilson, *Introduction à l'étude de saint Augustin*, Paris, Vrin, 1982; H. Marrou, *Saint Augustin et l'augustinisme*, Paris, Seuil, 1999.

67 On this, it will be very helpful to consult the arguments presented by Youakim Moubarac in his *Pentalogie islamo-chrétienne*, tome IV: *Les Chrétiens et le monde arabe*, Beirut, Cénacle Libanais, 1973.

68 An essential task is the reformulation of the Lebanese constitution; it seems to me that the contribution of the three parties involved – Christian, Muslim and secular – is so far unclear, and could be problematic. Is it possible seriously to envisage the possibility of a pluralistic Lebanese constitution, one that might be able to take account of the inevitably diverse sociocultural sensitivities of the Lebanese population? Paul Ricœur has quietly made some extremely helpful suggestions: 'In a contingent context (geographical, historical, social, cultural), the incumbent political personalities, for reasons not necessarily clear to them at the time, may be able to put forward to their fellow citizens a "good constitution". This is a new

approach to creating profound agreement and valuable support for the process of rehabilitation should be to take inspiration from the Universal Declaration of Human Rights. Lebanese society as a whole, however, must commit to a serious examination of the ways in which it proposes to receive and adapt the Declaration to its purposes. While respecting the spirit and the potential for subversion contained in the Declaration, Lebanese citizens should be able, through debate, to identify from it some legal notions to resource the establishment of a civil society keen to embrace its own form of pluralism – a pluralism necessarily shaped, in its turn, by the nature of Lebanon's religious plurality. A properly Lebanese secularism should be able to reconcile Lebanese faith, as expressed in its many religious bodies, and the demands of a reshaped, deconfessionalised politics.

---

example of political judgement in the moment, where *eubolia* rests on nothing other than the conviction of those involved, on their sense of justice, of the virtue of institutions, at the time that they make their "historic" choice.' (P. Ricœur, *Soi-même comme un autre*, Paris, Seuil, 1990, p. 302).

3

Theological thinking in Lebanon

The problem of the teaching of theology

The current situation

A description of the Lebanese context is the best way to approach an understanding of the issue of theology. The Lebanese Christian communities are seeking to live out their calling and to better understand the significance of their commitment in a context of perennial sociopolitical uncertainty. The uncertainty makes not only their own lives but the very life of the country precarious. Christian faith in Lebanon is conditioned by this shared challenge. This third chapter will explore how, against such a sociocultural and sociopolitical background, Christian faith is expressed and passed on within the Christian communities. Given that Lebanon lacks any properly formulated or coherent contextual theological thinking, this seems a reasonable approach. The thinking is as yet ill defined, and a critical examination of the realities of theological education will incidentally help to reveal its inconsistencies and the challenges it presents. The content of what is passed on in terms of theological education only tangentially corresponds to what might be expected of a properly contextualised theology. What is taught is more in the nature of theoretical elements taken from imported theological experiences, rather than what has been learned through a living faith. We must therefore start by assessing the Christian theological education currently available in Lebanon, before we can start to propose a new local theological thinking.

It is well known that there is a religious vitality to many aspects of life in modern Lebanon, especially in the teaching of theology, both Christian and Muslim. There were shoots of this vitality at the start of the Lebanese war (1975–1990), and since the end of the war it has grown, reaching a climax in fierce demands for independence from the different Christian communities in Lebanon. When the political voices were silenced in Lebanon, soon the roles within society were reversed, and religious voices, especially Christian, gradually took over from the gagged political voices that were being forced towards compromise. The vitality in religion thus failed to lead to a better theological understanding of Christian commitment, and instead betrayed a poorly understood political malaise. Religion, it turned out, was being systematically instrumentalised by politics.

Various factors explained the vitality: the confessional nature of Lebanese society, which deepens divisions and causes excessive rivalry between communities;[1] the identity crisis exacerbated by lethal conflicts not only locally, but also regionally and even globally;[2] the weakening of state structures that ensured that faith-based organisations and associations were integrated, protected and promoted;[3] and the challenge of life in Lebanon, which is precarious and therefore drives people to seek refuge in the strength they see in religious life.

Religious vitality, it appears, is largely due to the difficulties presented by daily life in Lebanon. Such difficulties naturally create a need for various kinds of sociocultural action. Lebanese religious practice is a faithful reflection of the hopes and aspirations of the Christian communities, but it is also the case that the teaching of theology reveals that in their religious practice the communities are keen to take on responsibility for the complexity and implications of practising a religious life in Lebanon.

Before we embark on this critical assessment, we need to note that the proper status of Christian theology in Lebanon, which is the focus of my approach here, has never been examined as an entity. Some investigations of specific aspects of it have been carried out,[4] but no monographic account has yet been given of current Lebanese theological thinking. No serious research has been carried out, or conclusions reached, about the facts of religious life in Lebanon[5] or the current state of theological thinking, let alone the teaching of theology.[6] Some sociologists of

1 L. H. De Bar, *Les communautés confessionnelles du Liban*, Paris, 1983.

2 G. Corm, *Géopolitique du conflit libanais. Étude historique et sociologique*, Paris, La Découverte, 1987.

3 É. Picard, *Liban. État de discorde. Des fondations aux guerres fratricides*, Paris, Flammarion, 1988.

4 I need here to cite an earlier work of mine, published in Arabic, on the renewal of contemporary Arab Christian theological thinking (M. Aoun, *La pensée arabe chrétienne. Requêtes d'une réforme d'actualisation*, Beirut, Dâr Al-Talî'a, 2007).

5 J.-P. Charnay, *Sociologie religieuse de l'Islam. Préliminaires*, Paris, 1977.

6 On the subject of the teaching of theology in Lebanon, there is a brief introduction by Élie Khalifé-Hachem ('La situation d'une faculté de théologie dans le monde arabe', *Proche-Orient Chrétien*, 1979, XXIX, vol. III–IV, pp. 306–313).

religion, such as Abdo El-Kahi[7] and Thom Sicking,[8] have expressed an interest in examining religious life in Lebanon. Some theologians, such as Michel Hayek,[9] Youakim Moubarac[10], Georges Khodr and Cyrille Salim Bustros,[11] have enquired into the state of theological thinking in Lebanon and in the Arab world. Samir Khalil Samir has attempted to pull together the Christian aspects of Arab Christian heritage with a view to introducing Christian ideas into modern Arab culture.[12] Some Lebanese philosophers have tackled the central problem of the cultural and political significance of the Christian presence in the midst of Arab societies.[13]

---

7 A. El-Kahi, *Valeurs religieuses au Liban à l'entre-deux siècles 1989–2003. Orientations culturelles et dynamique de foi*, Louaizé, Notre Dame University Press, 2003.

8 Th. Sicking, *Religion et développement. Études comparées de deux villages libanais*, Beirut, Dâr Al-Machriq, 1984.

9 Michel Hayek's main French-language theological works are: *Le Christ de l'Islam* (Paris, Seuil, 1959), *Le mystère d'Ismaël* (Paris, Mame, 1964), *Les Arabes ou le baptême des larmes* (Paris, Gallimard, 1972).

10 Youakim Moubarac has written a vast amount on theology. In addition to his scholarly works, he has written several works of personal theological reflection: *Abraham dans le Coran* (Paris, Vrin, 1958), *Pentalogie islamo-chrétienne* (Beirut, Éditions du Cénacle, 1972–1973), *Recherches sur la pensée chrétienne et l'Islam dans les Temps modernes et à l'époque contemporaine* (Beirut, Université Libanaise, 1977), *La chambre nuptiale. Approches spirituelles et questionnements de l'Orient Syriani* (Paris, Cariscript, 1995).

11 These last two Lebanese theologians have written mostly in Arabic. The great majority of their works have been published in Lebanon. Georges Khodr's works have been published by An-Nahar (Beirut), and those of Cyrille Bustros by Saint-Paul (Jounieh). They have written on closely related themes, driven by a shared intellectual and pastoral concern: the enculturation of the Christian faith in the Arab world, dialogue between Muslims and Christians, ecumenical dialogue, resourcing and renewing contemporary Christian Arab thinking, exploring the ambiguous and tense relationship between religion and politics in the societies of the Arab world, etc.

12 Together with the late N. Edelby, he founded a series on Arab Christian heritage (Patrimoine Arabe Chrétien, éditions Saint-Paul, Jounieh). Among the many works of Samir Khalil Samir, I suggest the following: 'Littérature arabe chrétienne' (*Travaux et jours*, no. 14, 1972, pp. 115–127); 'La théologie arabe chrétienne' (*Journées Romaines*, 12, Pontificio Istituto di Studi Arabi e d'Islamistica, 1979, pp. 93–98); 'Études arabes chrétiennes' (*Orientalia Christiana Periodica*, 46, 1980, pp. 481–490); 'Une théologie arabe pour l'Islam' (*Tantur Yearbook 1979–1980*, Jerusalem Tantur Center 1981, pp. 57–84); 'Pour une théologie arabe contemporaine. Actualité du patrimoine arabe chrétien' (*Proche-Orient Chrétien*, 18, 1988, pp. 64–98).

13 The current leading philosophers in Lebanon are Charles Malek, René Habaché, Kamal Youssef El-Hajj, Farid Jabre, Paul Khoury and Nassif Nassar. All these six Lebanese philosophers have been highly aware of the difficulties faced by Christians living and witnessing to their faith within the Arab world. Each, however, has interpreted the spiritual and cultural significance of these difficulties within his own philosophical frame of reference. What they share is a desire to see the Christian presence as a positive and modern influence.

The Institut Supérieur des Sciences Religieuses at the Université Saint-Joseph has recently appointed a group of young researchers to carry out a factual analysis of the Lebanese theological landscape in order to produce a report on the current state of theological education in Lebanon.[14] Apart from these small beginnings, the three topics mentioned above are otherwise unexplored.

This study, however, has no greater ambition than simply to establish some basic facts. Its first task is related to a debilitating drain on the country's religious energy: the fact that Lebanese theologians seem incapable of giving a theological account of the faith experience of those who share their religious affiliation. This is partly explained by the almost total absence of a conceptual framework within Middle Eastern Arab culture suitable for expressing the particular challenges faced by Christians in Lebanon.[15]

This is a huge task, so I am deliberately limiting my study to the three areas that I consider fundamental to engaging in a critical reflection on the ways in which theological knowledge is produced and transmitted in Lebanon. First, before discussing the teaching of theological thinking, I shall describe the current state of theology in Lebanon. Second, I shall write a summary analysis of the ways in which Catholic theology is taught at university level. Third and last, I shall evaluate the challenges faced by theological thinking in modern Lebanon, and the changes over time in the way theology has been taught within Lebanese society.

The history of theological thinking in Lebanon

The way in which theology is taught in Lebanon is of course closely linked to the characteristics of local theological thinking, which in turn reflects the circumstances of the Christian communities in the land of cedars. As we have already seen when describing Lebanese society, eighteen Lebanese communities share the same economic and political space,[16] of which thirteen are Christian and belong to the four main Christian families: Catholic, Orthodox, pre-Chalcedonian and Protestant.

---

14 F. Daou et M. Asmar (eds), *L'enseignement universitaire de théologie et sciences religieuses catholiques au Liban. État des lieux et perspectives*, Beirut, 2005.

15 The modernisation of the Arab language has always been a major concern of the Arab renaissance and of the present era. See M. R. Hamzaoui, *L'Académie arabe de Damas et le problème de la modernisation de la langue arabe*, Leiden, 1965.

16 E. Rabbath, *La formation historique du Liban politique et constitutionnel*, Beirut, Université Libanaise, 1973; A. Messarra, *Théorie générale du système politique libanais*, Paris-Beirut, Cariscript-Librairie Orientale, 1994.

It follows that the ways in which Christians practice their faith in Lebanon are influenced by diversity, both internally, because of the variety of their communities, and also externally, because they live in a Muslim–Christian society. The various conflicts suffered by Lebanon through its history – some peaceful and fruitful, some violent and destructive – have exerted a powerfully traumatising effect on the mindset of Lebanese Christians, who must nevertheless serve as a key reference in the formulation of a contextual theology. The vicissitudes of their history have convinced Lebanese Christians that Muslim–Christian coexistence, if not impossible, is certainly agonisingly difficult.[17] And ecumenical relationships between Christian groups are severely compromised by the history of conflict between the different Middle Eastern Christian communities. There have been attempts at fraternal hospitality and dialogue, but the strains of the past and fears about the future undermine any efforts at meaningful theological rapprochement. Indirectly, however, the Lebanese crisis has forced Christians to pull together, and to overcome their confessional divisions and ecclesiastical hesitations, much to the dismay of the religious authorities. Many Lebanese Christians feel a deep bond of unity as they live out a shared historical and political calling in the midst of the Arab world.[18]

Christian theologians must necessarily examine the implications of Christian faith lived out in a pluralistic society as divided as is Lebanese society, and they cannot overlook the important matter of Muslim–Christian coexistence.[19] One of the first distinctive marks of Lebanese theology must therefore be that it lives up to this serious responsibility. The first important point of reference for any Christian theology in Lebanon must be the very real presence of Islam. This lies at the root of a real wrench within Lebanese Christian theological thinking. In terms of individual reflection and writing, Islam is the most important and absorbing feature in any theological engagement with the many challenges faced by Christian thinkers. In terms of the teaching of theology, however, the issue is much less prominent, and indeed sometimes almost invisible. This may well be because

---

17 A. Brissaud, *Islam et chrétienté. Treize siècles de cohabitation*, Paris, Laffont, 1991; Bat Ye'or, *Les chrétientés d'Orient entre Jihâd et dhimmitude*, Paris, Cerf, 1991; Y. Courbage et Ph. Fargues, *Chrétiens et Juifs dans l'Islam arabe et turc*, Paris, Fayard, 1992.

18 J. Corbon, *L'Église des Arabes, op. cit.*

19 There are many mutual readings and interpretations The bibliographical register of theological dialogue between Muslims and Christians is endless. The international journal *Islamochristiana*, published by the Pontifical Institute for Arab Studies in Rome remains the best source for this. A remarkable issue of the journal *Concilium* (1976, no. 116) was given over to a thorough presentation of Muslim–Christian theological dialogue.

young Lebanese Christians have finally lost all hope of experiencing truly peaceful conviviality with Muslims. They therefore feel discouraged and rejected by the overbearing claims to monocultural hegemony from Arab Islam, a hegemony that is in woeful contradiction to the former open and tolerant pluralistic tradition of Muslims in Lebanon.

Islam, however, is inseparable from Arab culture and language. Arab identity is thus necessarily the cultural context into which the Christian message must be delivered within the Arab world, and especially within Lebanon.[20] In other words, Christian theology in Lebanon is called to live out and give voice to the demands of the faith within the mould of contemporary Arab culture. And here we see the second distinctive characteristic of the vocation of Christian theology in Lebanon. The political decline of the Islamic world, especially under the Ottoman empire, also entailed an intellectual decline.[21] One might have expected the subsequent Arab renaissance to have given rise to an appropriate and fruitful Arab Christian theology. Paradoxically, however, although Christians were very much a part of the Arab renaissance, this did not include the formulation of an Arab theology fitted to the expectations and aspirations of Christian communities in the Middle East. The fundamental paralysis affecting Arab thinking at the start of the twentieth century thus seems to have had serious consequences among Arab Christians. As a result, twentieth-century Lebanese theologians have not been able to draw on long dormant patterns in Arab thinking in order to construct a systematic and coherent way of expressing the incarnated nature of their faith. Because cultural Arab identity was in hibernation, Christian theology in Lebanon had descended into torpor.[22]

Both Islamic and Arab identities are of course challenged by modern and postmodern thinking. Modernism has evoked a variety of reactions in the Arab world and this has been reflected in the thinking of Christians too. Arab Christianity was suspected, throughout the twentieth century, of being in unsound collusion with Western ideas, which prevented it from introducing into the Arab world and into the various Christian communities any initiatives that might foster the growth of effective sociocultural, economic or political changes. The obstacles set up by Arab modernism[23] have therefore also choked off Lebanese Christian theology.

---

20 R. Khawam, *L'univers culturel des chrétiens d'Orient*, Paris, Cerf, 1987.
21 J. Berque, *Les Arabes*, Paris, 1973; J.-P. Charnay (ed), L'ambivalence *dans la culture arabe*, Paris, 1970
22 P. Khoury, *Tradition et modernité. Une lecture de la pensée arabe actuelle*, Würzburg-Altenberge, Echter Verlag-Oros Verlag, 1998, pp. 14–29.
23 R. Brunschwig (ed), *Classicisme et déclin culturel dans l'histoire de l'Islam*, Paris, 1956.

Fearful of confrontation with Islam, Lebanese Christians have been prevented from learning in any concrete or fruitful way from the experience of Western modernity because Muslims reject all that modernity might entail, and its potential for destabilisation and uncertainty. Looking at modernity, Christian theologians were tempted by what it promises and alarmed by what it might require. In their writings, they therefore watered down their representations of modernity, thereby sacrificing both its revolutionary and its beneficial potential. Their privileged relationship with the Eastern Christian tradition suffered as a result, reduced to repetitive arguments unlikely ever to give birth to real change.

Islamism, Arab identity, and modernity emerge, therefore, as the three major challenges faced by any Christian theology produced in Lebanon. All three should by right feature as the major thematic background in any reflection and commitment by the Christian communities currently fostering religious academic activity. Worryingly, it seems this religious energy may be wasted because of a reluctance to engage with these three major concerns that must surely characterise any serious future theological study in Lebanon and the Arab world. Existing theological scholarship risks becoming self-satisfied and narcissistic if it continues to take fright at the prospect of these three challenges.[24] Some contemporary Lebanese theologians have been brave enough to try to engage with this delicate and thorny intellectual ministry. It will be useful to assess the specific ways in which their conclusions – as yet only half formed – might be incorporated into the teaching of theology in Lebanon. I am describing here the personal commitment that drives these theologians to take on a mission of witness and intelligent approach to the Christian faith among their Lebanese compatriots.

This quick description of the current situation shows that theological thinking in Lebanon is still suffering from paralysis because of past difficulties and future challenges. It is in the teaching and passing on of the faith that there are the greatest grounds for concern. This aspect of religious life therefore deserves a full measure of attention. There are however two important limitations. First, we should examine especially closely theological teaching in the university sector. One might expect universities to foster freedom of thought and the development of critical faculties. Second, we must take into account ecclesial allegiance. We shall focus here on Catholic theological teaching for two reasons. There appears to be an exceptionally high degree of lively commitment among Catholic Churches in Lebanon and they have many links with the worldwide Catholic Church. In

---

24 Co-edited, *Les Chrétiens du monde arabe. Problématiques actuelles et enjeux*, Paris, Maisonneuve et Larose, 1989.

turn, this presents the risk that the local teaching might be driven by the teaching and writing emanating from Catholic university centres overseas.

The teaching of theology at university level in Lebanon: the current situation

The teaching of Catholic theology in Lebanon is shaped by the country's religious landscape. It has three distinctive characteristics: it is emphatically confessional, it is free of any political or state influences, and it is offered through a multitude of competing establishments which yet bear strong resemblance to each other in the ways in which they organise themselves. We shall use these three characteristics to analyse and illustrate our findings in this third chapter.

We shall analyse the geographical and thematic range of courses offered according to confessional allegiance, academic level, and pastoral concerns. In terms of confessional allegiance, there are four categories of university establishment in Lebanon, corresponding to the four Lebanese Christian families of faith: Catholic, Orthodox, Eastern pre-Chalcedonian, and Protestant. Within each of these, the courses of study follow either an academic or a more pastoral curriculum. In some places, academic study is determined in function of an overarching pastoral programme.

The teaching of Catholic theology is principally delivered through six academic institutions and university faculties, marked by a high level of scholarship delivered within university structures. Alongside them there are about thirty non-university pastoral establishments offering faith development courses to parishes and to teachers of catechism at secondary level. This study will focus on the academic institutions and university faculties.

Their diversity reflects the confessional diversity found within the Catholic community. Among the seven Middle Eastern Catholic Churches, there are four theology faculties belonging to the Maronite Church (The Pontifical Theology Faculty at the Université Saint-Esprit de Kaslik, the Faculty of Theology and Pastoral Studies of the Université Antonine, the Faculty of Religious and Theological Sciences at La Sagesse University, and the Seminary of Saint-Antoine de Padoue de Karm Saddeh), one higher education institution belonging to the Melkite Greek Catholic Church (Institut Saint-Paul de Philosophie et de Théologie), and one other university institution belonging to the Latin Church in Lebanon (Institut Supérieur des Sciences Religieuses in the Université Saint-Joseph in Beirut).

Two of these are particularly highly regarded, the Pontifical Theology Faculty and the Institut Supérieur des Sciences Religieuses, both of which are incorporated into a university structure. The Université Saint-Esprit de Kaslik and the Université Saint-Joseph each provide an academic environment that fosters best practice in the teaching of theology, and encourages theological research in a demanding multidisciplinary university context. Each institution moreover has a well established historical and academic presence.

All six university centres offer training for the priesthood and for life in a religious order. Most of those studying are aiming to enter a form of consecrated life. There is therefore a particular focus on the pastoral topics within the university theology curriculum. The institutional names may suggest a variety of offerings, but each of them assumes that their students in religious subjects adhere to the Christian faith. Christian theology as taught at university level in Lebanon is therefore exclusively reserved to those disseminating Christian pastoral care, in both ordained and lay forms of ministry. Because Lebanese society is so profoundly confessional, to date no institution offering a neutral or even multiconfessional curriculum has yet been created. The Lebanese state continues for this reason to maintain a distance from all forms of religious instruction. The state university, on principle, does not include a faculty for religious studies.

University level teaching of theology in Lebanon is both determined and limited by a number of factors: the ambiguity of religious calling among Christian communities in Lebanon and the Arab world;[25] the inevitable difficulties in formulating a systematic description of the Christian faith, in all its varieties, in the context of the challenges existing within Arab society; the principal focus in theological formation in universities on pastoral and practical matters; and the risk of alienation that threatens to divide Lebanese Christians from the Middle Eastern Christian tradition. In most cases, the teaching is offered under two main headings: the global presentation of official Catholic doctrine as it affects the various ways in which the Christian faith is lived out, and a basic training in studying biblical texts.

A recent study, mentioned above, analyses the content of theology teaching according to three categories:[26] the foundation subjects that give access to the primary Christian texts (exegesis, dogmatic theology, patristics); contextual subjects that equip students better to understand and situate the revealed truth (philosophy, Church history, ecumenism, spiritual theology, science of religions, ancient languages); and the mediation subjects related to the social sciences that

---

25 J.-P. Valognes, *Vie et mort des chrétiens d'Orient. Des origines à nos jours, op. cit.*
26 F. Daou et M. Asmar (eds), *L'enseignement universitaire de théologie et sciences religieuses catholiques au Liban*, p. 19.

help promote more effective Christian action (morality, liturgy, missiology, canon law, sociology, psychology, politics, modern languages). This taxonomy is chosen here as being particularly appropriate to the kind of analysis that is specifically relevant to the Lebanese context.

The six teaching institutions all teach a shared core syllabus. Each one of the faculties or institutes, however, chooses to prioritise the field or fields that are best suited to its own character and vocation. As a sample comparative study, these are the conclusions reached by the analysis conducted at the Institut Supérieur des Sciences Religieuses at the Université Saint-Joseph, and which correspond to the teaching in three university faculties: The Pontifical Theology Faculty, the Institut Saint-Paul, and the Institut Supérieur which was the body conducting the research.

The analysis shows that the Pontifical Theology Faculty teaches a programme that majors on biblical and doctrinal subjects. Foundation subjects and contextual subjects thus make up about two thirds of the overall curriculum, and the mediation subjects are given less prominence. Among the contextual subjects, philosophy and Church history are foregrounded. Among the foundation subjects, it appears that there is no particular emphasis on non-biblical sources within Church tradition, in particular the heritage of patristics and liturgy. The lack of mediation subjects, however, is highlighted because of its effect on the engagement of the Church in the world. In terms of subjects relevant to practical theology, those offered include liturgy, art, and dialogue between religions. Others, such as missiology, the teaching of religion, catechetics, political theology, and cultural studies are all omitted. In its conclusion, the study emphasises the insistence of the Pontifical Faculty on the speculative and classical aspects of the training offered; these suit well the intended student body, which is largely made up of seminarists training for the priesthood. The courses therefore tend to highlight the faithful transmission of Christian doctrine in conformity with the official teaching of the Catholic Church. The faculty's name, Pontifical, spotlights the institution's focus.[27]

This same study opens by identifying that the Institut Saint-Paul de Harissa presents a well-balanced curriculum in the subjects it teaches. The three categories appear to be evenly represented, which suggests that the programme has been designed to offer a plurality of theological approaches. Among the foundation subjects, however, there is a greater emphasis on patristics than on other areas, which suggests a desire to highlight integration into the Eastern tradition. The Institut also attaches considerable importance to the teaching of Islam and

---

27 *Ibid.*, pp. 48–49.

to familiarity with Arab civilisation. These two topics, however, are covered in such a way as to squeeze out any teaching on other non-Christian religions. In another of the categories, foundational morality and philosophical ethics are also not taught. Morality is studied only as it affects specific issues.[28]

The teaching at the Institut Supérieur des Sciences Religieuses[29] is marked by an emphasis on teaching practices and on personal faith development, with a view to gaining a better understanding of pastoral activity. The contextual subjects therefore carry less weight than the foundation and mediation subjects. Among the foundation subjects, there is a particular focus on cultural studies, which is treated as a stand-alone subject. There is a parallel course at the Institut on the Arab Christian heritage, which illustrates, using the context of the Arab world, the implications of using a foundational approach to cultural studies.

The proportional weight allocated among the mediation subjects suggest that the course places particular value on the role of practical theology in its curriculum. Courses are offered, for example, on culture and Christianity in the modern Arab world, on missiology, on the theology of vocations, and on spiritual guidance. It is worth pointing out that the majority of the student body at the institution are women, among whom a third are not members of a religious order. Given this last characteristic, which is peculiar to this faculty only in Lebanon, it is surprising to see no particular stress on feminist theology.

All six of the Catholic faculties are finding it increasingly challenging to deliver their syllabus in the depth they would like. Paradoxically, their desire to include the benefits of religious and social sciences within theological formation has meant that other subjects in the curriculum are taught less thoroughly than was previously the case. This change is due to the evolving motivations among the student body at the Institut Supérieur des Sciences Religieuses. The institute is not one that trains for the ordained priesthood, but rather to ensure their graduates have a more sophisticated understanding of faith in the real world. The courses offered have been designed with a boldness also in evidence at the Pontifical Faculty in its thematic selection of practical workshops,[30] which offer a contextual understanding of the theory disseminated in the academic lectures.

---

28 *Ibid.*, p. 50.

29 *Ibid.*, pp. 53–54.

30 A brief overview of the proposed workshop titles illustrates the genuine desire on the part of the Pontifical Faculty leadership to promote the contextualisation of theological expertise: 'Le Synode pour le Liban: étude critique de la recherche ecclésiale post-synodale' [The Synod for Lebanon: a critical examination of post-synodical ecclesial research]; 'Écologie et foi' [Ecology and faith]; 'La bioéthique dans les questions relatives à la vie naissante et à la vie

Challenges and opportunities for the future of theology in Lebanon

Any critical evaluation of the teaching of theology in Lebanese society must be approached from two different angles: the technical and the organic. From the technical angle, we should ask whether the curriculum is balanced, whether the methods used are appropriate, and whether the teaching is effective. From the organic angle, we should enquire deeply about the teaching as it is delivered, and whether the teaching and practice of theology in Lebanon might be improved and better understood. While these two aspects are inextricably linked, and I fully appreciate the importance of the purely technical questions, I shall deliberately focus here on the organic matters, because the quality of theological teaching in Lebanon depends on the establishing of contextualised Arab theological thinking.

We must remember that formulating any locally relevant theology must meet certain initial conditions, including the following: it should improve the survival chances of the Eastern Churches, both physically and intellectually, within Lebanese society and the other societies of the Arab world;[31] it should help to explain the religious, cultural and political calling of Christian communities in Lebanon;[32] it should enculturate the Gospel message within the fluidity and uncertainty of the modern Arab world; it should help to establish a new conceptual Arab theological language so that the fundamental truths of the Christian faith can be expressed in appropriate Arab terms. These are clearly much needed, given the indecisive ways in which local Christians express their faith both in their verbal witness and in their practical commitment. Unfortunately, the many university level establishments offering welcome, training and support have not yet yielded truly promising and relevant contextual theological outcomes.

---

finissante' [Bioethics in matters relating to the start and the end of life]; 'Lecture de la déclaration Dominus Jesus' [A reading of the Dominus Jesus declaration]; 'Dialogue des civilisations' [Dialogue between civilisations]; 'Textes philosophiques contemporains' [Contemporary philosophical texts]; 'Le fait confessionnel libanais: avantages et désavantages' [The realities of Lebanese confessionalism: advantages and disadvantages]; 'Églises catholiques du Moyen-Orient' [Catholic churches in the Middle East]; 'Droits de l'homme et mondialisation' [Human rights and globalisation]; 'L'Église et les moyens de communication' [The Church and the media].

31 A. Mahiou (ed), *L'État de droit dans le monde arabe*, Paris, CNRS, 1997; D. Rance, *Chrétiens du Moyen-Orient. Témoins de la Croix*, Bibliothèque Aide à l'Église en détresse, 1991.

32 In order to avert the risk that Christians might marginalise themselves in Lebanon, É. Khalifé-Hachem recommends that a Lebanese theology should engage in holding itself critically to account (É. Khalifé-Hachem, 'La situation d'une faculté de théologie dans le monde arabe', op. cit., p. 311. See also Y. Moubarac, *La question libanaise dans les textes du patriarche Sfeir*, Paris, Cariscript, 1989).

The six faculties mostly reckon simply to deliver – with varying degrees of success – the substance of Catholic doctrine as it has been created and developed in Western Catholicism. Any efforts in the direction of adapting to local circumstances have been conditional on the teaching staff being available and suitably competent. The adaptation required calls for the teacher not only to be thoroughly qualified to teach their subject, but also to have an exceptional and deep understanding of the Lebanese context. This particular combination is not, it seems, to be found. The lack is clear from the very small number of theological publications that truly address the issue of the life of Christians in the Arab world.

There is arguably a deep connection between the substance of Lebanese theological thinking and the ways of understanding the reality of Lebanese society. It is well known that the two traditions that exert the strongest influence on contemporary Arab Christian thought are the heritages of Antioch and Arab Christians. Since the twelfth century, when Arab Muslim thinking began gradually to weaken and lose its identity, there has been a long epistemological break in the pattern of Christian witness. The first modern Arab renaissance, at the turn of the nineteenth to the twentieth century, stimulated an assessment of the particular nature of Christian life in the Arab world, but only in literature. The second Arab renaissance, in the last three decades of the twentieth century, has made a deeper impression on Arab Christians, but has not led to the emergence of new ways to express their faith. As well as looking at these two periods of renaissance, we must examine the two heritages and what they bring to contemporary Christian theological thinking in terms of suitable methodology and approaches to formulating a new assessment of Christian faith. So it is still unclear how these two traditions will interact with a developing Lebanese Christian theology. A relevant question here is whether the mindset gained during their history by Arab Christians will be sufficiently adaptable to engage with the new approaches to human reality and to the new hermeneutic perceptions of *kerygma* current in contemporary Christianity.

There are three fields of reference that need to guide the development of Lebanese Christian theology. First, the existential challenge faced by Lebanese Christians at the dawn of the third millennium. Second, the possible approaches to assessing human life in the Arab world, in a process advocated by both modern thought and contemporary Arab thought. And third, the universal Catholic Christian *Weltanschauung*, which explicates the meaning and implications of the Christ event within the context of human life on Earth. A Christian theology wanting to be credible in Lebanon, and more generally in the modern Arab world, should therefore aim to create at the intersection of these three fields a space for interaction and osmosis from which might emerge a new theological vision better suited to the specificity of the Christian vocation. Any features of this vision that are distinctively marked by an Arab understanding of life and of the world will help to distinguish it from the character of the worldwide Christian faith, which is arguably anonymous and non-incarnate, since it is not rooted in any specific cultural landscape.

The requirements of this culturally determined approach will enable Lebanese Christian theology one day to liberate the teaching of theology at university level from an attitude that so lacks life and sensitivity that it is on occasion close to resignation. Chiefly, it must closely examine how Islam, Arab identity and modernity affect the thinking of Arab Christians, forcing them either to retreat or to confront.[33] When engaging in confrontation, Lebanese Christians must remember that the contribution of Middle Eastern Christians in assimilating and transmitting philosophy demands that Christians now commit in their turn to assimilate and transmit the gains of modernity. Although no longer a major influence, as they were under the Umayyads and probably also under the Abbasids, they are still able to highlight to Arab Muslims the best of what Western culture has to offer: an analytical approach and a constant striving to improve on the historic and social achievements of the human spirit.[34]

There is therefore an urgent need to identify in the heritage of Antioch and of Arab Christianity any cultural elements that might justify influences from Western modernity being brought into a truly Arab setting. Contemporary Muslim attempts to modernise Arab thinking offer a sample of what can be achieved in the way of preserving the authenticity of the Arab soul.[35] Lebanese Christians now have to explain how it is that their Christian faith brings them comfort and hope that they might succeed in their difficult task, since modern Arab thinking has not yet succeeded in this major challenge. Their reasons for hope will have to be found in the demands of the Christian faith as expressed within Arab culture.

---

33 One example of confrontation is evident in the writings of some nineteenth-century Christian authors (cf. J. Fontaine, 'Le désaveu chez les écrivains chrétiens libanais de 1825 à 1940', *Proche-Orient Chrétien*, 1973, XXIII, pp. 3–32).

34 The attempt by the former rector of the Université Saint-Joseph, albeit much disputed, serves as a particularly unusual example of encouraging cultural pluralism as a way of recognising fundamental human rights (see S. Abou, *Culture et droits de l'homme*, Paris, Hachette, 1992). In Muslim thinking, the issue of cultural pluralism is in fact linked to the issue of liberty (cf. M. Charfi, *Islam et liberté. Le malentendu historique*, Paris, Albin Michel, 1998).

35 The following names are a sample of some twentieth-century reformers within Arab philosophical thinking: Zaki Najîb Mahmûd, Hasan Hanafî, Muhammad Al-Jâbirî, Jâbir Al-Ansârî, Mohammad Arkoun.

No one is suggesting that the Middle East be deprived of its spirituality by inoculating it with a modern analytical approach. On the other hand, future Lebanese theological thinking must refuse any longer to foster within the Arab world a sense of the supernatural, since this must not become a major problem in Arab society. Rather, it should learn to harness the excitability of Arab religiosity. The Arab perception of God needs to be modified, so that Arabs may experience the divine as a place of welcome and fraternal encounter.[36] Ultimately, Arab Christian theology should aim to foster an understanding of God in the Arab world as one who offers to Arabs both liberty and a tool for self-examination. For these reasons, Christians in Lebanon and in the Arab world must respond to the challenge of the notion of conviviality. Theological renewal cannot work one-sidedly only. Christian theological thinking must tackle the issues in perfect synergy with both Muslim and secular Arabs.

It remains to be seen, however, how capable the university theology departments will be of contributing to the birth of this type of theological renewal in Lebanon. We are still faced by equivocation and indecision, not due to any obvious obstacles, yet without a clear road map. One thing, however, is clear: there is evidence in some university faculties of a desire to engage in serious and high-quality academic research in order to ignite the much longed-for renewal. Having myself taught philosophy and intercultural dialogue at the Pontifical Theology Faculty at the Université Saint-Esprit de Kaslik, I feel qualified to identify some possible developments in terms of the shape and direction of the theology curriculum at the faculty. The background to these developments is marked by the profound tensions that inevitably continue to affect the basic cultural options available to this Maronite university. Other Catholic universities in the country share the same background, so this analysis can be applied to them also.

The first kind of tension that affects the life of the Pontifical Theology Faculty arises from the dual cultural vocation of the Université Saint-Esprit. By vocation, not only is it open to Middle Eastern modernity but it also promotes integration into Arab culture. As a founding body of the university, and its spiritual heart, the Pontifical Faculty necessarily shares the resulting tension, and serves as the main forum in which that tension is felt and expressed. In response to the vocation of Middle Eastern Arab Christianity, and in accordance with the university's

---

36 Fraternity between religions is a major theme in contemporary theological thinking. The aim is to identify ways of living and organisational systems within multicultural society that reflect the diversity of world views and the differing approaches to rationality (see A. Touraine, *Pourrions-nous vivre ensemble? Égaux et différents*, Paris, Fayard, 1997).

vocation, the Pontifical Faculty should be able to facilitate the development of
an Arab theology adapted to the needs and priorities of local Christian witness.
At all levels of teaching, and in its research, the faculty needs to respond both in
its writings and in its actions to the challenges and the achievements of Western
modernity, which the faculty should make the object of close and critical study;
this in turn will inform both teaching staff and students in their interaction with
their native multiconfessional and multicultural Lebanese society.[37]

The second kind of tension is linked to the conflict that arises each time the
Pontifical Faculty is expected to honour its status as being under the ecclesiastical
authority of Rome. Like other Pontifical Faculties, it is also keen to demonstrate
its enlightened confidence in human reasoning. For it is clear that theological
renewal in Lebanon will only lead to a good outcome if academics are able to
work at theological research with full academic freedom. In the concrete sphere
of their teaching, the quality of academic freedom can be gauged by the ways in
which the questions and concerns of the students are met with serious consideration. It will require a bold intellectual approach to engage with the challenges
arising from the everyday experience of Lebanese Christians in such a way as to
promote a renewal of the Christian vision that truly responds to the lives of people
living in the modern Arab world.

The university theological community must also engage with another authority whose ecclesiastical power is clear and direct. The intellectual authority of
the scholars in the community of teachers and researchers in the theology depart-
ment of the Pontifical Faculty is sometimes held in check by their ecclesiastical
masters, and yet they also on occasion encounter resistance from more obscure
sources. The discernment and lucidity exercised by theology research scholars has
often been disputed by spontaneous outbursts from Lebanese popular religion,
side-lined by the sentimentality that periodically overwhelms the religious experience of students, or contradicted by the objections arising from the aberrations
of sociopolitical developments in the country, especially those that originate in
relations between Christian communities, and between Muslims and Christians.
Each of these contrary forces hopes by its activity to bend the authority of the
theological discourse in its favour. The theological community is well aware of
the danger that these potentially powerful voices can present, so in order to protect
its message about the vocation of Christians in Lebanese society they sometimes

---

37 It is useful here to mention the priorities identified for academic research in Lebanon in the
immediate post-war period (see Co-edited, *Perspectives et priorités de la recherche au Liban*,
Paris, CNRS, AUPELF-UREF, 1995).

avert the threat by clothing their concept in an abstract formulation that veils its dangerous reality.

The third kind of tension is one that most particularly concerns the teachers at the Pontifical Faculty who want not only to ensure that the faculty students receive a basic theological training, but also to engage with the major international theological debates rocking Christian thinking, debates that also make a deep impression on Lebanese society. Two obstacles lie in their way: they are severely held back not only by the limited timetable slots available to them but also by the academic freedom permitted by their supervising authority. The Pontifical Faculty would very much like to engage with these theological debates, if only because they would contribute to a more solid theological formation for their students. If it is able openly to engage in such debate, the faculty will one day be in a position to foster a spirit of religious enquiry within Lebanese society.[38] Until now, however, one has to acknowledge that there has been little obvious progress in terms of nurturing a critical awakening in the Arab world. Thanks to its teaching and its research, however, the Université Saint-Esprit deserves to be quoted in the media across the Arab world as a place of renewal for Arab religious thinking. For this to become reality, the faculty needs to engage in a serious and sustained exercise of evaluation and analysis.

The fourth kind of tension arises from the professional engagement of the teachers at the Pontifical Faculty: in most cases, they feel torn between their commitment to their religious status and their dedication to academic life. The Pontifical Faculty, as a place that nurtures both faith and research, seeks to help its teaching staff to manage the tension between, on the one hand, adherence to religious obedience and spiritual authenticity, and on the other hand, their academic research, in which they focus on academic competence and the practice of teaching. In order to become an excellent centre of renewal, the faculty is aiming to recruit more specialist academics. Mindful, however, of its theological vocation, it is nevertheless keen to support the religious commitment of its teaching staff. The quality of the theological research the faculty will be able to produce will be determined by the balance it can maintain between these competing calls.

The fifth and last kind of tension experienced by the Pontifical Faculty is related to its national identity and patriotic commitment. It is one thing to proclaim

---

38 In the 1960s questions were already being asked about the role and impact of universities in the sociocultural changes within the contemporary Arab world (cf. J.-J. Waardenburg, *Les universités dans le monde arabe actuel. Documentation et essai d'interprétation*, Paris-Hague, 1966).

that the experience of Lebanon's unique identity is at the heart of the national concerns of the university, but quite another to know whether this priority is one that appeals to the mind of their Arab compatriots. Arab identity, as currently experienced, is in conflict with the human aspirations of many Lebanese – and yet one might have expected the two to work in tandem. The energies of those who defend and promote religious thinking at the Pontifical Faculty need therefore to be directed towards initiating a critical yet empathetic dialogue with the thinking within the societies of the Arab world. The differences between Lebanese Christianity and other Arab forms of Christianity (Egyptian, Syrian, Iraqi and Palestinian) are minimal, albeit not absent; however, the sociocultural, political and religious differences between Lebanon and those other Arab societies are very much more significant and need to be treated with great care.

In its commitment to the life of the nation, the Pontifical Theology Faculty, if it is to propose changes to Lebanon's sociocultural life, must pay even greater attention to the differences in other Arab societies. In engaging with the rehabilitation of Lebanese life, it must thus take critical account of the forces for change and renewal currently being experienced in other Arab societies. Interreligious and intercultural solidarity is driven by a profound conviction that the sociocultural experiences of thoughtful religious Arabs are very similar, whether they be Muslim or Christian. Arab Christian theological thinking, if it is to experience an awakening and renewal, must ensure that it does not, either consciously or subconsciously, cut itself off from Muslim religious thinkers who might be seeking the same kind of reform. It is this delicate and thorny task that Lebanese Christian theology is called to take on, and the Pontifical Faculty intends to play a key part in fostering the enterprise.

*

We have made a brief *tour d'horizon*, outlining the work that lies ahead for theological thinking and the teaching of theology in Lebanon. I make no claim to have definitively identified the theological problems faced by Lebanon. I simply wanted to add my thoughts to the current theological debate. Until now, any demands for excellence in theology have presented as a confusion of tensions and even contradictions, especially in the context of Lebanese society. A few decades ago, any thought of modernising theology would have seemed mad. Now, all Lebanese theologians have to step cautiously into *terra incognita*. The Christian frame of reference in Lebanon is more familiar with the image of the shepherd leading his sheep than with the reality of a community that takes responsibility for its faith and is able continuously to call itself to account in the light of the influence and inspiration of the Word of God. We need of course to bear in mind that fundamentalist attitudes in Lebanon and in the Arab world have contributed to the poor reputation of theological renewal. But we must also have the courage to add that the higher academic standards have exposed a wide range of attitudes among the Churches in Lebanon, some of which might be, in extreme cases, exposed to suspicion. At all events, it is time to question the taboo that suggests that Middle Eastern Arab theological thinking can plough its own self-sufficient furrow. Modesty, however, is always a good thing. The most ambitious of theological projects needs to acknowledge the humble origins of Lebanon. And in any consideration of the religious meaning of human life, humility is a good starting point. Our project here, therefore, should see the hoped-for renewal as a distant precursor, seeds in the ground, or yeast in the dough.

So this critical analysis will not end on a pessimistic note, but it hopes instead to stimulate and motivate thinking that will lead to a new commitment to enculturated faith. The findings of this chapter will, I hope, serve as a launch-pad for the next, which aims to outline ways to identify the conditions that might give rise to a new contextual Christian theology in Lebanon. The journey ahead consists of interweaving themes, guided by the fundamental aim to encourage theological renewal. It is therefore essential now to discuss the current state of theological activity.

4

The beginnings of a contemporary Arab Christian theology

Contemporary theological studies published in the West do not mention the contribution of modern Arab Christian theology, for the very good reason that the theological thinking of the Christian communities of Lebanon and the Arab world is at an embryonic stage. As we have seen, the sociopolitical and sociocultural context goes some way to explaining the particular nature of their Christian witness. However, it is important to acknowledge that in Lebanon, and in some Arab countries, there is a genuine desire for theological reflection and commitment. In Part Two of this volume, we shall explore a selection of models that provide a clear demonstration of this.

But before we examine some of these models of contextual theology, we need to explore the conditions that would favour the development of such a theology. And this is where we begin to see clearly the difficulties of the project. The issue is complex and subtle, hard to capture within the conceptual framework of contemporary theology. This is an urgent problem, requiring serious and critical reflection that must be the responsibility of the Christian communities concerned. The issue is not a straightforward one. Theological thinking in Lebanon and in the Arab world is afflicted by a serious deficiency, which we shall analyse in the first part of this chapter. The rupture with medieval and Arab Christian theology has a long history, so it cannot for fear of alienation be that one might tread carefully and tactfully around difficulties. What is needed is a bold commitment to restoring the relationship. Some attempts have indeed been made to take a theological approach to the duty of Christian witness. The second part of this chapter, at the risk of some repetition, will present a noteworthy and very promising local theological endeavour. All such undertakings, however, are at risk of losing momentum and energy, a Lebanese and Arab fact of life with which one must always reckon.

The crisis in current Arab theological thinking

A shared fate

No one can deny that there is in Lebanon an epistemological impasse in which not only Christian but also Arab theological thinking is stuck. The latter is moreover prisoner of the *aporia* that has a general hold on contemporary Arab thinking. Indeed, a seriously damaging crisis is affecting Christian theology that is culturally Arab.

It is clear, however, that among the many shapes that could be adopted by Arab modernity, the options are heavily influenced by theology, both Muslim and Christian.[1] Religion may not display the full richness of Arab identity, but it nevertheless distils the essence of it. It is good to remember too other key characteristics of Arab identity, such as language, nationhood, soil and history; each of these serves as a backdrop to the conflict between tradition and modernity, which is deeply marked by the religious vision jointly safeguarded by Islam and Christianity.[2]

In some ways, it is the religious vision that lends logical and coherent agency to the range of characteristics. The internal tensions arising from the two strands of the vision are currently such that the resultant shockwaves are spreading throughout other aspects of Arab identity.[3] These characteristics are subtly linked, and interact in different ways, but there is nevertheless ample evidence that this scarcely mitigates either the widespread tensions or the leading role played by religion in the Arab mindset.[4]

This chapter will seek to expose, with care and circumspection, the causes of the current identity crisis within modern Arab theology; the first part will explore

---

1 In addition to the well-known text by Farid Jabre on the importance of theology in Arab thinking (F. Jabre, 'Être et Esprit dans la pensée arabe', in *Studia Islamica*, XXXII; F. Jabre, 'Le sens de l'abstraction chez Avicenne', in Mélanges de l'Université Saint-Joseph, vol. L, 1984; G. Jihami (ed), *Mélanges offerts au Professeur Farid Jabre*, Beirut, Publications de l'Université Libanaise, 1989), a lecture given by Louis-Joseph Lebret in 1964 as part of the 'Conférences du Cénacle', entitled 'Le Liban au tournant', expressed regret that there had been 'too few philosophers and theologians in a country where so many civilisations had successively lived and intermingled.' Lebret continued: 'Was it not in this country that the one and only God was sought out, in the midst of idolatrous cultures, and did it not take part in the great theological debates of the first ten centuries of our age? The history of Middle Eastern thinking is still lagging in this country.' (Conférences du Cénacle, Beirut, 1964).
2 See N. Nassâr, *Tasawwurât al-ummâ* (Perceptions of the nation), Beirut, Dâr Al-Talî'â, 1982.
3 See P. Khoury, *Islam et Christianisme. Dialogue religieux et défi de la modernité*, Beirut, 1997; P. Khoury, *Une lecture de la pensée arabe actuelle*, Altenberge, Oros Verlag, 1998.
4 See P. Khoury, *La religion et les hommes*, Beirut, 1984.

the problem in the context of the Arab Christian mindset. Theological thinking in Lebanon is an unusual example of this. To start with, some preliminary remarks are called for.

First, it is not easy to offer a clear and succinct definition that might encompass in a few brief and trenchant phrases the concepts used in this analysis, such as modernity, identity, tradition, or even Arab Christianity,[5] because of the shifting or even opaque nature of these concepts and of their wide fields of meaning.

Second, the analysis posits that there is a real crisis – a statement that calls for an explanation that I feel ill qualified to supply; this chapter will therefore not provide a full factual description of the crisis. However, the first part of the chapter will borrow confidently from the various existing analytical descriptions of modern Arab thinking.[6]

The analysis will highlight, but may not always present or justify in full, the explanations that specifically account for the current crisis in Arab Christian theological thinking. The lethargy afflicting Arab Christian theology is not due only to factors that it shares with Muslim theological thinking, so we shall therefore focus on the matter only as it touches Christianity. It is only the respectful format of methodological exposition that makes it acceptable to offer an explicit presentation of the specific identity crisis in Arab theological thinking. And we also note how difficult it is to disentangle the cultural, social, economic and political crises, always implicated because of their relationship of dialectical mutuality.[7] If we are able therefore to disregard other aspects of the crisis, the most important aspect of this initial analysis is the issue of Christian theological discourse, both where it comes from and how it affects the reality of people's lives in Lebanon and in the Arab world. This exposition will however be a descriptive summary, and will not attempt to include concrete illustrations.

Given these initial observations and reservations, it is important to point out that the exposition makes no claim to being exhaustive. It has far more modest ambitions, aiming only to outline a few thoughts that might serve to open and then guide the debate on the subject. And given that it will not be possible to address the whole of the issue within the limitations of this restricted canvas, I shall be obliged to omit, or rather make choices, in my analysis of the current theological

---

5 Cf. Collectif, *Les chrétiens du monde arabe*, Paris, Maisonneuve & Larose, 1989.

6 Cf. P. Khoury, *Tradition et modernité. Thèmes et tendances de la pensée arabe actuelle*, Beirut, 1983.

7 See J. B. Metz, *Pour une théologie du monde*, Paris, Cerf, 1971. See also G. Gutiérrez, *Théologie de la libération ou théologie progressiste?*, Paris, 1977; L. Boff, *Qu'est-ce que la théologie de la libération?*, Paris, Cerf, 1987.

situation. I am aware that this is a delicate undertaking, in which random irrelevancies might at any moment intrude into the theological reflection. It is not always possible to justify every choice. So this is, in the strictest possible sense, an essay, and I describe it as such in order to highlight its deliberate limitations.

The causes of the crisis

The first cause of the current crisis in Arab Christian theological thinking is clearly due to the fact that the conceptual mechanisms used in the Arabic language to convey the *kerygma* of the Christ event are ageing and rapidly becoming obsolescent. Some stale categories used to express the Greek understanding of Christian *kerygma* have been set up as golden statues around which a number of Arab Christian theologians dance with dismaying loyalty.[8] The Arabic language suffers from a panoply of deficiencies: worryingly rarefied dedicated neologisms;[9] a lack of linguistic innovation and advanced technological devices that might enrich the potential expressiveness of religious symbolism; and semantic ossification that stifles any variety in thinking. These obfuscate what is already an inadequate conceptual theological framework, due to a poor interpretation of tradition, and in turn cast an obscuring haze around the message of the Gospel.[10]

Any debate that fails to get beyond this initial difficulty must nevertheless acknowledge that theological Arabic, whether in Islam or in Christianity, is rooted in an ancient theoretical context. Any renewal in Arab thinking, whether philosophical or religious, must necessarily find expression within existing linguistic and conceptual structures in the language. The terminology available, especially as it is used within the Middle Eastern Arab sphere, will inevitably serve as foundation for any descriptive or apologetic Christian discourse. There is a danger here: the vehicle that must by necessity convey the *kerygma* of Christian experience, giving it coherence and enabling it to become incarnate in Arab culture, is vulnerable to habituation and passivity, thus stifling creativity and life. It will not be up to the task of expressing authentic attempts at updating and modernising the

---

8 See R. Arnou, 'Platonisme des Pères', in *Dictionnaire de Théologie Catholique*, vol. 12, col. 2258–2392; P. Khoury, *Paul d'Antioche. Traités théologiques*, Altenberge, Oros Verlag, 1994, Introduction, note 1.

9 An interesting example is the introduction of the suffix 'iyya', equivalent to 'isme', 'ism', 'ismus', in European languages.

10 See in Cl. Geffré, *Un nouvel âge de la théologie*, Paris, Cerf, 1972, the second chapter, entitled 'La théologie à l'âge herméneutique', pp. 43–66; *ibid, Le christianisme au risque de l'interprétation*, Paris, Cerf, 1988.

message. Linguistic renewal, it seems, is doomed to failure within current official Arab theology, but one can well imagine a grassroots initiative that might enable renewal in other ways.

The second cause of the current crisis arises from the variety of competing influences and frames of reference that play into Arab Christian theological thinking.[11] Arab Islamic theological thinking has drawn on Greek, Persian and Indian traditions, but in cultural terms there is widespread unanimity in drawing only on the widest possible understanding of Arab identity. Arab Christian theological thinking, on the other hand, is pulled between a number of powerful forces: its original Semitic nature has become overlaid by other forces, stratified elements deriving from various strands of both Western and Eastern theological influence. This multiplicity not only enriches but also complicates, bringing with it divergent and irreconcilable elements. Forces that might seem reconcilable can prove in the end to be mutually incompatible. From where we are now, the path ahead seems fraught with danger. Theological systems and movements of religious ideas, the quantity of information, and the variety of ways in which all these can be assessed, all change so fast that it is increasingly difficult simply to keep up with theological research in order to engage in an informed choice of ideas.

This perception should properly be better defended than it is here, but it is undoubtedly the case that Arab Christian theological discourse lacks a certain degree of internal coherence. The reasons for this are clear, and need not delay us much. In our disoriented age, in which we are prey to the confusing seductions of Western modernity,[12] it is highly risky to graft modern notions onto traditional wisdom, under cover of paying respect to a heritage that may be poorly tended and exploited but is rich in innovative potential. Arab Christian theology, in seeking to define its modern identity, must not only be aware of its own subconscious inheritance but also be on guard against the attractive charms of the many uncertainties and ambiguities, and the looking-glass messages, that are beamed out by the many paradoxical influential forces. Seeping in unchecked, rather than enriching and tempering this theology, those multiple contradictory influences will fissure and weaken its conceptual structure. Too awkward to define, this theological discourse should probably be seen as uncertain, and hobbled by its lack of control

---

11 The wide range evokes the notion of 'estrangement' used by Y. Congar to illustrate the split – now usually described as a schism – between Catholic and Orthodox Churches (Y. Congar, *Neuf cents ans après. Notes sur le schisme oriental*, Chevetogne, 1954).
12 See J. Habermas, *Le discours philosophique de la modernité*, Paris, Gallimard, 1990; A. Nouss, *La modernité*, Paris, Ouverture, Granger, 1995; G. Vattimo, *La fin de la modernité. Nihilisme et herméneutique dans la culture post-moderne*, Paris, Seuil, 1987.

from without or of self-moderation from within. For some, however, this apparent failing is a source of enrichment.[13]

The third cause of the crisis arises from the confrontation between two divergent perceptions of the deposit of faith: medieval and pre-conciliar, versus modern and post-conciliar. Modern Arab Christian theological writing suffers from the effects of this fundamental dichotomy in understanding the meaning of faith; this is arguably a major epistemological caesura. We are, after all, in the presence of two different worlds, or rather, two different visions of the world, suddenly and dramatically revealed by modern rationalism. They are linked by biblical revelation, burning brightly in the light of reason, but modern perceptions of the latter have a major effect on the ways in which we understand lived reality (the facts), and this in turn informs and extends the willingness of people to contemplate the absolute (the meaning).[14] Hence the divergences that currently encumber progress for theological thinking. Hence also the deep divisions between these two visions, presenting us with an insoluble dilemma. Each one exercises a polarising influence that may prove fatal to any chance of reconciliation.

Given that each of these worlds gives voice to a polarity, they should and must be drawn back into the original aims of the Christian mystery, so a way must be found to heal the rift by highlighting any shared perceptions in order to make up for deficiencies and foster a grafting process.[15] And here we have a crucial dialectic between the ancient metaphysical process adopted by Christian theology and the more recent rational forms of modern thinking that constantly challenge and influence a new Christian understanding of the world. For modern Arab theological thinking (both Christian and Islamic), the many nuances within Western modernity may yet threaten to exacerbate its present difficult impasse.

In other words, in looking at current Arab reality, we are not seeking to take an all-encompassing theological system of knowledge and use it as a crucible in which to forge together both old and new formulations of the Christian faith. Cultural transpositions and osmoses of this kind have been intrinsic throughout

---

13 An interesting example is Abbé Michel Hayek's suggestion that the different Lebanese confessions should be brought together around Antioch, a location shared by the Catholic and Orthodox patriarchs (see M. Hayek, 'Église Maronite', in *Dictionnaire de Spiritualité*, 1980, vol. 10, col. 631–644).

14 On the relationship between facts and meaning, and on the ways in which the author applies these terms in his studies of Muslim–Christian dialogue and the relationship between tradition and modernity, see P. Khoury, *Le fait et le sens. Esquisse d'une philosophie de la déception*, Paris, L'Harmattan, 2007.

15 Cf. the famous *coincidentia oppositorum* of Nicholas of Cusa (N. de Cues, *Trois traités sur la docte ignorance et la coïncidence des opposés*, Paris, Cerf, 1991).

history, but we must not forget that any such compilation and synthesis could plunge into deep despair the small group of Arab Christian theologians who are already clearly overwhelmed by the extent of the task facing them.

Even if these two aspects of any intelligible Christian discourse are seen as being in mutual dialogue – rather than mutually exclusive – we still need to guard against compromising the intelligibility of the Christ event by presenting it through a haphazard collection of unfocused ideas picked out randomly from any old corpus, and then cast in stone as the record of tradition. An efficient way of resolving the tension in this dichotomy is to apply a critical form of analysis that will identify the extremes of the divergence–convergence polarity between which lie the whole range of possible compromise and adaptation.

The fourth cause of the crisis is linked to the third; it lies in the split that modern Arab Christian thinkers identify between the content of the Gospel message and lived reality. There is indeed a dissonance between the official Gospel message and the daily concrete experience of Arab Christians; and it would be true to say that the discrepancies between the official theological interpretation of the Christian mystery and the ways in which Christians live out their faith commitment in the normal flow of daily life can only be explained away, or justified, in ways that perhaps owe more to ingenuity than one might like.

It is crucial for any current theological thinking, especially if it aims to engage with the sociocultural, economic and political experiences of the various societies in the Arab world, to expend energy and commitment on staying in touch with the daily lives, both individual and collective, of the faithful.[16] Its message will fatally damage and ossify any life, originality or variety in the world in which the faithful are engaged, if it degenerates into prescriptive verbiage, a sclerotic body of immutable lifeless propositions.

Hegel said that philosophy is its own time apprehended in thought,[17] but some Middle Eastern Christians have failed to grasp his statement's subtlety and continue to use archaic concepts to embroider irrelevant side issues, rather than engaging with the reality of life and the truth of the Gospel in order to weave a substantial and authentic enculturated theology truly concerned to preserve an unbroken link between words and their meaning. Anyone engaged in this kind of new and adventurous theology must bear in mind at all times that in order to be seen as true, and to be effectively communicated, the message must be fully lucid

---

16 See the essay by J. Mouroux, *L'expérience chrétienne. Introduction à une théologie*, Paris, Aubier, 1952, which is already a classic.
17 Hegel, *Phénoménologie de l'Esprit*, trans. J.-P. Lefèvre, Paris, Aubier, 1991, p. 389.

and unambiguous, clearly linking an authentic lived experience with its meaning, which draws on and is lit up by faith. Meanings and actual thoughts are thus kept grounded in the cultural realities of the relevant witnessing community, and firmly supported in clear arguments sustained within the tension between our two polar forces. Below, I describe a possible theological approach responding to this suggestion.

When the Spirit freely infuses life and energy into this differently lived experience, commitment and theological thinking evolve in harmonious interaction, enhanced within a cultural space which, in turn, is filled with the riches of the Spirit.[18] If Arab Christian theology can convey its message within the forms of language that faithfully reflect the lived experience of every Arab Christian and of every Arab Christian community, it will set a new standard by which those Arab people it aims to address will be enabled to hear a life-changing message.

And linked to the fourth cause, the fifth concerns the ways in which Christian theological communications are articulated within the various societies of the Arab world. Little is available in terms of experience of either hearing or experiencing the truth of theological content, which in turn betrays how little thought is going into formulating the ways in which these things might happen.

It results in inadequate Christian pastoral care in Lebanon and in certain other Arab countries, and it limits the ways in which the resources of social sciences might fruitfully be exploited; and moreover, it hampers the effectiveness of any linguistic tools in Arabic that might express, regulate and monitor Christian theological activity. Theological discourse, if it is firmly rooted in everyday life and in the opportunities that it offers, will evolve and thus lend increasing urgency to the question of how to define and enable a truly appropriate Arab Christian theology. Any contextualised theological discourse must, by its very vocation, be intimately connected with the whole of human experience within the Arab world. Clearly, the linguistic expression used in regulation and monitoring will therefore need to be sufficiently varied to accommodate the range of that experience, and to be regularly revisited and recalibrated, in order to take account of new stresses that may arise from the dialectical tension between theological pronouncement and day-to-day life.

---

18 See P. Evdokimov, *L'Esprit Saint dans la tradition orthodoxe*, Paris, Cerf, 1969.

The limitations of the diagnosis

We have reached a diagnosis, but we have not eliminated any ambiguity. Arab reality is complex, so extreme caution is called for. Before moving on from these reflections to suggest a path for theological recovery, therefore, I would like to offer three brief remarks designed to clarify the context of the theoretical developments presented in this chapter.

First, the above analysis of the causes of the crisis intentionally omitted any reference to the unavoidable issue of diversity within the Arab Church: doctrinal (pre- and post-Chalcedonian Orthodox, Uniate and Latin Catholics, Lutheran and Reformed Protestants), cultural (Syrian Aramaean, Byzantine Greek, Copt, Armenian, Chaldo-Assyrian, Roman Latin), and national ethnic (Lebanese Christianity is different from Iranian Christianity, Egyptian Christianity is different from Palestinian Christianity, Sudanese Christianity is different from North African Christianity).[19] Inevitably, such a multiplicity of Arabic-speaking Middle Eastern Christian communities will engender a diversity in theological thinking. This is awkward, and it is rendered more difficult still because the interlocutor for this diversity, modernity itself, engages with the world in a wide variety of shapes. For this theology to come to terms with all these aspects of crisis it must first get the measure of its disconcerting and complex partner in dialogue.

Second, the crisis we describe here affects not only Christian Arabs, whatever their nationality, but also Muslim Arabs. The causes for the crisis may be similar or different in one religious system or the other, depending on whether the underlying factors are purely external (sociocultural situation, the economic and political context) or purely internal (the form and content of revealed truth); Arab Christian theology must however strive to work in harmony with Muslim theological thinking.[20] This requires both a deep attitude of sympathy and the willingness to engage with a major challenge. Harmonious collaboration is able not only to highlight the values of conviviality and shared destiny,[21] but also to stimulate a local sense of mutual respect for theological discourse, even when the response from Muslim and secular interlocutors is not the one hoped for. It should not, however, be allowed to hinder the responsibility to express faith and

---

19 J. Corbon, *L'Église des Arabes*, op. cit.
20 Farid Jabre and Subhî Al-Sâlih voice this concern in L. Gardet and G. Anwati, *Introduction à la théologie musulmane. Essai de théologie comparée* (Paris, Vrin, 1948), the first in the section on Islamic theology, the second in the section on Christian theology. See also L. Gardet, *Les grands problèmes de la théologie musulmane. Dieu et la destinée de l'homme*, Paris, Vrin, 1967.
21 See I. Illich, *La convivialité*, Paris, Seuil, 1975; M. Buber, *Je et Tu*, Paris, 1970.

witness. Christian Arabs are in a minority, so they cannot hope on their own to bring healing to Arab ways of thinking, and such healing is a necessary precondition for Christian theological renewal.

Third, those who create the theology we are discussing here must be willing to live with the uncomfortable paradox that could compromise the prospect of renewal. It is especially clear in the contradiction between the attitude of openness expected within modernity and the inevitable restrictions due to the minority status of Arab Christian communities. This confrontation could crucially compromise the presence and identity of the Christian communities within the Arab world. A realistic pessimist might suggest that Christian identity could be dangerously compromised if modernity, as defined above, suggested the need to lend authenticity to Christian witness through an attitude of kenotic humility. This would call for sanitising the institutional involvement of Christian communities and reducing their hierarchical visibility; for work to sow the seed of the Gospel among Arab societies, into Arab culture, and into the hearts of fellow Arabs; and for sacrificing the legal right to be different, forcing Christian distinctiveness to be absorbed into an imported diversity. This last has yet to be given Koranic approval, and to receive legislative integration and practical acknowledgement by most Arab political regimes.

It is an agonising choice: physical survival or spiritual fruitfulness? To choose self-affirmation is to deny kenosis. If Arab Christians choose survival, they will be forced to formulate a polemical theology and an ethical stance of resistance. If, on the other hand, they prefer to adopt a strategy of quiet insemination into Arab culture, they may have to embrace self-offering and sacrificial love. Any future Arab theological thinking must take account of this dilemma, acknowledging the extreme difficulty in honouring these two contradictory calls on the conscience of Arab Christians.

The witness of kenosis cannot, however, be a reason not to exercise evangelical discernment, which at its heart is driven by the need for theological renewal. Witness to faith needs to find its place within the core of Arab culture. The contribution of Christian faith is fundamental, provided it is understood in a new way. It can be generally agreed that Arab culture has a religious soul, and its horizons must not be limited by a mechanical secular rationality. Christian faith can play its part in enabling Arab culture to embrace a more enlightened form of rationality, something that developments in Arab Christian theology must take into account.

Without its Christian dimension, Arab identity would be mutilated and narrow-minded. Without Christian theology, Arab identity, the joint creation of Muslim and Christian, would be robbed of its soul. Without the renewal of Arab Christian theological thinking, the Christian communities in the Middle East would suffocate and die.[22] In order to overcome the causes of the crisis, there must however be a selective approach to the resources offered by modernity. The aim must be that a reformed and revived theology, rather than dragging Christians down the path of slow physical disintegration, might enable them to blossom as a witnessing community.

The first part of this chapter has enabled us to reach the following conclusions. Just because the theological crisis is serious, this does not exclude the possibility of healing and renewal. A number of projects have assessed the recent history of the Christian communities in Lebanon. We therefore need to examine the issues that have been identified in order to confront the challenges that face Christian believers in the Arab world. The second part of this chapter outlines one possible option, but it in no way calls into question the value of other similar theological initiatives. In presenting the theological work achieved in this initiative I have chosen to limit the study to just one local theological project. I am aiming to suggest ways forward rather than to produce a detailed list of facts and texts. Many issues will still need to be explored. There is much that could be investigated, but will not be included here. The task may seem demanding and dangerous, but it must one day be attempted in order to safeguard the wide range of theological sensitivities that sustain and support the faithful witness of Christians.

Sketching out a contextual Arab theology

The parameters

An Arab, or Middle Eastern, theology is a description that embraces a variety of concepts. At the start of the twenty-first century, the Institut Saint-Paul de Philosophie et de Théologie (Harissa, Lebanon) launched a theological project described by its instigators as the most audacious in modern Lebanon, and identified its threefold purpose. First, to evoke a classical heritage by reviving the patristic tradition so much valued by Middle Eastern Christians. Second, to situate the Christ event firmly in modern culture. And third, to update the material used in preaching in order to highlight its contextual relevance. Within this epistemological triptych, they needed to give expression to the experience of faith as it is lived, rooted in the societies of the Arab world, and flourishing within the ambient Arab culture.

---

22 Cf. the rather alarming work by J.-P. Valognes, *Vie et mort des chrétiens d'Orient. Des origines à nos jours, op. cit.*

In doing so, it was important to live up to the expectations of a mosaic of Christian communities for whom their sense of ethnicity and culture are the most salient elements of their Arab identity. The third element, religion, has always served to distinguish Christian Arabs from Muslim Arabs. The second part of this chapter thus aims to identify and situate recent local theological thoughts and actions designed to engage with all the Christian communities of the Arab world.

Middle Eastern life is extremely complex, and in Lebanon itself shot through with conflict, so that the most challenging temptation among Christians is to perpetuate inherited reactivity; it was therefore essential to shine the clear and critical light of the Gospel into this charged atmosphere. Hence the establishment of a centre for theology in the Middle East. Given the cripplingly confessionalised context in Lebanon, it was important to find a relatively neutral venue from which to operate. The Melkite Greek Catholic Church is dedicated – sometimes at great cost – to ecumenism. Their academic home is the Institut Supérieur des Pères Paulistes, who were willing to take on this important task and welcome to Harissa a group of supra-confessional theologians and university professors. The moving spirit behind this initiative was an unusual Belgian theologian, Serge Descy. Working together with the Rector of the Institute, who would later become the archbishop of the Greek Catholic community in Boston (USA), Mgr Cyrille Salim Bustros, he created the core of what would become the Centre de Théologie pour le Moyen-Orient (Centre for Middle Eastern Theology).

The minutes of the initial plenary meetings define the Centre as follows:

The Centre has been set up under the academic patronage of, and is hosted by, the Institut Saint-Paul de Philosophie et de Théologie (Harissa). Its principal objective is to promote contemporary theological thinking relevant to the Middle East. Its activities and output are rooted in the theological heritage of the Christian Middle East, which the Centre is keen to ensure is made widely known and relevant. The principal aim is to anchor its theological thinking in the world, and more specifically, in the multiconfessional societies of the Middle East. The context for this theoretical approach is a multidisciplinary approach that will in particular encompass philosophy and the human sciences. Ultimately, it aims to meet the expectations of the very diverse Christian communities of the Middle East, and to reflect their witness and commitment. The Centre seeks to become a place of meeting and of interconfessional research, both in terms of its membership and of its fields of study.

Proceeding with clarity of vision, over time the Centre saw its ambitions begin to take shape. Over ten years, it established the distinctive character of its work, in spite of various obstacles, changes that have affected the stability of its membership, and the new theological challenges arising from the daily reality of Lebanese and Arab life. The original nature of the Centre's work can be summed up in three distinctive traits: an ecumenical sense of openness, as a starting point for any attempt at analysing the confessional diversity among Christians in the Arab world; a desire to give privileged attention to the reality of human life, which is necessarily the setting for any theological investigation; and a constant effort, when confronting the historic experience of the faith community with the deposit of faith, to call on the scholarly gains from the social sciences.

Overcoming local uncertainties and human reluctance, the Centre was able to organise four theological symposiums between 1987 and 1994; remarkably, given the turbulence of Lebanese life, their proceedings have been published by the Pères Paulistes in four separate volumes. I suggest that the best way to benefit from the symposiums and their distinctive contribution is to summarise here the contents of these volumes. First, a terminological observation. The members of the Centre have a variety of theological sensitivities, so it was thought best to reach a compromise. It was decided that the phrase 'Middle East' would satisfactorily convey faithfulness to the tradition of the Eastern Churches and the need to work towards integration in the societies of the Arab world. The reasons underlying this compromise have remained valid, but identitarian tensions have increasingly nudged Christian communities towards a disabling sense of nostalgia.

From 15 to 19 October 1987, the first interdisciplinary theological symposium ever held in Lebanon,[23] on the epistemological requirements for a contextual description, took place at the Institut Saint-Paul, and was introduced in the following terms:

> This meeting, which one could describe as exceptional, given the chaos of war that has surrounded us since April 1975, arose from some shared research within a focus group; ... the group was concerned that there was a lack of any theological thinking specific to the Middle East and capable of responding in a manner both relevant and prophetic to the current challenges presented by the multiconfessional societies in the region: Islam, as the dominant religion, Arab

---

23 *Pour une théologie contemporaine du Moyen-Orient. Actes du premier symposium interdisciplinaire, Institut Saint-Paul de Philosophie et de Théologie (Harissa),* Jounieh, Éditions Saint Paul, 1988, 332 p.

identity, as the dominant culture, political confessionalism, the Middle East's
state of economic dependency, the survival of the Christian communities,
and so on... A local theology that could be significant for this lacerated
Middle East should aim to set free the meaning of the Christ event from the
successive theological formulations that have evolved during the historical
and cultural contexts the region has lived through.

This was, however, the initial theological meeting, so it was necessary first
to establish clearly the frame of reference for the specialists to contribute their
thoughts, and they did indeed open up some wide and varied landscapes. Given
that this opening symposium focused on introductory and narrative material, I
suggest that there is little need to give a detailed account of the content of the
various presentations.

We must, though, take note of the various challenges identified. The Centre
places a high value on its vocation for incarnation, and therefore on any challenge
involving enculturation that refers to Islam and Arab identity. It also tackles the
issue of local theological thinking in the light of its sociopolitical responsibilities.
When matters relating to politics and the economy are mentioned, the Centre
aims to ensure that Lebanese Christians are aware of the issues, and to guide them
towards an appropriate contextual political theology.

The inaugural address by Cyrille Salim Bustros announced four themes for the
symposium. The first, entitled 'Religion and Society in the Middle East', aims to
describe the Middle Eastern society that our theological discourse must address.
The attempt is to offer a coherent if somewhat sketchy representation of this
society and its various constitutive parts: the geosocial and geographic context
(Antoine Ghossein); the socioeconomic and political context (Ibrahim Maroun);
religion and social and national integration (Bassam El-Hachem); the conflict of
ideologies (Sami Aoun); intercommunity problems, and the Muslim–Christian
problem (Tarik Mitri). Each problem in turn was examined in the light of the faith,
and the foundations for an appropriate theological reflection were established.

The second theme presents the various recent attempts at developing a theology of the world. The main aim here was to explore various theologies that have
arisen in very different contexts. As part of this, it seemed important to prepare
to defend our emerging theological approach from the ambiguities and lacunae
of theologies identified under the following headings: the Kingdom of God and
Jesus's social practice (Jean-Marie Van Cangh); the discourse of political theology and its mediations (Serge Descy); Metz and political theology (Jad Hatem);
aspects of Latin American theology (Joseph Comblin), liberation theology in the

context of Asia (S. Klappen); and the theology of non-Christian and Muslim religions (Augustin Dupré La Tour).

The third theme concerns a new reading of the theological inheritance from the East. The two lectures by Samir Khalil Samir (the Eastern Arabic-language heritage) and Mgr Georges Khodr (the Eastern Greek-language heritage) present the Eastern theological heritage in such a way as to identify its energetic capability for compromise, and its potential for renewal. The distinctive contribution of each Church is re-evaluated, and this reveals Arab Christians in terms not only of their commitment to a mystical inner life, but also, and especially, of the visibility of their ethical integrity.

The fourth and last theme is entitled 'Towards a new theology in the Middle East'. The work of the symposium then concludes with two lectures. One, by Boutros Labaki, reflects on the experiences of the social and political struggles of Lebanese Christians during the 1960s, and their outcome. The second, by Cyrille Salim Bustros, redefines the features of the ways in which the Arab world had begun rather tentatively to explore religious thinking during the previous few decades. Two working groups were established at the end of the symposium to prepare for the next one by proposing and discussing a set of statements. This first volume concludes its report of the initial symposium by presenting these.

This first endeavour was of course intended to define the sociocultural and sociopolitical realities of the Arab world into which any future theological thought would speak. The Gospel message must necessarily be relevant to its context, so the Centre engaged with an analysis of this context, accounting for it also in the light of the region's history. This approach arose from a deep-seated conviction that the call of the Kingdom can be read and heard in many ways, both written and spoken. The societies of the Arab world are distinctive in character; the Christian communities living and witnessing among them need to develop an appropriate theological format for their message, one that will foster a responsible attitude towards the life and the challenges that they all share.

The societies of the Arab world: a lieu théologique[24]

The wishes expressed by those who took part in the first symposium give shape to the theme of the second: 'The Societies of the Middle East as Theological

---

24 *Lieu théologique* refers to a new sociocultural situation that gives rise to a new form of theological thought (Cf. the theological collection *Lieux théologiques*, Labor et Fides, Geneva, Switzerland).

Space';[25] this theme addressed a shared need that is inherent in the nature of Christian presence in the Arab world. The introduction makes this clear:

> The intention of the inaugural symposium was to begin to clear the ground. This one will explore one part of the ground: couples, ecumenism, and the dialectic of tradition and modernity. The methodological aspect, which was emphasised during the first year, has not been omitted. It includes proper material for reflection: exegesis, epistemology, dogmatics, all of which are centred around political theology and aimed at dissemination.

In analysing the structure and behaviour of the different societies that together build lives and mutual relationships within the Arab world, any exercise in theological thinking must take a responsible and honest approach.

Following Jad Hatem's introduction, which focused on the part played by university scholarship within the Church, the first part of the volume presenting the second symposium begins with a lecture ('Bible and desacralisation', Augustin Dupré La Tour) addressing the power of the Bible to demystify. The lecture explores the conversion potential in the dichotomy experienced by Christians between what they read in the Bible and the reality of their daily lives. The religiously oriented societies within the Arab world are forever prey to the temptation to devalue not only their understanding of God, but also the nature of religion, by abusing it in order to justify a certain kind of sociopolitical order. The Bible condemns this kind of impoverishment and reductionism, and calls us instead to heal the world from its tendency towards sinfulness. A middle way is called for, one that reconciles the move to make political society religious with the secularisation of human understanding.

Jad Hatem's contribution on 'The Trinity in the context of political theology' seeks to identify the ways in which Trinitarian aspects of the divine might serve to inquire into human reality. Hatem enriches his exposition on the Trinity with references to patristics that provide dogmatic grounds enabling him to avoid a unilateral approach. Hatem makes use of the two concepts of *koinonia* and *perichoresi* and attempts to transpose and apply them to the privileged and sensitive aspects of human life. The first aspect is the family, where the example of the Trinity acts to bind together the members, whether peaceably or not. The second

---

25 *Les sociétés du Moyen-Orient comme lieu théologique. Actes du deuxième symposium interdisciplinaire, Institut Saint-Paul de Philosophie et de Théologie (Harissa)*, Jounieh, Éditions Saint Paul, 1991, 127 p.

aspect is that of society, where an exacerbated monotheism is held back by the despotism of a single power that annihilates diversity. The third aspect concerns the individual, in whom a sense of the physical self is resistant to anything that might lead to fusion or annihilation.

Serge Descy's lecture, entitled 'The problem of theological epistemology in the field of politics', examines the problem of theological method and epistemology within the limited field of the theology of politics. By focusing on two *epesteme*, social sciences and theological knowledge, theological discourse is expected to assimilate, conceptualise, and then reflect the innovation proper to Christian commitment. To achieve this task of extrapolation implies the exercise of an internal critical faculty, as deployed by the author when examining Latin American theology (Gutiérrez and Boff) – and in doing so he reveals areas in which a lack of clarity undermines the two theologians' work. It is therefore necessary, he argues, to leave aside forms of theology that are unable adequately to validate the practice of theology. He argues that a synthesis of the four fundamental mediations (analytics, hermeneutics, cultural intra-religious, and practical) will be a determining factor in the rebalancing and remediation of future theological writing.

The second part of the volume, entitled 'Pluralism and modernity', includes three studies. The first ('A theology of couples', by Juliette Haddad) emphasises the nature of the complementary relationship that Western societies have established between a man and a woman in the responsibilities they share. The true nature of a couple, she contends, emerges as each learns to model themselves on Christ's pascal sacrifice and abandon the focus on self, or ego; instead of being an obstacle that hampers the encounter between two people, the body becomes the space in which intimacy is revealed, inviting both to share in mothering through reproduction and nourishment. In the East, sadly, those roles are more firmly restricted to women.

In the second study ('A research question on Christian intercommunity relations in Lebanon', by Jean Sleiman), the author explores the different Christian communities in Lebanon: their specific history, the social structures and narcissism revealed in their coexistence as neighbours. A cognitive discontinuity – pathologically, it decouples accumulation and synthesis, reason and life, faith and existence – condemns these communities to a life of stagnation, in which a range of distortions can have tragic consequences. One can identify the most remarkable of these distortions through a series of collective pathological behaviours. For example, they neglect to learn the lessons of history in acknowledging the identity of the Other; they become paranoid in their obsession with persecution; they persistently fail to exercise any self-criticism; and by nourishing their history and martyrology they infuse daily life with drama and tragedy. In conclusion, the author points out that the two forms of ecumenism practised in Lebanon – between institutions and within theological dialogue – may in some ways be inadequate, but they are able to help build a triple strategy for reform: recognising the Other as they are, liberating reason and re-writing history, and harmonising the ways of witnessing to the Gospel.

The third and last study ('Complementarity and opposition between tradition and modernity in Middle Eastern theology', by Thom Sicking) highlights the false conflict that local theological thinking has set up between tradition and modernity. The conflict is false because Western and Eastern ways of living, and the values and certainties they entail, exist together – albeit with some signs of tension – within the space inhabited by Arab Christians, a space admittedly divided into silos defined by the spheres of their daily lives and how well these fit with the proposed principles. Three kinds of sphere (religious, professional, and private) are therefore regulated by a random amalgam of values and convictions that mainly derive from two ideological world visions. This gives rise to a fundamental contradiction that affects the ways in which Arab Christian theology is formulated and its practical outcome. It is therefore essential to acknowledge the tension that exists within the Arab world between tradition and modernity, and to bring to bear the resources of the social sciences, especially the sociology and psychology of religion.

A theology of critical resistance and clarity

In organising the third multidisciplinary symposium at Harissa,[26] the organisers decided, despite the pervading spirit of religiosity in the societies of the Arab world, that the time was right to engage in a cleansing and healing critique of the different concepts of God that are constantly emerging and being disseminated. This was a necessary premise for any relevant contextual theology. The aim of such a critical exercise is to identify and reject the ploys used to justify the behaviour of believers. The starting point is a theological conviction requiring great critical lucidity in any Christian religious thinking. In other words, the Arab world must now cleanse its theological thinking of obsolete cultural and sociopolitical notions that have become irrelevant, harmful even, to the extent that they get in

---

26 L'utilisation de l'idée de Dieu dans la société du Moyen-Orient. Actes du troisième symposium interdisciplinaire, Institut Saint-Paul de Philosophie et de Théologie (Harissa), Jounieh, Éditions Saint-Paul, 1993, 251 p.

the way of Christian witness and risk subverting it. For the future of Arab Christian theology, this purification process in its discourse is of major importance, hence the key significance of this third local theological gathering.

In his opening lecture, 'The Uses of God in the societies of the Middle East', Joseph Maalouf presents the nature of the problem and then, briefly, the regulating principles that could pave the way and situate a theological reflection that might undertake the task of purification. By design, his initial examination was in outline only. He does however identify topics that will lend themselves to critical revision and amendment.

In his text 'The Reign of God and the Holy Land in the Old Testament', Paul Féghaly focuses on a critical exploration of texts in the Old Testament; he seeks to rediscover as far as is possible the original textual content of the divine promise to the Jewish people on their definitive and irrevocable right to the land that is a token of His faithfulness. The author wonders about the spiritual interpretation of the text *Sur la terre de Dieu nul n'est étranger* (On God's Earth no one is a stranger): it might be legitimate to the extent that it fits with Yahweh's overall salvific plan, but could also be set up as a hermeneutical proof of the claims of the Jews. This requires the narrative of the return to the promised land to be subjected to thorough reinterpretation. In other words, this narration should not be used to interpret a problem play, however noble and transcendent it might be, but to give voice to a spirit of openness, a willingness to engage with the world to bring together the Holy Land and the Kingdom of God.

Augustin Dupré La Tour entitled his study of New Testament theology 'Jesus, critic of the way the idea of God is manipulated'; in it, he portrays Jesus as the only one who knows the identity of the Father, and is therefore best qualified to condemn, through both his message and his behaviour, erroneous understandings of the transcendence of God. The transcendence of God, he suggests, is robbed of its substance by the exaggerated anthropomorphism of the Jewish people. To support his argument, Dupré La Tour identifies three fundamental attitudes characteristic of the reductionism of which he accuses the Jews: a hypocrisy that involves deceiving others in order to gain their respect on the basis of religious gestures, and which gravely damages the authenticity of their alliance with God; a blindness which, linked with fundamentalism, inevitably leads to a totalitarian and exclusive ideological rigidity and thus to misguided interpretations; and a mistaken certainty that they are in possession of the whole truth, which in turn leads them into an idolatrous manipulation of God. The author inevitably concludes that it is only the *little children* who can grasp the truth of God's kenotic love.

In 'Myth and religious language', Adel Theodor Khoury aims to show on the one hand how myth is a necessary part of religious expression, and on the other that it is important to demystify religion, first, to prevent people from remaining fixated by one original and unchanging model, and second, to sustain their awareness that history brings with it not only changing needs but also successive and definitive improvements. This approach brings together several strands of critical theological thinking. It does not, however, espouse the radical demythologisation strategy advocated by Bultmann. Khoury maintains that human beings are naturally carried along by a sense of tradition that they cannot simply shed. The theological argument he carefully develops shows clearly the influence of Gademer's hermeneutics.

Camille Zeidan in his lecture 'The crisis in language about God' makes effective allusion to Paul Ricœur to support his contribution, which calls into question some of the linguistic strategies that distort the truth about God. The Kantian critique of metaphysical conceptualisation has enabled the indirect message of symbols to be well suited to expressing the nature of religious experience, which one might expect theology to convey. Zeidan identifies a tension that arises between concept, for which words are often inadequate, and symbol, which contributes allusion and deflects rigorous objectivity; from this tension emerges a space for listening that benefits from the awareness that neither the listener nor the listened to are set in stone. His argument subtly exhorts the Christian communities of the Arab world to learn from the hermeneutics of Ricœur in their exegetical practice. If they are prepared to do this, they could benefit by redefining the Christian mystery in terms intelligible to the historical context within which they live.

In his study entitled 'Religion and power among ninth-century Arab theologians', Samir Khalil Samir uses quotes from Arab theologians to examine how Christian Arabs defended their religion in the face of energetic Muslim expansion. Arab-speaking Christians were falling in numbers, offering as a representation of God in human form a proof of true religion: Muslims were powerful and superior in numbers, while Christians incarnated kenosis and humility. If indeed the effectiveness of the divine plan is most fully revealed when mankind subdues any thirst for domination, then for Arab Christian communities to abandon any form of power might enable them to engage in a more authentic form of witness, one that is true to the spirit of the Gospel.

Thom Sicking's contribution, 'The worship of the saints as a form of popular theology' took a sociological approach to attempt to resituate the saints as legitimate channels for mediation and intercession. There are risks to this form of popular worship, however: on the one hand, the impulsive origins of this type of devotion, and on the other the thoughtless harsh disapproval of such impulsivity on the part of theologians too caught up in lofty academia to pay attention to the daily expectations of believers. When everyday emotions are the main driver of theological understanding, a person may enjoy a special relationship with a saint who is a mediator; but they must not allow this to blind them to the danger of divergence – clearly signalled, for example, by a desire to exert ideological manipulation.

In 'God and the Earth in contemporary Judaism', Jad Hatem sketches out the variety of interpretations of the concept of the land of Israel devised by contemporary Jewish scholars who wish to give a theological account of the historical events of the great return and the reappropriation of the promised heritage. The principal hermeneutic theme linking most of the essays (Kook, Ellis, Wiesel, Fackenheim, Buber, Greenberg) is undoubtedly the dialectic of divine challenge and human response, and the dialectic centres around the question of the distinctiveness of Jewish identity. From this discursive stem various branches of reasoning soon develop. Some advocate the salvation of the whole Earth as a necessary precursor to any authentic relationship with God, while others favour the idea that election and a promise are the foundational manifestation of an irrevocable commitment, underpinned by a mandate to bear responsibility for universal good. This lends urgency to the task of dialogue between Judaism and Arab Christians, who are also Semites; by its very nature, the dialogue should be spared the accusation of the racism that is so often assumed in other cases. A persistent question here, however, is on the matter of assertions by Judaism to singularity in the relationship. Some contemporary Jewish voices have been raised against the intolerable exclusivity of claiming a unique relationship with God.

Two brief reflections on fundamentalism among Christians (Elias Khalifé) and Muslims (Adel Theodor Khoury) examine the origins and characteristics of the phenomenon and how the danger of reductionism might affect the two religions in the future. Muslim fundamentalism has been attributed to three factors: a reaction against colonialism, cultural disorientation due to the disconcerting and destabilising effects of modernity, and the failure of national revolutions. If authentic identity is achieved through struggle (to liberate Islam from alienation, to rehabilitate the universal validity of Muslim tradition, to re-establish a fair social and political Islamic order, as substitute for superannuated Christianity), there yet remains a pressing question: how and whether the claims of fundamentalism can accommodate modern religious plurality. Christian fundamentalism is described in other ways. The state of Christianity in the Middle East has little in common with the injustices and paralysis holding back Muslim societies over the past two centuries. Christian fundamentalism is closely linked with American Protestantism, and experiences local resurgences. Arab Christian communities, being a minority, are at risk of lapsing into similar identity-related tension and theological rigidity. The deepening sociopolitical crisis in the region is likely, even in the absence of appropriate scriptural justification in the New Testament, to force these communities into a defensive position.

The analysis of the daily activities of the Lebanese offers an insight into pastoral psychology. In 'The roles attributed to God in managing our actions', Francis Leduc examines two aspects: the role ascribed to the Word of God in relation to ethics, and the way in which the presence of God is visible in daily events. Leduc suggests that a fundamentalist reading of Scripture results in a lack of prudential judgement for the actions of most Lebanese believers. Such a reading lays bare inherent contradictions within the text of the Bible. The Christian interpretation of events is infantilised by poor judgement, which also upsets and weakens the equilibrium – highly prized by Eastern theology – between ethics and the quotidian, undermining human autonomy. An exercise in self-criticism is becoming urgent: one that respects the mystery and otherness of God, but also inhibits collective self-delusion and promotes an improved sense of ethical responsibility.

'The Copt discourse on God' by Fadel Sidarouss is an analysis of both the history of Copt theological thinking in Egypt and its possible future. Copt theology insists on the transcendence of God and on his impassive nature; in compensation it fosters in excessive measure the worship of saints as mediators and protectors; it highlights a type of Christology influenced by close polemical discussion with Islam and focuses mainly on the divinity of Christ; it exhibits an extreme exaltation of the Cross as a symbol of life in which suffering and martyrdom are prominent features. Contemporary Copt theology, as these characteristics suggest, is very much marked by tension between tradition and modernity, exacerbated by the influence of Islam. The three threats to the identity of the Copt Church (Islam, Catholicism and Protestantism, and modernity) are a major challenge, to which the Church will need to respond by embracing radically new theological thinking. The process will be something akin to replacing the scriptural concept of *mono-genes* with the philosophical concepts of *ousia* and *homoousios*.

In the final theological essay in this section, 'Towards a contemporary theological discourse on God in the Middle East', Cyrille Salim Bustros suggests some guiding principles for theological reflection on the realities of daily life in the Arab world. Two preconditions will make it possible to establish a reasonable Arab Christian theology, one that will pay proper attention to the experience of faith within the Christian communities living and working in the different societies of the Arab world: first, giving up thinking in terms of myth, and second, accepting the notion of interfaith dialogue. In boldly and urgently taking on the challenges of diversity, we must be mindful that in any message proclaiming the Gospel there is always a tension between promoting universal love and adhering to the demanding truth of the Incarnation. When we think about a theology of dialogue in the Arab world, we advocate adopting a respectful approach to the mystery of God and, as well as the establishment of an open and cooperative relationship, creating a space for coexistence and joint intellectual exploration. This optimistic thought is the final one in a contribution that, on a theoretical level at least, will have helped to elucidate a theological matter of undoubtedly grave importance. In an Arab world that is disastrously prey to all kinds of extravagant imagining, it is really not easy to portray God as a pure being, who sometimes veils his face and sometimes reveals his intimate self. If we can approach God not by misusing words that might misrepresent and devalue Him, but rather by emphasising that He is inexpressibly mysterious and beyond comprehension, then we will fit in with the Eastern tradition of apophasis. Such an exercise would lay a rational foundation for a new form of contextual theological thinking in and for the Arab world.

From liberating God to liberating mankind

The turbulent sociopolitical context in the Middle East has created tension and conflict throughout much of the Arab world. Threatened by instability, Arab political regimes have increasingly resorted to the unwarranted use of violence. Many experts agree that the issue of freedom has become the principal challenge facing Arab societies. The problem of religious freedom is a major preoccupation, crucial to both individuals and the communities in the region. Violence affects all groups and all individuals, whatever their religious or political affiliation.

Where political totalitarianism has been carefully grafted onto ontological totalitarianism, it is extremely unwise and dangerous to denounce the existential disfigurement that a perverted understanding of religion can inflict on human society. Especially in matters of religious freedom, Arab societies continue to behave in accordance with the medieval model of a single religion (to prevent religious pluralism) and a unique orthodoxy (to preclude diversity within a single religion). It will take a brave exercise in introspection to dig into the ideological depths of collective behaviour in order to disentangle the sociopolitical and socioreligious forms of extremism that pervade secular aspects of Arab society. In seeking to make God free, as humans we earnestly seek our own liberation. The fourth theological symposium[27] aimed to address this question, together with the religious aspects of oppression, and what follows is a summary of the analyses and conclusions presented.

In his preface, Cyrille Salim Bustros observes religious freedom through a double prism: critical realism and sympathetic open-mindedness:

> We must not ignore the truth about the use of religion to oppress, but rather face up to it critically as an adolescent phase in the history of the development of human intelligence. We must be both realistic and critical. In truth, when it comes to religion people have not always behaved honourably. We cannot blame the mistakes made by believers in various religions on God, but only on the inherent weaknesses of human beings. Open-mindedness, the second attitude, must be practised between religions and also between believers and atheists. We must engage in dialogue so as to understand each other, and see in the other person's religion, or their human understanding of each other, an alternative path to God or towards the best of mankind. The respect of religious freedom, in the end, is an acceptance of difference and otherness. We must fearlessly unmask the tendencies towards totalitarian violence that throughout history have prevented the promotion of religious freedom. Religions have tried, in vain, mutually to eliminate each other. For the future, believers of the various religions must engage in dialogue and collaboration [...] in a shared conviction that their different religions all lead to God, and aim to understand His will, in order to grow, in His image, into self-giving love. Religious freedom will thus become the means through which mankind becomes both more human and more divine.

The prophetic tone of this introduction makes it a true manifesto for a humanity liberated from the domination of false religious and ideological powers. This throws light onto the vocation of the religions. To the extent that they contribute to liberating mankind, they will also be fulfilling God's plan. Their plurality points to the limitless riches within the divine heart, whose divinity is better honoured through a diversity of approaches than through the hegemony of only one.

The successor to Mgr Cyrille Salim Bustros as director of the Institut Saint-Paul, Elias Aghia, gave a brief but detailed introduction to the research presented

---

27 *La Liberté religieuse au Moyen-Orient. Actes du quatrième symposium interdisciplinaire, Institut Saint-Paul de Philosophie et de Théologie (Harissa)*, Jounieh, Éditions Saint-Paul, 1995, 269 p.

in the fourth symposium; Paul Féghaly ('Religious freedom in the Old Testament') then highlighted the key factor in the increase in religious extremism in the Middle East, showing the two strategies of exclusion and open-mindedness that characterise the books of the Old Testament. If it is true that faithfulness to the Covenant and the coherence and homogeneity of the Jewish community have led them to develop an unduly defensive attitude, such that they despise and reject any other religion, it is also true that the universalism present in Isaiah stands against this disabling introspection, and casts aside the chains of chauvinism parading as religious exaltation. The tragedy for the Middle East – hinted at by the Old Testament's reticence on the subject – is unquestionably the collusion between religious and social factors: any passage dealing with the stranger and the non-believer is mystified as divine election and granted little human dignity. This critical approach rightly condemns the ways in which servitude is claimed to embody a more faithful obedience to the Word of God. Any critical hermeneutical approach must be able to expose the theological justifications for rejecting the Other. And if the Other is no threat to God, then it should not be seen as a threat by anyone wanting to inherit God's gentleness.

Mgr Georges Khodr in his 'Orthodox vision' explained that religious freedom derives from an attitude of kenosis, in which the emptying of the self confirms the freedom of others. According to Gregory of Nyssa, freedom is a gift from God and not only bears witness to the original likeness between God and man but also enables diversity, which in turn becomes conclusive evidence for the exercise of freedom. Freedom is rooted in the theology of communion, and takes on an emblematic significance in the general organisation of Christian life. Freedom means that wrongdoing, although acknowledged, need not lead to exclusion: human weakness is recognised as such, but need not be fatal. The contribution of orthodox theology thus appears to be decisive in the theological approach to otherness. If God Himself is free, then all that comes from Him and His power must necessarily also be characterised by freedom. Thus, by analogy, a person who is free clearly shares in the life of God. Those who claim to share in this life have a duty courageously to express their freedom through their lives and relationships.

Louis Khawand provides a historical overview of the social doctrine of the Catholic Church ('Religious freedom before and after Vatican II'), in which he outlines the evolution of the concept in papal encyclicals from Gregory XVI to John Paul II. Jad Hatem, in 'Christians in Lebanon and religious supra-confessionalism', examines the reasons why very well-known Lebanese Christian thinkers such as Rhani, Gibran, Neaïmy and many others, in their disappointment at the lack of any religious freedom in the space shared by the different Lebanese communities, developed a philosophical-theological description of the faith that overcomes the pitfalls of doctrinal differences and community disagreements. A Christian theological approach that seeks to extend its religious influence beyond the rigid limits set by ecclesiastical institutions is limited by the following factors: Lebanese Christians are a minority within the Arab world; they contend with the strong attraction of the deist appeal of freemasonry; the counter-witness of blindness and obscurantism of the Churches in Lebanon; the desire to abase the Christ event by presenting it as merely a prophetic mission in order not to alienate non-Christians; the rehabilitation of Canaanite monotheism which, out of concern for transconfessional ecumenism, includes Ishmael among the elect of God. Following on from this critical description, these Lebanese intellectuals reacted in philosophical terms by re-imagining religion as based on pluralism and tolerance. The only reason minority Arab Christians are able to live in peace is thanks to the ideas of the Enlightenment, which describe a way of life founded on fundamental diversity. The only way to respond to exclusionary fundamentalism, they maintain, is to reject extreme violence.

In his lecture on Islam and religious freedoms, Radwane Al-Sayed seeks to locate the problem of religious freedom in the legal debate on dhimmitude. His critical reading of the Muslim legal lineage divides the history of the Muslim community into several periods. Each period brought with it a pattern of legal adaptation. The Prophet of Islam originally wanted to give his nascent community an autonomous and distinctive identity. This was an attempt to establish a distinction from the legislative system then prevailing. When the Islamic state was then established and consolidated, the legal process featured economic and administrative emancipation from the Christians, who were at the time in the majority in public life. When at a later stage Crusaders and Mongols started to threaten political alienation and military destabilisation, the reaction in the Muslim community was one of violent self-defence. By stages, they then began viciously to attack the Christians, believing that they were defending themselves from renewed hostile incursions. There was through all these developments a clear contradiction between the Koranic text ('there is no compulsion in religion', 2, 256) and the legal text dealing with the freedom prescribed by the Koran and compromised by legislation that aims first and foremost to ensure community cohesion and political stability. Apostasy, in these terms, was indissolubly linked to defection, a fundamentally political form of treason, punishable by death. This means that the text of the Koran is always interpreted in the light of the best advantage to the Muslim community, and the Muslim concept of religious freedom does not recognise the modern legitimacy of the individual. In effect, this religious concept is dependent on a collectivist perception of humanity. The author deplores the fundamentalist exploitation of this reductionist perception, and invites Muslims to develop a new religious anthropology that might enable contemporary Muslim thinking fruitfully to benefit from the positive aspects of modernity.

In tandem with this approach, Adel Theodor Khoury's reflection highlights the right to be different in a society characterised by religious plurality. He is well acquainted with Muslim–Christian relations, and strives to identify in the two traditions, Christian and Muslim, not only similarities in the reproof of error, but also the hermeneutic potential for redefining individual identity, not over against others, but rather with others, and to their benefit. This could lead to a new form of anthropology based on the acknowledgement of interculturalism. The definition of a person's individual identity, and of the other's identity, would no longer be based on a dialectic of rivalry and exclusion, but rather on a movement towards openness and solidarity.

Jean-Louis Lingot, in 'Human rights from a religious perspective' presents the various theological positions defended by Catholics, Protestants and Orthodox who work hard to establish that human rights are based on theological principles drawn from Christian anthropology. One would not wish to reduce the substance of the Gospel to the Declaration of Human Rights, but theological influence and Christian inspiration in the Declaration are clear. The ethical content of the Declaration has worldwide reach, but it also shares many features with the moral demands inherent to the mystery of Christianity. The secular understanding of the rights of man may have a less extensive metaphysical frame of reference, but it owes to the story of salvation an openness that takes its reference from an absolute in the person of Christ, who warrants within Christianity the truth and validity of any normative statement about mankind. These statements have a modern flavour but they belong in a purely theoretical perspective. There is no mention of the checks and balances that might validate the relevance of the interpretations they offer.

Jean Corbon, in his 'Intolerance and ecumenism', scrutinises the enigmatic entity that is inter-Christian conviviality, which is sadly unecumenical, and is in danger of getting bogged down in inter-church group activities that sound a fatal knell to any future notion of freedom. The authenticity of any evangelistic witness can only suffer as a result. The freedom preached in the Gospel Beatitudes is ontologically communional, and therefore ill suits half-measures and uncertain compromise. To list the intolerant behaviours that emerge from the conviviality practised among Lebanese and Arab Christians (attempts to force others to join in; refusal to acknowledge the existence and/or pastoral activity of others;

misrepresentation of others' identities; neglecting and/or isolating others), is to reveal its theological inadequacy and ecumenical failings. It may seem fatal, but this ecumenical weakness can be transformed and stimulate a better and more respectful appreciation of what true ecumenism requires. All Arab Christians therefore need to receive this message. They are invited to take note of the twofold focus of what is needed in truly ecumenical spirituality: first, patient but active waiting for the realisation, in God's time, of Christian unity, and second, an appreciation of the urgent need for theological and catechetic training that will sharpen the sense of ecumenical responsibility in everyday ministry.

Joseph Maalouf's account, 'The exercise of religious freedom in Israel' argues that religious freedom is compromised by the Law of Return. This law contradicts the principle, so dear to the Jewish people, of a secular and democratic state. The legal texts of the constitution of Israel, far from promoting equality between Jewish and Arab citizens, are generally aligned to a dramatic narrative of struggle and self-defence, in which the foreigner, or the Other generally, is readily suspected of latent hostility. As a result, 'foreigners' are surreptitiously deprived of the privileges reserved to supposedly 'indigenous' citizens. If the state of Israel wishes to preserve its image as a democratic nation, it should really reassess its discriminatory practices, which are not in keeping with the legal tenor of the democratic principles that their constitutional texts theoretically advocate.

The Bishop of Baalbeck, Cyrille Salim Bustros, in 'Religious freedom in the diocese of Baalbeck', started by making a clear distinction between political freedom and religious freedom. In Lebanon, a majority Muslim society, it is extremely dangerous to transpose theological differences into the political arena. In Baalbeck, in which the Shiites are the vast majority, only left-wing political parties are permitted; the small Christian minority, however, shelters under the umbrella of the Lebanese state newly restored in the Bekaa Valley, and enjoys religious freedom which it is able to practise and exercise in various ways in civil life. They are free to build churches and worship in them, to teach, and to run businesses. Political freedom is still determined by the demographic imbalance that dominates Baalbeck, much to the regret of Christians who are in the majority in other Lebanese towns, but they are nevertheless permitted to enter mixed marriages (in the face of objections from Muslims) and to engage in meaningful theological debate. In a country where the history of the reform of ideas is sadly different from its present achievements, and where politics and morals are not in step so that even the logical application of good ideas can lead to bad results, the bishop of Baalbeck's critique is realistic and pertinent.

The contribution by Joseph Moghayzel, 'Laws and changing mindset', was the last in the series, and provided an essential final complement to the set of theological analyses in this fourth volume. He argues that citizens who wish to have their rights valued and maintained must work to exercise their freedom within a strong dialectical opposition between law and mindset. He took various examples and case studies: from the penal code (the permutation of the death sentence to life imprisonment); in the legislation relating to individual status (the fact that religious marriage is compulsory within Lebanon, while civil marriages contracted outside Lebanon are recognised); and the confessional allocation of power (verbally and in writing, confessionalism is abolished, but it persists in people's minds). In all of these, it becomes clear that in a pluralist society such as Lebanon's, the mindset differs from one community to the next, and this gives rise to legal processes that may be parallel but are divergent or asymmetrical. According to Moghayzel, when citizens gain an appreciation of universal human and spiritual values, then Lebanese society will be able to benefit from a real symbiosis between mindsets, and legislative processes will be able to evolve in a healthy way.

The conditions that might enable a new Arab contextual theology

This concluding section cannot hope fully to explain the theological significance of the consistent and regular publication of these four volumes. In this prospective epilogue, I would simply like to identify from them some signs of hope for the future that may equip local Christian communities so that they can address the task of theological witness in ways that seem to me to be especially important. Because some of these contributions present complex analyses, because of the approach used for some of the studies, and because the ways in which long-expected contemporary Arab theological thinking is produced, presented and disseminated are so far unsatisfactory, it is as yet a bit early to hope for a true local theological renewal. We cannot assume that by calling four theological symposiums in the space of ten years we shall be able to give substance to this hope simply by engaging with a certain number of issues of the highest importance in terms of life, witness and the future of Christians living in the Lebanon and in other societies in the Arab world.

It is clear that we shall by forced by a scholarly attitude, marked by patience and humility, to postpone for the time being the day when this kind of Arab theology will see the light of day and take its natural place among the modern local, contextual and continental theologies. It remains an open question, however, whether and to what extent this initiative might contribute to the development of such a theology, when it is considered alongside those that already exist – if in somewhat fragmentary non-academic form, and especially in Egypt and Palestine.

Here in Lebanon and in the other countries of a feverish Middle East, we are constrained by a paralysing level of expectation; it is therefore important calmly to reflect on the fundamental conditions that might enable deeper, relevant and fruitful work in theology. The concern is that the sociopolitical and sociocultural context might compromise such a plan. Christians might be prevented from entering more deeply into the process of reflection and theological conceptualisation by their inability appropriately to represent the voice of Christian witnesses engaging with the Arab reality of political oppression, religious violence and economic strangulation. To overcome these difficulties they will need to display outstanding theological courage, which in turn will empower them to proclaim their faith in terms so evidently genuine that they will convey both promise and salvation. It is therefore essential to free modern theology from the temptation to remain stuck in the retrograde interstices of traditional religious discourse.

What conditions, then, would enable Arab theological thought to be vital and relevant? They can be considered under two headings: theoretically, how to develop a system of thought; technically, how to manage it. Because of its importance and its serious implications, we shall focus heavily here on the issue of theoretical development. We shall enumerate some of the conditions, expressing them as somewhat fragmentary observations, in the light of the generally prevailing mindset in Lebanon and in the societies of the Arab world.

Our first observation – which does not necessarily bear the marks of modern epistemology – is that theology includes a triad of different but complementary meanings: the theology of prayer, of words, and of action. The theology of words includes an especially important notion. It can describe the dangerous attempt to describe in words the very nature of God Himself, or at least the ways in which He acts and reveals Himself. It can also include the apparently slightly less risky exercise of describing mankind's experience of God. A contemporary contextual Arab theology, therefore, must allow space for this threefold dimension, placing emphasis rather on the existential aspect of human experience, which itself is heavily influenced by the way in which Arab Christians receive the Good News of God's revelation and react to its concrete implications.

Local theological knowledge is expressed in terms of the triad of the theology of prayer, action and discourse, so when it brings together the diversity of Christian experiences mentioned above, it should be able to convey not only the epistemological categories of Western thought, but also some that are truly Arab and Eastern. Those exercising this theological knowledge will need to shape the Arab and Eastern categories that will best and most faithfully communicate the enculturation of the Gospel into Arab cultural soil. To develop these categories will require two points of reference within the cultural heritage: the local Lebanese and regional Arab culture, and the channels through which Arab modernity is currently expressed. At this point, we can no longer overlook the growing gap between the methods of analysis prescribed in modern Western thought and the specific reality of Arab life, which seems to many to be resistant to systematic dissection. Those keenly aware of this gap might favour taking a pluralistic approach that took account in its cognitive analysis of typically indigenous aspects. And similarly, the existence of the gap justifies the need to take proper note of Arab realities before including them in a potential synthesis with a foreign theological work. It could be helpful to enlist the sensitivity of Western Christian faith to bring its own theological light to bear and offer models of comparison and challenge.

Contemporary Arab theology needs to be aware of the particular challenge faced by Christians caught in the workings of a reality that constantly calls their Christian faith into question, and it must work to become a true reflection of the intimate and individual experiences of living witnesses. It needs also to avoid any ideological prejudice, for once the Christian experience of these witnesses has been discussed and summarised, they must also be offered support in their conceptual understanding. Any reductionism, therefore, that might threaten to limit the existential aspects of their faith to pre-set formats or concepts. For Christian commitment in the midst of everyday life is impossible to shrink into a notional uniformity or absorb into a greater ideal. This contemporary Arab theology must, however, exercise evangelistic discernment and allow that faith inspires, regulates and shapes practice; it must therefore highlight that when Christian practice is liberated from reductionist vagaries, it offers not only a demonstration of faith but also a touchstone and existential corrective, validating the authenticity of the witness.

This new theology, in aiming to be relevant and to convey the news of salvation, must enable a dialectical tension between the transcendent notion of the evangelical imperative and the immanent notion of the human response; its discourse must be founded on the essential balance between action and kenosis. Focusing on that balancing act not only responds to the challenges and constraints faced daily by Christian Arabs, so that it appeals to them on an intimate level, but it also finds echoes in the externalised intersection of their lives and their theology. Any theological discourse must therefore be shaped to take account of the historical situation of these communities, bearing in mind the fatal interference between politics and religion that has hobbled them since the eighth century. For these communities, their major concern is best expressed as an ontological desire for active survival, which in practical terms means a desire to be a Christian minority capable of seeding the core aspects of their faith into the dominant Arab Muslim culture.

If they achieve this, it would seem that a kenotic theology faithfully modelled on Christ offers the best and most historic opportunity to give shape to an appropriate collective theology. Islam, after all, which is the cultural base layer of Arab identity, is very unwilling to allow any visible or muscular form of Christian witness. Even if Arab Christians are able to convey their witness message in theological language that chimes with the Arab heritage they share – and this cannot be guaranteed – the authenticity of their words is under threat from the weight of history and the intrusions misinterpreted as undercover proselytism. Collectively, the community needs as a matter of urgency to engage in a decentring of the self, based in a theological understanding of kenosis that guides their daily living. This is not in any way a suicidal move: they are not to disappear, in order to please their Muslim fellow citizens. Rather, by practising kenosis they will percolate more effectively into the historical patterns of Arab life, which in turn conveys their genuine and major commitment to the dignity of the Arab population. In this way, a theology of kenotic commitment will enable Arab Christians to prove the credibility they so keenly need to demonstrate to the Arab world. And in response they can expect a peaceful and positive reaction from their Muslim neighbours, who might justifiably be suspicious of any hint of superiority from a Western civilisation that they so abhor, or any implication that the Christian theological thinking associated with it might claim supremacy.

Having chosen this theological approach, its proponents will need to test its relevance by reviewing the Greek, Syrian and Arab heritage of the Middle East, both theological and cultural, and also to test it against Arab modernity. Crucially, they will highlight and compare the theory guiding their action with what the post-conciliar Western Church, in its greater maturity, is seeking to express in all its expressions of innovation. The process will thus follow a logical approach entirely focused on the urgent need for decentring. Their theological review should include a closer examination of biblical figures, of patristic models – including Arabic-language Middle Eastern thinkers – and of the conceptual paradigms of modern Arab culture. In their review, they should seek to identify factors that might underpin their kenotic theology and its practical implications. The outcome of the review will be able to trace its ancestry along an unbroken line that includes interpretations of the Christian faith back through the ages, to the scriptural foundations of all authentic theological experiences.

In taking this long view back to its foundations, this new Arab theology will be able to identify problem areas and formulate suitable faith-based responses, which, taking account of the challenges and expectations of local Christian communities, should elicit a collective commitment, realistically tailored to the limits of its reach. I would like to suggest here some areas in which an appropriate theological response is called for. I shall list some of them here. First, religious alienation: the scandalous plurality of Churches that prevents an authentic prefiguring of Christian unity; the rigid Jewish attitude that adamantly refuses any contact with Arab Islam or Arab Christianity; the indefensible and intransigent claim by Islam to universal status. Second, economic and political alienation: the abuses of dictatorial political regimes; the inappropriate rehabilitation and justification of enlightened despotism; the tribal exploitation of natural and human resources; the slavish subjugation by Arab regimes of legislative, executive and judicial power. Third, cultural alienation: the Arabic language suffers from an inherent semantic deficit that could silence those wishing to express in theological terms their Christian faith as experienced both intellectually and existentially; the lack of academic rigour in the identification and expression of the religious, ethnic, cultural and sociopolitical history of the different societies in the Arab world; and the want of a space in which individuals and groups can flourish in an aesthetic and/or ecological sense.

These lacunae, and many others, challenge Christian theology to engage in reflection in order to present them in a critical light. This provides an opportunity to Arab Christian communities keen to offer a modest contribution to solving these problems to demonstrate their real solidarity with their Arab fellow citizens, both Muslim and secular. Together, they should address the challenge of modernity and work to improve the conditions for Arabs and to humanise the peoples of Arab countries.

*

This, in sum, is what is demanded of a contemporary Arab theology, and by the same token, the challenge that will both test and stimulate it. In deconstructing and analysing this theological work, I hope to have shown how much Arab Christian communities will need to pursue the practice of their faith within the crucible of their historic existence. These communities need not only to review their sociopolitical and sociocultural context in the light of their faith; they also need to review their faith in the light of their lived context. This two-way review should enable a better understanding and appreciation of their identity and their calling within the Arab world.

Part Two

THE THEOLOGY OF CONVIVIALITY: PATHWAYS AND MODELS

1

The Abrahamic heritage
(Youakim Moubarac)

Everything the Abbé Youakim Moubarac (1924–1995) wrote was in pursuit of
one single and clear aim: to enable Arab Christian theology to develop a better
awareness of the conviviality between people in the Middle East. The theological
foundation of conviviality in the region is the shared Abrahamic heritage. The
three forms of monotheism that arose in the Middle East can legitimately claim to
share the same heritage. A contextual Christian theology of conviviality could thus
help to justify the inherently diverse ways in which this heritage is experienced in
religious terms. To acknowledge the legitimacy of the three pathways – Judaism,
Christianity and Islam – is to recognise the vast range of spirituality within the
true Abrahamic faith in God. This chapter aims, in its first section, to condense the
key points of the theological thinking that re-examines the Christian perception
of Islam, in order, in the second section, to offer a new theological vocation to the
Christian communities of the Arab world.

To attempt to summarise the rich legacy of Youakim Moubarac[1] in a few pages,

---

1 Youakim Moubarac, a Maronite clergyman, was born in 1924 at Kfâr Sghâb in the north of
Lebanon. While still quite young he moved to Paris and concentrated on studying Islam under
Louis Massignon. He lived in France for some forty years, especially in Paris where he
exercised his priestly ministry in the parish of Saint-Séverin, and taught at the Sorbonne and the
Institut Catholique; he returned to Lebanon in 1984 in order to present his *Pentalogie
Antiochienne* and to direct the preparations for the Maronite synod. The Maronite Church was
forced by circumstance to postpone indefinitely the planned synod and instead joined in
preparing the Roman Synod for Lebanon; disappointed, Moubarac returned to settle in France,
where he died in 1995. His theological output is huge. Of the approximately forty titles, the best
known are: *Pentalogie islamo-chrétienne* (Beirut, Éditions du Cénacle Libanais, 1972–1973),
Pentalogie antiochienne – domaine maronite (Beirut, Éditions du Cénacle Libanais, 1984),
L'Islam (Paris, Casterman, 1962), *Abraham dans le Coran* (Paris, Vrin, 1958), *Recherches sur*

however, is a major challenge. His output on Islamology alone is so varied and multifaceted that it is almost impossible to give a fair account of it even through a carefully chosen selection. So, although this is an impossible task, and since there is as yet no monograph presenting his life and works,[2] I propose to pick out various approaches to his original thought and to seek to identify the invitations presented through its riches. His writings not only have indisputable academic value, but they also present an energetic call to action. His primary focus is a serious and patient endeavour to seek a just and appropriate renewal of evangelistic witness as it is lived in the various Christian communities living in the sociopolitical region of the ancient Church of Antioch. What is original in his thought is the slow and mature evolution of a triple theme, seamlessly linking the interminable efforts to reform the Maronite Church, the keen desire to share in rebuilding Christian unity in Antioch, and the unwavering commitment to promote dialogue between Muslims and Christians[3] in the Arab world. This chapter will concentrate only on the theological process seeking to provide justification for conviviality between people in the Arab world.

Towards a new Christian theology of Islam

In the first part of this chapter we shall seek to identify the guiding principles and main features that clearly characterise Youakim Moubarac's Islamology. There are two aspects to this. First, we shall explore the theological status of the dialogue between Muslims and Christians as Youakim Moubarac envisioned and established it; then, we shall examine the theological understanding of the status specific to the Islamic religion as a particular and challenging expression of the

---

la pensée chrétienne et l'Islam dans les Temps modernes et à l'époque contemporaine (Beirut, Éditions de l'Université Libanaise, 1977), *Le Renouveau liturgique* (Paris, Éditions Saint-Séverin, 1959), *Dossier sur Jérusalem* (Revue d'Études Palestiniennes, Paris, 1983). In homage to his teacher, he edited the *Opera Minora de Louis Massignon* (Cairo-Beirut-Paris, 1963).

2 A first step in this direction has recently been taken by the Friends of the Abbé Moubarac. A reference work has been published in Lausanne: a selection of studies presenting his theological thinking and some formerly unpublished works (J. Stassinet (ed.), *Youakim Moubarac*, Lausanne, L'Âge d'Homme, 2005). One part of this chapter is a slight reworking of my contribution to this volume in his honour.

3 Youakim Moubarac acknowledged having spent most of his time studying Islam and the improving of relationships between Muslims and Christians. 'I am coming late to the task (of studying the Christian Middle East), as my university work required me to focus on Islamology, only then to be limited by misfortune to Maronite affairs.' (Youakim Moubarac, *La chambre nuptiale du coeur. Approches spirituelles et questionnements de l'Orient Syriani*, Paris, Cariscript, 1993, p. 9)

divine economy. Moubarac considered the theology of dialogue to be a determining prelude to the way that Christians perceive Islam. Within the Christian
Weltanschauung, the theological status of Islam does indeed affect the ways in
which Christians envisage and practice dialogue with Muslims, but it is also true
that historic practice has generally promoted a more cordial human and spiritual
relationship between the parties, and one can hope that this will help Arab Christians to establish stronger fraternal relations with Muslims. This is really a *sine
qua non* for an intelligent, just and open theological attitude towards the Islamic
religion. Moubarac's theological intentions on the whole favour engaging first
in a thorough study of the theological basis for dialogue between Muslims and
Christians before attempting to define a theological perception of Islam.

Dialogue as prelude to theological conversion

Stages and markers

Moubarac's Islamological investigations were guided by two overarching sources
of inspiration. His first source of inspiration was a personal one: he found himself
driven by a paramount evangelistic need, as a Christian, to understand what he
experienced, and to live by what he believed, and this entirely shaped his approach
to studying the Islamic religion. When carrying out training among his parishion-
ers at Saint-Séverin in Paris, he frequently repeated: 'It is essential to understand,
but also to stay faithful. One might even say that it is impossible to be a Christian
and to say that we know God if we do not remain faithful to Him, if we are to bear
witness.'[4] Any attempt to deepen one's understanding and extend one's knowledge
of God's immense work in the universe is in itself a spark of openness and faithfulness. Any theoretical approach to Islam in the works of Youakim Moubarac
is therefore necessarily linked to a communal life with those who live and act as
those who are inspired by the religion and are constantly guided by it.

His second source of inspiration was purely theological in origin. Youakim
Moubarac's Islamology was motivated not only by personal factors but also
by the need for Christian and Muslim coexistence; it was also closely linked to
the assumption underlying all his work and that enabled him clearly to see, as
inspired by his teacher Louis Massignon, that the person of Abraham symbolised

---

4 Y. Moubarac (ed.), *Catéchisme pour adultes à Saint-Séverin*, Paris, Casterman, 1965, vol. I;
Le Credo, p. 175.

the communion of the three monotheistic religions.[5] Reference to Abraham thus becomes the theological locus par excellence of the meeting between Muslims and Christians.

Youakim Moubarac knew intimately, body and soul, the true nature of Muslim–Christian relationships as they have developed since the seventh century, and wanted to offer himself as a living link between the children of Abraham. To this end, he was always deeply aware of the mysteries of Islam and of its spiritual significance as he found it revealed in the light of the Christian faith. At the heart of this mystery he recognised the symbolic value of the call to Abraham and identified the key connection between the travels of Muhammad, the Prophet of Islam, and the spiritual meaning of that original call. He acknowledged in this connection his spiritual inheritance from his teacher, Louis Massignon, whose work 'was a key development not only of Christian thinking about Islam but also of Orientalism'.[6]

These two sources of inspiration drove Youakim Moubarac's energetic and dedicated efforts to serve the cause of dialogue between Muslims and Christians. He soon realised that an urgent task was to draw up a calm and objective history of Christian thinking about Islam.[7] Having identified this academic lacuna, he produced two doctoral theses[8] to remedy the situation; the second was published by the University of Lebanon Press. In these two historic pieces of research, and in his university work as a whole, he maintained high academic standards, which Arab Christians have successfully introduced into the cultural life of the Arab world. There are two key identifiers of this Arab modernity: research and critical analysis. Moubarac adopted wholesale the valuable analysis made by his friend Nassif Nassar,[9] and reiterated that the main contribution by Christians to Arab culture in modern times was rationalism.

---

5 Y. Moubarac, *Abraham dans le Coran*, Paris, Vrin, 1958.
6 Y. Moubarac, *L'Islam et le dialogue islamo-chrétien: Pentalogie islamo-chrétienne*, vol. III, Beirut, Éditions du Cénacle Libanais, Librairie Orientale, 1972–73, p. 100.
7 *Ibid.*, p. 94.
8 *La pensée chrétienne et l'Islam des origines à la prise de Constantinople*, Paris, Sorbonne, 1969, 576 pages; *Recherches sur la pensée chrétienne et l'islam dans les temps modernes et à l'époque contemporaine*, Beirut, Publications de l'Université Libanaise, 1977, 555 pages.
9 Y. Moubarac, 'Constantes de l'identité maronite', article published in Arabic in the Lebanese daily paper *An-Nahar*, 23 December, 1995.

The conditions and arrangements necessary for dialogue

Having composed his two *Pentalogies*, Moubarac was deeply convinced that dialogue between Muslims and Christians must above all be bold in its approach to all points of contention. There was a sense that this might compromise an allegedly delicate understanding between the two communities:

> In a true dialogue with sincere Muslims, we should not avoid any question or fear any response. If we lack the courage to speak out loud our message to its intended hearers, then it is not a message, it is what Massignon called a clerical tactic. We must have a firm and loyal belief that an open-minded Muslim deserves a valid response to any question. We should in any case, in the exercise of proselytism, both contemplate and achieve agreement between Christianity and Islam.[10]

Dialogue must be completely transparent, because the message, as understood and conveyed by the Church, cannot afford to be eclectic, distorted or diminished. If it is to be sincere, fruitful and effective, dialogue between Muslims and Christians and indeed any dialogue between religions must engage with the entire thought and all the life challenges particular to each of the religious traditions. And it is these two aspects that Christian and Muslim dialogue partners will need to open up and address in their exchanges. A striking facet of Moubarac's argument is his desire to prove that the perceived truth of the Christian message will depend strongly on the authenticity of the dialogue that Christians conduct with their Muslim interlocutors. From a missionary point of view, he is suggesting, this dialogue is called to become the touchstone of all Christian witness.

And while truth is called for, the Muslim conversation partner is quietly invited to approach the Christian with confidence, open to the prospects offered by the dialogue and attentive to the differences that inevitably arise between fellow human beings. True dialogue will only be possible if these conditions are consistently defended, and both Christians and Muslims wisely lay aside any desire to proselytise, to claim hegemony or to propose redemption. There should then be no grounds for fear in suggesting that the partners engaging in dialogue between Muslims and Christians should do so fraternally and freely, addressing all the issues that are significant in the life and faith of the Christian and Muslim communities. There should be no reason for any theological, legal or historical matters to limit the scope of the debate.

---

10 Y. Moubarac, *L'Islam et le dialogue islamo-chrétien, op. cit.*, p. 203.

Youakim Moubarac is fully aware and respectful of any hesitations that the Muslim partners might experience, but he thinks it inappropriate, and even illogical, to refuse to address the issue of dogma, despite most of those who do engage with it reporting that it is the most likely source of incomprehension, of bumps and distractions in the road. Moubarac even takes issue with the great French Islamologist Louis Gardet, whom he gently and respectfully chides for wanting to reduce 'the dialogue between Muslims and Christians to the three issues of secular culture, political and social matters, and the values in religious culture, albeit carefully stripped of dogma.'[11] Youakim Moubarac's categorical refusal to leave dogmatic theology out of the dialogue, notwithstanding all the risks that might ensue, is precisely because his whole understanding of the encounter between Muslims and Christians is based on the unshakeable conviction that at the heart of their respective theologies the two religions have points of affinity and opportunities for rapprochement that reach across the dividing lines of cultural and historic ancestry.

In other words, his refusal to exclude dogmatic theology shows how Youakim Moubarac is truly keen to revisit and benefit from the theological viewpoints of both Christians and Muslims. To explore the full riches of the theological investigations carried out by this spiritual son of Massignon is to gain a better appreciation of the great challenge of reinterpreting the theology of dialogue between Muslims and Christians. With great wisdom, Youakim Moubarac places the highest value on theology in his thinking. It is his firm belief that if the dialogue partners do not engage on a theological level, then issues of sociocultural interest will lack the proper grounding that might safeguard the security and relevance of the Muslim–Christian encounter. For it is in the last resort theology, as an expression of the historical revelation of God and of his word, that provides and justifies the religious and cultural structures supporting any religion.

In order to avoid historic anxieties, Youakim Moubarac advocates a systematic use of self-criticism. This exercise, if carried out with energy and high expectations, should liberate the dialogue between Muslims and Christians from the dross arising from apologetics and polemics that have marred and disfigured many an encounter between Muslims and Christians.

We should not shy away from admitting at some point that the Churches, and Christians, have not only been complicit, but have even been the instigators of

---

11 Y. Moubarac, *Recherches sur la pensée chrétienne et l'islam dans les temps modernes et à l'époque contemporaine, op. cit.*, p. 351.

various policies that have opposed Islam. This is not to rekindle old quarrels or to poison the atmosphere of any dialogue between Islam and Christianity. On the contrary, it is a careful de-mining exercise, identifying the precise times and places where Christian and Islamic regimes have been led to take opposing positions. An exercise in self-criticism should therefore not be an agonised penance. It should be a necessary step towards a healthy new basis for the relationship between Muslims and Christians.[12]

Clearly, then, self-criticism requires all parties to be prepared for some kind of conversion. A believer will only have the courage to conduct a self-examination in the light of faith if they truly seek spiritual authenticity. And it could then lead to a fitting reassessment of their theological perception of otherness.

Self-criticism involves not only a careful re-examination of each community's history – with a view to setting it on a healthy footing once again – but also an effort to identify the ways in which the evolution of their theological thought has in the past condemned and excluded the Other. In other words, each community is invited to cast a critical eye on its own tradition in order to root out unacknowledged prejudices that condition and distort their theological perception of the world, of history, and of others. This self-criticism, far from being a simple tactic for self-justification, should develop into a permanent control mechanism, a kind of regulatory authority that prevents dialogue from getting bogged down by suspicion and narrow-mindedness.

When the interlocutors in the dialogue between Muslims and Christians dare to open up to each other in the light of truth, they will be enabled to live up to the expectations invested in the dialogue and indeed to rise above any risks that might arise during their various debates. Thanks to the regulatory authority of self-criticism, the dialogue should then be able to reach deeper levels of fraternal theological agreement and courageously attempt some of the more painful or risky questions, such as the different approaches to God's self-revelation in Christian and Muslim thinking.

Self-criticism can help to keep the dialogue safe, while its fruitfulness will be ensured if the partners know each other – that is at any event Youakim Moubarac's strong recommendation. Any dialogue between those who do not know each other is bound to fail on a human level. So he specifies that any Muslim–Christian encounter must always require two preconditions:

---

12 Y. Moubarac, *L'Islam et le dialogue islamo-chrétien, op. cit.*, p. 195.

First precondition: the dialogue is with Muslims as Muslims. [...] Second precondition: in planning and carrying out every specific encounter, whether major or minor, one must bear in mind the thinking and concerns particular to Islam. Clearly then, as in the case of a certain vision of Islam in religious history, it is with an Islam under stress that dialogue must be engaged.[13]

The chosen way is radical, and must be faced with realism. It is especially important not to idealise historic realities that were jeopardised by challenging circumstances.

In this connection, it is important to remember that partners in the dialogue between Muslims and Christians have often been tempted to invent misleading images of each other. Fictitious dialogues have been composed in which the writer has sought insidiously to make the other partner fit a desired profile. These manoeuvres prejudicially hide the true nature of the dialogue. Both Christians and Muslims must avoid any invention or distortion if their hope is to exchange an honest mutual revelation of the truth of their faith.

A truthful dialogue, therefore, is one that takes place between people, not between religious systems. So long as Christians and Muslims do not dare to meet and to converse as faithful believers each in the truth of their own faith, then dialogue between Christianity and Islam will not be possible. When your interlocutor decides to open up about their own human struggles, it is therefore crucial to treat them with respect. In any dialogue, we must always resist the temptation to claim a comparable experience: to emphasise similarity and equivalence is to diminish the otherness of the interlocutor. In dialogue between Muslims and Christians, the partners are bidden to deny their self-centred instincts and to be prepared to be disquieted by otherness. Youakim Moubarac exhorts his fellow Christians to remain sensitive to, and acutely aware of, the very particular and historic challenges currently facing Islam. There is no point in wanting to free Islam from its tensions, hoping to enable it to be open and to interact with others, by detaching it from its historic context. Importantly, one therefore has to bear in mind the full range of the ways in which, through the course of history, Christianity and Islam have manifested and expressed their identity. This dialogue is stepping in with a challenge at a specific moment in their history. I have stressed here 'the thinking and concerns particular to Islam' because these are the two principal elements of the life of the Muslim community. For Muslims, it is their thinking that gives shape and expression to their whole community, and their concerns

---

13 *Ibid.*, p. 132.

reflect the positive attitude adopted by an Islamic community as it seeks out its true vocation.

The dialogue: implications and promises

Having established the preconditions for a true dialogue, Youakim Moubarac embarks on the delicate and risky task of identifying the concrete implications, and shedding light on what it might promise for the future. He opens with the following observation: 'Dialogue, then, is decisive, constructive, creative. Religious dialogue is crucial to the future of religion itself, and this is especially the case with dialogue between Muslims and Christians.'[14] So there is a close link between dialogue between Muslims and Christians and the historic moments when the two monotheistic religions were born. It clearly is not possible to isolate the inner life of each of these religions and to discount the many ways in which it might be directly influenced by the dialogue between Muslims and Christians.

The three adjectives used by Moubarac trenchantly describe the ways in which the internal development of the two religions is affected. Dialogue is decisive when it leaves a clear mark on the ways in which the two communities, Christian and Muslim, evolve and interact with each other over time. It is constructive, because the change it engenders contributes to the enriching and the growth of each of the religious entities. And it is creative, because it is only in dialogue that theological boldness can enable thinking to step outside the beaten path and emancipate life from recurrent cliché. Youakim Moubarac is therefore able to assert that the future of Christianity will depend on the quality of the dialogue it conducts with Islam:

If Christians truly believe in the future of their religion, they must acknowledge that they need to make a radical change in the way they encounter other religious worldviews, and therefore need to emphasise in their interreligious dialogue not only the method and the approach, but also the potential for achieving conversion. Christianity employed these means vis-à-vis Hellenism. It seems, however, to have become stuck at this first step. There are several more waiting for attention, and the dialogue between Muslims and Christians has been patient for fourteen centuries.[15]

---

14 Y. Moubarac, *Recherches sur la pensée chrétienne et l'islam dans les temps modernes et à l'époque contemporaine, op. cit.*, p. 554.
15 *Ibid.*, p. 553.

There was a time when Christianity was thought to enjoy a freedom of movement that enabled it to evolve in isolation, ignoring the influences to which it had always unwittingly been subject in the shaping of its history. The irrepressible development, however, of new social sciences, especially the sociology of knowledge and hermeneutics, have given rise to increasingly pertinent observations that bear out this notion. The illusion of complete autonomy is sustained by a lack of awareness of the invisible mechanisms that generate the structures of our thinking and our behaviour models. One of the determining factors in the evolution of the Christian religion is suggested in the way all the potentialities for conversion and mutation available through active interfaith dialogue have been deployed in the past.

According to Youakim Moubarac, dialogue between Muslims and Christians cannot simply be described as good neighbourliness. It is very different: it is a life choice that shapes the human relationships that evolve between the faithful in the two communities. This choice becomes a life-giving force for both individuals and communities, shaping the identity of each individual religious body. The history of Christianity supplies conclusive evidence here. The different phases in which the religion took shape, expanded and contracted, were moulded by its contact with the cultures that surrounded it. Greek thinking exerted a strong influence, supplying a paradigm and a foundation; Christianity should take its cue from this and explore the rich possibilities of further mutations. Youakim Moubarac suggests that Islam has been extending an invitation for fourteen centuries.

Arab Christianity, it appears, has been able to respond to the invitation by adopting into its theological categories some of the terminological nuances that might be correctly understood in Muslim theological thinking. This worthwhile and lively undertaking, however, has not been followed up in modern and contemporary practice, other than in a few isolated and incomplete attempts. It has therefore become urgent for Christian theology to wake up to the pressing need to make space for the Muslim Other and all that this implies, both theologically and anthropologically. The original dialogue with Hellenism led to the emergence of a strongly Hellenic Christianity; it is therefore not unreasonable to expect, as does Youakim Moubarac, that dialogue with Islam could lead to the development of an Islamised Christianity. Such a form of Christianity would have the virtue of soundly integrating into the revised articulation of its theological vision the adamant demands peculiar to Islamic monotheism, shown in the loyalty of Muslims to the calling of Abraham. A theology of conviviality should be able to draw motivating strength from such a development, since we can see in it the ultimate aim of any process of dialogue.

So far as I can see, Youakim Moubarac probably has not made use of this somewhat disconcerting notion. No clear statements on the status of an Islamised Christianity are to be found in his writings. Indeed, Hellenism is a cultural reference, whereas Islam is a religious body that identifies itself by its origin in divine revelation and its enclosed character. An Islamised form of Christianity should therefore be understood as a mutual interpenetration of two religious bodies sharing a desire to bring together two perceptions of the world mutually adjusted to achieve complementarity. If, however, one emphasises the cultural characteristics of Islam, which could influence the way that Christianity presents its historic truth, then the notion of Islamised Christianity mentioned above might help to recover the original underlying meaning on which the process of enculturating the Christian *kerygma* relies.

At all events, we must always remember that the ultimate goal of any dialogue between Muslims and Christians is to reveal to the whole world the economy of universal love that we receive from God. In the light of this economy, we should no longer think in terms of superiority and proselytism: 'From now on, our work of mission must leave out any ill-considered proselytism, rely in faith on indomitable hope, and remember that only love remains.'[16] Rather than lose its way in complicated games of intolerance and exclusion, the dialogue between Muslims and Christians aims instead to create among the Christian and Muslim partners a place of solidarity and communion as they seek to bring about God's unique plan.

In their shared hope and their absolute commitment to truth, Christian and Muslim partners should be able to take a responsible view of the history of their secular encounters. Looking at that shared history with a clear eye and an optimistic heart, they will be able to shine a light where darkness threatens, and rejoice where light radiates:

> Through thirteen centuries, political and social conflicts have shown little honour to God, but we must remember that in the background his Christian and Muslim servants have through all that time shared a valuable cultural and spiritual history. The fruits of that history have been varied, and have included some wonderful examples of sainthood.[17]

This calls for a fresh reading of history, in its entirety, and in its shared aspects. 'Fresh' in the sense that we need a salutary reinterpretation of the events and

---

16 Y. Moubarac, *L'Islam*, Paris, Casterman, 1962, p. 161.
17 Y. Moubarac, *L'Islam et le dialogue islamo-chrétien, op. cit.*, p. 95.

attitudes that have characterised the interfaith relationships between the two communities. Fearlessly, we need to expose the underlying messages – whether noble
or not – that have inspired the words and actions of the faithful.

Importantly, this reinterpretation of history must aim to show that the vocation
to dialogue, which lies deep within the revealed truth of both religions, is not tied
to any specific historic moment in their shared Muslim–Christian history. That
is not in the nature of this vocation. It acknowledges both success and failure,
but always offers the possibility of redemption and transcendence. By their very
calling, then, Christians and Muslims must be able both to preserve and to transcend the individual nature of their conjoined paths. This should help them avoid
the temptation to remain stuck and thus to arrest the course of a history in which,
as equal partners, they share the responsibility to manage the human city.

In reaction to some who have approached the shared history from an excessively realist or defeatist point of view, Youakim Moubarac is drawn to the
seductive ideal of spiritual communion. Theological dialogue is tremendously
important, but it is no substitute for the existential dialogue that arises from daily
life and shared challenges:

> Beyond religious dialogue, and lending it depth, there is a way of living
> life naturally, alongside each other; if we can appreciate this coexistence
> as a spiritual experience, then we are touching the core of what Christians
> and Muslims are able to seek together before God. As second-best to
> communication *in sacris*, Massignon used to advocate communion *in
> spiritualibus*, private shared fasting, pilgrimages to the holy places of each
> faith, Christian visits to Muslim cemeteries, and prayers borrowed from their
> prayer books and their Holy Book. And, alongside these 'works of piety', then
> also more private 'works of mercy' that gave them authenticity.[18]

Clearly, the two levels of dialogue serve an improved level of human
conviviality.

Beyond the theoretical and abstract plane, Youakim Moubarac sees the need
to rediscover a place where, knowing each other on an existential, immediate and
intuitive plane, Christian and Muslim believers could arrive at a communion of
heart and mind in the religious context of their faith, and he therefore emphasises
the importance of a 'dialogue of life' that allows the deepest level of spiritual
experience to blossom on both sides. He proposes a cycle in which, keeping these

---

18 *Ibid.*, pp. 135–136.

two levels of dialogue alive, one can move seamlessly from one to the other, without definitively settling on one or the other. The spiritual influence of Louis Massignon does not need to be further emphasised here, other than to highlight how mystical the full communion between the dialogue partners might become, if they dare to explore the energy hidden within the Christian and Muslim inner life.

The theological core characterising the particular nature of these two mono-theistic religions is most keenly visible in the heart of their spiritual life and their acts of mercy. This *Weltanschauung* claims to derive from a deep conviction that enables them to see life as an unexpected energy that can only be released and amplified by their existential engagement. Moreover, their practical commitment becomes the very locus of revelation, where the authenticity of religious truth is confirmed. When the dialogue between Muslims and Christians is understood as the best vehicle for believers to express their religious commitment, it will clearly contribute to fulfilling the divine calling to which both Christians and Muslims witness in their mutual encounter and in their common struggle to free mankind to become fully human.

Islam in the divine economy

In a spirit of fraternity, tested through dialogue, partners in that dialogue will appreciate the nuances and subtleties of the affirmations of truth that they hear. It is therefore essential to establish spiritual communion before launching into the intellectual aspects of faith. And of course, a fraternal dialogue can enable the development of that communion. Moubarac feels able to address the theological status of Islam because of the lived experience that protects his theological reflec-tions from misunderstanding. This theological status of Islam sits within a global understanding of the mystery of Islam.

The unifying thread in Youakim Moubarac's extensive Islamological work is his constant reference to his holistic vision of the religion of the Koran. This chapter seeks to identify the fundamental principles underlying his vision, in order to show the close link within his work between his Christian theology and his Islamological understanding. In other words, in the whole of his thinking, the ramifications and correspondences spring from a framework of fundamental cohesion. The second part of this chapter, therefore, aims to establish, situate and assess the basic elements of Moubarac's work that point to an emerging Christian theological understanding of Islam.

The theology of equality

To understand the nature of this cohesion, we need first to define its basic substance. This arises from a recognition of the fundamental equality of all human
beings. For Moubarac, the theology of original equality informs his approach to
the concept of the Other. Because of the Christian matrix of humility, when Christians meet with others they do so in search of a unique truth. Where theological
thinking leads them to put the requirements of inherent humility into practice in
their evangelical calling, they will find themselves better able to be open to the
individual nature of each Other that they meet. Moubarac sees his theological
approach to Islam as shaped by this intellectual discipline.

He seeks first of all to establish the fundamental requirement for any encounter between humans. He believes this to lie in the Christian acknowledgement of
that fundamental equality: 'Christians who describe themselves as the beloved
children of God should never interpret this as being superior to Muslims, or as a
privilege, so as in some way to see God as a gift for themselves and no one else.'[19]
This truth carries very serious theological implications for the Church, and Moubarac uses it to smooth the path towards fraternal encounter. Islam is a religion
that, in spite of its otherness, calls strongly upon Christians to remember that God
offers his universal love to the whole of humanity. The love offered so generously
by God to the children of Earth can never be limited by the capacity of humans to
receive it. The love given to one individual person cannot take away from the universal nature of that love – rather, it contributes to its radiance. So when Christians
feel the deep joy of being loved for who they truly are, they should never exclude
others from the radiance of this love. It is this free, unconditional divine love that is
the true foundation of human equality, and enables both encounters and dialogue.

We therefore need to see the truth of Islam itself, not through the lens of Christian truth. This is one of the most significant intuitions of Moubarac. In his book
Introduction à la religion musulmane (*Introduction to the Muslim Religion*),
which was welcomed approvingly by most members of the Muslim religious
intelligentsia, he is keen to show that although Islam came after Judaism and
Christianity, it does not derive from them. He even affirms that the two earlier
monotheistic religions became established in Arabia in order to allow Islam to
become the dominant force.[20] Whether one agrees or not, it is impossible not to
acknowledge the earnest desire for truth that Moubarac displays in his descriptive
and analytical Islamological work.

---

19 *Ibid.*, p. 201.
20 Y. Moubarac, *L'Islam, op. cit.*, p. 31.

A respectful understanding of otherness

A theologian committed to respecting the different nature of Islam will know not to use analytical and diagnostic methods suited only to Christianity. In a critique of a book about Islam published by an official Roman Catholic body,[21] Moubarac denounced as 'discourteous' the suggestion that Muslim families should be exhorted to look at the supposedly exemplary life of Christian families. 'It would be better to recommend that they follow the norms laid down in Islam itself.'[22] In any work involving Islam, we must always make use of its own points of reference. A Christian Islamologist should aim to base any exploration of the religion of the Koran on the theoretical possibilities offered by the religious texts themselves and their various subsequent interpretations. Muslims justifiably complain that Christians are perennially on the back foot, catching up on attempts at rapprochement and on a proper understanding of key aspects of the Muslim faith. Christians need urgently to become open to the message of the Koran before they attempt to assess its message on the basis of notions of justification and salvation drawn from the conceptual framework of Christian religious thinking.

What is needed is the development of an objective and cordial appreciation of the Muslim religion, and this demands that they choose exodus and disorientation. Christian thinkers seeking truly to understand Islam need first to put aside their own Christian nature and their set standpoints. They must then accept with patience and courage the hospitality of the 'other' world of Islam. Thus, and only thus, will they best discern the truth of the essential aspects of the Muslim religion:

> Although there are many texts in the Koran that bear a family resemblance
> to Jewish and Christian Scripture, both canonical and apocryphal, we need
> to acknowledge the clear and undeniable fundamental differences between
> these texts and the Koran. The Muslim community and the Book, which is the
> heritage that unites them, have their own distinctive features that must not be
> discounted simply because they somehow resemble and overlap with features
> of Judaism and Christianity. Given this fact, it is less instructive to consider
> the 'sources' than to absorb the message as a whole in the light of its own
> particular inspiration.[23]

The analyses and reflections deriving from the comparative study of religions

---

21 *Orientations pour un dialogue entre chrétiens et musulmans*, Rome, Ancora, 1969, 162 p.
22 Y. Moubarac, *L'Islam et le dialogue islamo-chrétien...*, *op. cit.*, p. 181.
23 *Ibid.*, p. 11.

should not allow us to overlook the distinctive nub of a religious system that is observed and examined as an object of study. The family traits and similarities discovered in Islam, for example, should not allow us to discount the originality and otherness of the faith.

The features and periodisation of Christian Islamology

Moubarac carefully revisits the various stages in the history of Christian Islamology, and notes that there is 'nothing that can be dignified with being a Christian tradition on Islam, merely a few attempts at a deeper discernment and understanding seeking to cure Christians of their chronic hostility towards the Arab and the Turk'.[24] He even points out, with some regret, that no 'post-Vatican II' vision of Islam has been formulated.[25] His emphasis on these omissions could be understood as a blunt exhortation to rethink the Christian wisdom gathered and garnered over several centuries of meetings, exchanges and debates.

Moubarac quietly celebrates the desire and determination of all those Christian believers engaged in dialogue and keen not only to set the past free but also to claim freedom themselves from historical burdens and failures. The slow, patient cleansing of memories needs to be matched by a proper acknowledgement of the real challenges inherent in coping with religious plurality. The ambiguities of the past make it important now to develop a fairer and more appropriate awareness of the flow of questions arising from Muslim–Christian encounters. In his commentary on the work published under the aegis of the Roman Catholic authorities, Moubarac emphasised the inadequacy of a simplistic Christian Islamology that focused simply on consolation, reconciliation and mitigation:

> This booklet offers polite Christian excuses, but what we needed was a
> rigorous work of ecclesial self-criticism; a declaration of sympathetic
> thoughts, when we needed an ecclesial programme of commitments. [...]
> And finally, it offers an ecclesiastical code for decorum in the Muslim world,
> when what is needed is a clear formulation of the problems that arise in the
> encounter between Muslims and Christians in terms of their thinking, their
> lives and their actions, problems that need *ab initio* analysis to identify the

---

24 Y. Moubarac, *Recherches sur la pensée chrétienne et l'islam dans les temps modernes et à l'époque contemporaine*, *op. cit.*, p. 346.
25 Y. Moubarac, *L'Islam et le dialogue islamo-chrétien* , *op. cit.*, p. 95.

principles involved, and any progress already established by individuals and organisations seeking to address them.[26]

The approach he advocates focuses first and foremost on clearly establishing the current state of Christian knowledge about Islam. This transitional phase is both sensitive and important for those who wish faithfully to assess the historic and cultural position of the Islamic religious system and of the worldwide Muslim community. So it is important to plan to assemble over time a body of knowledge that will discover and shape a coherent common ground, recognising the realities of Islam and fearlessly acknowledging the potential challenges of Muslim–Christian coexistence.

His various historical investigations allowed Moubarac to identify two discovery phases in the moves to draw near to Islam:

There have been two principal periods in which Christian countries have increased their knowledge of Islam through some form of exchange with the Islamic world and with scholars interested in it. The first phase was mainly theological in nature, and ended with the conquest of Constantinople, though in some small ways it has lasted until now. The second phase was scientific in nature, or perhaps more accurately philosophical; it ended at the time of the Algerian war.[27]

Christian knowledge of Islam cannot be considered separately from the cultural human relationships. The theological phase corresponds to the medieval era of Muslim–Christian controversies, which were hugely influenced by metaphysical considerations. The phase labelled as philosophical, on the other hand, includes the theoretical work done to encompass within the Muslim–Christian debate the new categories that emerged during modernism. It has some intersection with notions of Orientalism, which focused on seeing Islam through its cultural characteristics. Large-scale historical conflicts, and the many different and competing approaches, gave rise to amalgamations and ambiguities that can make it difficult to formulate a clear definition of each of these phases.

Islamologists seem not fully to agree with this chronology. There is another way, however, of looking at the important aspects here. Moubarac is keen to lend legitimacy to the various Christian approaches to Islam. An Islamologist seeking

---

26 *Ibid.*, p. 210.
27 Y. Moubarac, *Recherches sur la pensée chrétienne et l'islam, op. cit.*, p. 1.

to highlight an aspect of doctrine that especially fits with his preferences and expertise might realise that he needs also to take account of other equally important and essential elements of Islamic truth. When celebrating the mysticism of Islam and its many as yet undiscovered spiritual riches, he will need to counterbalance this with historical exegesis of the revealed text. If he has some notion of the history of theological thinking, he will readily appreciate that the main difficulties in interpreting the tradition (*sunna*) can only be addressed by someone with extensive experience of the sociopolitical context of the history of the different Muslim communities. The doctrinal formulation can therefore sometimes be presented as an objective outcome that invalidates debate.

The many different interpretations lead, not to an identity crisis, but rather to a potentially more fertile development of Muslim theological thinking:

> A Christian reading of the Koran is as normal as a Christian reading of the Old Testament. [...] Inevitably, there will be significant differences between Christians and Jews on the subject of the Old Testament, and between Christians and Muslims on the subject of the Koran. To either want to avoid such differences, or to pretend to do so, would be a failure of critical thinking; and in the case of the Koran, a failure on the part of Christian thinking and its fraternal acknowledgement of the very diligent work by Muslims to explore the meaning of the Koran's message.[28]

This of course bears out Moubarac's original intention, which was to develop a close collaboration between Christians and Muslims in exploring the wide range of religious thinking. Christians cannot carry out this exploration alone. They need to work with their Muslim brothers. For the main objective is to uncover the deep meanings and the existential implications of a cognitive universe that is chiefly grounded in faith conviction. The collaboration does not imply any kind of subordination or subjection. A Christian Islamologist must be able to enter into the Islamic religious way of thinking without constantly fearing excommunication or anathema, especially since his critical approach is shaped by a sense of communion with the inherent authenticity that religious thinking demands. For that very reason, it is not surprising that some differences may arise in hermeneutical readings of the text of the Koran. Indeed, this bears witness to the inexhaustible riches in the Koran.

When Moubarac argues for the legitimacy of Christian familiarity with Islam,

---

28 Y. Moubarac, *L'Islam et le dialogue islamo-chrétien*, *op. cit.*, p. 192.

he always means not only that Christians should acknowledge that the message of the Koran is in some ways undeniably other, but also that it is a fraternal sharing in the task of clarifying the particular nature of the message and its value. For this reason, he was not able to see this familiarity as simply and clearly in line with only one historical manifestation of Islamic thinking. He maintains that it is important for Christians to support all forms of Muslim exegesis that help to reveal the secret yet essential interaction between traditional interpretations of the Koran and the realities of the sociopolitical context within which such interpretations were defended. It must by now be clear to both Christians and Muslims that over time there is a gradual fading of the ambient culture that hosts doctrinal formulations, the careful explanations and clarifications articulated to express and develop them, and the different reasons why the community implicitly assented to them. In order to understand today the hermeneutic language of biblical and Koranic exegesis in former times we need to make an effort to re-examine the course of secular history, in order to revisit the context within which the analysis originally evolved, and those in which it was subsequently reshaped.

The legitimacy of multiple approaches to Islam

Moubarac conducted just such a bold reinterpretation when he examined the figure of Abraham in the Koran. As we shall see below, the person of Abraham plays a key part in Moubarac's Islamology. For now, we shall simply focus here on identifying the various ways in which his theological research might offer ways to foster renewal. When Christian thinking and Muslim thinking come together in a joint exercise in faithfulness and authenticity, new formulations can be created that will foster a deeper understanding of revealed truth not only in the Bible but also in the Koran. This at any rate was the profound conviction that drove all of Moubarac's work to nurture mutual understanding. But suspicion, ambition, proselytism and entrenchments, hostility, and violence sadly hinder the opportunity to develop an enriching mutual and continually evolving understanding each of the other. It is therefore becoming urgent to agree on the fundamental vision that will enable an initial attempt to acknowledge the identity of the Islamic religion:

> Taking Islam as a whole, we might think that for the time being at least it would not be impossible to reach a reasonably wide level of agreement among Christians to see Islam as a perfectly respectable 'religion of Nature', leaving aside certain aspects of family or social life which are determined, as with other religions in other places, by local circumstances and other cultures. [...]

We might then follow up with everything that has been said more or less since
the time of Abelard, characterising Islam as a philosophical position and thus
associating it with some kind of elemental association with Nature [...] If
our previous research had not drawn us as far as it did down the path towards
Abraham, then we might well have shared the vision offered. However, it is
not impossible to see our two paths converging. [29]

Until such time as a coherent harmonious Christian understanding of Islam
emerges, we need to agree on the essential aspects of Muslim religious identity.

Any Christian wishing to share the life of our pluralistic planet must learn to
acknowledge the inherently religious nature of Islam. The cultural ground we
share in our modern times makes it possible for Islamologists to identify these
traits within the religion of the Koran. As a result, Christians cannot truly know
about Islam if Islam itself is not recognised as an autonomous religious phenomenon. Conscious of the growing demand on the part of Muslim communities,
current Christian theological thinking is tending to re-emphasise the focus on the
symbolic importance of Christian discernment as a fundamental prerequisite for
any dialogue between Muslims and Christians. It is not possible to contemplate
that Christians should want to converse and collaborate with Muslims without
acknowledging Islam as a coherent and autonomous system of beliefs and practices that are linked to an authentic religious experience.

Reflecting on how such discernment might be achieved, Moubarac is keen to
point out that Christian thinking needs to go beyond the dogmatic *a priori* that
excludes Islam as an object worthy of theological research and thus justifies the
cultural reasons that led to its being treated as a primitive human system. It then
becomes much more meaningful to go back to the original genesis of the religion
and to examine the theological and philosophical evolution of Koranic thinking.
On the one hand, Islam is discovered to be an original movement that might
shape minds and structures. On the other hand, it becomes possible to see how
Islam fits into the evolution of history and the cultural affinities that link it to the
prevailing Semitic heritage in the ancient Middle East. When exploring these different specific affinities, Moubarac is keen that no aspect of studying the Islamic
religion should be overlooked. For example, he recommends a very thorough
study of Shiism as a fundamental component of Muslim religious identity. In
keeping with the Islamologist Henry Corbin's interest in mysticism, Moubarac
firmly believes that a wide range of the Shiite aspects of Muslim theology should

---

29 Y. Moubarac, *Recherches sur la pensée chrétienne et l'islam, op. cit.,* p. 534.

feature in the dialogue between Muslims and Christians. He appears to echo the statement by that famous Iran scholar: 'it is fundamentally impossible fully to explore the implications of any dialogue between Muslims and Christians without reference to Shiism, since the core of the theological challenge of dialogue lies there.'[30] It is therefore essential calmly and patiently to explore all the subtleties of the Koran corpus not only in its wider exegetic scope but also in its cultural and social implications.

In other words, any attempt to skirt around the thorny issue of a more thorough discernment of Islam might well be doomed to fail. The knowledge required for this discernment must maintain a sensitive approach to the ways in which the huge cultural bloc of Islam has manifested throughout history, and the tremendous hidden potential it represents. We can identify here a kind of magnetic dialectic between knowledge and discernment. The two poles are a key element of the openness and contact that Christians are seeking to offer to Muslims, an offer that will inevitably lead to a fraternal and peaceable enquiry:

> Christianity has two types of questions about Islam, some theoretical, others existential. The first type address the issue of Islam in God's plan and the economy of salvation. The second type are concerned with coexistence and the dialogue between Muslims and Christians.[31]

It is clear that discernment does not eliminate the need for questioning and for a critical and lucid approach. Moubarac knows his field, and gives an accurate assessment of the effect of truthful dialogue with Islam. Even if Christians accept and acknowledge the existence of Islam and its inflexible religious vision, that does not exempt them from vigilance and a desire better to understand the theological significance of the later emergence of the third monotheistic religion. They need to focus their attention on the theoretical coherence of the Muslim religious system and the legal and social implications of its beliefs. It would be deeply unwise to engage in an internal evaluation of the coherence of Islam from the point of view of the internal structure of Christian theology; we therefore have to consider Islam in the historical manifestations through which, over the centuries, it has consistently exposed the truth of its theoretical pronouncements

---

30 Henry Corbin, 'De l'histoire des religions comme problème théologique', in *Le Monde non chrétien*, 51–52, 1959, p. 146 (cited in Youakim Moubarac, *L'Islam et le dialogue islamo-chrétien...*, *op. cit.*, p. 128).
31 Y. Moubarac, *L'Islam et le dialogue islamo-chrétien...*, *op. cit.*, p. 96.

and ethical convictions. It is when Islam and Christianity meet in an interreligious and intercommunity encounter that they are able to demonstrate the authenticity of their ideals concerning salvation and happiness. Hence why Christian enquiry can only touch the visible aspects of Muslim truth, but these will suggest, second-hand, the internal patterns of coherence required by the framework for systematic theological thinking.

Following this line of thought, we need to remember that Islam has in the past been, and may still be, familiar with the unavoidable process of self-examination, self-regulation and self-regeneration. The insistence within the Muslim tradition on creativity, amendment and orientation does not mean that Islam exists within a closed universe, shut off from external influences. Rather than seeing Islam as caught within a sterile closed circle, we must engage with its intrinsic vitality, thanks to which it has at each stage of its historic evolution taken on the form that best fits with its legitimate desire to be relevant, its power to challenge, and its proven ability to integrate well. Christian Islamologists are therefore theologically bound to recognise that Islam has never stood still: 'In search of its own particular identity, Islam has evolved from its first beginnings through an infinite variety of situations.'[32] The basis for and justification of this perception are the theological assumptions underlying the theology of dialogue and also, perhaps especially, recognition of the historical force driving humanity's continuing ebb and flow of cultural expressions and experiences. As a revealed religion, Islam is inscribed within the course of history. To the extent that we can identify within the riches of the Koran's revelation the themes of progress and opportunities for agreement, then we shall better be able to see that the notion of evolution can be linked to the Muslim faith. Moubarac, in a spirit of theological realism, is keen to acknowledge that in its impetus to witness and to engage, Islam deploys inveterate defence mechanisms and self-censoring. A few rationalist theological movements have emerged and even flourished, such as Mu'tazilism which, for example, initiated a critical historical approach to the Koran. However, on the whole Koranic exegesis has very much followed dominant traditionalism. By the very nature of its revealed text, Islam could never submit its exegesis to the imperatives of modern biblical criticism. Theological reservations and purely exegetical caution have held back attempts at Muslim textual criticism:

The Muslim faith clearly prohibits subjecting the Koran to any historical or textual criticism, at least in any Western sense. This prohibition need not

---

32 Y. Moubarac, *Recherches sur la pensée chrétienne et l'islam, op. cit.*, p. 554.

prevent new interpretative attempts inspired by the spirit of Islam itself, which would not only be justified in refusing to apply the methods used on Christian scripture by institutions that have emptied it of any message, but would also be able to offer to modern Muslims a new hermeneutical approach to their sacred texts.[33]

Before rushing to the conclusion that Muslim hermeneutics are sterile, we should therefore hope to identify a bold and new form of Koranic exegesis. A comparison of the two theological worlds of Christianity and Islam suggests that there are differences at the level of principal motivations and major preoccupations. Islam places its principal focus on revelation within a textual corpus, and is thus less concerned by a reductionist critical analysis than by searching hermeneutics. The former searches the Koran relentlessly to detect the basic structures and matrices that convey the content and statements of Islam, whereas the latter seeks to identify the hidden meanings that shape the variety in expression and wording. The new Koranic exegesis mentioned by Father Moubarac appears to fit in with the concerns of another hermeneutic approach in which the text of the Koran is interrogated not for the truth of its statements but for the richness of its evocative expression.

The inherent tension within Islam and the richness of Koranic exegesis

Islam has accepted the demands of Koranic exegesis, provided it does not touch the sacred and unsurpassable nature of the Word of God as revealed in the Koran. The Muslim faith is fully focused on the transcendence of the divine word, which is authentically conveyed in the text of the Koran. This particular, unique status of the Koran as revelation has encouraged Islam always to take refuge in an attitude of firm loyalty to its revealed truth. The signs of divine authenticity are so transparently present in the way the message of the Koran is transmitted that everyone is bound to submit to it with gratitude. This is at any rate the view of those who think the divine word so lucidly clear that any human attempt to interrogate it or question it is unthinkable. The peaceful and legitimate coexistence of the four schools of Islamic law (Hanafiyya, Hanbaliyya, Malikiyya, Shafiyya) exhibited an original vitality in exegesis, but Islam soon succumbed to the temptation of rigidity. The tendency to intransigence that has affected Muslim theological thinking can at least in part be accounted for by the coincidence of unfortunate historical

---

33 *Ibid.*, p. 553.

and political circumstances. This has been exacerbated by the sacrosanct nature of the text of the Koran in Islam. The constant emphasis on the sacred nature of the written word in the message of the Koran in the end leads to suspicion of any attempt at innovative interpretation.

One of the theological reactions that has arisen out of the excessively literal approach to the Koran has been Sufi Monism. Moubarac uses this label to describe a wide range of Muslim theology that was attempting to break free from any subordination to the mediation of the word, and from any other mediation, in order to allow humans to merge fully with the divine. Moubarac's theological approach posits these two antagonistic poles between which Muslim thinking endlessly oscillates.

> Islam stands before the notion of a transcendent divinity as taught by the
> Koran, and is thus torn between two temptations. On the one hand, orthodox
> Fideism, and on the other, Sufi Monism. [...] Most of Islam has succumbed
> to orthodox Fideism and seems irremediably stuck there. [...] Because of
> orthodox Fideism, which is fixated with divine transcendence and discounts
> any kind of intercessor, intermediary, mediator, or any form of idolatry,
> the protestations in the Koran against the mysteries of Christianity are kept
> evergreen and undisputed. But because Sufism has not become completely
> mired in Monism, and there is an orthodox form of Sufism, it is fair to point
> out that Muslim orthodoxy has not become rigidly stuck in Fideism, but rather
> that in its highest forms it has faithfully adhered to the intimate mystery of
> God. The point here is clearly to present Muslim mysticism as the answer to
> the tension between Fideism and Monism, and as the true path – the Christian
> path, as it were – towards the mystery of God. This is indeed the purpose
> here, and the very reason why we consider the work of Louis Massignon to be
> essential to it.[34]

Moubarac here is describing an internal tension within Islam as an essential part of its most profound nature, and as a way to influence its own destiny.[35]

It is interesting to note that Moubarac, while remaining true to his own Christian faith, believes that he has here identified a real and true affinity between the two faiths. He suggests that the median path to reconciliation would be a Christian one, since the path to authenticity embraced by Muslim mysticism, as

---

34 Y. Moubarac, *L'Islam et le dialogue islamo-chrétien...*, *op. cit.*, pp. 126–7.
35 *Ibid.*, p. 130.

it seeks to avoid the two fatal temptations of Fideism and Monism, is similar to that of Christianity in its search for the mystery of God. Does Moubarac consider that when the two forms of mysticism, Christian and Muslim, seen as the locus of close communion and intimacy between mankind and the Creator, are the two best ways to achieve Muslim–Christian encounter? Or that Muslim mysticism is akin to Christian mysticism because Christianity, taken as a whole, is a mystical path par excellence? The underlying question here is whether Christianity can be reduced to its mystical dimension. In other words, can the full splendour of Christian truth only be revealed through an exploration of this privileged form of access to the divine mystery?

Moreover, if Sufi Monism overrides not only the demand in Muslim theology that the transcendence of the divine must be acknowledged without reservation, but also the reserve of otherness in Christian theology in any profession of faith in the mystery of the Incarnation, then Fideism cruelly blinds Muslim theology to the particular insights that Christian theology has to offer. The two temptations that are specific to Islam can thus not only obstruct the historic path of Islam and the Muslim community, but also thwart the dialogue between Muslims and Christians, and worldwide human conviviality. However, since the tension Moubarac is addressing here afflicts Islam specifically, we can arguably conclude that there is a certain inherent dynamism to the spread of the Koran message and its outworking. The tension thus seems to define the ways in which historical realities have shaped the message. Islam places great emphasis on eschatology, and this offers Muslim theology an opportunity regularly to review its approach to solving its original tension. In Moubarac's terms, all of Islam tends towards eschatology, that is to say, towards seeing God. If the monotheism of the Koran is at its core eschatological, it is because it desires always to be open to the as yet unseen future understandings of the word that God entrusts to mankind. It is probably in this sense that Moubarac tackles 'the notion of eschatology embedded in monotheism not only by the worldly forms it takes in daily life but also by the prophets. Islam can thus be defined in two words, 'eschatological monotheism', since the unique character of God is borne out by his role as judge.'[36] This approach has at its heart another basic tension, one that may fire up other aspects of Islam and its theological thinking. Specifically, it safeguards the pure demands of divine transcendence, as clearly required in Koranic revelation, and yet is constantly open to the different ways in which this transcendence can be expressed in its many and various eschatological challenges. In other words, the eschatological aim of Islam could

---

36 Y. Moubarac, *L'Islam, op. cit.*, p. 57.

make Koranic monotheism more sensitive to theological plurality, and thereby foster a real and fruitful openness within the Muslim community to the Other, and a firm and definitive determination to engage in friendly and cooperative human relationships. To make the endpoint of the history of human thinking the observation point for the mystery of divine transcendence would be a way of allowing current theological thinking constantly to correct itself as it seeks out the divine mystery. The notion of eschatology would then serve as a purifying corrective to the historical expression of Muslim faith and Muslim existence, both individual and communitarian.

If Islam can patiently engage with this double tension, it will over time be able to overcome what Moubarac has called its hereditary legalism. Muslims should not be led by their respect for Koranic law to adopt a rigid and intransigent attitude in their daily dealings with their fellow citizens. The implicit message of the full humanity of our fellow humans is in fact the main content of the explicit message of divine revelation. Indeed, the ultimate intention of all communication from the divine is to enable mankind to become fully human – and only an atmosphere of fraternal love can foster that. And here we meet a third source of tension, one that flies in the face of the historical message of the Koran:

> A Muslim, even the highest authority in Egypt, does not define Islam any more than one swallow makes a summer, or the 'high priest that year' defines the Israel of the prophets. And if the whole of Islam were to fall in with its hereditary legalism and condemn, in the name of its laws, the messengers of divine love sent to it, then Christian scholars should not take the side of this majority within Islam but firmly side with the messengers, if necessary with the people against their leaders, and in the face of legalist Islam highlight that which Corbin, with some energy and full justification, calls the best of Islam.[37]

Textual legalism stands in contradiction to human fraternity, just as the inanimate and petrifying word stands in contradiction to the liberating and life-giving spirit. So the key skill is therefore to know how to identify where signs of divine love can be found in the interstices of the Koran. If the ultimate message of the Koran is that it fosters the blossoming of humanity to its fullest potential, trusting fully to the life of joy God has designed for all human beings, then all of the law must take second place to the principle of human fraternity. Whatever side issues

---

37 Y. Moubarac, *L'Islam et le dialogue islamo-chrétien…*, *op. cit.*, p. 131.

and theological side-tracks legalism may seek to explore, this must not be allowed to drown the original inherent intention of the text of the Koran. A large number among the Muslim community confess to the primacy of the divine purpose over universal fraternity; nevertheless, Islam must remain faithful to the initial inspiration behind its revealed truth and resolutely resist all illegal manipulation, and any efforts to force the unwilling to adopt positions they do not agree with. The truth may not be accepted by the majority, but its intrinsic sincerity will shine through, and help establish a relationship of love between the messengers of light arising out of the two communities, Christian and Muslim. It is they who will need to fight off any betrayal of the original truth of Islam.

Islam as Arab Abrahamism, and the mediation of Ishmael

In the course of their struggle, Christians will discover the true face of Koranic monotheism:

> Islam could be defined as a negative or desert Abrahamism, specially designed to address Jews and Christians, challenging them on Mariology, eschatology and ecumenism. This summons arouses in Islam, for all its intransigent and unshakeable monotheism, a constant state of tension. Some privileged few among the Muslim faithful have responded to the challenge of this tension, and they are inspiring Islam to move beyond the religious reserve determined by its founder in order to live in loving union with God, an experience in which they also draw on the person of Christ in His Passion and judgement. [...] Christian thinking must seek to consider Islam as a whole, taking in its interior tensions and its constant dynamism.[38]

According to this original approach, Islam is faced with the urgent task of responding to the demands of its hidden spiritual vocation, which claims allegiance to Abraham as its central figure. Moubarac accordingly proposes an audacious vision of Islam, in that he likens it to an approach to faith which is expressed in its total confidence in the Word of God and which has over the centuries become a communion of love between mankind and God in the person of Christ. The whole of Muslim eschatology can be understood by enlisting these two human experiences of communion, in which should be included the Marian expression of complete human trust that gave birth to the Word of salvation. These three

---

38 *Ibid.*, p. 103.

models enable Koranic eschatology to remind mankind that it is only faith that
yields fruitful achievement.

Moubarac remains true to his theological position and his academic reserve,
yet he believes he has identified within Islam an internal force that pushes the
boundaries of its various theological formulations and its differing historical
expressions. If Islam is defined as a negative or barren Abrahamism, this may
hark back to the tension experienced by Abraham himself in the challenge to
his role as a father. His severe test seems to have birthed a double vocation.
The positive Abrahamism of Isaac is reflected, mirror-like, in the negative Abrahamism of Ishmael: these descriptions are not so much value-driven as expressing
a theological interpretation that seeks to capture the mystery hidden in the divine
economy. In order to identify the nature of this interpretation, Moubarac fearlessly invokes the need for an internal spiritual processing of the whole message
of the Koran: 'It is clear to see that we need to see this from the point of view of
the spiritual internalisation in the Koran of the primitive religious attitude of our
Father in Faith.'[39] So it appears that the revelation in the Koran is characterised
by an Arab reappropriation of the emblematic figure of Abraham. This reappropriation, via the notion of Arab identity, both safeguards and amends the future
of the Abrahamic vocation in that it perceives in the path taken by Ishmael a
requirement for lucidity and authenticity that has been tragically lacking in the
course of Jewish history.

Hence Islam cannot possibly be identified with Judaism, nor with Christianity,
nor even with any sectarian or syncretistic version of those two monotheisms.
Islam is eminently Abrahamic, but 'not because of a biblical pedigree, but by
some kind of quirk of the Arab world.'[40] The mediation of Ishmael has a crucial
role to play in Arab mediation, for the following reason: the Koranic revelation
shines a corrective sidelight on the story of Isaac, symbolically echoed in the
historic experience of the Jewish people, which gave historic expression to the
Abrahamic calling in a specific sociopolitical context. The figure of Ishmael thus
serves as a reference to explain the negative Abrahamism of Islam:

> The fate of Ishmael is in some ways essential to the promise of Isaac, in
> order to avoid it disintegrating into irrelevant racism. What would be the
> value of a blessing through Isaac 'for all nations' if it began by excluding the

---

39 Y. Moubarac, *L'Islam, op. cit.*, p. 61, note 6.
40 *Ibid.*, p. 34.

descendants of Ishmael on racial grounds? Surely this would be the start of anti-Semitism?[41]

Moubarac, the writer of the two Pentalogies, carefully and pertinently traces the parallel destinies of Isaac and Ishmael, who both received the blessing of Abraham. If Islam identifies itself with the destiny of Ishmael, then it becomes essential to the survival of Judaism, because it carries within itself the breath of life that is lacking within the traditionally exclusivist historical Jewish understanding of its destiny.

According to Moubarac, Islam presents within the succession of Ishmael a revolution similar to that which the Christian Scriptures in the New Testament present within the succession of Abraham through Israel. Islam is thus a 'spiritual Ishmael' in the same way that the Church of Christ is a 'spiritual Israel'. Both are clearly related to Judaism. The two forms of monotheism, Christian and Muslim, both arise out of Judaism and together have the task of correcting the historic destiny of the Old Testament, the repository of the first covenants with mankind. They may have moved in different directions, but these two forms of monotheism have a solid shared commitment to seeking truth and authenticity. Together, as equal partners, they are dedicated to revealing the full richness of the divine promise so as to share it with the world and showing how it meets the needs of the human heart. Each in its way, they make the promise of Abraham one that is for the whole world:

> The Koran, a provisional text, like the Qibla of Mecca, has cast a veil over the divine mystery; the Cross, in contrast, tore the Temple veil from top to bottom. But Islam has not yet acknowledged that the defeat of the Cross rid the Temple of the abomination of desolation that had intruded into it under the form of a national and triumphant God, and that Jerusalem has become a new city.[42]

The veiling of the mystery can only be understood in terms of Koranic eschatology, which says that knowledge of the successive phases of the same unique revelation will be granted and secured. The provisional nature of the Koran can thus be explained because it is mediated through history, via a succession of ephemeral human lives. To the believer in his enthusiasm for mysticism, the fullness of truth

---

41 Y. Moubarac, *L'Islam et le dialogue islamo-chrétien...*, *op. cit.*, pp. 111–112.
42 Y. Moubarac, *Recherches sur la pensée chrétienne et l'islam*, *op. cit.*, pp. 554–555.

appears as the final goal and crown of his spiritual hopes, which will be fulfilled beyond what the thirst in his own soul might be able to express. Seen from this perspective, the Koranic veiling of the divine mystery becomes a path of humility and discretion before the ineffable nature of the divine promise. While Judaism claims unwarranted exclusive right to the promises, and Islam casts a veil over the mystery, Christianity reveals divine love through the scandal of the Cross, to show the vast and unconditional passion of God to all mankind. In this light, the historical triumph almost serves as an obstacle to revelation. Islam appears to hide the mystery of God for fear that it might be tempted to exploit it by seeking to control both the world and mankind. In Christianity, on the other hand, frailty is revealed through the love of God, highlighting through that love the power of God among men to heal and to work wonders. Thanks to the veiling of the divine mystery, the spirituality of Ishmael, the original matrix of Islamic calling, prevents any racial discrimination. By revealing the divine passion through the Cross, the spirituality of the Incarnation removes any claim to controlling history or to seeking to exert force.

Islam thus seems to display the features of a strongly internalised Abrahamic calling. Moubarac describes Islam as an Arab Abrahamism. The expression may seem strange, but it fits perfectly with the fundamental intentions that shape the mystic Islamology of Massignon and his followers. Abrahamism, after all, can never be claimed exclusively by Judaism. The original promise can bear fruit in a multitude of blessings, and a variety of religious experiences can evolve from the spiritual covenant between God and mankind. It is therefore now no longer tenable to deny Islam its legitimate right to share, in accordance with its own vocation, in the religious experience of the human race:

> Islam has been designated by turns a Christian heresy and a pagan religion, and has not yet found its place in the canon of the religious history of humanity. However, we can now discern an increasingly clear and objective – indeed spiritual – vision of Islam. The following pages will attempt to describe it.[43]

We cannot credit Moubarac with imposing and defending the idea of an internalised Islam, nor assert that his mystical Islamology allowed him to see in Islam only the promise of beauty. The Lebanese theologian of Islam is sufficiently familiar with the Koranic religion to take a bold approach to his analyses of the intrinsic

---

43 Y. Moubarac, *L'Islam et le dialogue islamo-chrétien…, op. cit.*, p. 3.

vocation of Arab Abrahamism. He emphasised the aspect of internalisation, but precisely because he wished to show the riches and originality of Koranic spirituality, and thus to guard against any possible unwarranted assimilation or reductionism. The internalised Islamic pathway has revealed to him the Abrahamic challenge of the Koran's message:

> In this sense, Abrahamic Islam is Ishmaelite or Arab, a stranger in its own home and filled with a holy fear in its apprehension of the divine transcendence, whose sovereign will is hunting it down yet oppressing it so much that it dare not approach, but keeps a distance as did the Prophet in front of the 'jujuba of the limit'. We also need to reconcile this initial mystic, Abrahamic and 'Ishmaelite' vision of the Prophets with the famous *hadith al-ghurba* that is so typical of the fate of Islam. Islam was not born in the peace of a father's home, and is not destined to remain there as in the bosom of a legitimate wife: 'Islam was born a stranger, says the hadith, and will be a stranger at the end, and happy are those who recognise themselves in this fate as strangers.' And this way of looking at the Abrahamic message and heritage as a condition of spiritual existence is of interest not only in Islam. That might also be the perspective for Christianity, on different grounds, but fully justified through its descendance from Sara.[44]

To the extent that Islam is linked to the Abrahamic calling, it benefits from a form of dependent or incidental legitimacy by association. In Moubarac's theological perception, however, Islam enjoys a status that is autonomous and original in relation to the mediation of Abraham. As we have seen, it contributes a form of amendment and complementarity. Moubarac thus dares to assert that Koranic meditation is original and particular, in spite of the assertions in the Koran itself that confirm the secular continuity of the same unique divine revelation. This threatens a theological taboo, since Islam keenly advocates its own specific vocation, which legitimately aspires to universal status on the basis of its claim to benefit from the universal nature of the divine promise. If we therefore acknowledge the organic link Moubarac identifies between Islam and Ishmael's vocation, we must then draw all the conclusions that result from that shared destiny. Ishmael is the *outsider*, the *alien* and the *itinerant*. Each of these labels corresponds to a test of faith that affects the way in which Islam sees its own vocation.

---

44 *Ibid.*, p. 111.

The irrevocably original character of Islam

To the experience of the *outsider*, Islam in fact offers hospitality and free gifts. It is inclusive of those who are marginalised by the history of the powerful – those whose power derives from divine promises and those whose power derives from human works. Its mission consists in welcoming the abandoned and disregarded. And beyond this openness and human compassion, Islam witnesses by its lack of discriminatory actions that God will never be a God of exclusion, of elites or of privilege. To the experience of the *alien*, Islam offers the path of apophasis, that is to say, theological silence in the face of the unfathomable mystery of divine transcendence. According to its most authentic tradition, Islam was born as an alien, so it is important for all the members of the community of believers, in both their individual and their collective existence, to live out in all aspects of their lives all that this implies. Islam will live, now and throughout time, as an alien so long as it resists the temptation to behave in a superior way towards those whose lives have not historically been part of the Muslim community.

The alienness of Islam derives from the son banished as an alien by men, but rescued and blessed by God. Islam is therefore invited to bless those who are refused God's blessing by people, but who are welcomed and protected by God. A deep rift appears here in the mindset common to all human beings, separating the normal from the alien. That which, according to the criteria of human logic, appears normal is contrary to that which God, in his natural preference for the alien, considers true to his will and his plan. The alienness of Islam is therefore that its view is always that of the One who is totally other and different. The experience of the *itinerant* is echoed in the pilgrimage of a community of believers walking the way towards a place of sainthood. The itinerant Ishmael symbolises, in the life of Islam, the unending quest that is an integral part of the believer's daily life. Because of Ishmael's desert wanderings, there is in Islam a strong desire for improvement and knowledge such that the faithful are never satisfied that their present historical condition and identity fully match the inexpressible extent of God's plan. No definable manifestation would be capable of representing the vast spiritual and ethical implications of Koranic revelation.

An Islam as described above, that is excluded from the collusion of the powerful, alien in its own home and itinerant in its quest for greater reverence towards divine transcendence, cannot fail to have a positive effect on peace and harmony between peoples. Its foregrounding of the figure of Ishmael does not imply any propensity towards supremacy or exclusivism:

Through Abraham, God is the God of all believers. Islam does not say anything else about this; if on occasion it emphasises the person of Ishmael, this is not to value one race above another, nor one Semitic identity above another, but to heal the pride of the 'elect' by granting a spiritual Semitic identity to the mass of believers as a whole, whatever the path of their Abrahamic descent.[45]

Ishmaelite Islam, it appears, is a spiritual Semitic identity that is destined to counterbalance the elitist Semitic identity of the Jewish peoples. A religion that is willing to welcome others to share the pathway of its religious experience thereby sets up an effective protection within itself against sectarian divisions and exclusiveness. To adopt such an inclusive approach is to accept that the foundation and justification for the distinctive character of religious experience is a universal spirit that accepts and indeed transcends all the particular and inevitably distinctive features of the diverse and polymorphous spiritual quests of the different peoples and communities of the planet.

Semitic identity can only become a calling to universalism through becoming spiritual, and it is that calling that will enable hearts to find peace and souls to grow in stature. The very nature of its foundational vocation ensures that Islam stands against all forms of racism and ethnocentrism. By systematically casting aside any theoretical justification promoting the inimitable excellence of Muslim individual and collective identity, Islam should instead promote a human culture marked by gentleness and long-suffering. If God is the source of peace between people, and He is the God of all, then the vocation of the spiritual Semitic identity that Islam pre-eminently represents is to witness in thought and in action to the unsurpassable greatness of that truth:

> Muslims certainly do not close their minds to a form of universalism that, without denying the religious community, would accept real sacrifices for the good of all mankind and would respect the rights of all while expecting them all to do the same duty. But nowhere is this universalism to be seen clearly. Christianity itself, which they know designates itself a religion of love for all mankind, does not indisputably seem to them to fit the description. In the West, its worldly actions seem more closely linked to a desire to grow and become a world-dominating power, and a civilisation that Islam sees as harmful yet cannot neutralise. In the Middle East, Christians are in closer relationship with Muslims through shared language and race, and

---

45 *Ibid.*, p. 112.

even worldly interests, but they often keep themselves to themselves in
closed communities, showing greater openness to aliens than to their fellow
citizens.[46]

Moubarac's sense of history clearly lends a critical tone to his analysis of
Western Christianity, which has to a certain extent succumbed to the temptation
to connive with the nations of the West in their desire to extend their political and
economic power. In order better to highlight the universalism of Islam, Moubarac
unhesitatingly stigmatises the way in which Western powers have misleadingly
claimed to have a Christian cultural heritage. His critical approach alerts Christianity to the perils of collusion that lie in wait every time it chooses to rely on the
political power of the West; and that same critical approach invites Islam to realise
that it is called to make a major contribution to the emergence of a human society
that respects fundamental and inalienable human rights. This contrast is relevant
more to a historical description of the behaviour of the two religions, Christianity
in its dealings with Western societies, and Islam in its desire to find an important
and effective role in permeating and guiding the fate of mankind; beyond that, it is
important to appreciate how Moubarac helps Christians to discover the aspects of
openness and universalism that are specific to Ishmaelite Islam. Having conducted
a lengthy semantic analysis of Arab terminology relating to the different expressions of the word 'Islam', Moubarac concludes:

> Islam is thus in essence, according to the multiple aspects implied by the
> original Arabic forms of the word, a state of peace that can be gained, through
> God's grace, through a full submission to Him, by giving up and denying
> one's former self. The 'Muslim' is someone who lays down his arms in order
> to trust himself to God and find in Him protection and security.[47]

Moubarac's conclusion suggests that peace is an inherent part of a calling
through the Koran. The peace that God implants in the submissive and trusting
heart of the Muslim believer should then by extension extend and affect the historic behaviour of the whole Muslim community. If members of that community
live in peace, their witness as a body will inevitably be marked by gentleness and
compassion.

---

46 *Ibid.*, pp. 37–38.
47 Y. Moubarac, *L'Islam, op. cit.*, p. 69.

Islam, religion of peace

When we see the organic and permanent relationship between Islam and the supreme value of peace, then we are identifying the distinctive nature of the Koranic vocation: that Muslims are called to be witnesses to God on Earth. By distinguishing the two worlds of peace and war, Moubarac believes that 'Muslims are those who have submitted to God and become settled in His peace. If they are still engaged in war (*jihad*) it is to bring others, 'whether they will or not' (Koran 3, 77), to that same peace.'[48] If the ultimate aim of Muslim witness is to invite mankind to flourish in the enjoyment of that state of peace, of confidence and of healing, then there will be no need to exercise force in delivering that witness. To fight for a person to reach complete fulfilment in their being, that is, to live in the deepest peace granted to them by their Creator, is to fight for the happiness of that person and their life's salvation. Only this goal can justify the use of fighting, since it responds to the deepest aspirations of human nature. To be universal and to honour the original vocation of mankind, Islam must willingly agree to carrying out this spiritual battle in full recognition of the multiple paths towards that peace. Its distinctive and permanent value is its untiring commitment to that recognition.

The cornerstone of the Islamic vocation is that it shapes believers to be people of peace, for it is the religion of peace. Taking this theological conclusion as his starting point, Moubarac attempts to identify the ethical potential contained within Islam. One of Islam's theological promises as yet not clarified in law nor historically prominent is the promotion of human liberty. As Moubarac develops his historical Islamological investigations, he recalls the noble tradition of tolerance that marks the Muslim religion. Not satisfied with insignificant ephemeral reassurances, he boldly explores the more extreme demands of the tradition and emphasises the need for the Muslim world to undertake an ever deeper examination of the legal perception of Muslim theology in order to distinguish within the core of Islam the call to promote and defend people's freedom of conscience.[49] Such a call aims to incite Muslims to revisit their own distinctive theological origins. In other words, it suggests that it is the duty of Muslims themselves to draw from their own foundational documents the theological themes that would justify a renewed practice of tolerance adapted to worldwide pluralism. If Muslims themselves do not carry out this task, no one will be able to do it for them, for it is key to the destiny of Islam itself. A religion of peace must be able to evolve for itself the reasoning and arguments that will foster legal and political regulatory structures suitable

---

48 Y. Moubarac, *L'Islam et le dialogue islamo-chrétien...*, *op. cit.*, pp. 78, note 39.
49 Y. Moubarac, *L'Islam, op. cit.*, pp. 170–179.

for the emergence of a new era of human concord and collaboration. Moubarac, keenly aware of the delicate nature of such an exercise, has limited himself to quietly pointing to the potential that lies deep within the Muslim tradition for generating theological and juridical progress. In doing this, he has highlighted one of the best pathways forward for dialogue between Christianity and Islam. In this pathway, the two partners are encouraged to agree to the principle of fraternal emulation, in which each willingly lets the other critically challenge their truth. In each case, the critical approach from the other should help re-establish their own vocational authenticity. So the critical eye that Moubarac suggests is not in any way intended to dislodge Islam from its home territory, but rather to hint in a fraternal way at the best ways to support the truth of the message of Islam through commitment to Muslim identity and history. This pathway will continue to be the best only if the two dialogue partners rigorously resist all temptation to proselytism by assimilation, to reductionist strategies, and to any claims of hegemony or superiority.

Moubarac, remaining true to his vision, believes he may have identified the key to the summons that Islam could calmly address to Judaism and Christianity. He suggests that Islam could adopt a symbolic role as a reminder of the great covenants God has entered into with the whole of humanity. Islam summons Jews and Christians to remain actively faithful to their word and, by transcending all narrow forms of Semitism, to foster world unity via their shared Abrahamic faith:

> Islam's median role, which is not to mediate between the people of the Bible and those without scriptures, is that it must remain like the archer in the desert and neutralise within the *jihâd akbar* (the great fight) the internal tension that is integral to the fate of Islam.[50]

In addition to his exploration of the theological riches that are inherent to the identity of Islam, Moubarac believes he has identified a particular mission that has been entrusted to the Muslim community: to serve as a shock-absorber as Islam fights for the truth of both Judaism and Christianity. Moubarac suggests that Islam, a constant reminder of God's original plan, gives itself to humanity as the religion that sits in the midst of mankind in order to bring them closer to each other: monotheists, polytheists, atheists, all longing to regain their authentic humanity. By serving as a reminder to Christians that their vocation is to safeguard the Abrahamic Covenant, Islam has given itself a role in the future.

---

50 Y. Moubarac, *L'Islam et le dialogue islamo-chrétien...*, *op. cit.*, pp. 139–140.

Islam as a permanent challenge to Christianity

Moubarac audaciously considers Islam to be the challenge that will influence Christianity in building up its own future: 'If one can claim that Judaism is the past of Christianity, then perhaps we can allow that Islam can be seen as a gauntlet cast down among the religions and peoples of the world, as if to the future of Christianity.'[51] In Moubarac's enthusiasm, there is even a hint that he might see Islam itself as the future of Christianity. However, his theological clear-sightedness does not allow him to go that far. He does however sincerely believe that Islam challenges the conscience of Christians and encourages them to re-examine their faith in the light of the universalist demands of the message in the Koran. As a challenge, Islam is not so much a stumbling block for Christians but rather a locus for confrontation and stimulation, pushing Christians to enquire into the meaning of the Koranic revelation that suddenly irrupted into the world: 'For Christians, the extension of prophetism in time and space is something that bears re-examination, as does the classic thesis that revelation died with the last apostle.'[52] Moubarac seems to want to revise the notion of prophetism so that it includes Muhammad. He expects the theological debate to be fierce, and invites his fellow Christians to take seriously Islam's desire that its religious experience be acknowledged as authentic.

There have been many efforts to create an extra-biblical theology of prophetism, but Moubarac is still disappointed that the research on the subject has been fragmentary and basic: 'It may not be anyone's fault, but a properly theological Christian reflection on Islam, giving it its proper place in the history of prophesy, is still at an early stage.'[53] Certain bold theories claiming to confirm and recognise a derivative form of revelation in the Koranic corpus[54] lead Moubarac to emphasise the need for theological discipline. From an increasing awareness of the particular status accorded to Islam in the course of human history, and notes with surprise that each time Christian theological thinking is called to reflect on the meaning of the prophesy of Muhammad there is a sense of awkwardness:

Who among secular historians, examining the message of the Koran in good faith, would not recognise in Muhammad a 'high point on the path of

---

51 Y. Moubarac, *Recherches sur la pensée chrétienne et l'islam, op. cit.*, p. 555.
52 Y. Moubarac, *L'Islam, op. cit.*, p. 165.
53 Y. Moubarac, *L'Islam et le dialogue islamo-chrétien…, op. cit.*, pp. 85.
54 We should mention here the attempts by Massignon (negative prophetism) and Ledit (prescriptive prophetism). Some Lebanese theologians, such as Michel Hayek and Georges Khodr, have contributions to make on this subject.

moral and religious progress', with all the 'prophetic' qualities that such a description implies? And how, therefore, could we refuse to grant him a place in any representation of salvation history?[55]

The theological challenge of the Koranic Other is at its strongest here. Yet Moubarac is not afraid to carry out his theological responsibilities as a Catholic wanting to describe a global understanding of salvation history. He feels a deep sense of communion with all Muslims whose souls are moved by the demands in the Koran for authenticity, and he cannot fail to acknowledge that the messenger of Islam deserves the status of prophet. He formulates his acknowledgement as a question, yet everything in his writings and in his thinking suggests that he loyally subscribes to the notion that the Koran is prophetic. His thorough knowledge of Islam enables him to discern within the text of the Koran signs of a divine revelation to be given to the descendants of Ishmael, and offering a spiritual message of universal relevance for humanity.

Moubarac, in accepting that the Koran is by nature revelatory, does not in any sense compromise the unique salvation plan revealed and realised in Jesus Christ. The mystery of the mediation of Ishmael stands as an exhortation to Christians constantly to reassess their own theological perceptions:

> In truth, Islam does not itself need a response from Christians, but it does for the sake of the rest of humanity, in whose name Islam asks Christianity how it has made use of the message revealed to Israel. In that sense, and in that sense only, Islam speaks on behalf of the outcast to the elect, not to the Jews for the Arabs, but to Jews and Christians for the mass of people without scriptures.[56]

Given this level of expectation, Christianity cannot take refuge in silence, nor in indifference. When Christians are willing, however, to take up the challenge given by Islam and start to shape a response, they will demonstrate the truth of the spiritual impulse that invites them to see themselves in the closest available mirror image of their other self – Islam. Far from intending to impute the motives of Christians, Muslims are keen to discover the fate of the Abrahamic Covenant sealed for the benefit of all mankind. Since Christianity sees Christ as the fulfilling of that Covenant, Christians have a duty to show how this outcome opens up the possibility, at least on a theoretical level, for a diversity of spiritual paths for

---

55 Y. Moubarac, *L'Islam et le dialogue islamo-chrétien...*, *op. cit.*, p. 187.
56 Y. Moubarac, *Recherches sur la pensée chrétienne et l'islam*, *op. cit.*, p. 554.

different peoples and cultures to become open to the inexhaustible promises of the ultimate revelation of the Word of God. An admission that Islam is a spiritual path among others should not in any way compromise the unique nature of biblical revelation, since all these paths converge mystically and lead towards Christ. According to Moubarac, it is time for Christianity to settle the secular debate and acknowledge the possibility that there are many ways to meet with the divinely revealed word, which was made manifest in the person of Jesus Christ.

And in accordance with his theological imperative, Moubarac emphasises the ways in which Christ bears Koranic traits:

> Jesus is called the Word of God, who shares in his Spirit, and just as it is acknowledged that he has the power to achieve miracles, Jesus alone can speak the words of creation. His virgin birth is the equivalent in the will of God to the birth of all humanity in Adam.[57]

Interpreting Christ in this way as a Koranic figure betrays Moubarac's desire to expand Koranic Christology to fit with the Christology of the New Testament. The key question, however, is whether the commentary he offers fits with the intention in the text of the Koran as it is interpreted by the authors of Islamic exegesis themselves. There are many instances in the Muslim world of attempts in Koranic exegesis to refresh the image of Jesus, but it can be unwise to seek to inflect the sense of Koranic verses, however laudably, towards the implication of a spiritual reconciliation between the two forms of monotheism. Moubarac's respect for Islam is certainly such that in exploring the text of the Koran he never seeks to establish Christian or biblical parallels. As a Christian theologian of Islam, however, he does permit himself to offer new understandings – underpinned by his indisputable academic knowledge – of his own Christian doctrine and of Muslim doctrine. This is a risky path to take, as was shown in the debate that took place between Moubarac and Gardet[58] on the subject of Koranic Christology. It

---

57 Y. Moubarac, *L'Islam, op. cit.*, p. 63.

58 Moubarac is a firm believer in Muslim Christology and unhesitatingly criticises Christians who refuse to admit that there is such a thing. In his commentary to what was published by Rome in the volume introducing the dialogue between Muslims and Christians, he identified a lack of theological boldness where others might have seen methodical caution and a demand for objectivity. Specifically, Moubarac objects that the editors of the volume exacerbated the antagonism between Christianity and Islam on the subject of Christology: 'In particular, the comment on this page (*Orientations pour un dialogue entre chrétiens et musulmans*, Rome, Ancora, 1969, p. 55) should not have been made: 'But the Koran is clear, Jesus is neither God nor the Son of God'. This uncompromising and unnuanced statement is all the more surprising

is nevertheless the price that must be paid in order to leave the beaten track and explore new approaches identities, one's own and others'.

It is precisely on the level of this theological innovation that Moubarac deplores the inadequacies that paralyse and might even suffocate any Christian theological output on the subject of the dialogue between Muslims and Christians: 'there is no Christian tradition on Islam worthy of the description.'[59] And it is true that there is very little in the way of Christian theologies of Islam. This lacuna in recent theological output calls for a careful and detailed analysis of the reasons that might prevent, or at any rate slow down, the development of this field of research. The work of Moubarac itself makes a considerable contribution towards formulating a theology that invites questioning *by* Islam, before itself making inquiries *about* Islam. The theological view of Youakim Moubarac has been shaped and elaborated in such a way as to present Islam as an undiscovered, novel subject. Its undeniable originality derives from its ancestral affinity with the fate of Ishmael, and Islam as presented by Moubarac is highly spiritual and peace-loving.

The compromises of history have not spared Christianity, and in a similar way Muslim collusions with the sociopolitical realities of the Muslim world have left their mark on the historic evolution of the message of the Koran. In order, however, to identify the particular spiritual features of each religion, we need as far as possible to isolate in its purest form the kernel of truth that lies at the heart of Christian and Muslim beliefs. And their faithful are expected to bear witness by their individual and collective behaviour to the message of authenticity integral to each of these forms of monotheism.

Beyond this process of purification that is essential to the revival of these two spiritual traditions, we should not underestimate the theological rigour that pervades Moubarac's Islamology; he calls for a further council 'after Vatican II'[60] covering theological investigations into Christian understanding of the meaning of Koranic mediation. At the dawn of the third millennium, what is available to Christian theology in terms of a systematic description of worldwide human existence, that might enable it to develop a positive and analytical understanding of the phenomenon of Islam in all its dimensions and various forms? How can we in today's Christian theological discourse ascribe to the Koranic revelation a double status of autonomy and affinity, that allows not only for the unique,

because one of the authors has clearly stated elsewhere: 'The Koran does not deny the central dogmas of the Church' (L. Gardet, *Connaître l'Islam*, Paris, 1958, pp. 29–30 and 114).' (Y. Moubarac, *L'Islam et le dialogue islamo-chrétien...*, *op. cit.*, p. 190)
59 Y. Moubarac, *Recherches sur la pensée chrétienne et l'islam*, *op. cit.*, p. 346.
60 Y. Moubarac, *L'Islam et le dialogue islamo-chrétien...*, *op. cit.*, p. 95.

once-and-for-all redeeming mediation of Christ but also for the vital new contribution of the message of the Koran? How is it that Muslims can warmly welcome as
legitimate any approach by Christian theology, while in its turn Christian theology
works hard to reinterpret the revelation of the Koran in the light of preoccupations
that are inherent to its own patterns of thinking and according to the prejudices
dictated by the worldwide assumptions about Islam? All these questions, and
others not yet articulated, form the background that, according to Moubarac, justifies the need to develop a new perception of Islam in Christian theology.

The originality of the theological reasoning favoured by Moubarac lies in the
way he neatly links three different key features of his own spiritual and intellectual development. These are, first, his spirit of fraternal communion of heart and
soul with Muslims of all stripes and theological allegiance; second, his vigilant
and rigorous scrutiny of the significant depths of the Koranic message and the
Muslim calling; and third, a theological boldness that brings together his objective
knowledge of the inherited tradition and his creative exploration of the ways in
which the deposit of religious faith carries potential for growth. His theological
contribution lends urgency to the need for the 'after Vatican II' council that he
advocates. In summarising the conclusions of Christian Islamology over the past
few decades, Islamic theological thinking needs now to seek out its identity and
vocation by exploring the multiple pathways of diversity available to mankind.
Any new Christian theology of Islam must maintain a lucid and critical analysis
of its own methodology in the context of a world that is conducting a fundamental
re-evaluation of its epistemological evidence. There is a pressing need for both
Christianity and Islam to re-examine their mutual theological understanding in
order to ensure that their current discourse is relevant to the present human situation. They will be credible only when the ways in which they are recreating hope
for mankind have been critically reviewed. Moubarac's contribution is extremely
useful here. His novel theological approach suggests a new role for Arab Christian
communities as privileged witnesses.

The new theological vocation of Arab Christians

Moubarac's theological reading of Islam enables him to discern a new understanding of the status and roles of the Christian communities in the Arab world. The
focus of his reflection is the responsibility to be an authentic witness, in a way that
involves reassessing one's own life in the light of the urgent need to be open to
diversity. The inspiration for his work is the noble mission he sees as the task of
Middle Eastern Christianity. The mission will need all the different Arab Christian

communities to mobilise all their available energy. Before outlining the key features of the mission, Moubarac describes the reality of life for Christians in the
Arab world. And against this background he traces out the fine detail of the vocation
entrusted to these Gospel witnesses. The second part of this chapter aims to show
the links between these two crucial aspects of Moubarac's theological thinking: his
assessment of the current challenge, and his perspective on the future mission.

The current challenge

Features of a problematic identity

These Christian communities naturally develop different cultural sensitivities.
Their views are determined by four factors: their theological allegiance (Chalcedonian Orthodox, Pre-Chalcedonian Orthodox, Uniate or Roman Catholic, Protestant); their liturgical heritage (Syrian, Greek, Copt, Chaldean, Arab, Armenian);
their national identity (Lebanese, Egyptian, Iraqi, Syrian, Palestinian, Jordanian);
and their cultural ties (pre-modern or modern, Arab, pro-Arab or anti-Arab, Fran-
cophone or Anglophone). It is however not unusual to find miscellaneous combinations of these collective factors. The depiction here will aim to maintain any
nuances resulting from such combinations, so that readers may better be able to
appreciate the application of Moubarac's analysis.

In the first instance, his analysis focuses on a better understanding of the reality of
what he is writing about. When Moubarac speaks of Christians in the Middle East,
he has in mind those who live within the geographical boundaries of, on the one
hand, the three ancient patriarchies (Antioch, Alexandria and Jerusalem), and on the
other, the new constellation of the Arab world (the different countries of the modern
Arab world). Whether they are originally Arab or have become absorbed into Arab
culture, these Christians have been shaped by forces both internal (the monastic ideal
and the patriarchal structure) and external (the Muslim religion and Arab culture).

> The monastic ideal has clearly shaped and fuelled the patriarchal structure of
> these Churches. However, the fact that they exist within the Islamic empire
> has lent extra force to that way of being and the life in community. Might one
> even argue that it has encouraged them to rely on the sacramental expressions
> of their religious life, and to some extent to 'secularise' the patriarchal
> structure, granting extensive temporal prerogatives to the figurehead?[61]

---

61 Y. Moubarac, *La chambre nuptiale...*, *op. cit.*, p. 21.

I

The question suggests a keen view of the oxymoronic condition of the Arab Christian communities. On the one hand, their religious history is deeply marked by ancient monasticism. On the other hand, since the seventh century they have had to adapt their social life to the demands of Muslim sociopolitical legislation. Christians in the Middle East have thus made a twofold structural adaptation. To keep faith with their mystical origins, they have given pride of place to their sacramental practice. As a result, their faith has flourished most especially in its liturgical expression. This in turn made it somehow less easy to identify some historical aspects of their commitment as a community. Their communal identity was principally displayed in their worship rather than in the sociopolitical arena. They had greater difficulty, on the other hand, in fitting in with the constraints imposed on their sociopolitical integration, which was shaped by the legislative context of the Muslim *umma*. Without going as far as the caesaropapism of the Roman patriarchate, they nevertheless melded the religious and political seats of power into one in their communities. The patriarchate then became the chief vehicle of their identity, the symbol of their unity, and the Mecca of their aspirations.

The communities were deeply marked by this twofold adaptation. Instead of learning to adapt as times moved on and changed, the predominance of their sacramental and liturgical life, eclipsing the reality of ordinary daily life, has led the Christians of the Middle East to develop a kind of lethargy that still affects the Christian communities of the Arab world to the present day. To describe this lethargy Moubarac reaches for a term used in psychology: they have become withdrawn.

> In the Middle East, Christians are in close relationship with Muslims through shared language and race, and even worldly interests, but they often keep themselves to themselves in closed communities, showing greater openness to aliens than to their fellow citizens.[62]

For Moubarac, to be close to Muslims means to feel close affinity to their religion and their Arab culture. There is of course a question as to whether Christians in the Middle East belong to the Arab race. Moubarac, however, seems little troubled by the matter. On the one hand, he reckons that a considerable proportion of the Arab population was Christianised well before the arrival of Islam, and had to leave the Arab peninsula for different urban centres that are still active parts of the modern Arab world. On the other hand, in his view the Christian communities

---

62 Y. Moubarac, *L'Islam et le dialogue islamo-chrétien...*, *op. cit.*, p. 38.

that have lived for centuries within the geographical boundaries of the Arab world can no longer overlook the fact of their historical, cultural and sociopolitical roots. Indeed, if all the communities within the Arab world were to be returned to their primitive states, highlighting their religious, ethnic or tribal allegiances, then there would be no such thing as Arab identity in terms of a shared set of the character-istics belonging to the various sociopolitical entities in the Arab world. Moubarac clearly does not feel that religious identity should be sacrificed to benefit cultural or political identity. He therefore often mentions the Christian Middle East, which in his vocabulary appears to represent a crucible of infusions and sensitivities belonging to the Patriarchate of Antioch.[63]

Incomprehension and suffering

For Christians in the Middle East, the problem of identity clearly shows that with-drawal is one of several malign effects on their thinking and their behaviour, and it results from their lack of lucidity and courage in recognising the irreversible reality of their rootedness. Moubarac claims that two aspects of affinity with the Arab world support his thesis: language affinity and racial affinity. Elsewhere, as we have seen, he identifies significant links thanks to a shared Abrahamic faith. If this is truly the case, one might wonder how and why Christians have felt the need throughout the intervening centuries to live withdrawn, enclosed and fearful lives. There are two possible major reasons for this dramatic situation: the dis-crimination that affects the lives of non-Muslims within Muslim communities, and the inherent disparity between the different sociocultural expressions of the Islamic faith and the Christian faith. The first of these is freighted by the political history of the Islamic empire and the Muslim principalities around its periphery;

---

63 To describe the heritage of the Middle East of Syria and Antioch, Moubarac forged a neologism: *syrianité*. [His term *l'Orient Syriani* is translated here as 'Christian Middle East' – trans.] For him, it brings together the shared elements that are specific to the Arabic-speaking Christian Middle East. The integration of the Copt heritage is a persistent difficulty, but Moubarac appears to privilege the fact that being part of the Arab world represents for Eastern Christians a cultural link. This suggests that in chronological terms at least, *syrianité* takes precedence over Arab identity. The presence of Arab witnesses at Pentecost is not a reliable measure of the reach of Christianity into Arab tribes during the first three centuries: during this initial phase of Eastern Christianity there was lively growth among the Christian communities that spoke Syrian and/or Greek, and were under the authority of Antioch. Moubarac supports the theological status of his notion of *syrianité* by emphasising its importance for ecumenism: 'The *syrianité* of the East can play an active part in promoting Christian unity. It's tempting to think that it might even be the best part.' Y. Moubarac, *La chambre nuptiale…, op. cit.*, p.

the second is marked by the different attitudes to women and the different ways in which sacred texts are treated. Christian communities in the Arab world share a deep sense of communion, due to their common 'ethnic' and 'cultural' characteristics, and to a theological affinity in their monotheistic faith, yet their situation remains extremely problematic. Moubarac, wishing to alert the Arab populations to the need for them to become more aware of their historical responsibility in managing developments within the Arab world, makes the following rather bitter comment:

> I do not wish to be unduly pessimistic, but the position of the Christians of which we are speaking is that for most of their history they have lived in a state of 'humiliation and defensiveness'. These words... best express the way that Christians in the Christian Middle East have been treated, both by the so-called Christian empires and by non-Christian regimes.[64]

Clearly, Moubarac is keen to stay objective in his historiography. He is making every effort to disentangle the external influences and the hidden collusions. The identified culprit is power, of whatever religious stripe. Both Christian and Muslim empires persecuted the Middle Eastern minorities within the Arab world. It was not only the Christian minority that suffered martyrdom – Muslim minorities suffered similarly. His differentiated approach frees the collective Christian conscience from any potential paranoid obsession.

Moubarac does not issue an arbitrary massive condemnation of Islam and the Muslims, but rather seeks to identify the real reasons for the gradual extinction of Christian life in the Arab world. He is well aware that even in its very early days Islam was not one monolithic entity, that the Eastern forms of Christianity – Syrian or Arab, Copt or Greek – have never used political military power, and that sociopolitical infrastructure has often dictated the direction taken by Koranic hermeneutics in the different Muslim empires of the Arab world. Despite all this, Middle Eastern Christians have remained deeply scarred by their status as marginalised and persecuted minorities. Inevitably, this has led to a deep feeling of disappointment and fear among Christian Arab communities, and lent a keen sense of martyrdom to their witnessing. This in fact explains how it is that many communities feel torn between two opposing options: either to withdraw fully into their own mysticism, or to take the irreversible step of exodus. In the seventh century, the Christian Middle East was hoping for an unexpected liberation from the yoke

---

64 *Ibid.*, p. 16.

of Byzantium. But it soon became clear that Middle Eastern Christians were fated
to be perpetually disappointed. No political power could help them at long last to
shake off their minority complex, and no major positive change in Arab history
was able to provide deep healing for their secular bitterness.

For Moubarac, the sudden arrival of Muslim troops in the Christian Middle
East was a moment of liberation. He quickly emphasises, however, that the eupho-
ria was short-lived and fragile. The moment of liberation became the paradigm
for all the false dawns of political liberation that have afflicted Middle Eastern
Christians:

> For this reason, as is well known, Christian communities that were not
> affiliated to the Christian empire welcomed Islam as a liberating force.
> However, we also know that after this first impression, which lasted beyond
> the end of the seventh century, the reality for Christians in Islam was one
> of unexpected changes from the time of the Crusades onwards, and once
> the Arab empire weakened under the increasingly dominant Turks. Moving
> forward to our present century, we see a slow death, punctuated by massacres
> and movements into exile, which could lead to a pure and simple extinction of
> Christianity in the lands in which it was born.

There is an unimpeachable logic to this devastating statement. The truth of it
has sadly been confirmed throughout the final decades of the twentieth century by
all the bloody events that have caused not only grief among the Eastern Churches
of the Arab world but also a deep anxiety among the better-informed Muslim
partners, those who are the most worried about the future of coexistence among
Arab Muslims and Christians.

The purifying desert

It is therefore no longer surprising to discover that the Churches of the Christian
Middle East, soon after their inception, found themselves in a fierce fight for survival. The crisis was linked to the sociopolitical vicissitudes that created turbulent
relationships between the Churches and the Christian and Muslim empires during
different periods. If Christians in the Middle East are gradually sinking into torpor,
it is due to the deep-seated unhappy inherited memories in their Churches. There
are still some who, rather than choosing a geographical exodus, prefer to bear
witness by staying in their homes, albeit in some kind of spiritual exodus. They
remain on their native soil, but opt for a silent form of eschatological waiting:

For Christians in particular, the retreat 'into the desert' as experienced by
those who created the practice, becomes not so much a struggle with Satan as
a protest against the way that the Church and its clergy embrace compromise
and resign themselves to the temporal realities or their time. For us, it remains
a bastion where we can avert the sadness and horror of present-day evils by
longing for the times to come.[65]

There is no need here to rehearse the recent evidence of this sadness: bloody
conflicts involving Palestine and the Lebanon and, to a lesser extent, Egypt and
Iraq, provide irrefutable proof that mutual suspicion continues to jeopardise
Muslim–Christian relationships in the Arab world. Should we then see the desert
as symbolic of flight and resignation? For some Christians, this is their experience.
Others, and this includes Youakim Moubarac, boldly see the desert not as a site
of fear and resignation, but rather of desire for purification (*catharsis*) and active
conversion (*metanoia*).

In the desert, Middle Eastern Christians will be able, he avers, to discern the
meaning of their existence, or rather, of their survival in the modern Arab world.
They might also choose to invent new ways in which to respond to the challenges
of the present time. Nevertheless, there is an important and decisive aspect: a clear
sense of a new interpretative model that they intend to apply to the reality of the
experiences they share in living with their Muslim fellow citizens. There can be
a number of interpretations for a historical event. Depending on the perspective
of the person interpreting it, the same historical situation can be seen either as a
reason for decline or as an impulse towards regeneration. While not denying that
Islam has to some extent paralysed the life and witness of the Western Church,
Moubarac likes to say that the religion of the Koran has purified it of its tendency
to be hegemonic and egocentric. Indeed, he even suggests an interpretation that
gives a positive view of the fall of Constantinople. By occupying the splendid
capital of Byzantium, he claims, Islam may have encouraged the two Churches,
of the West and of the East, to overcome their theological differences in order to
focus only on the central message of the Gospel.[66] This bold theological reading,
however, cannot be applied indifferently to all situations, as Moubarac is well
aware. The Christian Middle East he describes has always tried to stay away from
the power game played out by the two sister Churches. And this interpretation

---

65 *Ibid.*, p. 99.
66 See on this Moubarac's contribution to this new historical-theological hermeneutics in his
L'Islam et le dialogue islamo-chrétien…, op. cit., pp. 136–139.

might also unduly associate it with the efforts to encourage Rome and Constantinople to share an experience of conversion.

History re-examined

Christians in the Christian Middle East, originally defenceless, experienced each successive tragic upheaval in the Arab world as a further challenge, adding to the burden of incomprehension and exclusion. Under the Ottoman occupation, the fundamental problem for the Arab world could be summed up as achieving cultural and political emancipation for Arab identity. Christians and Muslims engaged together in the fight. The problem however persisted, in a slightly different form, up to the colonisation period. The same battle was needed to achieve political maturity for the Arab world. As Arab countries, however, were on the cusp of achieving national status, the Arab–Israeli conflict emerged, an indirect outcome of the Ottoman occupation, and a direct outcome of Western colonisation.

The key elements in this brief historical overview, however, are the serious consequences that these different political situations provoked in the field of Muslim–Christian relations. Each of these three decisive turns in the modern history of the Arab world witnessed major political changes that dangerously rocked the delicate balance of Muslim–Christian coexistence. And distressingly, each time this happened there was the same pattern of mutual incomprehension and suspicion, and thoughtless exchanges of insults. It is in fact now well established that it was external interference (by the Ottomans, Western colonialists, and Zionists) that led to most of the violent attacks carried out by Muslims against Christians in the Arab world. According to the elders in the different Arab Muslim communities, the doctrinal differences and sociocultural particularities that identify the two respective identities, Christian and Muslim, cannot in any way justify the violence and the armed confrontations. Yet Christians and Muslims in newly independent Arab countries have never engaged in serious theological political discussion of the concrete implications of their desire to live together in the same shared human environment.

Given the lack of a theoretical basis, it is not surprising that relationships deteriorate and tensions are exacerbated between Christian and Muslim communities in the Arab world. The difficulties experienced in the Arab world, far from bringing the communities together for their shared future, are daily further poisoning relationships between Christians and Muslims. At the dawn of the third millennium, after the fall of the Ottoman empire and the end of colonisation, the Arab world is facing head-on the consequences of two major problems: the effects of the Arab–Israeli conflict, and the unavoidable challenges of modernity and post-modernity. Despite the efforts of Arab reformists on all sides, modernity, and the phenomenon of globalisation that it plays into, have remained peripheral at best, and have not touched the core of Arab culture. Moubarac's interest in relation to this is focused above all on the leading political issue in the Arab world, the Arab–Israeli conflict. He most probably believes that the consequences of the conflict have prevented the Arab world from becoming open to modernity in the past, and that indeed they still do. No one has admittedly yet produced a thorough study of the potential within Arab culture for flexibility and adaptation. Given the lack of serious research that might present and confirm compatibility in principle between Arab culture and Western modern and postmodern culture, the issue of political factors is highly relevant.

According to Moubarac, the conflict between Arabs and Israelis is a problem of human culture rather than international politics. It hinges on the encounter of three religious civilisations that each claim to be universal, effective and meaningful. Crucially, therefore, what needs to emerge is a peaceful and fruitful intercultural existence. Hence Moubarac's invitation to the three monotheistic religions to commit to finding a solution to the problem. In 1969 he wrote:

> Today, we are finding out that the conflict is between mindsets on two sides: Christian and Muslim on the one, and different Christians and Jews on the other. The conflict is even more serious than that. It appears that a mindset that I could call Western and Judeo-Christian is now deeply committed to an undertaking of a colonial nature, under the cover of humanitarianism and religious in character, to the extent that it seems to draw the associated religious communities into the fray. I am especially alarmed to note that worldwide Judaism, with some notable exceptions, has espoused the cause of Zionism in the same way that medieval Christianity became fully committed to the Crusades, which of course led to the disastrous consequences of which we are all well aware. If we think of the problem of the Holy Land as being the most important and the most urgent thing that any dialogue between Muslims and Christians needs to address, then we find that a third interlocutor must necessarily be brought in, and that one of the main preoccupations of the Muslims and Christians involved needs to be to instigate a dialogue with members of the Jewish faith who have remained uncontaminated and share our awareness of the present dangers.[67]

---

67 Y. Moubarac, *L'Islam et le dialogue islamo-chrétien…*, *op. cit.*, p. 225.

Thirty-five years after this lucid and intrepid analysis by Moubarac, the drama of the Holy Land is still breaking hearts and occupying conscientious minds. There are now only a negligible number of Palestinian Christians, but the Christian Middle East is nevertheless still intimately implicated in the conflict. For if Christian life is completely and finally extinguished in the Holy Land, then there is reason to fear that the same might happen before long in the remaining countries of the Arab Middle East. Christians in the Middle East are 'the hostages of a cruel conflict between Israel and Islam',[68] and as a result are suffering a double martyrdom: the martyrdom of unjust accusation, and the martyrdom of being involuntarily uprooted.

Each time they are tested, Arab Muslims seem to be somehow anaesthetised, and then to suffer the consequences of amnesia. Whenever the Arab world is attacked from outside, Middle Eastern Christians appear, in spite of themselves, to offer themselves up as scapegoats, against whom many Arab Muslims are then tempted to direct their anger and their desire for revenge. In the societies of the highly confessionalised Arab world, it seems that the distinctive feature of Christians is that they become a provocative lightning rod in moments of crisis. The reactions of Muslims betray their desire to suffocate and eliminate the Other. These desires are inherent in any religion motivated by proclamation and proselytism, and they are exacerbated in times of crisis. The recent history of the Arab world clearly shows that any aggression from the West leads to a dangerous confusion in Arab minds in the way they perceive different aspects of human life. Moubarac uses the word 'hostages' precisely because he is anxious about the harmful effects of this confusion. And it is why he invites thoughtful Muslims to avoid the worst, in other words, to make every effort to spare Christians in the Middle East any further experience of the double martyrdom he describes.

Peace in the Holy Land is likely only to emerge if there is a sincere three-way collaboration between Jews, Christians and Muslims. Only if these three spiritual powers willingly work together will they be able to break the fatal violence that threatens to engulf the Middle East in error and despair. This statement is not in any way a pious wish, but rather it offers a global assessment of the Arab–Israeli conflict. According to Moubarac, the solution to the conflict needs a threefold foundation: Abrahamism as the ultimate theological foundation, shared by the three monotheistic faiths; ecumenism as the spirituality of reconciliation and the instrument through which to manage diversity and to absorb tension; and citizenship as the concrete legal and political expression of the ideal of equality. In order

---

68 Y. Moubarac, *La chambre nuptiale…*, *op. cit.*, p. 103.

to 'promote an egalitarian Palestine in which Jews, Christians and Muslims jointly express its ecumenical and Abrahamic vocation,'[69] Moubarac argues in favour of a 'reconciliation within the framework of a Judeo-Arab Palestine, where Jews, Christians and Muslims would all be fully equal citizens – otherwise some might be excluded by the others, and this could lead to the worst possible catastrophe.'[70] Moubarac appears here to be advocating a unified, secular and egalitarian Palestine. His ideal solution is too beautiful to be actually possible. It is doomed to remain utopian, so long as daily experience in the Middle East repeatedly shows that secularism is unachievable without a radical reshaping of religious hermeneutics and a thorough modernisation of social structures. Moubarac's solution is fully relevant on a theoretical level, but in practice it is not achievable given the realities of human experiences in the Arab world. The exploitation of Middle Eastern oil reserves by the Americans in recent years, the uncontrolled demographic explosion in Arab countries, the exacerbation of Islamic and Jewish religious fundamentalism both in the Near East and in other third-world societies, the false equivalences alleged between secularism and the degenerate aspects of Western imperialism and the failures of liberal ethics, the unacknowledged despotism of Arab monarchies and republics, the illiteracy in Arab societies and the ossified tribalist mindsets, all these contribute to making such dream scenarios impossible. However, Moubarac's solution for peace is, as far as possible, open and faithful to the potentialities available in Semitic culture. Abrahamism and ecumenism are representative of the mystic experience available in each of the three monotheistic religions, while citizenship is unfamiliar to sociopolitical practice in Middle Eastern societies. His theological approach, however, is not principally aimed at negotiating a peaceful solution to the Arab–Israel problem. Rather, it proposes new perspectives of a spiritual nature. The chief reason for including any reference to peace solutions within the scope of this research is to highlight the importance attributed to Christians within the Arab world, and to re-examine what their future might hold.

Seeking a contextualised new evangelistic witness

Three conditions for the future

Three major issues in the societies of the Arab world will crucially affect the future

---

69 Y. Moubarac, *L'Islam et le dialogue islamo-chrétien...*, *op. cit.*, p. 208.
70 *Ibid.*, p. 222.

of Christians in the Middle East: a fair and lasting peace for the Arab–Israeli conflict; whether there can be a true and thorough process of modernisation in Arab societies; and the emergence of a Christian witness expressing the human values that best reflect the spirit of the Gospel. Moubarac's hope lies in this vision of the future. In truth, it should also be acknowledged that the contributions of Christians to the creation of this radiant Arab future are necessarily limited to the efforts they will need to make under the third heading. This is for a simple reason. Given how few in number they are, and their particular worldview, they will not be able from their own resources alone to instigate a modernisation process unless it happens as a consequence of the challenges faced by Arab Islam and Arab societies. And if that does indeed happen, then it is sadly clear that any claims that Christians in the Arab world have a prophetic mission seem somewhat unduly optimistic. Moubarac's call to recast the pattern of Christian mission in the societies of the Arab world therefore allows for the insurmountable limitations to Christian witness in the present circumstances. If they wish to do so, the one and only contribution that Christians in the Middle East can make to the Arab world – their world – will be the one thing they can prove in their own lives to be authentic: their witness to the Gospel.

The double witness: interior renunciation and fighting to defend mankind

This chapter does not aim to examine fully all the nuances of the reflection that Moubarac opens up here, but instead to provide a concise final summary. There are two key threads that pull together his theological reflection: evangelical renunciation (*kenosis*) and the secular fight to defend Arab people. Moubarac justifies his choices – evangelical poverty and the defence of mankind – by citing two major realities: the original identity of Eastern Christianity as conferred by its allegiance to Antioch and by its Semitic language (Aramaic, Syriac or Arabic); and the conditions experienced by the Christian communities currently living in the Arab world. Moubarac is persuaded that the mission of any social group can be seen in the interaction between the true nature of the group and the real circumstances of the lives of its members in their historical circumstances; he therefore persists in believing that at their core, these Christians in the Middle East have always been and still are kenotic and fragile (cf. the vocation to victimhood in Massignon), and that their challenge arises chiefly from the misrepresentation of Arab people. Their ability to build a mission that is lucid, relevant, consistent and effective will depend on a synoptic and interactive approach to the realities of fragile kenosis and misrepresentation.

Ideologies have been called into question, and philosophical and theological discourses that claimed to be universally valid have been disproved, so now Christian witness can no longer claim credibility based on theory alone. Only selfless poverty and solidarity are likely to convey the truth of Christian faith and to bear out its coherence as a world view. Moubarac identifies poverty as the only possible means of survival for the Christian Church if it wishes to survive and flourish in the Arab world. Hence his firm and critical tone when he questions the material comfort and financial status of Eastern religious orders: 'Which of the congregations of religious living in the land of Islam – barring two or three among them – can be described as having a living standard equal to that of the average Muslim?'[71] It is in sharing the same living conditions as their Arab neighbours that Christians can most effectively witness to their faith, not by claiming its supremacy or excellence, as some are still prone to thinking; modesty and faithfulness best convey the message of the Gospel. And beyond voluntary and fraternal material want, Christian poverty also aims to redress any pretentions Christian witnesses may have to exclusivity or self-sufficiency. In this sense, the one who is poor is the person who becomes dissatisfied with who they are, and willingly welcomes diversity.[72] We see here a dialectic of constant want and perpetual gift. Moubarac invites Christians in the Middle East to keep alight their testimony by rethinking the meaning for them of evangelical poverty. It will be their best way of acting as yeast worked into the dough of the Arab world. Being a minority, they are in some ways predisposed to take on this role. Their history, both ancient and modern, has always illustrated the relevance to them of this image. Sadly, however, this has often been proved somewhat late in the day. At the times when challenges arose, their reactions were not always perfectly suited to their evangelical ideal.

---

71 *Ibid.*, p. 204.

72 One of the many testimonies that confirm this sense of openness is what Moubarac calls the cultural mediation of Christians in the Middle East: 'I refer here to the translations that were mainly carried out by the Nestorians during the Middle Ages, and those that have been carried out since the seventeenth century by the Maronites and the Melkites. Medieval scholars translated Greek science and philosophy into Syriac, and then into Arabic. In other words, it was thanks to cultural mediation that the language of the Koran and of the Arab desert became a language of civilisation and, in its turn, provided an instrument of cultural mediation that enriched the Latin Middle Ages. As for the translations carried out by Maronites and Melkites in modern times, they have enabled the Arab Renaissance to engage in the path of modernity.' Y. Moubarac, *La chambre nuptiale...*, *op. cit.*, p. 19).

The thorny question of political engagement

The response to the first reality, the ideal of evangelical poverty, seems obvious, in that it is closely related to the essence of the Christian message; the second, however, might seem more problematic, given its political implications, and it therefore requires closer examination. This chapter will therefore take a longer look at the multiple ways in which Christians in the Middle East are engaged in political matters. Official Christian bodies disregarded this delicate subject for a long time. In order to avoid having to compromise with daily realities, the Churches of the Middle East preferred to adopt a peaceful and mystical silence rather than engage in the hurly-burly of political conflict.

The call to witness to faith by taking up the cause of Arab neighbours can trigger all kinds of distraction and heightened anxiety. Serving their Arab neighbours calls Christians to act and to engage with all aspects of the historic life of the Arab world. Taking up the cause of the Arabs becomes a political struggle, since nothing of this nature can be achieved unless within the political sphere. In spite of the dangers, Moubarac remains deeply convinced of the need for political commitment that is shared with all Muslim partners in the Arab world. And as concerns Muslim political choices, he is categorically opposed to the neutrality of Middle Eastern Christians.

> Although this does not reflect reality, often Christians are assumed to be aliens
> in Islamic countries by those who do not realise that in matters that relate to
> the countries of the Middle East, they are stakeholders and have their own
> opinions, not on a Muslim politics in these countries, but on a politics in these
> countries in which both Muslims and Christians are equally concerned.[73]

Although the earliest Christian theological texts may have exhorted the baptised to live as strangers and pilgrims on Earth (cf. the image of yeast in the dough),[74] this did not mean that Christians should renounce any political engagement. Quite the opposite: this foundational recommendation emphasised that the baptised should make every effort to be open and adopt a fundamental attitude of communion.

In this Christian understanding, the alien is the one who is free of self-interest and divests himself of all that is foreign to the humanity of mankind, because his

---

73 Y. Moubarac, *L'Islam et le dialogue islamo-chrétien...*, *op. cit.*, p. 206.
74 See the *Letter to Diognetus* (an anonymous letter written towards the end of the second century; source in French: collection *Sources Chrétiennes*, no. 33).

only interest is mankind, perceived through the dignity of being the chief creation of the love of God. To be a Christian in the Arab world, therefore, means to be in solidarity with the full humanity of Arab neighbours and to defend their cause to the very end. The human problems encountered in the Arab world, at whatever level, are by definition encountered both by Muslims and Christians, since they share the same living space and local affiliations. Moubarac distinguishes here two types of dialogue between Muslims and Christians: the theological and spiritual dialogue between the Christian West and Islam, and the existential and political dialogue between Middle Eastern Christians and the Muslims of the Arab world. He says that the 'dialogue with Western Christians is more easily engaged with religiously minded Muslims', while Christians in the Middle East are more likely to seek out 'an existential dialogue with the political actors in contemporary Islam'.[75] This distinction may have been true in the 1960s, but it is no longer accurate about the reality of Muslim–Christian relations which, at the dawn of the third millennium, are developing between the two great monotheistic religions on a worldwide basis, in the different human societies in which they are embedded. The disastrous consequences of Western colonialism, the intolerable injustice in Palestine, and the disappointing stagnation of Muslim theological thought under the Ottoman occupation, have all led to the emergence of a violent and fundamentalist form of Islam that has advocated, based on the Koran, an undifferentiated attitude of intransigence and armed militarism. The events of 11 September 2001 sealed the rupture and hostility between the Western world and the world of Islamic fundamentalism. This in turn ignited Western interest in a global dialogue with Islam, which would thereafter embrace all the sociopolitical aspects of the message of the Koran.

Christians in the Middle East, who were existentially implicated in the living history of the Arab world, turned out to be better aware than anyone else of the global nature of Koranic allegiance. The dialogue between Muslims and Christians in different societies around the Arab world can be violent and peaceful in turns, but there is always a desire to include in the exchanges and challenges the political demands arising from the Muslim worldview. While the West was enjoying exploring the spiritual resources of Muslim mysticism, Christians in the Middle East were daily coming up against the invasion of the shared social space by assertive Islamification. The Christians in the Middle East were not unaware of the potential within the Islamic tradition for spiritual elevation and sublimation, but they also had to endure the consequences of political claims by Arab Islamism.

---

75 Y. Moubarac, *L'Islam, op. cit.*, p. 79.

These claims would be legitimate within the context of a monolithic society that was uniformly Muslim, but they present risks in a multiconfessional and diverse society. Were they to be applied literally, without regard to the particular situation of other communities, they could prejudice human dignity and lead to doctrinaire intolerance, a hardening of attitudes, and to intercommunity conflict.

In other words, the unity and coherence of the Koranic *Weltanschauung* require a greater attention to the different sociopolitical aspects of Islamic doctrine as a whole. A fragmentary perception of the vision of the Koran is likely to distort the truths of Islam, so it is essential to take the claims of Islamic thinking as a whole. A further consideration is the fact of worldwide interculturality. Given the globalisation of communications, increasing mobility and the growth in migration movements, the world is now more like an immense village in which all the inhabitants have a duty of care towards each other. The opening up of national frontiers means that we all have a greater level of investment in our shared existential sphere. And the evolution of postmodern technology has created a worldwide pattern of reciprocity linking the most distantly separated regions of the world in a shared ecological destiny. It is therefore becoming ever more urgent to enter into dialogue with Islam as a legislative system that affects the whole of the human community:

> It might be possible, after centuries of open warfare and stealthy opposition, to believe that in approaching any dialogue between Muslims and Christians the world of politics should be left to one side, temporarily at least. The contemporary Church could, in a similar vein, work towards concentrating more effort on its spiritual duties, and leave temporal matters to look after themselves. The right time for Muslim–Christian relations, in the view of Muslims themselves, is a truly political *kairos*, in the truest sense of the word. [...] The time seems to have come to move from a Christian polemic directed against Islam to a Muslim politics of the Church.[76]

This quotation clearly shows that Moubarac does not agree with the recommendations of the post-conciliar Catholic Church and suggests that politics need to feature in discussions between Muslims and Christians. Muslims themselves consider politics to be the best possible way to express the friendship and solidarity between themselves and Christians. Since Muslims are not able to dissociate religion and politics, then Christians must boldly be prepared to link politics and religion in their efforts to be of service to humanity. A failure to present

---

76 Y. Moubarac, *L'Islam et le dialogue islamo-chrétien...*, *op. cit.*, p. 134.

the Christian faith as an incarnated faith would do a disservice to the dialogue between Muslims and Christians. It is nevertheless important to monitor the strength of the link.

Christians and Muslims in a shared secular political struggle

If Christians in the Middle East wish to respond positively to the challenge presented by their Muslim partners, they will need to deploy the full political potential of Christian *kerygma*. Concentrating on spiritual duties does not exempt Christian communities in the Arab world from seeking out in the Gospels ways in which they can justify a common Islamic and Christian politics that promotes and sides with all Arabs. And these same communities need to find a Gospel-inspired courage so that they can debate, in a spirit of critical sympathy, the sociopolitical demands of contemporary Arab Islam. Leaving temporal matters to take care of themselves might therefore be understood as a call to draw both Christians and Muslims towards a new perception of their human reality, which in turn should naturally lead to a shared system for managing the human city. To relegate temporal matters to second place behind Gospel priorities is to give in subconsciously to what Moubarac calls the structural eschatologism of Western Christianity:

> We should correct the possible collusion between its structural eschatologism
> and the temporal circumstances around it that are still relevant. So it would
> be necessary to imagine for it a new era in which it would no more be
> necessary to defend or protect Christians than to advocate a Christian state.
> That would be to play into the hands of the Islamic state and of the Zionist
> state. Christians should instead join in the effort to secularise the struggle and
> advocate taking the part of one's fellow citizens by appealing to the humanist
> values of the monotheistic religions to defend them against fundamentalist
> tendencies.[77]

The clarity of his words is in strong contrast to the complexity of Middle Eastern realities. Moubarac's dearest wish is to wake the Churches of the Middle East from their deep eschatological slumber. Their awakening must, to avoid worse consequences, be done in such a way as to condemn any surreptitious collusions between eschatological sleep and political lethargy.

To be clear: Moubarac is calling for a non-Christian struggle that will aim to

---

77 Y. Moubarac, *La chambre nuptiale...*, *op. cit.*, p. 98.

redeem the essential Christian nature of Middle Eastern Christianity. By 'non-Christian struggle', he means the kind of commitment that aims to promote the humanity of the Arab peoples. The core of Christian action here is not so much to save Christian structures as to defend the cause of mankind in general, regardless of individual affiliations and beliefs. Any Christian institution wanting to secularise the struggle must have the courage to give up its own identity as a Christian social structure wielding direct or indirect political power. Intuitively, Moubarac sees that when Christians defend the cause of the Arabs this is a guarantee of real and authentic political commitment. Because of their vocation, Christians in the Middle East are more likely to see their political commitment as separate from any collective narcissism or the banging of any confessional drums. If they can highlight the value of forfeiting any desire for hegemony or exclusivity, they will demonstrate to their partners and neighbours the salvific value of total theological conversion.

Moubarac is profoundly convinced that the monotheistic religions will be saved from their own demons only by embracing the cause of mankind. A strong confirmation of his conviction is that he sees in the three Abrahamic faith paths clear similarities in their recognition of the same human values while also prizing the same spiritual resources. So the central truth towards which the spiritual aspirations of the three religions converge is therefore mankind:

> Rather than simply, as in the past, setting a life pattern, the spiritual path
> we have inherited from our teachers should prompt us to commit ourselves
> afresh to our own times; and if possible, to halt the slow process that has over
> the centuries stifled Christianity in the Middle East because it has relied too
> strongly on the force of arms for its survival, and when in trouble looked only
> to the eschaton. Christianity will be more likely to last and develop in the
> Middle East when the fight there is no longer for Christians against Islam, but
> instead for humanity – each person, and the whole person; that fight must set
> its own rules, shared and agreed by all sides, whatever differences there may
> be in the energies that drive them.[78]

Moubarac's boldly evangelical words identify the two fatal temptations that Christians in the Middle East have succumbed to over the centuries: spiritual resignation, dressed up as passive anticipation of the last times; and armed struggle, interiorised as a sublime act of defence of Christ Himself.

In framing these two temptations, Moubarac is no doubt thinking of the land of

---

78 *Ibid.*, p. 98.

Lebanon, an expression that he only rarely uses in his writing. When he does use it, however, it reveals a key motive that shapes all his theological thinking. The extent of its significance is that it points to a specific insistence on the particular nature of the vocation to which Lebanon feels called. The tragedy of the Lebanese war (1975–1990) threatened to undermine all the theoretical efforts of members of the Lebanese intelligentsia to establish what many Lebanese scholars saw as their country's distinctive identity, historical mission and contribution to human society. Some, however, think that the ordeal only emphasised the relevance of the vocation. The threat of possible conflict on a global scale between what have until now been thought of as the blocks of the civilised world proves beyond doubt the need to safeguard the Lebanese model of interreligious and intercultural coexistence, and to extend it worldwide.

For Youakim Moubarac belongs to the category of scholarly Lebanese Christians who firmly believe in the unique nature of the experience of Lebanon within the Arab world. If, however, a number of scholarly Lebanese Muslims fail to focus on the human dimension, it is precisely because of a fundamental difference in their perception of religious identity. Lebanese Muslims tend to see Lebanese identity as dilute within the vast world of Arab identity, or even Islam, whereas Lebanese Christians persist in seeing in the particular composition of their country elements that mark it out as having a deeply seated and truly distinctive cultural identity. Because of the symbiosis within the world of Koranic thinking between religion and politics, Lebanese Muslims are unable to envisage that politics might not be integral to the Muslim *umma*. Some religious Lebanese Muslims are in fact aware that in modern times such an integral involvement is not really possible, but they continue to look with suspicion on any Muslim–Christian efforts to modernise politics within Lebanese society.

Hence the continuing preoccupation with the issue of Lebanon in Moubarac's thinking. The issue of Lebanon is therefore central on two counts. First, because of the sensitive position of Lebanon, at the crossroads between modernity and some of the most extreme forms of fundamentalism; and second, because Lebanese Christians have suffered in Lebanon from the consequences of their two temptations, fight or resignation. In the series 'Libanica', which Moubarac served as editor,[79] there is a clear emphasis on the urgent need for profound changes in Lebanese society. The motivating principle claimed for the collection is to defend the ideal of a secular and egalitarian Lebanese conviviality in which the religious experience of those involved enables liberty to prevail over fundamentalism.

---

79 Series published by Cariscript, Paris.

If the struggle is refocused onto human issues, the perils of the two temptations can be averted. Beyond the struggle, people will see no sense in the Christian faith. Seen from this angle, faith becomes political commitment to serve humanity. Anthropology will redeem theology by providing historical substantiation. For religion, in order to become incarnate in human history, must espouse the cause of global human happiness. Whatever their religious allegiance, anyone holding such a faith will always be called to take up the cause of mankind.

> Clearly, Christian faith, just like Islamic faith and indeed any other
> personal motivation, can and should inspire, feed, urge and sharpen the
> drive to fight for justice. To confuse the political fight for justice with one's
> personal spiritual fight to attain the Kingdom is to run the risk of coming
> under the thumb of the ayatollahs or the Gush Emunim, or to succumb to
> caesaropapism. The two battles merge in the mind of the fighter who feels
> called to battle on both fronts. In such cases, the non-violence of the spiritual
> battle can seep into the political battle, thus making it both more just and
> more effective. On the practical level, and in terms of principles, however,
> the two should not be confused or given the same level of priority, for fear
> of depriving the temporal battle of autonomy and the spiritual battle of its
> distinctive nature.[80]

Moubarac is keen to be theologically meticulous, so he protects the distinctive spiritual nature of each theological body, while still highlighting the shared and universal character of the temporal battle. Since Arab populations, regardless of their religious affiliation, have suffered the same traumas and the same sufferings, they necessarily share the same aims and ambitions in their political battle. Some aspects of the ordeal of Christians in the Middle East seem to be specific to Christian religious affiliation, but the healing of Arab societies will eventually reveal that the suffering of Christians in Muslim countries is due more to sociopolitical disfunction within the Arab world and to a failure correctly to interpret the anthropological aims of the message of the Koran. Their human struggle focuses on the same preoccupations, shared through the human experiences of all Arab populations, but the religious aims of Christians and Muslims can lead to very different spiritual sensitivities. Their shared human destiny should not obscure the legitimacy of these differences within the Arab world. The cultural expression of religious faith can vary widely between one spiritual world and

---

80 Y. Moubarac, *La chambre nuptiale…*, *op. cit.*, p. 98.

another. Moubarac maintains that there must nevertheless be harmonious agreement about the concrete implications for the shared political battle for justice and peace in the Arab world.

By making the battle a secular one, Middle Eastern Christians will no longer be fighting on their own behalf, but on behalf of their Muslim partners and neighbours. The heart of the battle will be where they discover the true meaning of the Gospel: they will be living it. The distinction is an important one. There was a time when the excessive politicisation of the Gospel message led the Eastern and Western Christian empires to present Christian witness as an armed struggle to extend the power of Christianity to provide self-affirmation and the cult of individual and collective identity. The Christian Churches were committed to varying extents in this attempted compromise with worldly values, and in various ways they gradually changed the message and objectives of their evangelical mission. Instead of focusing on freely given personal witness and peaceful spiritual maturity, Christian missionary activity degenerated to become an expedition leading to forced conversions and dogged attempts to 'heal' humanity. The emphasis in present times should be on the theologies of evangelical conversion that highlight dedication to improving social justice within human societies that have now blossomed into pluralism and encompass a wide range of motivations and aspirations. The witness of Christians in the Middle East should present as an open and fraternal invitation to campaign together to identify and be grateful for the benefits of global interculturality. To this end, Christians are called to love Islam, and the Arab world, for who and what they are. In other words, to love that in Islam which is the distinctive nature and beauty of the Koranic vocation. Moubarac chose to write his book about Islam[81] precisely in order to show what Islam is capable of in terms of potential openness and growth, and to reveal the extent of its inherent universalism. Islam's vocation inclines Muslims naturally to consider it healthy and enriching for all people to coexist with members of other religions within newly created states. So if there is a sense that Islam is loved and acknowledged as a religion of openness, then Muslims will feel able to appreciate and foster the presence and the witness of Christians in the Arab world.

In other words, the new Christian mission Moubarac sees as the responsibility of the Churches in the Middle East is to love and defend not Christianity in and for itself, but Arab Islam and the Arab world, so that they regain the ability truly to love Arab Christianity. This fraternal exchange is reminiscent of the *Badaliyya* of Louis Massignon, and it both conveys and enables the best of the Christian

---

81 Y. Moubarac, *L'Islam*, Paris, Casterman, 1962.

vocation. It will not transform the Church of the Middle East into the Church of Islam, any more than the mission of Islam to Eastern Christianity would make the religion of the Koran into the Islam of Christianity. The Arabic lands are the same for everyone. They are located in the Middle East and they are generous hosts to both Christianity and Islam. The latter has made the greater mark, generating a veneration for the language itself of the Koran. But Christianity has also made its mark through a wide range of cultural influences. There may be differences in extent and sensitivities, but Christianity and Islam remain the two principal guests to have made their home in the Arab lands. A fraternal welcome to a third guest, modern Arab secularism, should encourage both the others to abandon any tendencies to insularity or to selfish doubling down on their prerogatives. This secularism is not akin to ancient Arab paganism, which the two Semitic mono-theistic religions have so violently rejected, but rather is keen to foster a form of creativity among the most audacious in contemporary human society. Christians in the Middle East, thanks to their religious sensitivity, are thus tasked with the delicate mission of reconciling Arab Muslims with their own secular brethren.

*

Having explored the work of Moubarac, it is important here to emphasise its theological significance. His is a fresh understanding of the identity of Arab Chris-tians, arising from his global reinterpretation of Islam. It has led him to develop and formulate a contextual expression of Arab theology, which achieves two pur-poses. First, it enables Arab Christian communities to give expression to their faith, as it is enculturated, in a coherent and intelligible fashion. Second, it allows them to integrate better in sociopolitical terms, because of the foundation it offers for a better form of Muslim–Christian conviviality. These purposes both depend heavily on the fundamental aim of the faith of the two communities. Both wish ultimately to be such an integral part of the Arab world that neither will be per-ceived as communities distinct from the Arab population as a whole. Only when they are perceived in this way will Arab Christians daily be able fully and finally to engage alongside their Arab neighbours.

2

The Ishmaelian fraternity (Michel Hayek)

The work of Father Michel Hayek (1928–2005) is thoroughly original in character. As both a theologian and a man of letters, he is a past master at marrying profound thought and elegance of expression in his thinking. For many years he preached at St George's Cathedral in Beirut, proclaiming to the Arab world a contemporary Gospel message. In the early 1950s he moved to Paris and then spent some fifty years researching, teaching and writing both theology and literature. He advocated radical reform for the Maronite Church of which he was a member, and dedicated his life and his writings to the cause of evangelical authenticity.[1] He had many friends among the great Christian prophets and theologians of his day, and was keen to demonstrate to his fellow Maronite believers that the Christian faith is not a haphazard conglomeration of traditional ideas drawn from Greek metaphysics. On the contrary, it is a dynamic commitment to the human race, whatever their allegiances and beliefs. This type of radical thought pervades the whole of Michel Hayek's work, which is extensive and marks a milestone in Muslim–Christian

---

1 'Father Michel Hayek was a man of many talents but was not fully absorbed by any one of the many tasks he took up during the course of a long ministry marked by many diverse challenges. […] Michel Hayek laid down markers, opened up paths both new and forgotten, inspired many through his widely ranging intuition, was a faithful friend and companion to many, and yet was always a solitary figure at the meetings of all the paths he took and then, without regrets, eventually left. He stood alone in his personal challenges, in the path he adopted in his church life, and in his university career, which touched the intersections between philosophy, theology, psychoanalysis, anthropology, linguistics and history. If we fail to approach Father Hayek with all this in mind, we might not fully grasp his full nature.' (Ch. Chartouni, 'Michel Hayek. Les méandres d'un prophète', in Ch. Chartouni (ed), *Christianisme oriental. Kérygme et histoire. Mélanges offerts au Père Michel Hayek*, Paris, Geuthner, 2007, pp. 10–11.)

studies especially.[2] His relationships with his homeland and his Church were marked by bitterness and disappointment, but it is greatly to his credit that he was nevertheless able to identify the priorities for an authentic Christian life in Lebanon and in the societies of the Arab world. His theological thinking is based on the urgent need to return to the fundamental notion of salvation to be found in the Good News and its message of liberation for all people from the chains that hold them down, starting with the chains of preconceived ideas and clichés. His desire was to renew Arab theological thinking, so he worked to develop a new approach to Islam, which he hoped would enable Arab theological reasoning to establish Muslim–Christian conviviality on the basis of a bold reinterpretation of Christian and Muslim traditions. The reinterpretation would enable Islam to reveal its true Ishmaelite vocation, which characterises Islam as condemned to wandering in poverty, while yet being sensitive to diversity and hospitality.

Islam in the calling of Ishmael

One of the major preoccupations of modern contextual Lebanese theology within Arab culture is to identify the place that Islam occupies in the economy of salvation. Breaking away from the sterile apologetics of the medieval period, Michel Hayek attempts to rehabilitate the dialogue between Muslims and Christians by seeking out a new approach to Islam. His approach follows the faint trace of the shrouded figure of Ishmael. It is impossible to perceive Ishmael without taking a new look at the person of Abraham. This explains the sense of tidal motion that pervades Hayek's masterpiece, *Le Mystère d'Ismaël* (The Mystery of Ishmael), seeking to understand the long-hidden relationship between a father longing to secure his lineage and his son, condemned to exclusion. The vocation of Islam, it becomes clear, depends on the outcome of this relationship. In order better to understand the tidal motion, this chapter will explore the analyses and meditations contained within Hayek's above-mentioned study. The exploration of the person of Ishmael provides us with the centrepiece for an Arab Christian theology of conviviality, which should in turn enable Arab Christians to explain their faith from a position of better integration with current Arab life.

---

2 Among Michel Hayek's many published works in Muslim–Christian studies are *Le Christ de l'Islam* (Paris, Seuil, 1959); *Le Mystère d'Ismaël* (Paris, Mame, 1964); *Les Arabes ou le baptême des larmes* (Paris, Gallimard, 1972). Two further studies were never published (*D'Abraham à Mahomet. La rupture et la continuité*; *L'Islam dans une vision chrétienne*).

The privileged status of Islam

The person of Abraham is unanimously acknowledged as a symbol of unity between the three monotheistic religions.[3] Michel Hayek appears, however, to distance himself somewhat from this point of theological unity in that he identifies differences in their interpretation of the figure of Abraham as father between the religious thinking of Jews, Christians and Muslims:

> Of all the prophets shared by the Bible, the Gospels and the Koran, it
> is Abraham who highlights the divisions between the three religions.
> Genetically, he nominally unites them, but on a visceral level, he is torn and
> this divides them almost irremediably.[4]

As Hayek describes him, Abraham is endowed with the dual ability to bring together and to disperse. Modern interfaith theological thinking must surely be able to free Abraham from the compromises that have obscured the truth about him. And this is indeed the task that Hayek takes upon himself each time he addresses the less unfortunate of the two inheritor sons, and the less fortunate of the three monotheistic religions. Following in the tradition of Massignon, Christian theology is called to do justice to Islam. To do this, there is no better way than to explore the real promises made to Ishmael.

In his general introduction, Hayek faithfully presents the theological arguments used by Islam to justify its calling and its distinctiveness. And indeed, the Prophet of Islam

> [...] also claims his share of the heritage of his ancestor Abraham. He is
> conscious that in spite of being a direct descendant he has been excluded from
> the inheritance, and claims his right as the older son, a right that nothing could
> abolish. In order better to take charge in the conflict between Judaism and
> Christianity on the subject of the Abrahamic legacy, although he came after
> Moses and Jesus, he claims legal and theological precedence over Jews and
> Christians. He [...] seeks out an undifferentiated, pre-biblical Abraham, who
> was not yet either Jew or Christian, nor yet polytheistic, a hanif Abraham.[5]

---

3 'If we look back to this generative moment in sacred history, it seems we should find in him
a figure that promotes peace, and acts as arbiter, the only one able to reconcile on mutually
acceptable ground all monotheistic parties, otherwise so divided on so many points' (M.
Hayek, *Le mystère d'Ismaël*, Paris, Mame, 1964, p. 23; henceforth MI).
4 MI, p. 24.
5 MI, p. 25.

Beyond its uncertain beginnings, Islam claimed the person of Abraham as the source of its own identity, of its dignity and of its distinctiveness. Yet Abraham would never have had this crucial theological significance were it not that he was the guarantor of the promises made to his son Ishmael:

> What can we say of Ishmael? Surely Abraham would have remained as simply one prophet among others, of average or even mediocre significance, if his firstborn Ishmael had not borne him – as reported in Muslim tradition – to the summit of the Kaaba so that he could look out from that original high place over the immutability of time and the monotony of the desert.[6]

In other words, Abraham owes his Muslim reputation to his son Ishmael, who was 'reborn' some twenty-five centuries later in the person of Muhammad.

Islam therefore values Abraham[7] not only because he is their ancestor in the faith that places full confidence in God, but also, and especially, because he is the father of Ishmael and of the Arab peoples. Muhammad is fully certain that Abraham is 'the father of Islam whose chief work was to restore the Temple at Mecca',[8] an assertion that demonstrates the close link established in Islam between Abraham, Ishmael and Muhammad. Muhammad simply restores the ancient promise made to Ishmael. The vicissitudes of human history having led to tragic blindness among Jewish and Christian believers, it became necessary to seek out the original purity of the foundational event and rescue the inheritance promised to Ishmael. In other words, Muhammad saw the incipient Muslim community as the repository for the original promises given to Ishmael through Abraham:

> Islam, a religious and social phenomenon Arab in origin, revives Ishmael, whose race and heritage it safeguards. He stands to attention, sword in hand, at the door to the Bible, freezing sacred history at that moment in Antiquity, and temporarily refusing to follow the 'elect' over the threshold without sufficient guarantees: Produce your proof if ye are truthful. [Koran 2, 111].[9]

---

6 MI, p. 35.

7 'Islam starts with Abraham but goes back to Adam, seeking to reclaim the original, ancient, immutable faith, nursed in the dawn of a primitive civilisation. Islam also belatedly claims the promise that will be fulfilled in Muhammad through the Ishmaelite line, but to acknowledge this does not change the content of the promise, it simply rehabilitates a monotheism that is as old as the world itself.' (MI, p. 26.)

8 MI, p. 28.

9 MI, p. 35.

Islam thus openly rejects any attempt to reclaim and monopolise the person of Abraham, and at the same time deplores the particular way in which Ishmael has been written out of history. If the Word of God given to Abraham is true, and if it is revealed in the flourishing of Ishmael's lineage, then the understanding of that word must no longer be exclusively explicated within Judeo-Christian thinking, however much it may be relevant there, but within a new life of faith experienced within the burgeoning Muslim community. This is how Islam would discover its path, its vocation, its destiny.

Islam: the religion of dawn

According to Michel Hayek, Islam aims to be scrupulously faithful to God's original divine intentions. To highlight this faithfulness, Muhammad is careful in the message of the Koran to follow on from Abraham's paradigmatic religious experience. But even as he does this, he introduces a few changes to the traditional figure of the great spiritual forefather: 'Abraham ... becomes the only prophet altered in the Koran in such a way as to present him as the father of Islam.'[10] And in his further investigations Michel Hayek identifies the evolution of the figure of Abraham in the Koran. Prior to the Hijra, Muhammad did not identify any link between Abraham and the Arab people.[11] This was because there was a state of communion before the final confrontation.

The many theological controversies upsetting both Jewish and Christian believers, however, led Muhammad to seek a third way through. He wanted above all to give tangible shape to the original purity of the call from God. In order to overcome differences and defuse hostility, there was an urgent need to rediscover the original unity of the three religions. It was only when he reached Medina that Muhammad felt able to announce the truth of that unity:

> To start with, all the communities were just one, which gradually disintegrated into multiple sects due to disagreements between people. This foundational faith, which is in essence monotheism, is the religion of the prophets and of those sent by God, without any distinctions or exclusions.[12]

---

10 MI, p. 57.

11 'There is no hint that he established any particular links between the patriarch and the Arabs of Mecca, other than as exemplars, as proposed during the mediation with the absent-minded of Mecca, on the threshold of divine damnation.' (MI, pp. 69–70).

12 MI, p. 76.

Discord does not reflect God's will, and nor do either the promotion of some or the exclusion of others.

According to Hayek, Islam not only explores the relevance to salvation of that original unity but also re-examines the emblematic figure of the first one excluded, Ishmael. Muhammad himself was misunderstood and rejected by those closest to him, and purposely identifies himself with Ishmael. He therefore emphasises the genealogical and spiritual links between the lineage of the rejected son and the Muslim community that was banished by Jews and Christians.

> He learned from his contact with the Jews in Medina that the scriptural authorities would not accept that his message was inspired because he was descended from Ishmael. He belonged to a race that they rejected by name; being already a motherless and fatherless orphan, he found himself also an orphan spiritually. Having been expelled and rejected by the city of his fathers, he found himself also to be descended from a son who had been cast out and deprived of his family heritage. Being a typically tenacious Arab, however, and determined to prove that God is the one God of all, he maintained that Ishmael's rejection did not forfeit his rights but rather confirmed them, since it established his physical relationship with the person of Abraham, with whom the Jews jealously guarded their fleshly paternal link. Muhammad traces his *hanif* faith back to his ancestor Abraham and is faithful to his message, since he worships no other god besides the one God.[13]

The genealogical link is thus justified on theological grounds. The two cases are so similar that it is impossible to turn down his desire for appropriation. Michel Hayek's line of discussion seems to mesh well with the message of the Prophet of Islam: if Ishmael is the father of the Arab nation, then the promises made to him should be fulfilled in the ultimate revelation from God. And that revelation is majestically exposed in the text of the Koran. Muhammad, who both bears and safeguards its message, has come to fulfil the promises made to Ishmael about his inheritance.

His careful argument demonstrates that God's faithfulness to Ishmael casts another light on the divine wisdom. According to Michel Hayek, Muhammad was gradually led to giving clear reminders to the People of the Book that God's generosity was not limited to Jews and Christians. 'God is free to choose who he showers his gifts on, who to guide towards the Straight Way, without being limited

---

13 MI, pp. 78–79.

by the Synagogue or the Church.'[14] The theology of origins thus paves the way to
a theology of a diverse divine economy. The historic reality of Ishmael's lineage
elicits a new understanding of the economy of salvation. According to Muhammad's Islam, God could not possibly exclude a section of the human family that
sincerely claimed Abraham as its father.

> It was necessary that a descendant of Ishmael should lay claim on behalf of
> the Gentiles, who were unaware of their right, to the universal heritage of
> Abraham, and to do so on the strength of his own relationship with Abraham
> according to the flesh: Islam thus helped the People of the Book to gain a
> wider understanding of God and His promise.[15]

This line of argument closely links the justification of Koranic faith with the
experience of banishment and exclusion shared by Ishmael and Muhammad. The
providential burgeoning of Islam has enabled both Jews and Christians to gain
a deeper experience of the vast extent of the mercy of God. The divine promises made to the first prophets of the faith should encompass all human impulses
towards sincerity, all desires for authenticity, and all spiritual quests.

Michel Hayek's theological reflections therefore bring him by a logical path
to a positive observation. He expresses it in terms of a sincere and irrevocable
acknowledgement of the distinctive nature of the message of the Koran and thus
of the Muslim religion. Muhammad is depicted here as the messenger whose
delicate duty is to remind his hearers of the purity of the original Word of God:

> The Koran that he has provided is recognised globally as a prophetic book,
> in theological terms pitched at the historical moment of Muhammad's
> engagement with religious history: not, within the chronology of sacred
> history, six centuries after Pentecost, but at the moment in Antiquity when
> Abraham cast Ishmael and his mother Hagar out of their home. His prophecy
> addresses only that section of sacred history. An ethnic prophet, an *ummi* born
> from among the nations, the *ummiyin*, excluded from Scripture, the very type
> of all the excluded [...], he brings a message from the archetype, the 'Mother

---

14 MI, p. 81. Michel Hayek frequently returns to the theme of evidence for the internal
coherence of Muhammad's understanding: 'Faced with the exclusivist attitude of the biblical
writers, and the pressure of controversy on the subject of the descendants of Abraham,
Muhammad learns to value his genealogical link with the patriarch through Ishmael.' (MI,
pp. 82–83).
15 MI, p. 83.

of the Book', in order to establish a mediating mother community between the idolatrous peoples and the revelation of truth. By returning to these origins, to the archetypal maternal bosom of human nature in its first and generous iteration, its *fitra*, he immediately sees the danger of God, his presence, or rather the path that he forges that both destroys and regenerates all things. What he witnesses here is true for all.[16]

In the light of this reinterpretation, Michel Hayek appears to make a symbolic shift that transgresses historical inevitability for both events and persons. In an exercise of retrospective redemption,[17] he reinserts the prophetic acts of Muhammad into the lived experience of Ishmael, thereby cancelling the time and distance between them marred by error, straying, falsification or misrepresentation. Muhammad's prophecies are presented as belonging to a time and a century other than his own. In spite of this theological anachronism, Islam as portrayed by Michel Hayek is restored to its original and best contours, since the Koran sums up the core of God's call to the whole of humanity: preserve the unity and transcendence of God, and proclaim His extraordinary mercy. All those who profess these two truths, and give themselves over in complete trust to the will of God, will find happiness in His promises, whatever their religious allegiance, their ethnicity or their ideological adherence. From the start, it is God who rules all. To long for that inaugural dawning moment is to experience the royal path of salvation that God generously offers to all of humanity.

Islam is the religion of absolute unity

As Michel Hayek examines the figures of the great prophets among the ancestors, he outlines a vision of Islam that sees in the belief in the one and only God the basis for all of Koranic doctrine. In returning to the origins of the religious experience of humanity, we find that clearly the first act of faith was to proclaim that God is the one and only God. Humanity's first spiritual impulse in its purity is thus clearly and directly linked to recognition of God's uniqueness. The research of scholars of religion does not bear this out, but Islam tends to state that humanity

---

16 MI, pp. 84–85.
17 'The genealogical relationship between Arabs and Muhammad ensures that they enjoy an honoured place among the Islamic peoples, just as the relationship according to the flesh of Muhammad with Abraham ensures that he has a distinct and privileged place among the prophets.' (MI, p. 87.)

was first monotheistic before falling into polytheism;[18] or rather, monotheism was always present and within sight, and religious experience was drawn to its demand for rectification and correction. For this reason, it is important to emphasise the fundamental demand of Muslim faith:

> Islam is older than the Covenant of the Last Supper made in the blood of Christ, older than the Covenant at Sinai, where the Torah established the Jewish people, older than the Covenant with Abraham based on the promise; and older too than the Covenant with Noah in which God promised to respect the order of the cosmos, since an atomistic understanding of the history of time and space implies no time, no continuity, no immutable laws. The only solidly fixed point in the inconstancy of the universe and the fragility of all things is the monotheistic truth as perceived in the very essence of created nature. From that fixed point, we can look out over the whole of creation; and from there, differences vanish into the monotony and flatness of the desert. Mankind can see only one exception; and that exception is God, fixed at a high point of the horizon, to the north of history: 'There is no God but God'. By witnessing to this truth mankind remains faithful to the witness of the original pact.[19]

In terms of its original pact, Islam makes every effort to prove its unwavering faithfulness to the original Covenant between God and mankind. The person of Adam embodies the innate spiritual impulse of humanity.

By evoking the emblematic figure of Adam, Islam is able to graft itself onto the original stem. In searching for its own authenticity it needs a primary point of reference, a key event. From there, stray variations can be aligned historically. Changes introduced into the practice and organisation of the religion will no longer be rejected as sinful:

> Beyond Abraham, Islam aims to reclaim the religion of Adam. The *hanif* beliefs championed by Abraham and thought of as the innate religion, the very practices of the religion, and especially pilgrimage, are all traced back to the origins of humanity. The faith and the law are jointly seen as the fundamental facts of religion. And Islam is right in claiming to be a religion older than Judaism or Christianity when it takes its reference from a primitive revelation.

---

18 See MI, p. 238.
19 MI, pp. 148–149.

The very best symbol of its more ancient status within the history of religion
is its practice of celebrating its services on a Friday, before the Jewish Sabbath
or the Christian Sunday. For all three religions, that day within the course of
the week is the day on which Adam was created, and the day of the end of
history. In an act of apocalyptic compression, Islam brings the two poles of
time together in order to place time itself under judgement, and describing
history itself, and any substantial length of time within it, as merely an
'interval', 'the blink of an eye or even less'.[20]

This sets up a dividing line between Islam and the other two monotheistic
religions. A chronological delay cannot overpower theological precedence. The
content of the Muslim faith claims to be profoundly linked with the as yet intact
substance of the original revelations. Anticipating accusations that might be
thrown at late arrivals in religious history, Islam insists on its claim to original purity. Muslim religious thinking was quick to adopt this obsession with its
origins, to the extent that the teaching of the Koran asserts its perfect identification
with mankind's religious nature. This gives rise to Islam's exorbitant ambition to
satisfy the deepest longings of the human condition.

Although Adam is, arguably, clearly the prototype of the universal believer,
Abraham is also clearly the model Muslim who knew how to respond to the
demands of pure monotheism. Islam therefore clearly feels it is viscerally attached
to Abraham. In order to confirm the credentials of the new religion in the desert
spaces of ancient Arabia, it was crucial to establish Abraham as an Arab:

[...] In Medina ... the religion of Abraham and Islam became interchangeable
terms. [...] Now, the link and the attachment to Abraham do not exclude any
of the other prophets, since they are all declared to be Muslim; however, none
of them are described, as he is, as the 'father of the Muslims'.[21]

Following in the footsteps of Louis Massignon,[22] when modern Islamologists
– including Michel Hayek – examine the emblematic figure of Abraham, they are
thus able to resituate Islam in its true vocation; as a Semitic monotheistic religion that appeared belatedly for reasons that were providential for the religious

---

20 MI, p. 158.
21 MI, p. 131.
22 In his doctoral thesis entitled 'Abraham dans le Koran', Youakim Moubarac played an
active part in the development of this theological project, focusing his reflection on the calling
and role of Abraham in the economy of salvation.

experience of Arabia, Islam is perfectly attuned to the theological teaching of the two preceding monotheistic religions. However, since the new Koranic calling could not integrate peaceably with the religious life of Jews and Christians, Muhammad decided to alter the calling of Abraham in such a way that it reclaimed the hitherto hidden destiny of Ishmael:

> This nationalisation of Abraham, or his 'Arabisation', throws a new light on purely Arab traditions; the Prophet integrates the cultural forms of Arabia Sacra into his religious vision, after also bringing in elements from the Bible. It seems he only looked at the Bible in order to pull from it – in spite of objections from those who claim it as their own – the section about Ishmael that had been sequestered, tied down and monopolised by the People of the Book. Coming away again, he opts for voluntary exile and inadvertently inhabits the calling assigned in Scripture to his ancestor Ishmael. This is the point at which the Abrahamic schism is fully realised. In all these events, it seems that a new and hitherto unsuspected dimension of Abraham's destiny is rediscovered. It identifies in Abraham's exodus a forgotten section of his life that has now been reclaimed [...] a wandering through the Arab desert as far as Mecca.[23]

Clearly, the Koranic description of the story of Abraham is more akin to a free retelling, and not to an updated interpretation. The Koran revisits the Bible not in order to reiterate it line for line but rather to discover what is said between the lines. In what is said between the lines of the Bible, Muhammad sees a deliberate shrouding of the figure of Ishmael. Islam therefore sets out to enable the People of the Book, Jews and Christians, to rediscover the riches buried in their scriptures. They are then invited to reappraise the journey taken by the one who was marginalised in the history of humanity. As the value placed on Ishmael's experience is restored, the vocation of Abraham is restored, fulfilled and authenticated; Abraham is once more the father of two children, not only one. If, however, Jews and Christians reject this paternal role of Abraham's and its implications for a wider horizon for the fulfilment of God's promises, then clearly they wilfully connive in the sinfulness of human nature: 'There is ... an Ishmaelite section of sacred history that is no longer mentioned in the Bible, which has been corrupted by those who guard it; Islam, as a descendant of Abraham, has reclaimed it.'[24]

---

23 MI, p. 91.
24 MI, p. 98.

In this way, the Koran reminds the People of the Book that it is still possible for them to gain enlightenment from the salvific power of the latest revelation. The absence of the Ishmaelite sequence in the Bible is not due to divine decree; on the contrary, it is due to human failing, an inadvertent manipulation, or even to deliberate falsification.

In Ishmael, Islam rejects all forms of exclusion and distinctiveness

Michel Hayek seeks to identify the distinctive traits of Ishmael in the three mono-theistic traditions, Jewish, Christian and Muslim, and he therefore focuses his theological interpretation on the delicate issue of exclusion. This is indeed the most lethal of the temptations that lie in wait for the three monotheistic religions. In turn, and from perspectives that sometimes converge and sometimes diverge, they exclude each other or declare that they have been excluded, or even wish to be exclusive. The internal logic of the Koranic calling, as presented in the most open forms of Muslim theology, rejects all forms of exclusion, isolation or elitism. Michel Hayek therefore promotes a new interpretation of the unfinished biblical itinerary of the key rejected figure in human history.

Islam deliberately denounces the unjustified rejection of Ishmael in the Bible. Seeking reunification and reconciliation, Muhammad reflects deeply on Ishmael's fate. His reflection gives rise to new enlightenment:

When the Prophet discovered the family relationships of Ishmael he experienced a psychological process of liberation and doctrinal realignment that enabled Islam to identify its definitive path and its status as a distinct religion, original and unchangeable.[25]

His thorough examination of the unjust and unjustified exclusion led Muham-mad to establish the link between his community and that born of Ishmael's lin-eage.[26] The Prophet of Islam thought he had discovered, moreover, the ultimate proof of his theological claims. He presents himself as the messenger of a religion that seeks to heal, to recall, and to return to the origins. He resolves to form a new community of the faithful who are entirely devoted to the will of God, in order to enable humanity to harvest the fruits of divine mercy, a mercy that will

---

25 MI, p. 202.
26 Throughout his theological investigation, Michel Hayek constantly reminds his readers that 'in the Bible, the Arabs are of Abrahamic descent' (MI, p. 217).

be revealed in the reconciliation of all the children of the promise. The Muslim community is therefore revealed as having a calling to moderation and gathering. In this sense, it is par excellence the community of Ishmael.

> The community that was born from Ishmael [...] becomes [...] a mediating community between two types of extremists: on the one hand, the polytheists who multiplied God in the image of their clans, and on the other hand, the biblical writers who reduced God to the level of a tribal god, wanting to restrict his infinite generosity to their community only.[27]

In describing the two extremes that are to be avoided, he identifies the gap that defines the new community. A double correction is needed in order to establish the much-needed amendment to the itinerary. What was needed was a new Ishmael to assume the task.

Among the great prophets of humanity, Ishmael does indeed have a unique vocation. His task is to furnish what is lacking in the biblical narration. Since mankind is by nature drawn to God, and God's plan is open to all of humanity, no one should be prevented from fulfilling the destiny to which their nature calls them. Those who become aware that this aspect of human nature is universal will find Ishmael to be a figure who brings healing, and who defends the marginalised by restoring to them the dignity of being called to share in the divine promise of happiness: 'Ishmael becomes the conscience of all those who have not received the message of the Bible but who, by their allegiance to his faith, bind themselves to a section of the Bible through which they gain salvation.'[28] According to Islam, humanity is a homogenous whole, all of it longing to surrender to the will of God. Ishmael therefore takes it as his mission to show to all humans that God is in his very essence just, as is clearly shown and made real in that all people are equally his elect. We therefore need to identify a missing section of biblical history that tells how Abraham's excluded descendants could be included in God's plan. It would enlarge the notion of 'the elect' and redefine them as being part of a newly integrated creation. The people of the elect would be the people of the whole of humanity, and the promised land would expand to become the whole of the inhabited world:

> Ishmael takes provisional revenge: he pits his own land and people against

---

27 MI, p. 204.
28 MI, p. 205.

the Holy Land and Isaac's descendants. In contrast to the exclusive claims of that particular lineage, he proclaims that all believers who claim descendancy from Adam are collectively elect; in response to the Torah, he raises the Koran. These facts that are ranged against Israel are not presented as a parallel development alongside the corresponding passages in the Bible, but are claimed by Islam to be values and institutions older still than the Bible.[29]

Islam, by insisting that it was the source of this radical reform in the under-standing of the will of God, claims to predate the initial divine revelation. The Koran, in seeking to boost its credibility, defines itself as being true to the very first expression of the will of God. At the very core of that divine economy a royal path conveys the call from God to the whole world. In returning to the origins Islam is able to escape the exclusivism of Judaism and to show its solidarity with all the religious experiences of humanity. The more the Koran is shown to be universal in its appeal, the more it is true to the authenticity of the call from God. The universality justifies invoking the original message of revelation. According to Michel Hayek, Islam claims the right to defend itself against repeated attacks from Judaism and Christianity. And if the two preceding monotheistic religions seem unable to agree over their crucial differences in understanding divine elec-tion, Islam offers a reminder that the authentic Word of God is to be found in the original content of the Koran, the message of which is that all the peoples of the Earth can be saved by submitting whole-heartedly to the all-powerful will of God. This Islamic understanding raises a key question concerning the conflict between claims to openness by the two pre-Islamic monotheistic religions, and the herme-neutic twists of biblical texts, twists that are related to the falsification of Jewish and Christian scriptures. It is therefore legitimate to wonder why Christianity opted for an aggressive and exclusivist interpretation of the biblical narration of the casting out of Ishmael: 'The verse in the Bible "sent away the servant and her son" had become a kind of scriptural argument repeatedly invoked in the calls by Popes to repel Islam from the Christian holy places.'[30] Christianity is reputed to be open-hearted, so this challenge is fully justified. From the point of view of the Koran, Islam intends to put right the aberrations in Christian exegesis on the subject of election and exclusion. Indeed, as the religion of the dawn, Islam

---

29 MI, p. 250.
30 MI, p. 219. The Pauline reinterpretation of that same narration itself condemns the errors of such an interpretation. In Islamic understanding, however, Paul's writings are questionable, and of doubtful value.

denounces the changes that have been imposed on the authentic Word of God throughout biblical history.

Towards a Christian theological understanding of Islam

The legitimacy of Islam in the divine economy of salvation

If this is the case, then Islam is well able to justify its claim to be a religion that is faithful to the original Word of God. The principal grounds for this are clear. In Islam, the notion of faithfulness means the restoration of the original revelation. For this restoration to be achieved, Islam needs to be able to give free expression to the nature of its vocation. And according to Michel Hayek the process instigated by Sara against Hagar and her son needs to be re-examined:

> Thirteen centuries after Islam discovered Ishmael, [...] the Church should surely, together with the Synagogue, think about reconsidering its assessment of Sara and Hagar in order better to understand the effect of the divine sentence carried out on the Mother of the Emigrants and her children: Hagar and Ishmael ...[31]

This calls for a re-examination not only of the Christian theology of Islam, but also, and especially, of the internal structure and thematic coherence of Christian theology itself. The present chapter is concerned only with the first of these two revisions, but the role of Muhammad was arguably to reinforce the value of the Bible by including it in a move to promote a more authentic openness to the Word of God. For the Koranic vocation calls not for the discrediting of the Bible, but for a search to identify its hidden potential. And one of the hidden aspects of the revelation of God is its invitation to restore and integrate those whom history has excluded. Islam knows that it is called to carry out this mercy mission that is essential to the equilibrium of humanity.

In order to reveal all the possible hidden riches, the theological revision must not skimp its examination of the central figure of Muhammad. And this leads to the crucial question of the prophetic nature of Muhammad. Before we explore the distinctiveness of the Koran, it is important to define more closely what we mean by Muhammad's prophetic nature. According to Michel Hayek, Muhammad can be called a prophet in that he becomes aware of a message of salvation destined

---

31 MI, p. 220.

for his own people, his own race, the Arabs. The message, and the means of its transmission, are related to his ethnic and linguistic community, and therefore deeply touched all Arabs to the core. The heart of the message was the exhortation to monotheism and the invitation to be open to the world:

> At the very moment when he was protesting against the Bible and against the election to grace by divine adoption, he was unwittingly confirming a part of sacred history and, in accordance with his own vocation, was serving the cause of that very Bible by exhorting monotheism and thus fulfilling one of its prophetic truths.[32]

Without rejecting biblical revelation, Islam confirms its truth while at the same time correcting its content. The correction is manifest in a fierce opposition to any suggestion of association with God or of excluding humanity. The distinctiveness of Muhammad's prophetic nature is shown in two ways. On the one hand, he insists on the uniqueness of God and a pure and unbending acknowledgement of monotheism; on the other hand, he is concerned to offer the gifts of God to all of humanity. The Arab peoples are thus rewarded by knowing that they gifted the person of Muhammad to the world and with him the privilege of experiencing submission to the will of God. The issue of chronology becomes a background issue, since despite the historic delay in the revelation of the Koran it is neverthe-less integral to the primitive phase of the divine initiative:

> Muhammad and the Koran can be described as 'inspired'; the inspiration is pre-biblical, Abramite, primitive; it is a stage on the road towards a positive revelation, offering a major justification for a part of that revelation: that monotheistic faith is possible for mankind thanks to human intelligence, in which the divine grace is constantly at work.[33]

Michel Hayek's classic approach to Koranic revelation enables him to consider a further theological interpretation that could offer a renewed Christian percep-tion of the distinctiveness of Islam. Albeit belatedly, Islam inclines Christianity to welcome divine transcendence, and offers it a prefiguring of its own destiny. The sacrifice of Ishmael prefigures the sacrifice of Jesus. The pre-Islamic exclusion of Ishmael symbolises the fate of Isaac in the divine Christian economy:

---

32 MI, p. 221.
33 MI, p. 241.

The exclusion of Ishmael was the first sacrifice imposed on Abraham's family, in order to prepare if for the next sacrifice, that of Isaac at Moriah, and of Christ at Calvary. Before his time, he was the scapegoat sent into the desert to die there willingly in order to purify the chosen posterity of Abraham. [34]

And it is here that we find the climax of Koranic distinctiveness, which can however only be clearly expressed in explicit reference to the revelation of the Bible itself. In this sense, Ishmael in Islam becomes the symbol of a propitiating sacrifice reminiscent of the sacrifice of Christ Himself. Ishmael's sacrifice, however, is particular in two ways: its salutary effect for both Judaism and Christianity is retrospective; and it is fully explained and effective only through the ultimate sacrifice of Jesus Christ.

So if Ishmael is a distant herald of the sacrifice of Jesus, he can neither be a substitute for the sacrifice of Christ Himself, nor can he therefore nullify the act of sacrifice. The Islamic version of Ishmael, as depicted by Michel Hayek, does not offer a redemptive sacrifice but instead serves to purify Judaism and Christianity by cancelling out the dross of human history. The ordeal he freely agreed to suffer is an eloquent appeal to others to submit faithfully to an all-powerful God. So it could perhaps be said that in Ishmael all people are the slaves of God:

The essential servitude of Ishmael is towards God, in whom he acknowledges the sovereign Lord who sees and who provides, and whom all humanity must serve. Islam reveals that this attitude of servitude is inscribed in the heart of each being, angelic or human [...] History has no purpose other than to produce this race of slaves, chosen to adore rather than to love, and to serve rather than to befriend. [35]

We see here the furthest reach of the theological examination of the person of Ishmael. Even if his double mission is contemporary and relevant in the context of interreligious coexistence on Earth, ultimately Ishmael's demands will not undermine the distinctiveness of the Christ event. Ishmael exhorts us to submission and trusting self-abandonment, whereas Christ encourages friendship, offers love, risks communion. The different types of relationship offered are complementary, but initially they are different. This is why Michel Hayek never attempted to align the Koranic figure of Ishmael, even in the best possible light, with the Gospel

---

34 MI, p. 226.
35 MI, p. 233.

figure of Jesus. It would however be wrong to liken Ishmael to a Gentile. Through the power of tears he was given a baptism of salvation.[36] Although he is not to be confused with Jesus, Ishmael is not foreign to Jesus.

And it is in this median, interstellar status that lie the origins of the burdens borne by Islam. Michel Hayek, keenly aware of the serious problems faced by Islam throughout history, does not intend to prettify its image. He finds that Ishmael gives Islam a new theological relevance, but does not turn a blind eye to its pervading faults. He considers that Islam has not moved on from animal sacrifice and has not been receptive to the saving relationship offered in Christ's sacrifice.[37] In spite of every effort, Ishmael's Islam is unable to understand the unique mystery of Incarnation and redemption. Paradoxically, Ishmael remains the symbol of those who exclude themselves from a full understanding of the love of God offered through Jesus Christ to all of humanity. In this sense, Ishmael also symbolises Israel, which has rejected the love of God:

> If God saves Israel, it is because 'his gifts and his call are outside of
> repentance.' But in the meantime, Israel is assimilated to Ishmael, who, in the
> flesh, was born in slavery, and was cast out from the house of Abraham with
> his mother, the servant Hagar. A new Isaac, the son of the free woman, Sara,
> takes his place in the family of Abraham: these are the pagans of old who
> were converted to Jesus Christ, the savages grafted onto the Abrahamic stem.[38]

Henceforth, to show you acknowledge the love of God displayed and fulfilled in Jesus Christ you no longer need to be part of this race or that, or to be in receipt of this or that message from heaven, or to submit to a particular form of spiritual asceticism. The only thing needed to show you acknowledge God's offer is to accept the sanctifying grace granted through communion in the self-offering sacrifice on the Cross of love. 'Ishmael is none other than the natural way for the man Abram to help embody the divine promise; his very failure points to a further stage, and leads directly to another means of salvation, which is grace.'[39] As Ishmael accepts the promises of grace, he freely abandons the asceticism of self-redemption and casts himself in full trust onto the love of God. Will this transfigured Ishmael, the symbol of human failure, be able to follow the divine

---

36 MI, p. 220.
37 MI, p. 226.
38 MI, p. 223.
39 MI, p. 226.

adventure through to the end? Will the Ishmael of Islam be able to concede that the logic of grace pushes divine love to the very edge of dispossession, destitution and kenosis?

The Islam of Ishmael rejects all forms of exclusion, and yet has to exclude itself by refusing freely to accept the economy of Incarnation and redemption. Paradoxically, in order to safeguard the purity of the original faith, Islam is unable to protect itself from premeditated and accepted exclusion. Its passionate defence of the archetype of monotheism forbids it access to the mystery of divine passion. Islam therefore seeks to be seen as a boundary set by God, limiting on the one side His own agency within human history, and on the other the agency of humans in the history of God. This suggests that Islam is simply an initiation:

> To the extent that Islam is the fulfilment of Ishmael's destiny, he can be seen
> as an initiation pathway to the supernatural revelation and promise, since
> he reconciles the nations with a natural revelation that extends to belief in
> a unique God who is Creator and judge. But he can also be, as he was for
> Abraham, an obstacle, tempted to allow himself to be limited by human
> factors, refusing to join the adventure towards the ultimate and true end to
> which God is leading nature. Faith could then suffocate hope and no longer
> become 'the assurance of things hoped for, the conviction of things not seen'.
> It was the true faith of Abraham the patriarch, to which he came only after the
> destruction of the human means and instruments: the loss of Ishmael.[40]

The question is therefore how to evaluate the Koranic religion as an initia-tion pathway. An emphasis on Ishmael's readiness to engage with the mystery of exclusion shows Islam to be the religion of integration and of the universality of salvation, a vocation to tolerance, to flexibility and continuing adaptation. On the other hand, an emphasis on the monotheistic insistence of the message of the Koran discredits the figure of Ishmael so that he loses his power of attraction and his aura of human compassion. Islam thus sits on the borderline between two theological domains, on the one hand unconditional openness and heightened sensitivity towards human suffering, and on the other a radical intransigence in condemning and rejecting any attempts to draw close to, or commune with, a transcendent God. Such a radical approach could soon degenerate into indefen-sible harshness.

---

40 MI, p. 225.

Christianity and Islam: towards a salutary confrontation?

Michel Hayek's approach is original, and it affects his perception of interfaith relations, in particular those between Muslims and Christians. Because he defines Islam as a preparation for Christian revelation, he therefore has to identify the distinctive natures of these two monotheistic experiences. According to him, Islam is well attuned to the theology of divine restraint and human submission: 'For Islam has not been given an official mission to announce "the secret hidden in God since the foundation of the world", his love, but to remind humans that they are the servants of the only God and if necessary to force them to adore.'[41] The mission of Islam is therefore to call all people to adoration; if they refuse, Islam is given powers to force them, with the sole object of revering the supreme power of God and, together with all humanity, of complying with the merciful will of God. If this is the case, then Islam can only engage with others through the prism of this divine injunction.

Wanting to gain a better understanding of this somewhat analytical theological attitude, Michel Hayek attempts to link it with Ishmael's own vocation. According to the biblical narrative, Ishmael is sent to attempt to conquer nature. He is to earn his bread by the sweat of his brow; as a fighter, he will learn to conquer in order to live and to survive. His conquests extend to the ends of the Earth, the space within which he roams: 'In fulfilling the destiny given for Ishmael in the Bible, he (Islam) will be an archer, always ready to "lay a hand on anything"; but since he was the subject of quarrels between nations, as Islam is today, "all will lay a hand on him".'[42] This comparison is evocative, for in faithfully following the actions of Ishmael, Islam continues to stretch its bow and to believe it is doing the right thing. Attacking in order to survive inevitably provokes a defensive counter-attack, and from there it is but a short step to an attack in order to conquer. And here we see the pattern of the tragic confrontations between Muslims and Christians that have marked their fourteen long centuries of coexistence. Islam attacks, and then finds itself attacked.

In Islam, conquest is founded on the idea that the world belongs to God, that it is Allah's possession. This understanding encompasses the Koranic truth to which Islam fully subscribes, and which is uncompromising in its lucidity and clarity. In Christianity, on the other hand, since its foundation, truth has been somewhat subjected to the changes and chances of history. When he compared the two versions of truth, Muhammad felt compelled to place a higher value on Koranic truth. He

---

41 MI, p. 235.
42 MI, p. 236.

therefore chose to oppose Christianity, and thus refused to promote the development of religious history that preceded Christianity, as he was not convinced by
the newer Christian truth.[43] So he preferred to remain faithful to the monotheism
of Abraham.[44] And here we see the second reason why Islam not only clearly
disagreed with Christianity but also opposed it and hoped to convert its adherents.

The third and final reason is linked to Islam's strong expectations of Christianity and of Christians themselves. According to Michel Hayek, Muslims take very
seriously the Christian's heartfelt desire for self-offering, most clearly exhibited in
the Gospel text of the Beatitudes. When this desire is not fulfilled, then it becomes
grounds for reproach to all Christians who live in indifference and lack of faith:
'Without knowing or acknowledging it, [they] expect [Christians] to live a life that
witnesses to the gift of the self out of love; and when this does not happen, then
[Muslims] take up arms to make martyrs of them, as if to avenge the disappointment of their secret expectations.'[45] In other words, Muslims expect Christians to
be martyrs to love, and if they fail, then Muslims themselves impose martyrdom
on Christians. In their disappointment, Muslims become fearful and powerful
aggressors and conquerors.

Beyond these three explanations provided by Michel Hayek for the confrontation between Muslims and Christians, it is important to emphasise that the figure
of Ishmael represents the real desire for reconciliation in the wounded theological spirit of Islam. This perspective implies that Ishmael is destined to serve as a
focus for communion between the three monotheistic religions. Michel Hayek's

---

43 In the context of ecumenism, M. Hayek understands Islam's reticence and defends it by
referring to the incoherence of Christian witness in the Middle East: 'It remains true that the
key problem in the Middle East, and the most urgent, is one of unity. Even if we assume that
all parties have the best intentions, it will still take fifty years to solve it, and there is no
guarantee that history, which we have abused, will grant us such a length of remission. What is
the point of fighting over the chairs when we commit to occupying them only with words?
Antioch is Turkish, Jerusalem is Jordanian, Alexandria is Egyptian, and all of them are in
Muslim hands. [...] Quarrelling about former glories is no use either, for we have not survived
thus far thanks to our personal merit, and whoever we are, we are all wild ones adopted by
grace. Sons of pagans from Phoenicia and Mesopotamia, 'our father is an Amorite and our
mother a Hittite'. The Melkite patriarchate may have the liturgy of Byzantium, but it does not
have its glory; and the perpetual orthodoxy of the Maronites is no claim to honour if it is now
overlaid with religious orthodoxy. What good is it to the Syrians to have produced James of
Edessa and Bar Hebraeus, if modern Syria is mediocre? [...] We may now be in the final stage
of our lives in the Middle East, remembering an existence that lasted fifteen centuries, troubled
more by ourselves than by others, and will now soon be extinguished.' (M. Hayek, 'Les
Églises antiochiennes face à l'unité', in *Orient Syrien*, vol. X, 1965, p. 400.)
44 MI, pp. 245–246.
45 MI, p. 252.

bold interpretation suggests that Judaism and Islam will be reconciled when Jews
are able to see in Jesus Christ the blessing Abraham gave to Ishmael. 'Ishmael
is doomed to dissent and to shadow his brother until he is granted the rights that
his brother already enjoys and from which he had been excluded: a blessing,
the full Baraka of Abraham, Christ Himself.'[46] This will require two theological
discernments: the restitution to Ishmael and to his descendants of the blessing
given to Abraham and through him to all of humanity, and the acknowledgement
of Christ as the one who came to reconcile not only the Jews, the Christians and
the Muslims, but also all of humanity, now revealed as the privileged recipient of
the blessing of God's love. Using the metaphorical style peculiar to the oral tradition of popular religion, Islam thus foretells in its own way the glorious return of
Christ to Earth in the shape of a married man with two sons. Islam thus 'foresees,
in some of its marginal traditions, that there will be a reconciliation of all the
monotheistic religions under this "sign of the hour": by taking a wife, Jesus will
have two children, one called Moses and the other Muhammad. The Church and
the Synagogue are similarly expecting this universal messianic reconciliation.'[47]
In this representation, the Christ of Islam will reconcile through his marriage
Muhammad and Moses, Ishmael and Israel, Muslims and Christians, bringing
them all together within the one family of the children of God. Islam does not have
a way, other than explicitly referring to Christ, of retrieving the blessing that was
stolen from it. So Christ becomes the symbol of divine justice that is then transfigured and becomes self-giving love. For the only agent of reconciliation cannot
introduce a new confrontation between forces. Through Christ, there is no question either of removing from Israel its blessing in order to restore it to Ishmael,
which would be a new injustice, nor of dividing the same and unique blessing in
a way that might lead to disintegration of the human family and an unthinkable
divine incoherence. Only an act of self-giving will bring peace to all hearts.[48] Only

---

46 MI, p. 250.

47 MI, p. 254.

48 Thanks to his loyalty to the Aramaean Church of Antioch, Michel Hayek offers as an
example the kenotic model of the spiritual experience of these Christian communities who
have never either been able, or wanted, to dominate in the power of the name of Jesus Christ:
'Byzantium, the city of victorious Christianity, founded an empire under the sign of the
Pantocrator enthroned in glory at the highest point of the apse, and Latin Christianity, in
following Christ and as part of its work in the world, devoted itself to building a temporal city
in order to serve the city of God; the Aramaean churches, on the other hand, never built either
empire or kingdom, despite the fleeting successes of those who were working for the often
ungrateful multitudes who rushed from the desert of Arabia. Byzantine Christians pray
standing, draped in light and imperial splendour, and Roman Christians fall on their knees

an act of passionate love for all humanity will be able to defuse the conflict and reconcile divided siblings. On the Cross of love, and in the destitution of death, Christ displays the truth of divine blessing: his renunciation of all forms of power and his compassion for all mankind.

Islam reinterpreted: the limits and the opportunities for a new theological interpretation

In order to assess the challenges presented by Michel Hayek's theological thinking, we need to bear in mind the themes in his multiple output, which cover philosophy, theology, poetry and politics, and in which concise statements jostle with conceptual analyses, poetic ambiguities and political allusions, all presented using a range of textual devices of tremendous complexity. Michel Hayek's theological writing extends considerably further than a simple investigation of the Bible and the Koran centred on the figure of Ishmael. However, his tremendous perspicacity in opening up as yet unexplored theological aspects of this figure in both the biblical and the Koranic narrative provides him with a framework for his theological system focused on recognising a major principle of the divine economy: the multiple ways in which the love of God is revealed and, as a corollary, the multiple ways in which the Abrahamic faith is experienced.

Given that Michel Hayek's aim is to reinstate the humanity of Christ, his reinterpretation of Islam is related to a plan to reformulate the statement of Abrahamic faith. He revisits the religious experience of the ancestor of the faith in order to condemn injustice and reveal a promise of communion. The Christ he calls upon dwells as much in the long history of the experience of Abraham as He does at the limits of human experience. It is this Christ who provides the point of reference for both the start and the completion of the healing of humanity. For Islam, this healing should also include the rehabilitation of the figure of Ishmael as the beneficiary of the same divine promise, and a transfiguration of the vocation of the Koran in order to bring its readers closer to acknowledging the mystery of the Incarnation. His reinterpretation thus features an acknowledgement that

---

before the Good Friday figure of Christ as they follow the journey of the Cross; Aramaean Christians meanwhile prefer the posture of metanoia, bending forward like a foetus in supplicant prayer, over the tomb of the Master, diving with him into the limbo of Sheol, the darkness of Easter Saturday, to convey that the light of Easter has not yet dawned for them, but it is the darkness before the dawn: like the symbolic Easter of the desert, it is situated 'between two evenings'. (M. Hayek, 'Spiritualité maronite', in *Dictionnaire de Spiritualité Catholique*, Paris, Beauchesne, 1979, p 640.)

the religious experience of the Koran is legitimate, and an invitation to Islam to convert so as to receive in full the blessing of Abraham in the person of Jesus Christ. In working towards that conversion, Muslims must surely be deeply grateful to Michel Hayek for his fraternal attitude in seeking to find a place for them to be received by right into the heart of the family of Abraham. The call to conversion may however irritate more purist Muslims who seek to remain true to the exclusive understanding of the final 'descent' of the first revelation in the Koran of the Word of God.[49]

For thoughtful Muslims, this gives rise to a sense of tension, of being pulled between wanting to acknowledge the value of Michel Hayek's Christian theological endeavours while yet remaining scrupulously true to the universality of the calling of the Koran. This sense of tension is yoked to the ambivalence of Hayek's Islamology, in which he wants to be faithful not only to the particular nature of the Muslim way but also to the way in which God's plan reached fulfilment in the Christ event. This dual faithfulness is challenging on both theological and practical grounds. It is probably also what emboldened Michel Hayek to encourage his Middle Eastern Syriac-language Arab Christian community to take on the sensitive task of contributing to the salvation of the Arab world: 'The inheritors of the Syriac tradition are responsible before God and before the history of the salvation of the Islamic world.'[50] His statement is expressed in a way that highlights his keen sense of the urgency of the mission in terms of Christian presence in the Arab world.[51] What salvation is he speaking of? Are we to understand it

---

49 Michel Hayek very often identifies in the religion of the Koran its double claim to specificity (Abraham, Muhammad, the Arab race, the Arab language, the Arab temple) and to universalism (Islam is the religion of all the prophets). See MI, pp. 131–132. Islam therefore often appears to oscillate between these two key positions, retrenchment and openness.
50 M. Hayek, *Liturgie maronite : histoire et texte eucharistiques*, Paris, Mame, 1964, Introduction, p. XV.
51 Some of Michel Hayek's other writings might be seen as contradicting this description of an urgent need for mission. In contexts related to the rigour of the Churches of Antioch, Hayek appears to downplay the role of Arab Christians in giving shape to a Christian theology of Islam. The experience of the Maronites in their dialogue with Islam seems to be limited to daily neighbourliness. Indeed, for the Maronites, their 'vital dialogue with Islam – history has not yielded any better example – [...] know very well that their encounters rest on flimsy grounds. Minor numerical considerations ensure that the dialogue is balanced and give their voice an advantage, but this cannot be sustained for ever. This is why they are very aware of matters relating to the unity of Christians in the Diocese of Antioch, not as a distinct Maronite community but simply as Christians living in the Middle East, since by definition the unity they are thinking of would cause them to lose the name they take pride in and that serves as a symbol of their common life and their resistance. They are invited to sacrifice this sense of identity. Maybe they will be compensated for past sacrifices through choosing this, the greatest

as conversion to Christianity, or as conversion to the profound truth of Islam, a truth related to the vocation of Ishmael as he has presented it? It may be that none dispute the urgency at this time of seeking the salvation of the Arab world, but it is far from clear whether and how the offer of salvation so freely tendered by Christianity might meet the needs of contemporary Islam. If Islam is reinterpreted in the light of Ishmael's vocation, might that present a possible way forward for rapprochement between Muslims and Christians, or might it be misinterpreted as unwelcome attempts at proselytisation? Only Muslims can give a fully informed reply here. However, we should remember that Michel Hayek's theological rein-terpretation is as useful as is this crucial question, for it is a real invitation to the practice of conviviality, a practice that is common to the three monotheistic religions who have an interest in the person of Ishmael. Despite divergent inter-pretations in Judaism, Christianity and Islam, clearly the shared recognition by the three monotheistic religions of Ishmael's ordeal of exclusion should encourage them to reject the notion of enmity. Yet the only enemy threatening to undermine Abrahamic faith is the claim to hold the absolute truth, a claim that wraps itself in all kinds of justifications. The time has therefore come for all three monotheistic religions to undertake an authentic exercise in theological conversion. It is also time for the faithful in all three religions to learn to respect the Other as the guest in whom they offer a welcome to the divine Other. A sincere and coherent practice of hospitality is the most truthful vehicle for the monotheistic religions to witness to their Abrahamic faith. Michel Hayek's great achievement is to have effected a hermeneutic reshaping within the world of Middle Eastern and Arab theology that might throw a different light on the potential openness of Christian faith. The person of Ishmael exemplified what that hermeneutics of conversion might look like. A complete theology of conviviality can thus be elaborated on the founda-tion of the initial plurality inherent to the movement of faith. Freed from tenets about supremacy or exclusion, the figure of Christ as interpreted by Michel Hayek offers Christians, but also Jews and Muslims, a way to access the gentleness of the divine. If God's plan is that in Jesus Christ all mankind will be able to share the blessings of divine love, then Christians will need to stop limiting the work of salvation to the members of the visible Church. According to Hayek, the theol-ogy of conviviality is the only Christian theology that is credible in the context of interfaith dialogue. Ultimately, it is the only theology that is still possible when one takes account of the religions of the whole world.

---

of sacrifices. "He must increase, but I must decrease".' (M. Hayek, 'Les Églises antiochiennes face à l'unité', op. cit., p. 402).

3

The divine economy as the foundation for conviviality (Georges Khodr)

The Greek Orthodox Metropolitan of Mount Lebanon, Georges Khodr (b. 1923) is clearly an eminent theologian in the Christian Middle East and the current Arab world. As a creative pioneer, a precursor and a visionary, he has worked tirelessly for the renewal of Middle Eastern theology in the context of the Arab world. He is deeply rooted in the patristic tradition of his Orthodox Church, and has skilfully allied his theological knowledge with a mystical detachment and simplicity. His ardent Orthodox faith has exerted a deep influence on the positions he has adopted in terms of ecclesiology and ecumenism. He is a keen defender of the Eastern Christian tradition, and yet has most energetically developed a contextual theology that carefully adapts the *kerygma* to the challenges of Arab identity and modernity. In the light of his experience as a member of the Orthodox Youth Movement (Mouvement de la Jeunesse Orthodoxe, MJO), of which he is a co-founder, he has tried to renew emphasis on a living experience of Christian faith in a world where mankind seems to be floundering among the mind-numbing chaos caused by decades of dictatorship. The influence of his reflection and the example of his life shine through in his works of Arab theology that are bold and original, and challenge the thinking of both Christian and Muslim Arabs.

We should emphasise from the start the distinctive nature of the way he expresses himself. All theologians develop their own language. In the case of G. Khodr, his owes much to the Arabic language. No other Christian theologian has been as successful as he has at moulding the Arabic language to the demands of expressing Christian theology. Nor has any other exhibited the same dexterity and delicacy in using to best advantage the language of the Koran and Muslim theological tradition. Characteristically, he will choose a word with multiple meanings, one drawn from the rich tradition of Arab polysemy; one meaning is the principal one, but others are present as harmonics, enabling a number of approaches and analyses. Nowhere in his output, however, is there a systematic theological presentation of the whole of his thinking. His work is creative and avant-garde, particularly in its openness to Arab identity and Islam.[1] It comes over as powerful bursts of ideas, fruitful intuitions, unexpected revelations, and bold ideas that have yet to be unpacked. It may be that his mistrust of a highly systematised and rationalist Catholic theology has made him reluctant to formulate a global and coherent dogmatic structure.[2] But this certainly does not imply that his influence has been limited in any way. Indeed, a number of his theological intuitions came to be regarded as offering inspiration and guidance in intellectual and spiritual Lebanese and Arab Christian circles. His influence has also extended into the Muslim Arab intelligentsia, where the tremendous riches of his thinking and the huge variety of subjects that he has engaged with were neither arbitrary nor improvised. The global vision

---

1 Throughout his life, G. Khodr has constantly encouraged his readers to look again at Islam. He has invited them to resituate this monotheistic faith into the very particular context of the spiritual experiences specific to the Arabian peninsula. On 22 June 2007 he was awarded an honorary degree by the Institut Saint-Serge in Paris, and he went so far as to announce his disagreement with scholars of the East who, like Louis Massignon, place Islam alongside Christianity and Judaism as one of the Abrahamic religions: 'Abraham occupies a very different place in Judaism, in Christianity and in Islam.' (*La Croix*, 25 June 2007, p. 19.)

2 For readers of G. Khodr, the surprise is in the great variety of styles he uses. His most frequent mode of expression has been, and remains, a short commentary in the editorial section of the Lebanese daily paper *An-Nahar*. This kind of text gives full rein to the excellent writing and the intellectual genius of the Orthodox Bishop of Mount Lebanon. Sermons are another medium, the one he uses for the spiritual edification of the faithful. A third type of writing is found in the many prefaces he has written for books published by his friends. These prefaces are carefully crafted and display the scope of his generous and analytical perceptiveness. He has shown himself to be a well-informed reader, intent on fostering fruitful dialogue. His interpretations are instructive, and offer a new way of engaging in intellectual exchange and addressing the core of any issue. He is also an accomplished speaker in major public lectures, which he is often invited to give as a special observer of the Christian Middle East. There has been just one work differing in content: his autobiography, *Law hakaitu masrâ-t-tufûlah*, published in French under the appealing title *Si je racontais l'itinéraire de l'enfance* (If I should tell the path of my childhood), Beirut, Éditions An-Nahar, 2nd ed, 2001) and more recently in a new translation into English under the title *The Ways of Childhood* (New York, St Vladimir's Seminary Press, 2016). Because of its thematic unity and the coherence of his aims and focus, his output is most effective when published independently to create its own intellectual orbit. See in particular the linguistic study of his sermons by T. Wehbé, *L'Église dans la modernité. Les structures du texte et de la communauté dans neuf lettres de Georges Khodr; Al-kanîsa fi-l-hadâtha. Bina-n-nass wa-l-jamâ'a fi tis'î rasâ'il lil-moutrân Georges Khodr*, Kaslik, Publications de l'Université Saint-Esprit de Kaslik, 2009.

of his theology can be guessed at between the lines. This examination aims to give an account, if possible, of its fundamental coherence.

There is as yet no exhaustive study of all his work. Some young Lebanese scholars are making every effort to produce a thorough study of his writings in order to establish a coherent and unified picture of his output.[3]

A group of his disciples recently initiated the task by assembling in his honour a selection of texts, most of which tend to bear witness to their loyalty to him rather than provide a close and focused analysis of his thinking.[4] So we do not yet have an overall survey of his theology. There are many reasons for this. A major feature of his output is its poetic and mystical character. It therefore naturally resists systematic definition. In spite, therefore, of his clearly trenchant and fixed views on some matters, G. Khodr's theology is still a work in progress, evolving in step with the challenges that face Christian faith in the modern Arab world and affect the lives of the Christian communities living there. In other words, as an Arab theology it is still on a journey of discovery, for a number of his statements are often phrased with hesitation. His uncertain approach casts doubt on

---

3 Two Lebanese scholars are arguably best acquainted with G. Khodr's thinking. They have studied it carefully and see themselves as ongoing disciples, called to promote it and to further it. They are Georges Massouh, professor of Muslim civilisation and of Muslim–Christian dialogue at the University of Balamand (Tripoli), and Assaad Elias Kattan, professor and scholar at the Centrum für religiöse Studien at the University of Münster. Massouh has produced a monograph on the Islamology of G. Khodr entitled: *Monseigneur Georges Khodr. Un regard chrétien sur l'islam* (Paris, 1992). Kattan has published a number of articles on the terminology, the theological hermeneutics and the Islamology of the Lebanese Orthodox theologian: 'Hermeneutics: A Protestant Discipline for an Orthodox Context?', *The Near East School of Theology Theological Review*, 23 (2002), pp. 47–57; 'Some Aspects of George Khodr's Attitude Towards Modern Western Culture', *Chronos*, 14 (2006), pp. 139–150; 'Das Kreuz als Hingabe (islām) an den Willen Gottes: Zu den Besonderheiten der Kreuzestheologie Georges Khodrs im Blick auf ihren islamischen Kontext', in *Christliche Gotteslehre im Orient seit dem Aufkommen des Islams bis zur Gegenwart*, ed. Martin Tamcke, 'Beiruter Texte und Studien', 126 (Würzburg, 2008), pp. 213–224; 'Les lignes directrices de la pensée théologique antiochienne contemporaine', *Istina*, 56 (2011), pp. 379–391; *Shirā' fī 'uyūn mustadīra: Dirasāt fī fikr al-muṭrān Jūrj Khuḍr* (Beirut, 2012) [in this book : *Al-kalima wa-l-jasad : fasārat Jūrj Khuḍr fī siyāqiha ath-thaqāfī al-islāmī*, pp. 43–56]; '"Anziehung und Repulsion wie zwischen zwei Verliebten": Zur Wahrnehmung der westlichen Kultur bei Georges Khodr', in *Christsein in der islamischen Welt: Festschrift Martin Tamcke*, ed. Sidney H. Griffith (Wiesbaden, 2015), pp. 513–523; 'The Cross as "Islam": Georges Khodr's Approach to Islam as a Paradigm of Contextual Theology', *The Journal of Eastern Christian Studies*, 69 (2017), pp. 69–78; 'L'incarnation du Logos dans le cosmos, l'Écriture et l'histoire: Origène – Maxime le Confesseur – Georges Khodr', *Contacts*, 266 (2019), pp. 150–165.

4 G. Massouh, A. Kattan, G. Tamer (ed), *Wajhun wa wahjun (Visage d'incandescence)*, Beirut, An-Nour, 2007, 278 p.

acquired certainties and opens up unexplored horizons for the interpretation of the revealed word. When he speaks of Islam, for example, he often uses a questioning tone. This creates an elegant invitation to his Muslim interlocutors themselves to engage with the work of renewal in contemporary Arab theology that he hopes for.

Georges Khodr's theological thinking and his fundamental assumptions

Christian truth: God is love

The fundamental premise of G. Khodr's theology is the experience of being in communion with the God of love. Based on revealed truth, the experience of shared love shows believers the immense extent of God's gift so generously offered to all of humanity. Christian truth is therefore characterised in G. Khodr's thinking as an act of love more important than anything else. It remains true that no one in this world has seen God Himself. When a Christian looks at Jesus Christ, he does not see the inexpressible glory of God Himself but rather, since the Incarnation, the glory of unconditional love reflected in the human form that is the Word made flesh. Such an experience of love thus does not compromise the otherness of God, nor his transcendence, provided that otherness and transcendence are understood as a superabundance of love requiring no conditional justification.[5] Through the Incarnation, love is given out of pure love. This mystic vision pervades the whole of G. Khodr's theological thinking.

The key initial notion is that this divine gift is completely freely given. A believer can recognise the gift only through faith, and not through speculative reasoning. For G. Khodr, faith is an act of love, of commitment, a place of experience:

God reveals Himself in the world as love, always in the fleshly reality of history, yet completely independently from history itself, in the intensity of

---

5 G. Khodr is faithful to the classic terminology used to express the dynamic of the Incarnation: 'The divine is thus implanted in nature. The supernatural becomes inlaid into nature itself as a grace.' (G. Khodr, 'Le christianisme oriental et l'homme moderne', Lecture given in Geneva in September 1996, published on the website of the Greek Orthodox Archdiocese of Mount Lebanon, www.ortmtlb.org.lb). And at the same time, he seeks to use anthropology as he interprets divine events. He makes a tremendous hermeneutic effort to offer an accessible interpretation of the mystery of the Incarnation and to show how the divine can be implanted into the human.

prophetic truth, in Matthew's reading of the prophets, and in the Philonian and Plotinian Logos understood and presented as the Eucharist by Saint John. All this is true, for God could not call for the love of humans unless he made contact with the historical reality of flesh, and could not save them without transfiguring their life.[6]

Beyond the importance of the historical aspect of the mystery of the Incarnation, this text is a wonderful example of the relational character of G. Khodr's theology. This is not a unilateral divine initiative imposed on humans without any reference to what defines the nature of humanity, which could be described as an ontological need for contact and interaction. In throwing Himself open to contact with mankind, God inscribes Himself into the historical limitations of the human condition. As understood in Christian faith, He is willing to be measured against the hopes and expectations of any individual who seeks fulfilment through accepting the mystery of relationship with the divine.

In this divine initiative, however, God characteristically and patiently acknowledges the importance of historic contingency. In order truly to encounter human beings, God effectively had to become man in a gesture of immeasurable love:

The pedagogical genius of Scripture is to be found exactly here. Without a specific instance, something that is of universal value might be considered a theoretical abstraction. And moreover, without the revelation in a specifically historical event of a significant truth, then lived experience might be considered insignificant. The revelation thus appears as the face of the concrete world, of the existential, of the moment of eternal value. Revelation is not limited to teaching, it also saves. In the Epistles, revelation adopts a certain number of events from human life and uses them to represent and reveal the characteristics of the Kingdom. This is none other than the reality of Incarnation.[7]

The encounter, from the start, features a harmonic correlation between God and mankind. It conveys the project of love that had, from the beginning, decreed a mystic affinity between the overflowing love of God and the endless impulse towards Him in the human heart. We should therefore not describe it as a stratagem

6 G. Khodr, 'La communication du message en terre d'islam', *Études Théologiques et Religieuses*, 64, 1989, 3, p. 375.
7 *Ibid.*, p. 381.

for divine hegemony but rather as a longing for communion that reveals the sincerity of mutual desire.

And here we see how it is that Christian truth is a relational truth, and not a speculative truth expressed only through thematic messages. It consists in the random and unforeseeable encounter that over time is forged between God and mankind:

> Christianity is founded on the fundamental conviction that the best form of
> revelation and candour between God and mankind is personal relationship,
> a face-to-face experience that banishes doubt, misunderstanding, or
> misrepresentation. God spoke once and for all in a human life, one that was
> lived among us. We are called to see and to return the look that God expresses
> in the mystery of a face: 'Whoever has seen me has seen the Father.' Here lies
> the truth of the Gospel.[8]

If this is true, it is because God fully identifies with the work of love expressed in His body. God and this monumental act of love are therefore in close relationship. The author of the act lives on in his masterpiece, and the masterpiece in turn ensures that the author is present and active within history. In the case of the divine initiative, the act of love through which God offers Himself in Jesus Christ faithfully represents who that person is. To know God in Christianity, it is not sufficient simply to think of Him. He is to be experienced through deep relationship. And even if the Orthodox theology of G. Khodr is vulnerable to anthropomorphic slip-ups, the act of love remains the most secure locus for the authentic revelation of the divine being.

God is beyond any system: the structural fallibility of theological discourse

From the point of view of the relational theology recommended by G. Khodr, God is forever an evasive mystery, an abyss supporting the life of creation but not identified with it. God's supreme impulse of divine love puts Him beyond the hold of human understanding. Even in the revelation of Jesus Christ, God is beyond comprehension and conceptualisation. This is a constant feature of the apophatic apprehension of God in Orthodoxy.

Similarly, Khodr suggests that mankind cannot know God Himself, but only apprehend His force. A person is illuminated by God from within, with an

---

8 *Ibid.*, pp. 376–377.

illumination that touches both body and spirit. The Orthodox faith teaches about a deification that bridges the void between God and mankind while still maintaining the 'unbridgeable space between the Creator and the creature in their respective essential natures'.[9] Theology can express itself only through mystical and apophatic words, since God is greater than all our representations of Him. I am compelled to give up any attempt to understand His essential or deepest nature, and therefore to define Him. As humans, we are called to adopt a modest and discreet attitude. At the most, we can hope to explore bit by bit the divine dimension of human life. That is to say, we can achieve a growing awareness of the mysterious absolute who dwells within the human heart.

Any theological discourse that claims to define God, however, jeopardises the truth of the Incarnation. God revealed Himself within the limitations of the human condition. The lived experience of the revelation leads Christian believers to situate the revelatory event in the very substance of historical reality. It is in no way uncharacteristic of the outpouring of God's love that He deliberately located His self-revelation in a place of poverty and humility, in the sociocultural context of human life: 'We are inexorably thrust into the course of history, but there is nowhere that the Church could not exist as a mystery and a place of revelation.'[10] We have to assert that Christian truth is profoundly historical by nature, or grounded in history. Its historicity in no way undermines the foremost importance of the love of God, but rather it facilitates its insertion into the frame of reference of human expectations.

By acknowledging its profoundly historical nature, Christianity as a religious system, and indeed all other religious systems, will be better able to resist the temptation to try and manipulate the person of God and His will. To the extent that religions no longer ascribe to God their own ideas and theological perceptions, their plans and their ambitions, they will be less likely to draw the ire of God. G. Khodr maintains that the monotheistic religions have not stopped fighting wars in the name of God:

---

9 G. Khodr, 'Le christianisme oriental et l'homme moderne', op. cit. In his study of Islamic spirituality in the writings of G. Khodr, Professor Mahmoud Ayyoub, the great Lebanese Islamologist, agrees with Khodr in believing that human speech not only reveals but also shrouds God's being (M. Ayyoub, 'Le dépaysement de la foi et le lien de la charité. L'islam spirituel dans la pensée de Georges Khodr', in G. Massouh, A. Kattan, G. Tamer (ed), *Wajhun wa wahjun* (The Face of Incandescence), *op. cit.*, p. 38).
10 G. Khodr, 'Le christianisme oriental et l'homme moderne', op. cit.

All monotheistic people make use of God. They have all waged war in His
name. When a man as saintly as Bernard de Clairvaux preached the crusade,
that lays a foundation for all religious wars by making alterations, however
small, to the symbols and standards carried by the armies.[11]

The Orthodox Bishop of Mount Lebanon judges that there is an urgent need
to condemn the manipulation methods used, which most often degenerate into
claims of superiority. God tolerates human babbling, but that is no reason for
people to try to sanctify their own words by attributing them directly to God.

A critical approach to such an underhand strategy could call into question the
collective instinctive decision to safeguard its faith by a community with its own
legal rules and social bonds. One of the deep reasons for religious fundamentalism
is therefore linked to the very nature of religious communities:

> It seems to me that a certain type of fundamentalism is linked to the reality of
> religion because religion is always framed by a human community. There is
> always a risk that its members will seek safety and security within the group
> itself. They will not aim to reach the heights of contemplation, and the work
> of ministry will seek to promote mass salvation. And all will be covered by
> the pious intention to avoid judging one's fellow believers. Since Constantine,
> there has been no period in history that did not include some level of
> fundamentalism. It is only persecution that reintroduces purity, since that is
> when history falls apart. What I am saying here about Christianity is even
> more clearly true of the other two monotheistic religions, in which the concept
> of God is indissolubly linked to legal ordinances: in the case of Judaism, that
> the land is blessed by the very Word of God, and in the case of Islam, that
> the Koran is omniscient. It is also clear that 'all honour and power belongs to
> Allah'. (Surat 4, 139). But it is equally true, as often stated, that in the reality
> of Islam 'power belongs to God, to his Prophet, and to the Muslims'.[12]

If all religious systems are fundamentalist, it is precisely because of this need
for salvation that is only poorly expressed through submission to an institution
claiming to be the only one capable of granting it. As soon as a religious institution

---

11 *Ibid*. See As'ad E. Khairallah, 'The Way of the Cross as a Way of Life. Bishop George
Khodr's Hope in Times of War', in Th. Scheffler (ed), *Religion Between Violence and
Reconciliation*, Beirut, 2002, pp. 481–495.
12 G. Khodr, 'Le christianisme oriental et l'homme moderne', op. cit.

focuses on itself and promises to remedy human frailty, then it claims for itself the right to stand in the place of God, whose activity is impossible either to foresee or to control. It would be a grave error to attempt to find deep ontological security without being open to the mystery of relationship with God. History shows that relying on any other kind of assurance makes people rely on themselves and become egocentric. Christian faith, however, enables a person to trust in the love of a God who offers Himself to all unconditionally. It can only undermine the generosity of this divine gift if it is channelled through the legalistic structures of a religious institution. Indeed, according to G. Khodr, God surpasses all endeavours to understand Him intellectually and all the legal structures of religious institutions. If the divine being exceeds our perceptions, then the relationship that we develop with this being must also transcend any strategies to contain or manipulate Him. In order to enter into a full communion of love with God, however, humans must be creatures whose deepest nature will truly thrive in that relationship. This calls for a renewed theological reflection on the Christian understanding of human identity.

Christian anthropology: the image of God as a synonym for liberty

G. Khodr declares early on that a human being is created in the image of God and that this creation has highly significant anthropological and ethical implications. In spite of the revelation through Jesus Christ, God remains beyond our understanding, but we are better able to grasp the nature of humans. And yet the divine transcendence comes and permeates the human heart, signalled by our many varied human interactions.

To have faith in God thus implies having faith in mankind. The Christian faith, therefore, cannot tolerate an enclosed universe that lacks a transcendent dimension. Yet this faith also acknowledges the existence of a void, of limitations that can only be overcome if and when a Christian progressively grows closer to the image God has carved deep into his soul.

We now need to sketch out the identity of this person; this will be an enquiry that will take us almost into the realm of the unthinkable. G. Khodr is keen to emphasise here the relevance of the patristic approach that interprets the image of God in terms of freedom, not reason: 'From the beginning, it is the *imago Dei* that Saint Gregory of Nyssa understood as freedom that mankind bears within him. This image is not within us thanks to reason. [...] Mankind is essentially freedom.'[13] The approach taken from Greek thought reduces a person to their

---

13 Ibid.

rational dimension, while the patristic approach highlights the ontological nature of personal autonomy. The greatness and the dignity of a person is revealed not through reason but through their naturally deep-seated freedom. Before we were ever rational animals, we were free beings.

According to G. Khodr, the Christian faith is characterised by this profound autonomy, gifted to human nature through pure love. For this reason, Christian faith must always foreground the freedom of humans. It is a freedom that in no way diminishes the greatness and the transcendence of God, since God Himself planned it when He created mankind in His own image. When we as humans take pride in our own wise laws, it does not necessarily deny the transcendence of God. From a Christian point of view, the greatness of mankind is proportional to the greatness of God. This very delicate equivalence underlies all of G. Khodr's anthropology. In other words, the freedom of mankind reveals the greatness of God:

> God must be rescued from any ambiguity about His greatness in order to
> maintain His integrity. An impassive God torments and dominates mankind.
> He becomes the Great Inquisitor because humans created Him in their own
> image. This God who wears his grandeur as a privilege and the power of death
> is not able to grant humans their freedom. This understanding makes no sense
> to those who have not received Jesus of Nazareth, who is gentle of heart and
> has *Walâyat*, the seal of sanctity, says Ibn 'Arabi. He is the one who unveils
> the mystery of God.[14]

In G. Khodr's mind, a person can even be afraid of their own freedom, and for that reason might try to create God in the image of their own frailty: a God who might be dominant and rescue them from the responsibility for their own freedom.

Clearly, if humanity is subservient to an utterly despotic divine will, it will be nothing other than infantilised. A false conception of the greatness of God denies human freedom. It is only the greatness of love that can safeguard and foster the freedom of mankind. G. Khodr believes that the Christian faith is made meaning-ful by being fully immersed in the life of the world. The God of Jesus Christ is a God who wants to free mankind from all forms of servitude. The Gospel is thus the cry for freedom from those who no longer wish their freedom to be subject to

---

14 G. Khodr, 'Grandeur et humilité de Dieu', in Collectif, *Grandeur de Dieu. Perceptions chrétiennes et musulmanes*, Journées Romaines, XX, Centro Nazaret, Rome, 6–12 September 1995, p. 21.

the laws of the Sabbath. Over and above religious, social or political constraints, the message of the Gospel prioritises the dignity of each individual. This highlights freedom as the site of authentic human relationship. To be free, according to G. Khodr, is not to double down on one's own individuality in order to protect it from the compromise of relationship. On the contrary, to be free is to be open to diversity and otherness:

> The individual as a creature of communion, who continues to be themselves because of communion – that is to say in self-revelation to the Other and in welcoming the revelation of the Other – originates in freedom and is thus the cornerstone of religious freedom. I will not explore further the notion that this sense of communion with the essential being of the Other is only possible in a mutual kenotic revelation, person to person. Mankind's space becomes the space of God. The Other may be in sin, or in error. I can suppress the shortcoming by inclining myself in the generosity of *metanoia* before the mystery of the person, by taking his individuality into my own, and thus into God. His individuality is an essential part of my being. I can only welcome him by listening to his self-revelation.[15]

Humans are creatures of communion because their most intimate need is met in communion with their fellow creatures and with God Himself. In this sense, Christian freedom would have no value if it were only for the benefit of each person's individual need. Christian humanism can claim to have given the world this illuminating insight. It bears repeating here that human freedom is a free gift from God. Humans are clearly free to use it as they judge best. But if it is stripped of its relational dimension, can it still be seen as the true freedom that meets the deepest needs of humans and makes them most fully human? Christians, after all, do not worship their own freedom. Jesus Christ Himself provides the model for freedom in human relationships, making Himself freely available to his brothers and sisters.

This is the freedom through which mankind can attain salvation. According to Khodr, a Christian soul is not saved simply through rational lucidity, but far more through enlightenment and heartfelt conversion:

> Lucid reason is not sufficient, the heart too needs illumination. [...] Mankind

---

15 G. Khodr, 'La liberté religieuse. Vision orthodoxe', in C. Bustros and M. Aoun (ed), *La liberté religieuse au Moyen-Orient*, Würzburg-Altenberge, Echter-Oros Verlag, 1996, p. 61.

is no longer held hostage by mechanical reasoning, nor by a search purely for knowledge. Gnosis is not how mankind achieves freedom. The knowledge of the exact sciences preserve people's autonomy yet without separating them from their divine origins.[16]

The gift of freedom makes mankind human and yet also supernatural. So the grace that frees us by making us increasingly fully human also frees us further by enabling us to participate in the life of the divine. Participation in the life of the divine is a fundamental pattern for human salvation and requires full commitment from the human heart. When freedom liberates our powers of reasoning, this paves the way for the freedom that converts the heart and liberates it from suffocating self-centredness. Mankind is thus only truly free when both reason and heart have embraced liberation. We humans are made for freedom, and all that is required of us is humbly to accept the divine grace that establishes us as inheritors in the Kingdom of love.

The world is the locus of salvation. Dialectic of the Church and the world

G. Khodr perceives the work of salvation as being intimately linked to freedom. Salvation would be inconceivable without the gift of freedom, as it results from a long process of emancipation and sanctification. Humanity is suffering from a deep ontological wound and therefore needs to find a space for communion. Such a communion, to be soundly established, requires those involved to have attained the fullness of their humanity, a place of full freedom in which their deepest longings are in complete and harmonious accord.[17]

Without tipping into an outdated medieval spirit of suffering,[18] the Orthodox theology of salvation to which Khodr claims allegiance runs counter to the

---

16 G. Khodr, 'Le christianisme oriental et l'homme moderne', op. cit.
17 'The challenge of the separation between matter and spirit, nature and history, individual and society – the challenge experienced by contemporary human beings – is swept aside by the spiritual experience of the eucharistic community and the hope of the Church in glory, with all humanity redeemed' (G. Khodr, 'Le christianisme oriental et l'homme moderne', op. cit.)
18 'Not only are the cross and the resurrection inseparable, but [...] the cross itself is already the place where sin and death were conquered. In all liturgical texts [...] the mystery of the cross of Jesus displays his victory, thus excluding the notion of suffering and the interpretation of redemption, long attributed to St Anselm, as satisfying God's anger' (G. Khodr, 'Le christianisme oriental et l'homme moderne', op. cit.; see G. Khodr, *Law hakaitu masrâ-t-tufûlah, op. cit.*, p. 114). According to G. Khodr, in essence, Christianity is 'resurrectional' (G. Khodr, *Law hakaitu masrâ-t-tufûlah, op. cit.*, p. 107).

negative spirit so widespread in the modern world. It does not attempt to engage with the perversions and the corruptions of the world, nor with the tragic forces rivalling to pull mankind either towards perversion by sin or towards sanctification through grace. The world is the theatre for the encounter and symbiosis between humanity and divinity, between the human need for freedom and communion, and the freely given gift of freedom and communion.

> In the light of the end of all things, the Church and the world are co-extensive. There is only one locus of salvation for them both. The Church is therefore not seen as in opposition to the created world, and the history of salvation is not on a different timescale from the course of history. In God's eyes, both the world and the Church stand before Him. And in the Kingdom too, both the Church and saved humanity will stand face to face with the Lord, as they must, as bridegroom and bride. The Church is the life-breath of humanity, and those who – by whatever mystery – are granted the breath of life belong to the Church. In the mind of God, the Church is the icon of that which people are called to be, the promise of transfiguration for all mankind.[19]

In line with this approach to the doctrine of salvation, since God's salvation is granted to all of humanity, any dividing lines between the world and the Church are erased. And since the work of divine love is to sanctify the whole world, there is no theological justification for any such division. Given the history of the Incarnation, it is impossible to draw a boundary between the human and the divine.[20]

Having said which, the Church cannot simply exist in parallel to the world. As G. Khodr judiciously observes, the world is the theatre in which the Church works towards enabling humanity fully to realise its vocation. A prime task, therefore, is to establish a happy and fruitful coexistence between the Church and human society. Christians, while avoiding meaningless neutrality or any ambiguity that might undermine the authenticity of the witness of the Gospel, are called to reveal to the world its true religious nature, and to remind the Church that it is set in the world, the privileged field for the deployment of salvation.

This, its first and foremost calling, is where the Church can rediscover its soul and refocus on the core of the Gospel message. And it is at this human, earthbound

---

19 G. Khodr, 'La responsabilité et le témoignage prophétique du chrétien dans la cité', Lecture by G. Khodr given in Geneva on 22 November 2001 and available on the website of the Greek Orthodox Archdiocese of Mount Lebanon, www.ortmtlb.org.lb.

20 In Christianity, the human cannot be dissociated from the divine, and vice versa. The two dimensions mingle with each other (G. Khodr, *Law hakaitu masrâ-t-tufûlah, op. cit.*, p. 24).

level that the Christian community, united in the Church, finds its essential vitality
and energy. It is in the witness of love and fraternity that G. Khodr believes that
the ultimate meaning of the mystery of the Church is to be found:

> Acts of charity strengthen the sense of fraternity among people if they are
> inspired by an understanding that we are honoured by the poor, and they
> therefore build up the inner life of the Church. But if the Church only exists
> for acts of charity, it becomes too easy to have a view of it only as a social
> organisation limited to visible tasks. The parable of the Good Samaritan
> shows us two things: first, that love came from a man who was a heretic and
> an alien, and second, that extending care for others beyond the sphere of
> religion or tribe establishes a human communion under the gaze of Him who
> is the God of both believer and unbeliever, and reveals a unity that reflects the
> unity within God. For surely the unity of God is this love that binds together
> the three divine persons, each of which lives from self-giving to the other
> two and from receiving the gift of the other two. The foundation for social
> action by the Church is less the dogma of Trinitarian unity than that of the
> divine economy. It is the Trinity *ad extra*, that is, the solicitude of the divine
> hypostases for the universe. It is the Trinitarian love offered to all humans,
> into which they are invited through the mystery of its economy. There is a
> kind of salvation given by the Church simply through the act of loving.[21]

This dense theological reflection exposes the Orthodox understanding of the
work of salvation; in it, G. Khodr chiefly emphasises the act of love that is the
intrinsic characteristic of the being who is God. The communion of the baptised
who gather in the witnessing church are born of the communion of the Trinity
and are the incarnation of this unique pattern of sacrificial love gifted by God to
all of humanity. The way in which each baptised person embodies the principal
challenges of the Gospel in today's fluid intercultural plurality lends vitality to
the Christian community. This kind of human life is authentically shared and celebrated in communion with the source of all gifts. The Church's whole being then
flares up in love and solicitude for all its human brothers and sisters.

In other words, Christianity should profess one and only one truth: the fraternal
love that transcends all confessional barriers. It is love, not the Church as such, that
saves the world. G. Khodr insists on this fundamental aspect of Christian life in
order to show that the absolute priority is the witness of the life of each individual

---

21 G. Khodr, 'La responsabilité et le témoignage prophétique du chrétien dans la cité', op. cit.

given to today's world. This incarnation of the Kingdom of love becomes real in the most personal of ways thanks to the baptised, who are so variously implanted in the living substance of social, political and cultural life.

G. Khodr wants to celebrate within the Orthodox Church the coherence of Christian lives and the harmonious rooting of the Church into the world. In a text that illustrates his deep attachment to the Orthodox faith, he portrays the way – which he sees as unique – in which Orthodox theology understands the authenticity of a fully committed Christian life:

> In contrast to Protestantism, Orthodox Christianity does not accept that faith
> should be privatised. Faith cannot be understood without the tradition of the
> Fathers, of the councils, of liturgy, of canon law and thus of the community.
> And the community is integrated and comprehensive. It is based on the notion
> that Alexis Khomiakov called *sobornost*, a form of symphonic concord of
> one and many, of the existence of all in the one. It is not integrated in the
> same way as the Roman Church, which is highly structured, pyramidal –
> even though Yves Congar rejects this term. The great freedom of Orthodox
> Christianity is a life outside of state structures, lived in eschatological hope,
> almost indifferent to the historical context, especially the tragedy of the Fall,
> in spite of the extraordinary significance of the Paschal event. Resurrection,
> however, is experienced in the Eucharist and in the keen expectation of its
> fulfilment in the *parousia*. This may partly explain how despotism has existed
> alongside intense religious life in both Byzantium and Russia. It may also
> explain the Church's servility towards the lawless former Soviet Union, where
> life was a dichotomy that in the end was a monstrous form of schizophrenia.
> Maybe it is only possible to have a healthy relationship with modernity if
> Pope Peter, Pastor Paulus and the monk John, whom Vladimir Solovioff
> described as the representatives of the three Christian confessions, were to
> come back to life to face the Antichrist.[22]

With analytical lucidity, G. Khodr shows how Orthodoxy, by ignoring the structures of the world, can also ignore the political aberrations of human society. Importantly, however, this reflection highlights the comprehensive nature of the Orthodox understanding of the world. It brings together the world and the Church into the same dynamic of salvation. If in Christianity everything comes down to love, then in the midst of a complex reality beset by uncertainty it is important

---

22 G. Khodr, 'Le christianisme oriental et l'homme moderne', op. cit.

to identify criteria for discernment. In this light, the ecumenical call for agreement among Christians and for deep collaboration conveys their desire for joint
conversion efforts, in solidarity and fraternity, to satisfy the requirements of the
Kingdom.

In seeking to identify the distinctive vision of Orthodoxy, our Orthodox theologian does not shy away from exposing the fragility and lacunae of ossified
approaches to the Christian faith. If the Church is to take its place at the heart of
the reality of the world, then Christians need to become increasingly aware of the
demands of everyday life. The wise course of action is to observe daily life and
learn from it rather than seek to impose set patterns. The baptised should therefore
not rely on preconceived religious ideas to engage with the world, but start from
the human needs that surround them. If and when the world and ecclesiastical
tradition act in harmful concert,[23] then Christians need to condemn and foil their
unhelpful strategies.

Ultimately, Christian faith is designed for the world and seeks to become
incarnate in the world. Even though the appearance of the world is constantly
changing,[24] faith remains a force for conversion to the supreme treasure of sacrificial love. And because it acts on the human heart, the seat of all hopes and
dreams, this force can adapt to variations. The Church, as a body set in the
unforgiving stuff of life, is inevitably subject to the inherent vulnerability and
changeableness of historic reality. G. Khodr therefore states realistically: 'As
long as there is sin, the Church will not succeed in being completely faithful.'[25]
This fallibility, characteristic of the Church, in no way prevents it from being the
locus for *metanoia* and permanent healing. G. Khodr suggests that renouncing a
now obsolete historic form might be one way to demonstrate the force for conversion that inhabits the Church. 'I am convinced that even if the world loses its
sense of direction it will never prevent lives of prayer and fraternal love. Starting
now, the Church needs to prepare for a probable future worldwide civilisation.
Our church life has a heaviness to it that will eventually lift. But we know that

---

23 On the matter of liturgical conservatism, for example, G. Khodr has formulated an
extremely bold sociological analysis: 'It seems to me that the the origins of a certain stiffness
in Orthodox liturgy lie at least in part in social conservatism. Social and liturgical contexts
work in tandem. This seems clear, even though liturgy develops according to its own laws.'
Ibid.
24 See J. Hatem, 'L'épiphanie du visage chez Georges Khodr', in *Contacts*, 141, 1988,
pp. 50–68.
25 G. Khodr, 'La responsabilité et le témoignage prophétique du chrétien dans la cité', op. cit.

the truth of Christ will last eternally and will find its own words.'[26] If the truth of Christianity first and foremost relates to the freedom of humans so that they may better find their place in the dynamic of sacrificial love, then it is important for Christians to see more clearly the differences and similarities in their experiences of relationship with the Other and of communion with God. In the midst of a changeable and unpredictable world, the most basic Christian truth remains that it depends not on a historic form of the Church, but on the reality of conversion and sanctification as experienced and blessed within the heart of the Christian community itself. G. Khodr thus prepares the theological ground for the probable development of a world in which the institutional Church will no longer have any significance, even if that world will still be thirsting for a true communion of freedom among humans.

The most important commitment for a Christian: to combat injustice and poverty

The Word of God, a word of life and of freedom, needs to be heard in the very midst of the world. Contemporary humanity, now more than ever, needs a word that will bring freedom from its own demons. Illusions of power have invaded our world and blocked the way to conviviality and communion. It is G. Khodr's profound conviction that the Gospel is a word of judgement. Instead of feeding the horror of inquisitions and condemnations, however, this judgement is a word of love that urges us to open up in solidarity to each other. All selfishness and indifference are then clearly the work of the human demon who sows division and discord: 'The Word exposes all peoples [...], the strength of Yahweh is deployed over the world and his justice terrifies Israel in its faithlessness.'[27] More precisely, the Word of God comes to abolish all dividing walls and separations. His word has the capacity to criticise and to discern salvation, and through it anyone can be emboldened to help build up humanity.

Humanity, however, suffers from injustice, segregation and oppression. The Word of God reminds us of the urgent need to take the side of the oppressed and the poor. The most telling confirmation that the message has been understood, the sign of truth, is simply a concrete gesture of fraternal solicitude. The poor then become themselves the altar for the great sacrifice:

---

26 G. Khodr, 'La responsabilité et le témoignage prophétique du chrétien dans la cité', op. cit.
27 *Ibid.*

You will be well aware that liturgy is not only the destination when we convert, but also the point of departure for our love, according to the beautiful words of Saint John Chrysostom, who speaks of the altar of the poor as being greater than the communion table: 'You can see this altar (the poor), he says, raised everywhere in the streets and you can sacrifice upon it at any time'.[28]

A sacramental theology is strongly linked, or even subordinated, here, to an explicit and bold theology of liberation. When we take into account the judgement of God, the altar that is the poor becomes the first altar, against which others are measured, the very best liturgical altar.

If this is the case, then any commitment by Christians on behalf of the poor must follow this strong lead that evokes the purification of the Temple. Any force used merely symbolises the determination that drives activity undertaken for the sake of the poor:

For today's Christians, Christ's purification of the Temple must be constantly repeated in the Temple of the nation on behalf of the poor, and throughout the world on behalf of the disinherited peoples who today are those that God favours especially with his love because they reflect the image of his Son nailed to the Cross.[29]

Liberation theology, as understood and commended by G. Khodr, does not advocate violence[30] but rather embraces a firm determination to defend those who suffer humiliation across the world. This same Word of God draws those held down by suffocating torpor and death and calls them to life and joy. The Cross becomes the symbol of the fight to ensure the emancipation of all. If the world

---

28 *Ibid.*
29 *Ibid.*
30 According to G. Khodr, Orthodox theology condemns all forms of violence, even when it claims to be holy: 'Saint John Chrysostom condemns as anathema anyone who says it is his duty to kill a heretic. The Orthodox Church itself refuses violence and thus accepts religious diversity as a mystery and a mark of human conviviality. No human group has to the same extent embraced a spirituality of gentleness. [...] Nor has any group created the same link as has the Orthodox Church between glory and suffering. The Orthodox Church is thus par excellence the Church of John, of the Light of Thabor, the one that shows the magnificent splendour of the glory of Christ. Hence it has been effective as the Church of the poor, the Church of true destitution, of impoverished priests.' G. Khodr, 'Le christianisme oriental et l'homme moderne', *op. cit.*). See also G. Khodr, *Law hakaitu masrâ-t-tufûlah, op. cit.*, p. 122–123.

is a battlefield on which the powers of life face the powers of death,[31] then the Christian can longer remain neutral or, worse, simply use empty words.[32] The first duty of the baptised, therefore, is to snatch humanity from destruction. That is the greatest commandment of the Gospel. Accumulated injustices seem to threaten mankind with annihilation. Such a deadly threat must be met in the spirit of the Beatitudes, which restore human dignity. The mysticism of the Beatitudes, however, does not fit well with the kind of liberation theology that aims to change the structures of injustice. G. Khodr wants to find space within contemporary Orthodox theology for the thesis, so feared by official Catholic theology, of unjust structures that invalidate any temporary material assistance:

> The blessed Augustine wrote: You give bread to the hungry; but it would be better for none to be hungry and for you to give to no one. Augustine dreamt of radical social change. The Fathers hardly envisaged a state order that would include social measures. Modern revolutionary thought has created the notion of structure. We need to involve ourselves in it so as to avoid as far as possible finding new victims along the path of our life.[33]

For such a theology does indeed demand a radical change in the social, economic, political and cultural structures that alienate not only individual spirits but also, and especially, the collective mindset of mankind. The primary aim here, therefore, is radical evangelistic commitment. The Beatitudes allow no room for half-measures or lukewarm compromise.

The Christian who truly commits to the Beatitudes needs to learn to tread warily around the gentle kindness that mires anything uncertain in inextricable and intolerable confusion. By resolutely choosing the conversion of the heart, Christian faith as lived and understood by G. Khodr condemns mystical and false irenics.

---

31 In the same spirit of analytical lucidity, G. Khodr wonders whether the Orthodox Church is truly aware of the realities of human history as it evolves, wrenched, crucified and suffocating: 'I do not know whether our Fathers were as obsessed by Greek thought, which was insensitive to the drama of history.' (G. Khodr, 'La responsabilité et le témoignage prophétique du chrétien dans la cité', op. cit.)

32 'If the Orthodox Church displays in its visible life a detachment from earthly treasures, then it will be truly present to the suffering of mankind. And this presence will be far more eloquent than any words timidly urging charity.' (*Ibid.*)

33 *Ibid.*

I am aware that political peace is only one option for us: it is a way that we can express our faithfulness to God, but it does not necessarily do good to the soul. But we should not be quick to judge the spiritual consequences of peace. It can pave the way for hedonism, for a levelling of spiritual life. But we should not resign ourselves to the flagrant injustice that denies the dignity of the weak, the hungry, the illiterate on Earth.[34]

If God's word is radical and opens up the prospect of emancipation, do these words constitute an involuntary reversal? They pinpoint how solidarity could be compromised by unfocused moves towards peace, so they do not diminish the urgent need for commitment. In fact, the comparison he suggests sounds a loud alarm for all those who allege the superiority of the spiritual kingdom as a way of evading their responsibility as citizens. The Gospel, if it is not firmly integrated in the course of history, degenerates into a place of alienation. Christians need therefore constantly to exercise evangelical discernment so that they stay attuned to the suffering of their human brothers and sisters.

The deliverance of mankind will only come about thanks to the witnesses of life and truth. Following in the footsteps of the man Jesus, it is Christians who can take on the serious responsibility of being such witnesses. G. Khodr says that love is the preferred name of God who became man, and that therefore all words that come from Him are an opportunity for a truly human conversion:

We have here a community of disciples born again through water and the Spirit, obeying the command of love, united with their Master through the history of mankind and offering Christ through the power of love. The word is a sign, a reminder, the presence of this Master. It refers to Him. It is He who transfigures it. He is both below and beyond the word. He is secret and marks the presence of God. He is the name of the God who cannot be named, as Maximus the Confessor suggested.[35]

In truth, commitment on behalf of the poor is the only action that truly reveals the identity of God. When Christians give themselves both body and soul to the cause of mankind,[36] God will be carried into the midst of humanity through a

---

34 *Ibid.* He counts the dialogue among the poor as the truly authentic form of dialogue. Neither Christianity nor Islam will be able to engage in true dialogue if they succumb to the temptation of riches (see G. Khodr, *Law hakaitu masrâ-t-tufûlah, op. cit.*, p. 35).
35 G. Khodr, 'La communication du message en terre d'islam', op. cit., p. 374.
36 Being present with others is an act of identification through which we can share profoundly

deep outpouring of authentic human cooperation. The words that announce this are only signs. Christ will appear in the world only through active commitment. In other words, only this kind of action can make the world more Christlike by transfiguring it in the image of the perfect Man, Jesus Christ, the love gift of God.

We have examined the theological background that determines the thinking and commitment of G. Khodr. These introductory reflections will, I hope, have pulled together and briefly presented the theological convictions that G. Khodr has presented through various texts and in various places. The core notion that drives the entire body of his thought is nothing other than love offered freely to mankind. It is a love that only makes sense when it is realised in the crucible of human reality, expressed in material flesh and blood individuals still thirsting to be wholly human. Any person truly and fruitfully experiencing that realisation must however first know themselves to be authentically free in their choices of both action and commitment. Here we are moving towards a definition of theological anthropology in which human dignity is founded upon liberty. And here begins a struggle that demands both patience and perseverance to reclaim the freedom that has been alienated through institutional structures. Work towards the freedom of mankind will then go hand in hand with an unconditional spirit of solidarity with the poor of the Earth. Before they can fully celebrate Christ, the baptised need to have celebrated the restoration of full dignity to mankind. G. Khodr builds on this fundamental understanding in formulating his theology of conviviality, a theology which seeks to be open-hearted towards the Other while fully respecting the free will that is integral to the mystery of divine love.

The unicity of divine love as foundation for an Arab theology of conviviality

The unfathomable mystery of the liberty of God

In his search for a solid theological basis for Arab conviviality, G. Khodr counts today's worldwide diversity as a force for good. Guided by a great optimism, he sets out to examine intercultural and interreligious diversity in order to unearth signs of divine wisdom. In the diverse environment that is characteristic of contemporary humanity, if no one can claim to hold the whole truth, then we must prioritise joint reflection on how best to nurture the various sensitivities and

---

in the condition of the poor of the world. This alone will guarantee true conviviality (see G. Khodr, *Law hakaitu masrâ-t-tufûlah, op. cit.*, p. 36).

approaches which create an urgent need for dialogue. Khodr chooses to explore the patristic tradition in search of ways in which to promote a new theological interpretation of diversity.[37] The Arab experience of Muslim–Christian conviviality remains the fundamental point of reference and the appropriate sphere for this work of reflection.

If the fundamental principle underlying G. Khodr's theological thinking is the freely given love of God, then the fundamental and unique characteristic of that love is freedom. In that, it faithfully reflects the nature of God's Kingdom. Love, if it is to be genuine, must be able to act freely. And freedom without love degenerates into arbitrary madness. G. Khodr maintains that there is a diversity of religious paths precisely because God dispenses a plurality of love:

> The gift of God is free, because God is not tied to the text of Scripture nor to the forms of worship through which he relates to us. The freedom of God is clearly announced in the sacred book: 'God desires everyone to be saved and to come to the knowledge of truth' (1 Tim 2, 3). Surely this great universal hope is undergirded by a respect for all religions as religious systems? And might not each of these religious systems somehow be one of the sites of revelation and thus an aspect of God's plan for the salvation of all peoples?[38]

In this text G. Khodr dissociates the God inscribed in Scripture from His revelation. God, being totally free, is thus well outside any specific historical context. Even the Bible cannot exhaustively describe God, whose very essence is love and freedom. Because of this dissociation, belief in the divine nature of Jesus is no longer a thoughtless abstract certainty, a kind of ahistorical truth, and becomes instead a way of interrogating reality, an attitude of openness to the mystery of divine transcendence. The notion of God is set free, and the ways in which humanity variously perceives and experiences religion become relative.

We should note here that contemporary Orthodox theological writing rarely exhibits such prophetic boldness. In his openness of mind, Khodr suggests that the freedom of God even sanctions a plurality of instruments for salvation. The term has yet to be endorsed by contemporary Orthodox theology. His recognition, however, of the legitimacy of various religious systems, which is explicitly present

---

37 Being anxious to spread the word of God, G. Khodr engages with the impasse that is human language. The challenge was to preserve the transcendence of the Word in the context of the finite history of human life (see G. Khodr, *Law hakaitu masrâ-t-tufûlah, op. cit.*, pp. 26–27).

38 G. Khodr, 'Le christianisme, l'islam et l'arabité', in *Contacts*, 1980, XXXII, 110, p. 106.

in this text, hints at an evolving theological position that will clearly support the notion. The Bible, as a covenant text with an infinite horizon, itself bears witness to the many paths offered to the peoples of the Earth:

> God is not only the God of Israel, but also the Saviour of the world, and he must therefore, in his multifaceted wisdom, take care of the whole world. The various ways in which the Creator rescues mankind were called by the Early Fathers of the Church 'promises' or 'provisions'. According to Saint Irenaeus, at the Last Judgement the Lord will say to all who have died: 'Come to me, you who have been blessed by my Father'. The same saint added: 'The Word, who always helped mankind according to various provisions, who does mighty works, saves from the first those who are saved: those who love God and, in their own way, follow the Word of God'.[39]

Clearly, Christian theology of religions cannot discount a divine wisdom that works in many different ways to bring about the history of salvation.

In this patristic hermeneutics, G. Khodr prefers to avoid the equivocal notion of instruments of salvation. He firmly chooses the vocabulary used by the Early Fathers. The 'provisions of salvation', the 'various ways', the 'multifaceted wisdom', the 'signs placed by God within religions', the 'enlightenments and illuminations' are some of the expressions he uses to convey the range and riches of the divine economy. The ultimate conviction of the Orthodox Bishop of Mount Lebanon is that God never ceases deploying his plan of salvation for the joy of all mankind, expressing it each time in the particular way that will register with the ways in which the beneficiaries will listen, receive and interact. In closing this meditation, he concludes that there truly is a plurality of economies of salvation, generously offered to the whole of humanity:

> This patristic reflection can all be more or less expressed through this thought from Irenaeus: 'There is only one God who, from the beginning to the end came to the aid of mankind through various dispensations' (*Adv. Haer.* III, 12–13).[40]

---

39 *Ibid.*, pp. 107–108.

40 G. Khodr, 'Christianisme dans un monde pluraliste. L'économie du Saint Esprit', Irénikon, 1971, 2, p. 194. According to G. Khodr, God dwells in the heart in his own way, for divine love transcends all human dogmas and institutions (G. Khodr, *Law hakaitu masrâ-t-tufûlah, op. cit.*, pp. 14–16).

The divine unicity is thus shown to be the unifying principle for all the scattered manifestations that have adorned the religious history of humanity. Each divine manifestation is received to the extent that mankind is able to apprehend it. This is necessarily the filter for any response to the mystery of God. By becoming present and active deep within the particular history of the peoples of the Earth, God commits His own self within the limits of a culturally relevant relationship. In other words, He freely, and within the limits of contemporary relativity, presents Himself to people who then receive Him in the light of their current lives. The context makes for tentative understanding, inevitably limited and imperfect, expressed, if at all, in incomplete words that cannot be completely fulfilled.

The diverse economy of the Spirit

In order to achieve openness to the mystery of God, G. Khodr suggests that Christian theology should commit more fully to the work of the Spirit. The Spirit is the aspect of the work of God that most clearly intervenes in the historical context of incarnation. This means that the Spirit of God can work towards achieving salvation alongside the mediation of Jesus Christ. Khodr's audacious reflection on the status of the Spirit in the economy of salvation appears to confirm a wider scope for the divine economy.

> The economy of Christ is not limited to His historical appearance, but rather it makes us partakers in the very life of God, which therefore brings in the notion of eternity, and the activity of the Holy Spirit. The very notion of the economy is a notion of mystery, and when we think of mystery, we also think of strength, of the impetus of an event, and of the freedom of God, whose work of providence and redemption is not bound to any specific event. [...] The Church's work is to read – through the veil of the mystery of which the Church is a sign – all the other signs that God has planted in various successive historical times, and even in religions, so as to reveal to the world of the religions the God who is concealed within, in preparation for the final and concrete revelation of the mystery.[41]

The God who does not depend on any scriptural tradition and is not bound by any redemptive activity is, according to G. Khodr, the source of the generous

---

41 G. Khodr, 'Christianisme dans un monde pluraliste. L'économie du Saint-Esprit', op. cit., pp. 196–197.

diversity of gestures of love and solicitude. Rather than limit the mediation of Christ to within the confines of His historical sociocultural context, the Spirit extends it to embrace the whole of mankind. Extended, it is able to adopt a wide variety of forms, according to the cultural contexts within which it operates. Despite the unity and solidarity of the three messengers of Trinitarian love, the Spirit is especially able to use cultural media to bring about the work of salvation, in ways that differ considerably from the traditional Christian norm. A theology of the Spirit thus preserves Christology from the temptation to limit its cultural and institutional ambitions. As we shall see below, the Church should gratefully acknowledge signs of the presence of the Spirit beyond the frame of traditional Christian sociocultural expectations.

G. Khodr, faithful to the intuitions of Eastern patristics about the Spirit, emphasises the freedom of God by conceding the principle that divine love might be able to work for redemption outside the Christian tradition. Rather than engaging with this work of emancipation from outside, that is, from a position of religious neutrality, he works from inside, by revisiting the question of the Spirit. And here he posits that there are two distinct divine economies:

> The Spirit is present everywhere, making His presence felt in an economy distinct from that of the Son. The Word and the Spirit are called by Irenaeus the 'two hands of the Father'. Here, we are not only confirming their hypostatic independence but also conceding that the coming of the Holy Spirit into the world is not dependent on the Son, and is not the work of the Word. [...] It is the Spirit that enthrones Christ here and there, as Irenaeus so eloquently puts it: Where the Spirit is, there is the Church (*Adv. Haer.* III, 24). The Spirit expends His energy according to His own economy and we can thus consider non-Christian religions to be sites where He is inspired to operate.[42]

A new theology of the Spirit takes shape here as these ideas point to the development of a space reserved especially for the work of the Spirit. The distinction that Khodr introduces between the activity of Christ and the activity of the Spirit suggests that some of humanity can be saved by the Spirit, and that this is fully in accordance with his most authentic religious hopes.

Even if a work of redemption is not explicitly attributed to the Spirit, this new theological perception, deriving from Orthodox teaching, presupposes a scope for

---

42 *Ibid.*, p. 200.

activity that is similar to Christ's own. 'All those whom the Spirit visits are the
people of God.'[43] So it is through openness to the Spirit of God, the spirit of mercy
and fraternity, the spirit of goodness and gentleness, the spirit of authenticity and
creativity, that the people of God realise their vocation. This vocation cannot be
judged by defining an assumed metaphysical relationship with the divine being,
since any such relationship cannot be apprehended or measured, but rather by
looking at human attitudes to openness to others, to solidarity during an ordeal,
and to fraternal communion. Because they are the people of God, members of the
religious community who have been touched by the work of the Spirit develop
the characteristics of those who have been saved through the mediation of Jesus
Christ.

In any case, the universal economy of salvation will only come to pass in the
ultimate perspective of the fullness of time: 'True fullness will be experienced at
the Second Coming. The economy of salvation will be realised in relation to that
final, ultimate meaning of things. The economy of Christ cannot be comprehended
without the economy of the Spirit.'[44] The real meaning of true fullness is linked to
the mystery of divine solicitude. That there is such a variety of religious pathways
shows us the divine desire to honour the rich breadth of hope for sincerity in the
human heart. Those who are moved by the work of the Spirit try to express in
many and various ways the mysterious and exhilarating presence of God in the
midst of human history. Rather than simply reciting a non-committal dogmatic
formula about their faith in the work of God, they devote themselves to a relationship of love and a covenant of faithfulness. The lifestyle that the Spirit inspires
in them gradually evolves into an attitude of openness and commitment to the
loving plan God has for each individual person. This is the experience of those
today who, each in their own way, try to respond to the bidding of the Spirit and
find that through Him they discover the transcendence of love and of freedom. The
Spirit is working in the very heart of each of us according to the divine strategy
that also set in motion the redeeming work of Jesus Christ. The Spirit thus not
only permeates all human attempts at sincerity but also, and especially, undergirds
the work of Jesus Christ Himself. It is the Spirit Himself who powers the reviving touch of Christ in the human heart. If this is true, then through the Spirit all
people, whatever their religious allegiance, can know Christ; better still, they can

---

43 *Ibid.*, p. 200. According to G. Khodr, 'the Holy Spirit is the editor of our spiritual life' (G.
Khodr, *Law hakaitu masrâ-t-tufûlah, op. cit.*, p. 70).
44 G. Khodr, 'Christianisme dans un monde pluraliste. L'économie du Saint-Esprit', *op. cit.*,
p. 199.

know the essence of Christ in their own way, according to the sensitivities of their own hopes and expectations. Thanks to the Spirit, we humans will experience the coming of Christ in a multitude of ways within our own specific place in history and culture.

The vast spaces where the Word becomes incarnate

We must conclude, then, that the variety of human religious experiences are stimulated by the Spirit of God Himself. The same Spirit continues to work and to manifest Himself in different ways through time and space, in different cultures and traditions. G. Khodr insists on this fundamental aspect of the work of the Spirit, yet in his theological writing he also emphasises the centrality of the person of Christ in the context of the Christian faith. The Word of God epitomises within Himself the key authentic truths that are quietly seeded in the soil of human diversity:

> I think the believer normally starts from the *Logos* in order to perceive the *logoi spermatikoi.* When we receive the *Logos* in faith, he refers us to the *logoi*. Once revealed as wisdom, He awakens in us the wisdom inherited from human culture. Without the Spirit, who leads us into all truth, we remain prisoners of our own mortality.[45]

G. Khodr's *Logos* is Himself an unconditional open embrace to the whole creation. He is present in all the efforts within cultures and societies towards achieving authenticity.[46] His identity is defined though relationship. It is therefore unthinkable that Christians should isolate themselves within their own particular way of understanding the Incarnation of the Word of God.

The profound theological conviction that illumines all of G. Khodr's writing is that faithfulness to the Word of God necessarily involves an openness to all the

---

45 G. Khodr, 'Grandeur et humilité de Dieu', in Collectif, *Grandeur de Dieu. Perceptions chrétiennes et musulmanes, op. cit.*, p. 20.

46 G. Khodr appears here to support the theology of the anonymous Christian advocated by K. Rahner in his inclusivist approach to other religions. Any of us, according to G. Khodr, can behave in a paschal way, as a person truly resurrected in the Kingdom, even if on the theological level we remain unaware of it (see G. Khodr, *Law hakaitu masrâ-t-tufûlah, op. cit.*, pp. 87–88). Beyond this Christological focus, in our innermost souls, each of us humans belongs to the intimate family of God and is fully involved in the communion God has established with the cosmos (*Ibid.* p. 97).

manifestations of the Word offered in other religious traditions. If the Word is essentially a relational being then he will not allow his activity and influence to be limited by the institutional framework of the Church. The Christian faith has a relational force that energises Christians to admire the presence of that same Word in the diversity of other religious traditions:

> If the Son of God is the light of the world, a light that has been active since
> the creation of the world, then in all places and times He will have left flashes
> of His light and signs of His touch. Light anywhere implies also shadow, and
> this is why we say that the shadow of Christ is picked out in the Bible. We are
> walking towards God through the shadows, through the most deeply hidden
> places in the Old Testament.[47]

Using this image, we could think that the flashes of light available to other religions faithfully reflect the splendour of the light of the Word. We still need to know, however, whether the wide variety of light flashes might compromise the unity of the light. In other words, we need to identify the limits of what is acceptable among the infinite variety of convictions and religious practices of the many parts of our one human race.

Here G. Khodr seems to want to exercise his prophetic boldness in a completely fresh direction: he wishes to a certain extent to relativise Christian salvation history. He has two intentions here. On the one hand, he wishes to ensure that Jesus Christ's achievement through the economy of redemption remains a central tenet of Christian faith. On the other hand, he hopes to enable other paths towards the economy of salvation to achieve their own legitimacy. These two aims appear contradictory, but he attempts to reconcile them in the following statement:

> This has persuaded me to relativise the notion of salvation history. This idea
> is certainly linked to the tendency for Eastern thought to understand through
> historicisation. The vision of Christ as simply the end of the history of the
> Old Covenant cannot, it seems to me, be reconciled to the eschatological
> aspects of the faith and of life in the Church, as it seems to overlook the aspect
> of mystery. Mystery is the force and the breath of the event. It cannot be
> historicised, just as the Church does not become an institution, but remains a
> charismatic place. [...] The Church therefore does not remain a closed society,
> nor simply an expanding society. It does not constitute a nation. And it is the

---

47 G. Khodr, 'Le christianisme, l'islam et l'arabité', op. cit. p. 105.

same Christ who is present not only within it, but also beyond its historical boundaries. And those who have not been baptised by the Church, as Saint Nicholas Kabasilas well understood, have been baptised by the Bridegroom of the Church. Christ is genuinely present less in the event than in the Epiphany. This last statement is truly prophetic.[48]

According to G. Khodr, the event of Incarnation and redemption should not be understood as a universal principle that can be understood by anyone, is valid always and everywhere, and is able to be incorporated into the lives of cultures and societies. If he prefers to speak of mystery rather than event, it is most probably because mystery offers a unique access into the reality of history. His theological statement reflects his bold thinking in that it embraces the full energy of ecumenism among Christians and religions.

For Christ did not come in order to set the event of the Incarnation in stone. Rather, He seeks to relativise the absolute fact of the love of God by making it accessible to everyone. Relativising the absolute of God in this way does not in any way diminish the divine transcendence. Rather, it allows Christ to reveal Himself freely to the very heart of each person, and in the crucible of their experience. This is why G. Khodr advocates seeing the presence of Christ not as a factual event but more as a disclosure or Epiphany in which the God who longs to define human life, and to be the frame of reference for the fullness of life, offers Himself again and again.

This theologically bold position enables G. Khodr to see Christ as an epiphanic manifestation of the absolutely free love of God. His epiphany is a generous response to humanity's quest: the God of the future has already appeared in the lives of mankind, bringing the joy of sincerity and fulfilment:

All study of religions is a study of Christ. It is Christ, and Christ alone, who is received as the light when a Brahmin, a Buddhist or a Muslim receive grace through reading their scriptures. And whenever a martyr dies for the cause of truth, or a person is persecuted for what they believe is justice, that person dies with Christ. The Islamic mystics who witnessed crucifying love were experiencing the unique *Agape* of John. If the tree is known by its fruits, there is no possible doubt that the poor, those who live in darkness in all nations and

---

48 G. Khodr, 'Les chrétiens d'Orient dans un contexte pluraliste', Lecture given in Geneva on 1 March 2001, and published on the website of the Greek Orthodox Archdiocese of Mount Lebanon, www.ortmtlb.org.lb

look to God for their hope, already receive the peace that the Lord grants to
those whom he loves (Luke 2, 14).[49]

The various religious experiences of humanity can be infused and irradiated
by the presence of Christ. So we are justified in thinking that this Christ reveals
Himself in different ways, according to the context within which he is received.
The many different forms of these revelations enable the Christian faith, without
undermining the unity of Christ, to understand and respect the diversity of religious traditions.

This kind of approach thus clearly derives from Christological inclusivity, in
which Christ remains the central reference point for any understanding of the
divine presence in the very heart of human history. To display such theological
open-mindedness, however, a person must above all be willing to accept a wide
range of manifestations of Christ that claim adherence to the complete freedom
of God. We would in such a case be looking at an attitude of inclusiveness and
implicit pluralism. Even if G. Khodr does not explicitly defend the idea of multiple revelations of salvation, he accepts the notion that there might be a range of
religious experiences in which Christ offers Himself freely in a culturally appropriate language of faith. In such cases, Christ might not be the name officially,
explicitly and necessarily invoked in any religious experience, but may nevertheless be the path towards the truth. When no particular historical manifestation can
lay exclusive claim to mediating the whole truth, then the only place where that
truth is revealed is and always will be the life that God so generously offers to all
mankind. Yet the Christ of the Christian faith claims to be life itself, overflowing
with energy and generosity, a life in which meet sharing and fulfilment. If the
truth of Christ is life in all its fullness and authenticity, any theological approach
to truth must therefore translate into commitment and action. The truth of Christianity is none other than the truth of the life that God grants in Jesus Christ. This
is not a truth that is merely theoretical or conceptual, but rather one that should
be borne out in the midst of lived reality. And in consequence, other religions can
be received and interpreted in the light of Christ, who is the ultimate symbol of
truth in life.

---

49 G. Khodr, 'Christianisme dans un monde pluraliste. L'économie du Saint-Esprit', op. cit.,
pp. 198–199. According to G. Khodr, Christ is the crucible or the meeting point for the
generosity of the whole universe (see G. Khodr, *Law hakaitu masrâ-t-tufûlah, op. cit.*, p. 88).

The true status of the Church as mediator

G. Khodr's ecclesiology occupies the mid-ground between the homogenising effect of the centralised Catholic Church and the diversity of the dispersed Protestant Churches, and is inspired by patristic theology, in which the nature and function of the Church is ostentatiously subordinated to the liberating work of Christ. He therefore has a far more nuanced sense of the Church and its mission at the heart of the world's diversity. He attempts to pinpoint where it is that the truth of Christianity is most clearly revealed: 'There is a sense in which Christianity is not exclusive. It is depth, but it is not everything. I wrote a few years ago that it is anathema to equate the one with the whole.'[50] Only this kind of boldness can shake the official view of the absolutely central nature of the Church. If Christianity, as a historic development and a spiritual tradition, can be seen as a need for depth, then it will better serve Christ's fundamental mission to emancipate all people and help each person achieve fullness of life. If, on the other hand, Christianity sets itself up as a strict framework of reference, compulsory for any authentic experience of human life, then Christ's fundamental mission will be pushed aside by the power structures of the Church.[51] G. Khodr therefore prefers to invite people to experience Christ for themselves rather than force them into a systematic adherence to the Church:

> There is no need to draw people into the Church. They will come of their own accord when they feel that it is the house of their Father. But there is a need to identify the Christlike values in the other religions, to demonstrate that Christ is the link to them, and that His love extends from them. The true mission does not take mission seriously. Our only duty is to identify and trace the marks of Christ through the shadows of the religions. [...] The missionary activity of the Church is to wake Christ where he slumbers in the shadows of the religions.[52]

---

50 G. Khodr, 'La liberté religieuse. Vision orthodoxe', op. cit., p. 60.

51 By identifying itself with ethnic groups and sociopolitical realities the Church has followed a risky path and jeopardised its mission to serve the kingdom of God. A critical historical approach on this subject by Khodr aims to analyse how this has happened: 'We should also examine the extent to which the wars between the Byzantines and the Arabs defined the *oikoumene* as being coextensive with the Church in the Middle East. In other words, ecclesiology, because of the armed struggle of medieval Christianity – both Latin and Byzantine – became a historicised ecclesiology: the Church adopted the sociological clothes of the Christian nations.' (G. Khodr, 'Christianisme dans un monde pluraliste. L'économie du Saint-Esprit', op. cit., p. 195).

52 G. Khodr, 'Christianisme dans un monde pluraliste. L'économie du Saint-Esprit', op. cit., p. 202.

By definition, the Church is a site of service and fraternity, and should bear the Christ-child first within and second beyond its walls. The first of these is the form of witnessing that is familiar in the traditional secular understanding of Christianity; the second is more problematic. It involves engaging with the absolute freedom of God and the profound humility of Christians who witness to the sovereign divine freedom:

> The Church retains its whole value as mediation. The freedom of God, however, is such that beyond the sociological boundaries of the New Israel He can inspire prophetic vocations as he did outside the boundaries of Ancient Israel. The voices of prophesy and wisdom outside the sanctuary, however, have a secret link to the power of the resurrected Lord and are not in conflict with the uniqueness of the economy of Christ.[53]

There is therefore no need to decree, for the sake of the freedom of God, that the Church has a central role. For this same freedom is able to elicit instances of service and fraternity beyond the visible institutional boundaries of the Church.

We therefore need to ask: where are the boundaries of the Church? Could it, indeed should it, involve the full range of human wisdom? G. Khodr's response is infused with mystic humility:

> The world, once exorcised, will be the Church. This requires us to examine where the limits of the Church are. Ever since Jesus stretched out His arms on the Cross, He has abolished all boundaries. I know that everything should be baptised, but when, and how? What, in the world and in the religions, is not the Church? This is the full mystery of it. However, if the reality of Christ does not subsist in the Church, is it not somehow latent beyond our historical frontiers?[54]

In the last analysis, G. Khodr's theological vision is strongly Christological, in spite of the major part played by the Spirit. The work of the Church as a whole crystallises around the figure of Christ witnessing to the fraternity and communion that embody the fundamental values of the Kingdom. At the heart of these values,

---

53 *Ibid.*, p. 199.
54 G. Khodr, 'La responsabilité et le témoignage prophétique du chrétien dans la cité', op. cit. Christianity, according to G. Khodr, cannot in fact be identified with a human institution. It is an ocean of light filling the whole world, freely and transparently given. Our task as humans is freely to surrender to it (see G. Khodr, *Law hakaitu masrâ-t-tufûlah, op. cit.*, p. 98).

all authentic human life is driven and ultimately drawn by love. The Church is therefore only meaningful and consistent if it is fully dedicated to this mission:

> Christ is not, in the end, a name, or a system, or an institution. Rather, He is a value, an action, He is the force that makes hearts become gentle, simple, humble, and encourages *jihad* on behalf of the suffering. The Church was instituted to proclaim this truth, to live it out and disseminate it. Perfection and fulfilment are not part of the Church as a historical institution, but rather they are part of the Lord who established the Church through the Word, water, the Spirit and blood, so that they would bear witness to God through it. Fulfilment is a description of what the Church will be in the last day, when it will gather the just from every nation and every race, when all the different paths will have disappeared in the face of the love of which they were merely a symbol. And since we are still journeying towards the Kingdom, the Church is our guide and our witness, making every effort transparently to channel the divine light that gives light to all of mankind. Scripture does not explicitly confirm that before the last day, mankind will give the name Jesus Christ to that light. For us, our vocation is to become pure so that we can be the servants who deliver *agape*.[55]

His theological position is crystal clear: the Church must not in any circumstances become the objective of Christian life. The Church only has legitimacy and temporary historical substance thanks to the presence of Christ, to whom it bears witness by word and deed.[56] It should never suggest that it is itself the subject of its own witness. God's coming into the midst of the world is for the Church the supreme critical achievement of its real existence. Indeed, the Church

---

55 G. Khodr, 'Le christianisme, l'islam et l'arabité', op. cit. p. 109. G. Khodr on occasion despairs of the Church as a powerful institution. He is often horrified by the increasing gulf between the Church of theoretical splendour and the Church of prosaic reality (G. Khodr, *Law hakaitu masrâ-t-tufûlah, op. cit.*, pp. 118–119).

56 It is interesting to note how G. Khodr interprets the evangelisation methods used in the Nestorian Church: 'Quite independently of this tradition, the Nestorian Church evangelised in a way that was more or less unique in its contribution to the spiritual development of the religious it encountered, 'improving' them from within (Tibetan Buddhism, China) without any attempt to alienate them. Their mission takes on a spiritual ambition that embraces the whole of creation. The Persian Church in Mesopotamia made the most audacious attempt to welcome Islam. The prophetic character of Muhammad is defined in Nestorian texts in relation to its intrinsic analysis of Muhammad's message. It does not lose any of its key logic or of the ontological unity of Jesus Christ.' (G. Khodr, 'Christianisme dans un monde pluraliste. L'économie du Saint-Esprit', op. cit., p. 196).

will not be able to embrace the fullness of the Kingdom until it gathers together, in a way that only God can direct, the many different spiritual traditions among humanity. In other words, in order to be authentic, the Church needs to be not only ecumenical but also – especially, even – interreligious. At the risk of shocking my readers, I suggest that G. Khodr's theological boldness might attain that level of cosmic universalism.[57]

The implication of a theology of diverse divine economy

What we have seen above suggests that worldwide diversity is in some way an intrinsic part of God's plan of love. His plan came to life when Christ brought peace and redemption. For every person, God desires happiness, and asks Christ to meet that person where they are, at the heart of their socio-historical experience and their daily challenges. Given the diversity of the paths that lead each of us to our most profound truth, which is nothing other than the gift of love written in our heart, Christ's movement towards us cannot possibly be limited to one specific form of religious experience. G. Khodr is well aware of this. He therefore advocates a wider conception of Christ and of His work, one that extends beyond the Incarnation:

> The Logos is more than just His Incarnation. He is in it, but not limited to it. When we say Christos, we also say Chrismation, or anointing by the Spirit, where the Spirit has dwelt from all eternity in the Word. Saint Maximus the Confessor confirmed that the Logos was incarnate in the Word of the Bible and, before Jesus' manifestation – His coming into the world – was also incarnate in the world. A major question still needs addressing: where and how does Christ slumber in the shadows of specific religions? There are legitimate limits to this line of questioning [...] as we do not have the appropriate criterion for an answer. Missiology, especially in the case of Hinduism, has been able to identify aspects of rapprochement, both similarities and divergences. Islamologists have also attempted to outline a Christian theology of Islam. The task is not an easy one, as discerning Christian theologians will be well aware. The apparent similarities can hide differences, or at least nuances, on a variety of matters, possibly even the understanding of God.

---

57 If, as G. Khodr maintains, 'The Church is more than its prelates' (G. Khodr, *Law hakaitu masrâ-t-tufûlah*, *op. cit.*, p. 44), it is because its openness is far more significant than its purely institutional character.

Positive theologies are not easy to superimpose on each other, and therefore to reconcile.[58]

The matter that acutely preoccupies Christian theologians is how to discern the two ways in which Christ is present, within the sacramental life of the Church and outside of it. It is important to remember that although Christ may have appeared in different ways, the unicity of the love of God gifts to Christ Himself an internal coherence and an underlying continuity in all His manifestations. There is therefore no point in asking whether the Christ who offers Himself to the experience of Christians is markedly different from the Christ who makes Himself mysteriously available in the experience of others. It would even be theologically indecent to try to measure for each of the different ways that Christ makes Himself present the extent, the dynamic, the distinctiveness of that experience. The truth is found elsewhere. Mankind needs Christ and all that He means for each person. Whether His truth is attested only within or also beyond the limits of traditional Christian institutions, this does not in any way diminish the radiance of God's love among mankind: 'There is but one difference between people: Christians have a name for their Saviour, whereas the others do not. In each case, the Saviour is one and the same.'[59] G. Khodr is effectively preaching that there is one salvation, reached by a diversity of paths. The diversity can find expression in other cultural forms of salvation. This is true in Islam, for example. There is therefore a pressing need for a new Christian theology of interreligious diversity. The coherence and supreme value of the person of Christ is not jeopardised by different names, nor is the unity of the plan of salvation.

His keen awareness of this need lies behind G. Khodr's call for the apophatic method to be used when looking at other religions:

We need to perceive, behind the symbols and historical formats, the deepest intentions of the believers and link their understanding of divinity to that which is our hope as Christians. That is to say that the apophatic method needs to be applied not only when speaking as Christians about God – since all concepts can be idols – but also, beyond that, to the way we speak of God in the context of non-Christian scriptures. In our understanding of people whose beliefs are different from ours, each person offers a learning experience and

---

58 G. Khodr, 'Les chrétiens d'Orient dans un contexte pluraliste', op. cit.
59 G. Khodr, 'Le christianisme, l'islam et l'arabité', op. cit.

an epiphany, so we should look at them and describe them to appreciate their unique characteristics.[60]

The apophatic method is one we have inherited from the Church Fathers, and enables us to understand the key features of the spirituality of other religious traditions. It also enables us to separate out theological discourse from the more transient cultural vehicles through which it is expressed. Christians are thus given a better understanding of the key aspects of religious experience and its expression in its many socio-historical contexts. At this level, a true encounter becomes possible between religions, and can open the way to a fuller understanding of faith.

Christian theology then becomes a path to appreciating otherness as a challenge to embrace solidarity and complementarity:

> It is completely inconceivable that theologians should give expert opinion on the relationship between Christianity and other religions if their theological thinking has not engaged in a spirit of creative critical analysis with non-Christian religions. Theology, if it is to be substantial, is a process of continuous exchange between biblical revelation and the reality of lived experience. And if we are to follow the Master in true obedience, we must seek out authentic spiritual lives among the non-baptised; this in turn raises the issue of the presence of Christ outside of Christian history. The extraordinary gifts and characters of many non-Christians is such that we need to evolve an ecclesiology and a missiology in which the role of the Holy Spirit takes pride of place.[61]

If we as Christians are to respond to the demands of this innovative approach, we need to re-evaluate the key aspects of different religious paths, and what makes them original; we must start with the Christian path itself, in which the vulnerability of the Cross reveals the depth of God's unconditional love. Christian theological discourse, in seeking to establish a new form of credibility, must have the courage to resist the temptation to superiority and intellectual hegemony. Engagement with non-Christian religions demands an attitude of respect towards their different traditions. G. Khodr may appear to privilege the position of the Christian

---

60 G. Khodr, 'Christianisme dans un monde pluraliste. L'économie du Saint-Esprit', op. cit., p. 201.
61 Ibid., p. 192.

faith by the way in which he situates others in reference to it, but he does constantly remind us that the Other is the place where we find fulfilment:

> Christians will be able to engage in full encounters only when they exclude
> any confessional pride, or sense of superiority related to culture or civilisation.
> Such humility requires Christlike behaviour towards others.[62]

This challenge calls upon Christians fundamentally to reshape their thinking, and indeed the whole of their personal attitudes. Abandoning self-centredness in order to open up to the Other, they should seek to embrace complementarity between religions in a spirit of patient optimism. If Christ is to be found in the shadows of the religions, then He can be wakened when people meditate on, and invest in, the riches and the spiritual ideals of all religious traditions. This could lead to a fresh formulation of Christian discourse, arising from the wonder of encounters between Christians and the believers of other religions.

To achieve such a creative development in Christian theology will require before all else a thoroughgoing trust in the work of the Holy Spirit. The theology of religions, G. Khodr asserts, can be nothing other than a pneumatological theology that examines the extraordinarily fertile yet unobtrusive work of the Spirit in the quiet depths of societies and cultures, and identifies how it compensates for the lack of the religions' identifying characteristics. The new theology of the Spirit rejects all forms of syncretism[63] since it takes a positive view of the existence of other religions, and makes every attempt, from its own point of view, to understand them. This will require a thorough theological conversion, one that will enable Christians to acknowledge the limits to any human approach to the mystery of God. Placing their trust in the Spirit, they will dare to believe the inalienable value of those who are other, different, alien.

A credible and responsible Christian theology of Arab conviviality can thus lay claim to three forms of justification: the absolute liberty of God, the multifarious radiance of the Spirit, and the multiple places in which Christ revealed

---

62 *Ibid.*, p. 201.

63 G. Khodr categorically rejects any form of syncretism that might devalue distinctiveness or erase difference. While seeking out the splendour of truth in its scattered and diverse manifestations, he still insists that this diversity shares a luminescent origin in the person of Christ. He is clear in affirming his inclusive Christology: 'Tertullian was right when he said: every soul is by its nature Christian. In this sense, Christ is constantly born in all the beauty of the world's religions.' (G. Khodr, 'Les racines du Christ', in the Lebanese daily *An-Nahar*, 13 December 1987).

Himself. This new theology advocated by G. Khodr offers a new interpretation of the history of salvation, and demands that we look anew at the work of the divine energy as it accomplishes God's unique plan outside of what we have always seen as the remit and institution of the Church. The lights of the Logos of God illuminate the world and thus contribute to the salvation of all those who wish to embrace the mystery of sacrificial love. Theological open-mindedness of this kind includes an ability to acknowledge the intrinsic value of the great religions and religious traditions of mankind. This kind of Christian faith will enable all the baptised to identify these spiritual riches as coming from God and to understand their message of life and joy in relation to the fundamental values of Christ Himself. And the Spirit Himself will illuminate the mutual understanding and the reciprocity of the exchange. G. Khodr situates his own interpretation of Islam – the otherness that so clearly challenges the Christian communities of the Arab world – in the light of this global approach to religious diversity.

Towards a Christ-inspired Islam: a new theology of Otherness

Existential motivations

G. Khodr sees Islam as far more than simply an object of curiosity for an Arab Christian. Rather, it is a living reality that offers a constant challenge to the mind of Arab Christians. Since the seventh century, Christian communities in the Arab Middle East have had to face up as best they could to the emergence of a new understanding of the universe that embraces theology, spirituality and morality. The new way of thinking and of life preached the absolute transcendence of God and His infinite mercy. And still today Christians in the Arab world have daily and spontaneous contact with Islamic believers. G. Khodr's Islamology can therefore justifiably be labelled an Islamology of proximity:

> I seek signs of Christ everywhere [...] Islam is so very evident around us
> that our first duty is to understand it [...]. We share in the sufferings of this
> population and their daily difficulties are ones we have in common with them.
> This is why I see the interest I have in Islam as a prospective intellectual and
> spiritual partner as contributing to our Orthodox renewal.[64]

---

64 G. Khodr, 'La nature de l'islam', *Courrier œcuménique du Moyen-Orient*, 2007, 54, pp. 48–49.

Given the existential imperative linking Arab Christians to Islam, I consider it inappropriate to attach the label of Islamology to the deep knowledge that G. Khodr has gained about Islam. Islam, as a spiritual dynamic, and as a cultural and socially practical movement, is fully integrated into the character of Arab Christians. The Orthodox bishop is deeply convinced of this, having been born and brought up to the sounds and rhythm of Muslim daily prayers in his native Tripoli, in the north of Lebanon. The future of Arab Christianity therefore seems to depend upon this Islam, which many contemporary theologians rightly see as the frame of reference for the challenge presented to the Christian faith in the context of the Arab world. Any renewal of Christian faith in Arab lands needs to rely on a good understanding of the values and ideals of the Koranic vision of the world.[65]

Even if the Islamic faith is an indivisible whole, many Arab Christians respect the Islamic spirituality of asceticism and trust, the literary elegance of Koranic phraseology, and the authenticity of its spirit of hospitality. Evoking these many riches, G. Khodr often refers to cultural Arab identity and makes a close link to Islam and its basic values:

[We should] remember that the Koran was written in the most beautiful style of our literary history, and that Christians cannot ignore this if they are to address their audience, especially in a church context, in the best Arabic. For us, the language is one of the vehicles for the message. Sometimes, as Christians, we discuss our stylistic preferences in the text of the Koran. Arab cultural identity does exist. If you do not excel, your words will be seen as belonging to everyday language and will not be acceptable. There is a shared Arab sensitivity, and fundamentally, it derives from Islam. And Islam is clearly still a linguistic phenomenon, so in linking with it your witnessing will gain in force. This means that the Church of Antioch, which has an exclusively Arab membership, is especially well equipped to convey the message of the Gospel to Muslims. There is already a real dialogue, based simply on conviviality.[66]

G. Khodr's principal concern at all times remains focused on Christ and his

---

65 G. Khodr, in the light of his responsibilities as a pastor, is quick to express a profound interest in the lives of Muslims. The Orthodox Bishop of Mount Lebanon feels keenly the vital importance of his relationship with Islam and Muslims, not 'as an Islamologist, but as the pastor for the whole population of a country, in the language of that country, on the basis of the one underlying foundation, that is to say, Christ' (*Ibid*, p. 50).
66 *Ibid.*, p. 49.

message of life. Arab Christians, however, cannot announce a Christ who is not incarnate. And any presentation of Christ as present and radiant must be capable of expression in the Arabic language – the only language that is able to reach the furthest corners of the Arab soul. Arab Christians are by their very nature infused with Arab culture. To understand Islam, they need to improve their knowledge of Arabic. In seeking a better command of Arabic, however, they will by the same token discover the splendours of Islam. For the special character of Islam is such that it requires us to see the inextricable link between the content and the vehicle of doctrine. To reach the heart of Islam, we need to enter through its gate. Because they are naturally grounded in Arab culture, Arab Christians can legitimately aspire to this theological, spiritual and mystical transition, which leads to a better understanding of Islam as a whole. In the light of this understanding, they will be better able to find the necessary words and categories to help them speak of Christ.

A Christian understanding of the Koranic 'Other' can make demands and cause difficulties

Through the centuries, the Christian perception of Islam has become freighted with some interpretations that can obscure its meaning. There are any number of examples of hastily drawn conclusions about Islam that have betrayed the core of the Koranic vocation. Throughout his life, G. Khodr has worked to elucidate the true religious vocation of Islam. In his writings, and in the arguments he made, we see the determination of an informed theologian who has undertaken to present to Christians, and sometimes even to Muslims, the true meaning of Islam as a religion of complete trust in God. This has led him to suggest a number of different approaches whenever attempting to identify the true teachings of Islam.

In his theological approach, which underpins his whole understanding of Islam, he recommends first of all to 'examine Muslim theology using the comparative method, in order to seek to discover [...] the nature of Islam'.[67] His ultimate aim in his Islamological research, however, is to highlight the deep affinities between Islam and the Spirit of Christ Himself. In doing this, he is able to see in Islam an autonomous consistency between its ideals and its practices. He therefore rejects all forms of reductionism or hegemony: 'I disagree with Saint John of Damascus, who stated that Islam was a sect of Christianity.'[68] He thus clearly discards as unhelpful an entire medieval Christian polemical tradition. In spite of

---

67 *Ibid.*, p. 39.
68 *Ibid.*, p. 39.

concern for comparison and mutual understanding, generally informed by Christian faith, Islam needs to be acknowledged on its own terms and in reference to its own criteria. Even the Islamological tradition that claims shared descent from Abraham is thoroughly revised. G. Khodr is realistic in his assessment that the thesis suggesting a shared monotheistic perception of the person of Abraham is improbable. 'Thus there is no "objective" Abraham who might provide a place of communion for the three monotheistic religions.'[69] In other words, the three monotheisms cannot claim communion in Abraham, as might have been hoped by some pioneers of dialogue between the monotheistic religions: 'If you like, there is no objective Abraham who might serve as the focus for communion between the three monotheistic religions.'[70] These two very clear statements show that Islam may have developed a different understanding of the identity of Abraham. The biblical emblem of faith can be portrayed as perfect submission and pure faithfulness to God's order:

> Allah, the God of the Arabs, has become the only God and, starting from
> his position within Arab cultural identity, Muhammad has met with the only
> God of the Jews and the Christians. Another element of the Arab identity of
> Islam seems to me to be the concept of *hanif*, which describes someone who
> does not associate any subsidiary divine figure with Allah. The group called
> *hanif* is mentioned in more than one Surat and Abraham was their ancestor.
> We therefore have here a monotheism that is clearly Arabic, not either
> Jewish nor Christian. This excludes the possibility that the Koran is simply a
> compendium of the two preceding monotheistic doctrines.[71]

In the text of the Koran, Abraham is clearly different from the figure given to us in the Bible and handed down through tradition. His distinguishing attitude is that he rejected all forms of associationism. This particular characteristic means that Islam can claim to be a properly Arabic monotheism. It is not directly modelled on Judaism, nor is it partly shaped by Trinitarian Christian monotheism. It is a truly Arab monotheism that reveals the distinctiveness of the religious challenges of nomad Arab identity.

In other words, G. Khodr is wanting to emphasise the specificity of Islam not

---

69 G. Khodr, 'Les chrétiens d'Orient', in Collectif, *Juifs, chrétiens, musulmans. Que pensent les uns des autres?*, introduction by A. de Pury and J.-D. Macchi, Geneva, Labor et Fides, 2004, p. 64.

70 G. Khodr, 'Les chrétiens d'Orient dans un contexte pluraliste', op. cit.

71 G. Khodr, 'La nature de l'islam', op. cit., p. 40.

only in its Arab monotheism but also, and especially, based on its foundational document, the Koran itself. Unlike a number of Arab Christian apologists, both contemporary and historical, G. Khodr recognises the intrinsic value of Koranic revelation:

> None of the great or small prophets to whom sixteen books in the Old Testament are attributed are mentioned in the Koran. This book is not aligned with the revelation to the Hebrews or in the New Testament. [...] We therefore need to seek out the truly Arab foundations of this religion. If the Koran is not biblical, then it is prophetic in nature: it announces the will of God to Arab paganism.[72]

The rejection of any affinity between the Koran and the Bible is less a sign of radical schism between the two types of revelation than a trenchant acknowledgement of the irrevocable distinctiveness of Islam, as is clear in the reference to the contextual nature of Arab culture, in which it is primarily Arab populations who are addressed.[73]

Seeking to emphasise still more clearly the Koranic traits of autonomy and distinctiveness, G. Khodr patiently enquires about other extra-biblical forms of affinity. He analyses the literary style and the internal expressiveness of the Koran's text, and concludes that the Arab religious text appears to be closer to Mediterranean Greek literature:

> The Koran gives us a revelation of the absolute, of an asceticism in which the concise language of the divinity encounters the Hellenic spirit. Among the scriptures of the monotheistic religions, it is above all the Koran that is patterned upon Greek wisdom. For if anyone is Greek, it is the person whose

---

72 *Ibid.*, p. 40. In another lecture, G. Khodr reminded his hearers that Muslims themselves interpret the Koran as belonging in the same line of monotheistic revelation, and therefore patently global and universal: 'This book, which is quite clearly Arab, places the Arab revelation in the wake of the previous revelations. Arab identity, in terms of religion, conveys biblical catholicity. It claims only a duty to proclaim the eternal truth received by the prophets of old.' (G. Khodr, 'Le christianisme, l'islam et l'arabité', op. cit. p. 95)

73 G. Khodr identifies two aspects in the Koran: the Koran that treats of the inaccessibility of divine transcendence, and the Koran that speaks in language that is accessible to mankind: 'To read the Koran is thus a flight through the looking glass of Allah. There is a dumb, or rather, a silent Koran (the face of the inaccessible God), and a manifest Koran that comes down to the human face reading it.' (G. Khodr, 'La communication du message en terre d'islam', op. cit., p. 375).

nature is not corrupted by original sin, who is capable of harmony, peace and wisdom, whose greatest dignity is the power of wholesome, just reason that feeds on the fruits of the Earth, and who welcomes gifts from their merciful Lord – excluding that of the Cross.[74]

These words are surprising and even disconcerting. For we are all aware of the contradiction between the thought world of Arabs of Semitic origin who believe in the faith of the Koran, and the thought world of the Greek world, both in terms of literature and of philosophy. Yet here G. Khodr seems to want to minimise the disparity by suggesting ways in which they might be reconciled, or even be similar. First on the level of style, and then in terms of anthropology, where ontological optimism is key in both worldviews.

This leads us to the conclusion that Islam is especially distinctive in terms of its own internal configuration. If we note a certain discrepancy between the nature of the Arabs and the values of Koranic Islam, then it specifically helps us better identify the ways in which Islam, in its pure original form, improves the spiritual lives of believers. The vicissitudes of history and distortions over time have together undermined the reforming energy of the original Islam. A multitude of sociopolitical factors have distracted Islam from its primary orthodoxy. As an example, G. Khodr describes how the egalitarianism of Islam has been jeopardised by changes in the Arab personality.[75] Yet the distinctive character of Islam cannot be tarnished by lack of faithfulness or historical compromises. G. Khodr's whole approach, therefore, has been to cleanse Islam from the weight of prejudices that hold it down and obscure its image. No form of conviviality could be satisfied with neutrality if the fate of an interlocutor unjustly accused of guilt for all the failings of the human condition is at stake.

The particular status of Islam in the divine economy

A second hermeneutic task is linked to the first, and it helps to identify the theological status of Islam in God's plan for salvation. It is here that we find the truly theological understanding of our Orthodox theologian. The openness to diversity in Christian faith, as perceived and lived out by G. Khodr, is in truth the

---

74 G. Khodr, 'Le christianisme, l'islam, l'arabité', op. cit., pp. 95–96.

75 'The pride, individualism, and racism of the desert peoples always get the better of egalitarian Islam. Pre-Islamic civilisation is constantly present in history and is difficult to discount. The impulsivity, vengefulness and passion of mankind continue unabated, despite the essentially Muslim virtues of moderation and thoughtfulness' (*Ibid.*, p. 94).

background to this process of justification. Seeking out a unique status within the divine economy is a task for the kind of theological hermeneutics that is capable of meshing in an intrinsic way with the very nature of Koranic truth. This investigation therefore frames the attempt to widen the scope of prophetism in order to deploy it legitimately beyond the scope of strictly biblical revelation:

> The relationship between the Creator and the universe both precedes the Law
> of Moses and exceeds it. In terms of history, it does not necessarily need to
> involve Jesus of Nazareth, nor evangelisation. It is based on direct inspiration.
> If we accept that the most basic form of prophecy tells of this relationship,
> then there is no reason why we cannot see prophecy outside the Church.
> The Old Testament reports Canaanite prophecy (I Kings 18), and in the New
> Testament there is nothing to suggest that Christ might have brought prophecy
> to an end in the world.[76]

So if Christ has not ended prophecy, then it is possible for new messages about the will of God to appear. The only condition, however, is that these subsequent messages do not contradict the salvation plan devised by God in Jesus Christ for the whole of humanity. If it seems that a message or a prophecy is incompatible with the cultural expression of historic Christianity, then it becomes highly desirable to distinguish its fundamental content from its culturally conditioned format. In truth, the divine will is far greater than the attempts at making alliances with the people of Israel or even with the Church of Christ in its many cultural forms.

In accordance with the leading theological principle of God's absolute freedom, a prophetic word given to the Prophet of Islam can quite legitimately be seen as part of God's plan. So it is not surprising when G. Khodr states that Islam, as an autonomous religion and a method of spiritual mediation, is truly part of God's plan:

> I know that everything I have said about the truth of Islam calls for a detailed
> study of the attitude of the religion towards Christian dogmas. However,
> the position I have described is rooted in Christian tradition: it is optimistic,
> makes a positive assessment of religions, and sees them as fitting in with
> God's divine teaching plan. The religion of the vast majority of Arabs is one
> part of God's plan and thus earns a place in the Christian vision of the world.
> We are a long way here from an expansionist or imperialist view that might

---

76 *Ibid.*, p. 108.

prevent most Christians from seeing any light in any creed other than their own.[77]

For Islam to feature in a Christian view of the world, we need to ensure that it has a place in the plan of God's love. This is in some way G. Khodr's ultimate goal: following other contemporary Lebanese Christian theologians, he is seeking to understand Islam theologically without reducing it to a tentative, incomplete element of the tradition of the Bible. Islam is thus a depository for a divine light that shines continuously for its faithful. It is the place of a specific revelation expressed in the language of Arab culture.

Not wishing to isolate the Koranic revelation in a place totally separate from the economy of salvation, nor wishing to annex it, G. Khodr prefers to describe it as having a profound affinity with the Christ event itself:

The departure for the desert and Mecca [...] offers us a new meaning to the Christian universalism in which we believe: this universalism is not the Church, its canons or its historicity exercising totalitarian power, but rather the absolute universalism of Christ who is apparent in the Church and hidden elsewhere. If the Church, as defined by Irenaeus, is where the Spirit is, then Islam can seem to be of the Church, like the robe of the Master which, when touched by the woman who suffered from bleeding, transmitted the power of the Lord and granted healing to this woman, who was an alien in Israel.[78]

The key element in this reflection meshes well with a long Christian tradition emphasising that Christ is independent of the Church. In other words, it is not a matter of setting the Spirit, Christ and the Church against each other, but rather identifying the scope of influence and action of each. Clearly, therefore, the Church cannot place any limits on the action of Christ, nor of the Spirit. The notion of the Church, in its widest sense, can in any case describe anywhere that gives expression to the work of God: that is, the widest possible field, in which the divine energy emanating from the Spirit and from Christ work quietly together. If Islam is of the Church, as the Orthodox Bishop of Mount Lebanon so eloquently puts it, then it is so in the sense of a mystic convergence towards the shared space of the vast work of God in creation.

G. Khodr rejects excessive focus on the Church, choosing instead to see Islam

---

77 *Ibid.*, pp. 109–110.
78 *Ibid.*, p. 110.

as an integral part of God's global plan. There is no question of pushing Islam into an ecclesial straitjacket, which it has consistently resisted. On the contrary, Christian theology will need finally to accept that there are perhaps many ways in which God, in His freedom, works to convert and regenerate the heart of humanity. In order to drive home this fundamental truth about Christian faith, G. Khodr draws on the deep history of mankind's religious experience:

> Dialogue becomes possible in the light of the rejection of Ishmael, the father of the Arabs, by Isaac, the father of the Jews. The Byzantines knew that as Christians they were inheritors of the promise of Isaac, and in their liturgy have always referred to the Muslims as 'Hagarene'. Muslims, in some sense, are also part of that promise and should not inherit the tears of Ishmael.[79]

Echoing the original work of Fr Michel Hayek, G. Khodr acknowledges that Islam is legitimised even in the Bible. Following Muslim theology, he links Islam to the divine blessing given to both Isaac and Ishmael in theological terms, thus according to Koranic revelation a direct affiliation to the original covenant between God and the peoples of the Earth, and especially with the people of Israel. Islam is therefore granted joint status as inheritor of God's promise. The blessing of Ishmael leads ultimately, through the working of the Spirit, to the descent of the Koran, the revelation of God's mercy and of his plan of salvation, which he conceived also for the Muslim faithful.

Christ's mediation in this was decisive, and the plan includes the Muslims on two grounds: their status, first, as children of God, and second, as the inheritors of the blessing given to Ishmael, the honoured ancestor of their Koranic faith. Islam offers to its faithful guiding mediation inspired by the notion of salvation, as is clear from the massive presence of Christ in the Koranic revelation. Islam thus has a distinctive place in the Christian view of the history of salvation:

> Islam is privileged, perhaps above even post-biblical Judaism, because of the special place given to Jesus, unlike in any other religious sphere. I mean here that Christ is called by his name in Islamic sources, which means that we can include them in our specifically Christian reflections.[80]

No other Orthodox theologian has dared to suggest so great an inversion of the

---

79 G. Khodr, 'Les chrétiens d'Orient dans un contexte pluraliste', op. cit.
80 G. Khodr, 'La nature de l'islam', op. cit., p. 37.

status of Islam and Judaism.[81] It is extremely unusual to come across a Christian theologian prepared to take such a position on biblical and post-biblical Jewish heritage. His theme is, of course, Christ and His central role. Indeed, G. Khodr suggests that the Christ of the Koran is perhaps closer to the Christ of the New Covenant than is the Jewish Messiah of the Old Covenant.[82] Even if the biblical texts of the Old Testament describe the figure of Christ in ways similar to the figure in the text of the Koran, post-biblical Jewish exegesis, and indeed Muslim exegesis, both differ considerably from Christian Christology based on the foundational experience of the Easter faith. Khodr remains conscious of the reductionist Koranic exegesis, but believes that the Word of God and the Spirit of God are Koranic expressions conveying a certain deep affinity with the official Christology of Christianity. The recognition in the Koran of the particular status of Christ in God's plan brings Islam back into the orbit of the economy of Christ Himself. So we have here a Christological sensitivity that is particularly attuned to Arab spirituality.

The hermeneutics of evangelism in the lands of Islam

The third hermeneutic effort is related to the requirement for evangelisation, and it has two aspects: a Christian interpretation of Islam, and a Muslim interpretation of Christianity. The first of these arises from the explicit will of Arab Christians who wish to give free expression to their most deeply held Christian faith, while the second can be better understood as a discreet suggestion to Muslim interlocutors. These two aspects, however, share the same ambition for authenticity and conviviality.

From the start, the first interpretation excludes any form of mission.[83] The

---

81 G. Khodr, however, invites Christians to engage in intense dialogue with Judaism once hostilities have abated (G. Khodr, 'Christian Mission and Witness in the Middle East', Lecture given in Washington DC on 7 February 1994).

82 'Arab Christians have been encouraged over the last three decades to privilege dialogue with Islam because the Koran, unlike Judaism, allows that Jesus is the Messiah, even if it diverges from Christians on the matter of Christology. The major reality in the revelation to Muhammad is that the Son of Mary is given a place of honour. Jesus is omnipresent in Islam, whereas he is completely absent in Judaism.' (G. Khodr, 'Les chrétiens d'Orient dans un contexte pluraliste', op. cit.)

83 According to G. Khodr, mission is not possible in Islamic lands: 'In the Middle East, the mission as a system of organization is unthinkable at any time. However, this did not inhibit a Christian presence which appeared especially in the field of literature and the national life where we live together. There is an evident sensibility to the Gospel in this part of the world, yet without adherence to baptism.' (G. Khodr, 'Christian Mission and Witness in the Middle East', op. cit.).

Orthodox theology of conviviality, according to G. Khodr, discredits any attempts at forced proselytism. What Arab Christians are able to offer to their Muslim partners must however be spontaneously and boldly conveyed in the most expressive aspect of Arab culture, the spoken and written word: the word of life incarnated in commitment, transmission and communication. This is why it is crucially important to use a Christian hermeneutics that foregrounds reference to the Word of God:

> In Arab lands, therefore, the spoken word is our main hope for
> communication, the best bridge between us and the Other in their own world.
> We need to undertake a work of translation, to take a series of symbols that
> are intelligible in their own context and make them coherent and intelligible in
> a completely different context. In the Arab context, therefore, our task is not
> to engage in dialogue with a partner who denies the existence of God [...]. To
> deny God, in the non-believing milieu in which the Church of Antioch exists,
> would be to deny the Trinitarian God.[84]

Despite the strong kinship due to their shared point of reference, the word, Christianity and Islam offer two different perceptions of divine revelation. The Trinitarian God of the Christians presents a challenge to Muslims because traditional exegesis of the Koran offers no corroboration, or even a suggestion of it. As we shall see below, this is a stumbling block for Muslim–Christian conviviality in the Arab world.

The word, however, remains the only workable way of conveying the Gospel in Arab countries. So it is urgent to learn the 'Arab and Muslim' language in order to use it to sing out the Good News. The shared point of reference, the initiating Word of God, may just enable us to develop the skill. The anthropological understanding towards which Christian and Muslim theology converge is that humans are privileged in their ability to listen. If God speaks, we as humans are able to listen and receive. If we are listening out for revelation, then both Christians and Muslims are able to receive with humility the message of love sent by God to the whole of humanity:

> In this sense, the Bible is a written word that is radically different from the
> Koran. The core of the Christian message is still that God speaks. This is the

---

84 G. Khodr, 'La communication du message en terre d'islam', op. cit., p. 376.

common denominator between Christianity and Islam: Only God can reveal his nature to us, and he does so in his own way.[85]

This is the message that reveals to both Christians and Muslims, but also and especially to all of mankind, the true nature of God. It is therefore necessary to agree not only that the word is a particularly important aspect of God's work, but also, and especially, that it is the fundamental basis for revelation, for the full expression of the love of God.

Every Christian and Muslim is thus called to highlight within their own receiving tradition this specific and original truth about divine revelation. If the Word of God remains the common denominator bringing together Christians and Muslims in a similarly open and listening attitude, then Christians should remain committed to witnessing, in words and in actions, to the incarnation of that divine love in the person of Jesus Christ.

> Personally, I am not convinced of the ultimate usefulness of the comparative method used to expose the two religions, but Christians must always seek to find and recognise the marks of the Master in any heritage, whether religious or not. Seen under this light, Islam is one of the themes linked to Christ in the Koran far more than we might imagine. And we can track His footsteps in Muslim literature, both the Arab and the later Persian.[86]

Instead, therefore, of comparing the twin Christian and Muslims theological systems in order to pick out the similarities and differences – a laudable but inadequate exercise, according to G. Khodr – it is better to seek out the marks of Christ in Islam. This is what a truly Christian interpretation of Islam should aim for. For our Orthodox theologian, Christ Himself is the enduring centre of gravity, Christ as depicted in biblical and patristic hermeneutics. His person can be seen and interpreted in very many ways. The path of Islam, therefore, can be considered one particular reception of that same Christ.

G. Massouh,[87] in his review of G. Khodr's theology of dialogue, suggests that his own approach is closer to recommending interpreting the Koran from a clearly Christian perspective. When reading it in this way we will be able not only to seek

---

85 *Ibid.*, p. 376.
86 G. Khodr, 'Le christianisme, l'islam et l'arabité', in *Contacts*, 1980, XXXII, 110, pp. 104–105.
87 G. Massouh, *Monseigneur Georges Khodr. Un regard chrétien sur l'islam*, unpublished typescript, Institut Saint-Serge, Paris, 1992.

out similarities and differences, but also to identify affinities between verses in the Koran and verses in the Bible. Since the Bible is the ultimate frame of reference for all Christian revelation, it is important to re-examine the particular way in which biblical revelation is received in Islamic religious experience. Similarly, G. Khodr maintains that the Christian interpretation of the Koran should explicate any Christological or evangelical content that might be found in verses in the Koran.[88] The task, then, is to reveal the spiritual and theological depth of the text of the Koran in the light of biblical revelation. Hence the hermeneutical strategy that focuses on seeking out the spiritual meaning hidden in the Koranic revelation.

One of the aims of such a process is to bring out the Koranic texts that encourage openness, tolerance and respect for individual liberties among Muslims. As a witness to Christian faith in the societies of the Arab world, G. Khodr maintains that the most appropriate form of evangelism is one that encourages spiritual renewal among Muslims. If Christians in their witness can involve their Muslim interlocutors in searching for the fundamental human values within the Koran, they will indirectly promote a recognition in Islam of true Gospel values.[89] Neither

---

88 According to G. Massouh (*Monseigneur Georges Khodr. Un regard chrétien sur l'islam, op. cit.*, passim), the hermeneutics of G. Khodr are ambivalent. On the one hand, he identifies certain verses in the Koran and gives a Christian interpretation (2, 138; 57, 27; 5, 114); on the other hand, he appears to leave out part of the verse in question, when he seems to think that it might undermine the internal coherence of his own theological thinking, or the underlying logic of his re-evaluation project (see his interpretation of verse 27, 57). In certain very limited cases, he cites a verse of the Koran in an exclusively Christian context. However, this Christian hermeneutical approach, dictated by circumstances, is probably not symptomatic of an inclusive theology of redemption, since it acknowledges the integrity of the Koran while emphasising the theological and spiritual values that characterise Koranic revelation and do not have an identical parallel in the Bible, such as verses 5, 28 ('If you raise your hand to kill me, I will not raise mine to kill you, because I fear Allah – the Lord of all worlds.'); 5, 32 ('whoever takes a life – unless as a punishment for murder or mischief in the land – it will be as if they killed all of humanity; and whoever saves a life, it will be as if they saved all of humanity.'); 22, 69 ('Allah will judge between you on the Day of Resurrection concerning that over which you used to differ'). By highlighting them, G. Khodr emphasises their distinctiveness and suggests an interpretation that might reveal both the Christian and Muslim meaning.

89 According to G. Massouh (*Monseigneur Georges Khodr. Un regard chrétien sur l'islam, op. cit.*, passim), G. Khodr's thinking and actions are shaped by the witnessing of the Christian minority in the Arab world. As an Arab Christian, a member of a minority community living at the heart of a traumatised Middle East, the Orthodox Bishop of Mount Lebanon 'has taken on the mission of reconverting Muslims to religious tolerance, so that they can have restored to them a sense of the liberty that the Koran says is the right of every human. Khodr simply reminds us of the Koranic texts that mention liberty' ('no compulsion in religion', 2, 256; 'You are not over them a controller', 88, 22; 'If you raise your hand to kill me, I will not raise mine

Christian nor Muslim can fail to see the universal character of some verses in the Koranic revelation. This then establishes a clear link to the universality of biblical revelation, which reached its climax in the self-revelation of God in the person of Jesus Christ. In reality, therefore, G. Khodr is choosing not a simple academic form of Islamology but rather an Islamological form of witness, which aims to 'waken Christ in the shadows of the religions'. The word 'shadows' here has two meanings: first, the universal dimension that is not yet accessible to the Muslim interlocutor; and second, the imperfections and inauthentic aspects that might hinder that same interlocutor from gaining the best possible understanding of the mystery of Christ, and therefore becoming open to the promise of salvation.

The whole Koranic hermeneutics of G. Khodr is for this reason focused on the centrality of the person of Christ. According to him, 'if we seek the face of Christ where He sleeps in the shadows of the religions, we must follow His traces through the Koran'.[90] By doing this, we not only bring Koranic revelation and biblical revelation into closer relationship, so that we can show that the salvation mediated by Jesus Christ is universal, but we also can develop an enculturated Arab Christian theology, one that respects the particular demands shaping the witness to which Christians are called in the different societies of the Arab world. G. Khodr's commitment to the development of such a theology is far more than a simple rhetorical wish; he has engaged in serious and responsible examination of the resources and materials gleaned from both the religious experience of Islam and Arab culture itself. A favourite topic in which work is necessary for an Arab theology of enculturation is the meditation on the notion of Koranic mercy in relation to the Christian theology of the Fatherhood of God.[91]

---

to kill you, because I fear Allah – the Lord of all worlds', 5, 28). G. Khodr also holds that a number of Koranic verses can be read and meditated by Christians, for they contain edifying spiritual and moral teaching and can thus 'teach Christians about specific matters and help strengthen their faith'. For ultimately, 'the end purpose of all dialogue should be, according to him, a desire to better discover the beauty of others'.

90 G. Khodr, 'Bible et Coran', in *L'Ancien Testament dans l'Église*, Chambésy, Éditions du Centre Orthodoxe, 1988, p. 226.

91 The hermeneutical process referred to by G. Khodr consists in scrutinising Koranic terminology in order to find the semantic affinities with Christian theological language. This is highly relevant, if we accept that the religious experience made possible by the revelation in the Koran is rooted in the Bible. G. Massouh reviews this hermeneutics through an examination of the ways in which the Koranic notion of Rahmân has been used. In an article entitled 'L'Orphelin' ('The Orphan'), G. Khodr cites verse 6 of Surat 93: 'Did He not find you as an orphan then sheltered you?' The Koran here is referring to Muhammad, who was an orphan under the guardianship of his uncle Abou Taleb. He then cites the letter of James: 'Religion that is pure and undefiled before God, the Father, is this: to care for orphans and

The Semitic context makes this somewhat easier, and it is indeed the main asset claimed by Arab theological thinking. A renewed formulation of the *kerygma* cannot discount the Semitic lands in which it originated. Islam claims the same cultural universe, so it falls to Arab Christian theology to rethink its heritage from Greek conceptualisation and turn instead to Syriac patterns of thinking about Christian mystery.[92] This call, coming from an Orthodox theologian, is born of a particularly lucid mind and a boldness of thought that defies all forms of Eastern conservatism.

The hermeneutics of evangelisation require Arab Christian communities fundamentally to rethink the conceptual approach of their theological discourse. The criteria they use in adapting their theological language can provide a basis for setting the norms for evangelical witness. It will not be possible to take our message to the societies in the Arab world until we have worked through this normative methodological preparation. If it goes well, with care and circumspection we will be able to identify the places in which our witness will be most likely to

---

widows in their distress, and to keep oneself unstained by the world.' (1, 27). He also cites the Lamentations of Jeremiah: 'Our inheritance has been turned over to strangers, our homes to aliens. We have become orphans, fatherless; our mothers are like widows.' (5, 2–3) Following a brief commentary, G. Khodr notes that for the apostle James, the best way for a person to express love is to act in this way. Similarly, he points out that for the prophet Jeremiah, the most important thing for mankind is to experience the fatherhood of God and His love. And finally, he concludes that 'the image of God as Father in the Old and the New Testament is his image as Rahmân in the Koran.; (G. Khodr, 'Al yatîm', *An-Nahâr*, 5 November 1988). In support of his view, he explores the root of the word *rahma*, which is *rhm*. He points out that the *rahma* is *si'a* (largesse), which gives us the name of Jesus in Arabic, *yasû'*. The name comes from the Hebrew *yasa'*, which is the same in Arabic, the one who saves through the *si'a* of God, that is, through God's infinite largesse. God is *rahîm*, merciful, just as a woman is *rahîm* in the sense of the largesse of her *rahem* matrix. He ends his meditation with a quotation from the Psalms (Ps 144, 8): 'The Lord is gracious and merciful, slow to anger and abounding in steadfast love.' [Quoted in the French original as 'Le Seigneur et compatissant, *rahîm* et miséricordieux, patient et plein de miséricorde *rahma*.' – transl.] (G. Massouh, *Monseigneur Georges Khodr. Un regard chrétien sur l'islam, op. cit.*).

92 G. Khodr advises, in order to remain respectful of the Semitic sensitivity of Islam and Judaism, a deliberate return to Syriac theological language: 'The message which is addressed to both Jews and Muslims, could not be creative nor could it flow from the land of the East unless it is the message of the Eastern Patristic tradition, and in particular, of the Semitic theology in a terminology that should be worked out by a critical usage of the Greek philosophy which gave its modes of expression to the Christian dogmatic. The Semitic mind in general, and the Muslim in particular, is alien to Greek categories. An intelligent biblical theology read through the Syrian tradition can become the tool of the evangelic[al] message. It is to this task that all churches should settle down. It is the work undertaken together in the mission and the witness which will free the churches of what opposes them.' (G. Khodr, 'Christian Mission and Witness in the Middle East', op. cit.).

speak to the Arab and Muslim heart. Then we shall need to tailor the core themes of the evangelical message for the ways Arabs today live and think.

This highlights the importance of the other aspect of evangelisation – developing an appropriate Muslim interpretation of the Christian *kerygma*. Here, we shall not be able to do without the kind help of our Muslim partners. In the last analysis, it is the *sine qua non* for any fruitful encounter between Arab Christians and Arab Muslims. Any such approach by Muslims to Christianity must also be seen as an aspect of evangelisation. For if Muslims are better able to understand the truth of Christian faith, they will be able to appreciate its distinctiveness and advocate for better conviviality with their Christian partners, something that would not be able to grow and flourish if there is confusion or misunderstanding.

In reviewing the ways in which Islamic hermeneutics need to be re-examined, G. Khodr emphasises the fundamental issue of Christian revelation. He points out first that Islam finds it difficult to integrate the idea of history into its global vision of divine transcendence: 'Islamic thinking as a whole is not attuned to the reality of history, maybe because of the absolute transcendence of God. Its being thus independent of time may be partly due to the fact that the Koran is contained within the Preserved Tablet, preserved with God from all eternity'.[93] Despite the historic inscription of Koranic revelation, Islam prefers to preserve the essential being of God in a sacred, separate and inaccessible sphere. The only relationship between this divine being and history, however, is a commerce understood as communication and solicitude. This does not call for direct contact, but simply for superabundant generosity and absolute omnipotence. Incarnation, as taught in the Christian faith, is therefore unintelligible to Islam: 'The revelation thus appears as the face of the concrete world, of the existential, of the moment of eternal value. Revelation is not limited to teaching, it also saves. In the Epistles, revelation adopts a certain number of events from human life and uses them to represent and "reveal" the characteristics of the Kingdom. This is none other than the reality of incarnation. It is completely unintelligible to Islam.'[94] And here lies the peril of incomprehension that endangers the Muslim interpretation of Christian faith. The Incarnation mobilises the whole of the divine being and draws Him into the drama of human life. When, extraordinarily, the divine initiative breaks into the human condition, the event of the Incarnation is transformed into the place of redemption and salvation:

---

93 G. Khodr, 'La nature de l'islam', op. cit., p. 41.
94 G. Khodr, 'La communication du message en terre d'islam', op. cit., p. 381.

We need therefore to help our Muslim partners to accept the reality of a
personal revelation whose action is to illuminate, not to reduce to passivity,
the minds of people who are thus 'Christified' and regenerated in the image
of God, so that they become partners with God, full co-creators, who give
expression in human language to the understanding of the Word made flesh.[95]

The Muslim understanding of Koranic revelation does not assume any form of
direct divine involvement in the course of human existence. At the most, it aims
to guide people and steer them towards the right path of monotheism and virtue.
There is no mention in the Koran of humans being regenerated in the image of
their Creator. Nor is there any allusion to the ultimate purpose of inner illumination by the Holy Spirit: that we grow more godly.

Islam in fact appreciates and endorses the initial conception of the Abrahamic
faith. Yet this conception excludes any personal involvement of God in the progress and intrigue of human history.[96] This is at the root of the fundamental difficulties Muslims have in accepting any personal manifestation of God in the
crucible of human existence, so the concept of the Incarnation thus loses the force
of its impact in challenging the Muslim interpretation of Christianity. G. Khodr
therefore offers Muslims the possibility of seeing in Christ the fulfilment of the
perfect man. There is, incidentally, an equivalent notion in Islamic mysticism –
the Man of God who brings to completion the work of creation by restoring and
energising the divine image written in the deepest part of the human heart:

To present the person of Jesus to Islam might consist not in insisting on Christ
as the Son of God, which would be interpreted as blasphemy, but from the
point of view of Christian anthropology, starting from Christ the new Adam in
order to interpret Christ the Word.[97]

According to Christian anthropology, God urgently comes to rescue us in our

---

95 *Ibid.*, p. 379.
96 'There is never any question of seeing the face of God or of sharing in uncreated energy.
There is no substantial difference between the nature of a person on Earth and their nature in
eternity. For Islam does not consider the notion of the glorified body. This is, I believe, the key
difference between Islamic heaven and Christian heaven. Islam uses the word "heaven" only
to describe the dwelling-place of God. God does not share his own glory with the beings he
has created. God never inhabits human beings.' (G. Khodr, 'La nature de l'islam', op. cit.,
p. 46.)
97 G. Khodr, 'La communication du message en terre d'islam', op. cit., p. 382.

fragility by offering that we might transcend our condition and share in His plan. He desires to involve Himself in the worldwide kingdom of love that persists throughout the centuries. The person of Adam can thus serve as a starting point shared by both Christian and Muslim theological perceptions. In order to ensure, however, that this hermeneutical accommodation does not paradoxically obscure the core aspect of Christian faith, G. Khodr is keen to safeguard the fundamental element of Christ's work, his true and final victory over sin.[98]

If the Muslim interpretation of Christian faith enables Muslim interlocutors to accept some aspects of the personal character of revelation, then it may also allow them to encounter other Christian truths – in particular the Trinity and redemption through the Cross – with greater equanimity. So it turns out that the principle underlying God's revelation of Himself in Jesus Christ acts as an essential prelude to understanding the full picture. The divine being is committing in person to walk with mankind. Such an outcome could not come about if there were not, in God Himself, a kind of dynamic of love, which the Christian faith describes in terms of Trinitarian energy: a relationship of embrace within the divine being that does not in any way jeopardise His unity. According to G. Khodr, when the Trinity is described in this way it should not seem alien to the Koranic understanding of divine mercy. It describes the activity of taking on, and assuming, the whole of human reality. According to the Islamic faith, the Word of God as written in the Koran can reveal the huge solicitude of the Creator. The Koranic revelation, therefore, describes a divine communication to reveal God's plan designed for the joy of mankind. And at the heart of this message, a Christian might justifiably perceive a description of the Trinitarian dynamic of divine love.

G. Khodr certainly remains deeply convinced that it is not impossible to perceive the Christian notion of the Trinity in conjunction with the Koran: 'I do not think that the Koran, taken on its own, seems anti-Trinitarian.'[99] This theo-

---

98 'We can only present Him to others in the words He Himself used. We must present the complete picture of His nature, of His relationship with the sin of mankind, and of our faith in Him as the incarnate Saviour.' (*Ibid.*, p. 381.)

99 G. Khodr, 'La nature de l'islam', op. cit., p. 44. Thanks to his analytical textual approach, he also reckons that those to whom the refutation of the Koran is addressed are not Christians who hold the orthodox faith of the universal Church, but Judeo-Christian groups who in the seventh century were propagating a deformed representation of the Trinity in the Arabian Peninsula. 'We have shown that the dialogue with Islam is based on the fact that the Koran is not as anti-Trinitarian as had formerly been believed. We have established that the word Naçara, used by Muslim commentators to describe Christians, is in fact more properly applied to Judeo-Christians who were the only ones living in Arabia at the time of the Prophet. The supposed anti-Christian statements in the Koran were in fact designed only to refute

logical approach does not have any ambition beyond offering Muslims certain elements that might promote a more accurate and appropriate understanding of the mystery of the Trinity. Part of this is to identify in Koranic hermeneutics the underlying tendencies that could be seen as compatible with the Christian impulse of Trinitarian faith. And here, Christians have a serious duty: they need to articulate intelligently the basis of their *kerygma*. This is a delicate task, but it could be very fruitful in terms of their conviviality with Muslims. Ultimately, after all, Christianity professes monotheism and thus values the unity of the divine being.

> It is therefore time for Eastern Christians to draw on their own resources, starting from their present witnessing, in order to live with dignity and stature. When they remember that they are yeast in the dough, they will be freed from the complex of being a minority lost in the vastness of the Arab world. As they are themselves Arabs, they do not need to enculturate themselves as would a missionary from an alien country, but they still need to learn to 'speak Muslim'. In the Middle Ages, Islam thought in Greek. Now, it is returning to the simplicity of the Koran, it is adopting technology, and knows nothing about Christianity. How should we unwrap the message of the Gospel without freighting it with the language of ecumenical councils? Some Christian and Muslim authors are calling for the introduction of the critical method in reading the Koran, but this has so far not borne fruit, at least in the Mashriq. It is perceived to be an attempt to undermine the basis of the faith. At a discursive level, I think we may need to attempt afresh the grand plan of the Arab Christian apologists to show that Christianity believes fundamentally in the unity of God, not wishing to hide the mystery of the Trinity, but rather to link the unity and the Trinity as did the Greek Fathers. This is a clear challenge to the Koran. Given the divisions among Christians, it is also very important to identify the other challenge in the Koran, described in terms in two verses of the revelation, since Muslims are convinced that divisions among Christians are focused on the nature of God.[100]

This hermeneutical effort by G. Khodr to reinterpret the Koranic concept of

---

Judeo-Christians and Sabellianism. The anti-Christian apologetics were not drawing on the New Testament. The Koran remains for Muslims their only reference for knowing about Christianity.' (G. Khodr, 'Les chrétiens d'Orient dans un contexte pluraliste', op. cit.).
100 G. Khodr, 'Les chrétiens d'Orient dans un contexte pluraliste', op. cit.

Christianity appears to invite both Christians and Muslims to an extraordinary effort to convert. In each of the two theological worlds, believers are asked to pull away from focusing on their own subjectivity and put themselves in the place of the Other. The problem of the Trinity is a fundamental issue, and can seem more like an impasse in which the two partners become trapped by the illusion that they alone are in possession of the truth about God. G. Khodr's first observation, however, is that that the Christian experience, and Christian theological sensitivity, are distinctive. They are the crucible in which is refined the theological language that aims to convey how God reveals Himself in Jesus Christ. To acknowledge their distinctiveness is crucial to the Christian message.

We can therefore say that the Christian understanding of personal revelation and of the Trinitarian mystery of God can be seen as a common core from which devolve the other truths of Christian faith. Islam is still seeing these truths from its own perspective, which does not coincide with the distinctiveness of the Christian perspective. The question of the suffering of God is also the object of a long and painful controversy between Muslims and Christians. The Cross, to Islam, represents the failure and impotence of God, but from the Christian perspective, it represents the infinite love of God for His whole creation:

> The Son of Man is the suffering servant, the wounded divine love. Islam shows a Christ who is alien to us. The Christ in the Gospels in completely different from the Christ in the Koran, who has come down from the Cross, who has refused the cup given to Him by the Father, who in some way denies his own surrender, his 'Islam' to the will of the Father in unconditional dedication and obedience. Faced with the negation of Islam, we can only respond by presenting the scandal of the Cross. Without the Cross, the Resurrection is meaningless. Islam believes in a coming Resurrection of this same Jesus, who will return to die. We, however, are asked to state that the Cross 'proves', confirms the Resurrection here and now as the inescapable consequence of the very nature of God who is love. For us, the Resurrection is not some kind of arbitrary finale. It is the proof that love has conquered death.[101]

---

101 G. Khodr, 'La communication du message en terre d'islam', op. cit., p. 384. According to G. Khodr, Islam cannot include the concept of redemption, since it cannot implicate the divine transcendence in the drama of contingent human existence and history. 'Islam still cannot entertain the notion of a mediator between God and mankind. There is a personal reconciliation between mankind and God. There is a response from the penitent to divine forgiveness that has no connotation of redemption.' (G. Khodr, 'La nature de l'islam', op. cit.,

It is not G. Khodr's intention, in emphasising the difference, to undermine the hermeneutics of conviviality. Quite the opposite: he is attempting here to stimulate a profound reflection among Muslim theologians in order to encourage openness to the differences with Christianity. Instead of describing the divine being as impotent, the Christian theology of the Cross emphasises the true strength of divine love, which leads Christ towards the victory of Resurrection. While moderating the language used for the Muslim audience, the hermeneutics of evangelisation offer the opportunity to see the power of God through the lens of what love can achieve. The divine transcendence, out of infinite love for mankind, can destroy the power of evil and death through sharing in the fragility of human life: it is a different way to demonstrate credibility and to proclaim the power of salvation in the very heart of human history.

This summary has outlined G. Khodr's bold and promising hermeneutics, painstakingly elaborated to guide Christians and Muslims towards better mutual understanding. In all the points addressed in his work in contextual theology, he has plumbed depths that contemporary Arab theology does not yet seem ready to explore. There are any number of texts bearing witness to the seriousness and wisdom of this novel approach in the context of the theological confrontation between Muslims and Christians. The most important aspects of this theological exercise are its rigour and its sincerity. For each of the elements that he examines and reinterprets, our Orthodox theologian assesses where possible misunderstandings lie and lists where there could be misapprehensions and accidents. He strongly recommends that one should show respect for the distinctiveness of Islamic faith, and seek patiently and confidently for points of reconciliation, but he resists not only intolerant fundamentalism but also any irenic levelling that lack firm beliefs and fail to discern true Christian identity.

The absolute priority for the witness of love

It would be safe to assume that there is always a risk of misunderstanding in this kind of hermeneutic process. Muslims could accuse the Christian exponent of hermeneutics either of proselytism, of theological incompetence, or of evangelical naivety. G. Khodr boldly steps out of the mainstream, while yet aware that

---

p. 46.) This difference is a key identifier of the distinction between Christianity and Islam: 'The fundamental difference between us and them remains the scandal of the Cross, and this alienates the Muslims from the core of the Gospel message.' (G. Khodr, 'La nature de l'islam', op. cit., p. 45.)

the whole of his thinking on dialogue might be under threat. He prefers to leave dialogue on theology to the specialists. He does however advocate witnessing through daily life and through personal relationship with Christ.

The first duty of Arab Christians is to live an authentic Christlike life, which encompasses both suffering and resurrection. The hermeneutics of lived faith does not need the complications of problematic theology:

> There is no need for us to seek to explain Christian faith when Islam objects to 'theological' details, as if we were engaging with our interlocutor in dogmatic theoretical discussions. We are called to give voice to the crucified Christ, 'the power of God for salvation to everyone who has faith' (Romans 1, 16). We should proclaim the fact of the Cross in the same spirit as Christ Himself who bore it.[102]

If we are to give up on a dangerous and compromising debate, let it not be in order to spare our dialogue partners any confrontation with others. The unspoken motive for such reticence is a theology of mysticism that places a high value on an inner sense of God's closeness:

> Leaving aside the language of the heart, any denial of God is essentially to be assessed on the level of objective concepts. The mystery is not that which we understand, but that which understands us. Concepts are idols. It is only the impulse of wonder that truly understands something. According to the Fathers, the mirror of the soul does not reflect the idea of God, but the face of God. By looking at it, we look at God. We say His name not as one states an idea, but as a confession of faith arising from an immediate sense of the divine presence, of His burning proximity.[103]

The Orthodox Bishop of Mount Lebanon arms himself with these great theological convictions when he ventures into the territory of Christian interpretation of Islam and Muslim interpretation of Christian faith. He is not denying the significance or pertinence of theory, but he places the greatest importance on the witness of daily life. When we base our life on commitment to daily relationship, it establishes and highlights the core of the Christian *kerygma*, and in turn our life is enriched and energised to challenge those around us.

---

102 G. Khodr, 'La communication du message en terre d'islam', op. cit., p. 384.
103 *Ibid.*, p. 384.

For in the end, it is not a conceptual theological approach that will enable those engaged in dialogue between Muslims and Christians to gain an intimate sense of the living and loving presence of God. Only a heart on fire with the Spirit will truly witness to the unconditional and universal love of God:

> This theological work would be in vain if it were not supported by what Bergson terms a supplement of soul. Before we think about how to encounter Islam, we need to remember that Muslims have always been fascinated by the lives of Christians, by their gift of tears and their humility. This was the description that Muslims received. It is those who are passionate about God, using the language of passion, who have most moved Muslims. For a Muslim the path to reach God goes via a Christian heart. [...] So it seems to me that in working towards a shared life it is less important to talk than to be in Christ. Any talking that is not nourished by being in Christ seems to me to be in vain. Sociocultural diversity among our peoples is enriched by great courtesy, nobility even, hospitality, and respect for the spoken word. These virtues are foundational for Arab tradition. Christians are called to nourish them with love.[104]

If there is a choice between the witness of fraternal love and that of theological knowledge about faith, then Arab Christians must every time unhesitatingly choose the first. The ontological dimension of the heart's communion with Christ is more important than the gnosiological approach of theological reason. Rationality will always be inadequate in describing the mystery of the divine being, so rather than trying to decorate its delicate tissue with subtlety and nuance, in the context of Arab conviviality it would be far better to take hold of solid Arab reality and marry to it the concrete demands of the Gospel Beatitudes, so as to create an experience of authentically shared life with our Muslim partners.

The fact is, life in Christ comes before knowledge of Christ. Without flattening

---

104 G. Khodr, 'Les chrétiens d'Orient dans un contexte pluraliste', op. cit. The meaning of Christian witness in the Arab world derives from an authentic commitment to fundamental Gospel values: 'Christians are not asked to produce good recipes from the great kitchen of ideas of this world, but rather, first and foremost, to be present with the name of Jesus in their hearts and on their lips. If we sometimes think that the look in the eyes of people in the Middle East is perhaps vacant, it is because those eyes have never met the eyes of a saint. Only a praying person will be able to witness to the Word made flesh, given a face, to Christianity as a religion of faces.' (G. Khodr, 'La communication du message en terre d'islam', op. cit., p. 391).

the fundamental certainties of Christian faith into two-dimensional simple human activity, we should aim to bring our Muslim interlocutor to a personal inner experience of the love of God, a love that was fully revealed and realised in Jesus Christ.

> We are called to bring our brothers to God in Christ before seeking to offer
> an intellectual defence of doctrine. In the chronology of Christian experience,
> knowing the nature of God comes after, not before, meeting the incarnate
> Christ who died and was raised to life again.[105]

Lived experience takes precedence, above all because the inner life is key to all spiritual development. In other words, G. Khodr prefers to trust Christ Himself to work on the inner conversion of Muslims. It would indeed be dangerous to trust that Christian faith could rely on the somewhat shaky foundation of earlier theological discourse. This is all the more true since the Arab world in which Christians are witnessing has been traumatically scarred by manipulation and marginalisation. And in addition, there is in Lebanon a long history of personal Muslim–Christian conflict. The Orthodox Bishop of Mount Lebanon, faced with this difficult and fruitless history, has bitterly revised his position: 'For some time I have been tempted to think that it is only in the context of culture, humanitarian efforts, and the construction of a sound nation that we shall be able to meet with Muslims who resist theological dialogue.'[106] This helplessness in the face of Islamic theological reasoning sums up the evolution of all of G. Khodr's thinking on Islamology.[107] For Islamic theological reasoning preaches that the truth is whole, and is unwilling to acknowledge any dialectical movement through confrontation and complementarity. This is in many ways similar to monotheistic

---

105 G. Khodr, 'La communication du message en terre d'islam', op. cit., p. 389. Even if Islam remains uncertain about the way in which Christians understand the plan of salvation, Christian witness must persevere in following the demands of this path: 'We are asked to explain, not a doctrine, but a personal encounter on which doctrine has then been elaborated. The divine strategy is the meeting itself. Muslims cannot accept the reality of this strategy, but we should at least ensure that they are fully aware of what it is they are rejecting. (*Ibid.*, p. 382.)

106 G. Khodr, 'La responsabilité et le témoignage prophétique du chrétien dans la cité', op. cit.

107 From the point of view of G. Khodr's hermeneutical analysis, the lands of Islam are very different from any other ancient civilisation (Roman, Chinese, Indian, African) because Islam is integral to the civilisation and draws everything into itself (G. Khodr, 'Christian Mission and Witness in the Middle East', op. cit.).

theological reasoning, though Trinitarian logic enables Christians to integrate diversity as a sign of the gift of self-sacrificial love.

This is a serious impasse, and G. Khodr seems to want to leave open the issue of theological debate; understandably, however, he has exposed it in terms that reflect his own personal struggle. He came late in his personal journey to this indecision, and it does not in any way affect the relevance of his hermeneutics. Indeed, he adds to his theological aims a humanist perspective. Given that he thinks theological dialogue with Muslims may be unfruitful, he exhorts both Arab Christians and Arab Muslims to engage together in defending the Arab peoples. Thus the Arab peoples themselves become the locus for the contextual dialogue with Arabic Islam:

> To strive together for peace turns out to be the *sine qua non* for interfaith dialogue. No one will believe that the Christians are sincere if they offer dialogue but do not also work for the justice and peace that is the right of each person.[108]

So faithful Christians should ensure that their positive contribution to building up a just and equitable human city lies at the very heart of their commitment of faith. If Arab partners join in this building up on the basis of reason only, it will not succeed. If, however, a breath of spirituality flows from the deep heart of God's love, offered through Jesus Christ to all the Arab world, then it will bring life back into the Arab soul. It is therefore urgent, from an intellectual point of view, to denounce the

> national illusion that consists in imagining that some social or institutional political arrangement would be sufficient in order to calm deep personal anxiety. The heart of mankind is made for the infinite, for limitless love. Suppressing this longing for the infinite is the reason for many contemporary troubles in the Arab world.[109]

Theology thus becomes 'theopraxis' [theory fused with practice], since the

---

108 G. Khodr, 'La responsabilité et le témoignage prophétique du chrétien dans la cité', op. cit.
109 G. Khodr, 'La communication du message en terre d'islam', op. cit., p. 386. In a private conversation in the summer of 2010, G. Khodr told me that he was thinking of writing a theological treatise on the key concept of love, as it is understood in the Christian faith. Such a project would not make sense without reference to a wider theological aim, which in his case was to identify the distinctiveness of the Christian understanding of divine love.

context of the Arab world demands a commitment to human solidarity. At a time when spirituality is sadly lacking, and when the Arab peoples are suffering from oppression and injustice, it would be an act of faith by Arab Christians to hold themselves fully and unconditionally available in the service of Arab humanity. This strategic line is not in any way dictated by the requirement to preach:

> If, as Gregory of Nazianzus put it so well, 'anyone who is not cared for is not saved', then we shall not be able to speak about salvation if our words do not come from a place of limitless love for Muslims. This love will make a major difference to our conversion and our seeking out of our brethren in other Churches throughout the deserts of Arabia.[110]

To love the Muslims is for Christians themselves a form of profound conversion, one that will help them reach the heart of the other: the other Muslim and the other Christian, but also the other person of any description – each of these is a place where divine beauty is revealed. In the final analysis, only the witness of love can be the most appropriate hermeneutical vehicle for engaging in Muslim–Christian conviviality in the Arab world, and it is the best way to show profound and heartfelt understanding of the high stakes involved.

G. Khodr has clearly received and understood Islam as Christlike. It is Christlike because he sees within it the person of Christ, quietly dormant. It is Christlike also because of the hermeneutics of the gentle attitude that the Christian faith adopts when looking at the Koranic vision of the world and mankind. G. Khodr's Islamology thus consists in finding Christ in Islam and then revealing Him to Muslims who wish to open themselves up to God's sacrificial love. The ultimate aim, for our Orthodox theologian, is to identify the truth of Islam, where it is incompletely understood, as a Christlike truth. He also hopes to create a harmonious synergy in which the Islamic faith can live with the gentleness of Christ, without making Islamic believers share all the explicitly Christian theological formulas on the nature of Christ. G. Khodr's ambition, then, in his Islamology, is to carry out a work of gentle seduction. He would like Muslims to love Christ in their own way. The ideal scenario for Muslim–Christian conviviality in the Arab world would be that Christ is loved without all the paraphernalia of speculative Christian theology. In this sense, to be Arab is also to acknowledge the inexhaustible richness of the Christ event in the history of the Arab world.

---

110 G. Khodr, « Renouveau interne, œcuménisme et dialogue », in Collectif, *Les chrétiens du monde arabe*, Paris, Maisonneuve & Larose, 1989, p. 28.

Arab Christianity and conviviality

Revisiting Arab identity

If G. Khodr uses the Christ event as a measuring stick in his hermeneutical approach to Islam, it is because he considers Arab identity to be a vast crucible in which various strands and spiritual infusions meet and interact. The fertility draws its nourishment from the original seed, the first Logos, which inspires and energises engagement with the mystery of divine love. Arab identity is not merely geographical, but providentially it is tied to a region that symbolises the diversity of human spiritual experience. Any explanation of this theological position would be incomplete, and indeed incoherent, if it did not include a specific and explicit analysis of the concept of Arab identity. G. Khodr's entire theology is presented within its specific context, in this case the Arab context. It is therefore unthinkable to end this chapter without having identified the fundamental challenges of this particular context.

From the first, Arab identity is clearly a site of cultural identity rather than racial or even national identity:

> We should therefore speak of Arab identity, as we might of Roman identity
> or Spanish identity, without prescribing a specific political or national
> connotation. For now, we are simply looking at a cultural and geographical
> definition, a place of renewal in which all who live within that frame are
> welcome, however diverse their origins and whether Arabs or not. [...] This
> definition that we offer is different from systematic Arabism as preached
> by nationalist thinkers, who longed to recreate what they saw as a golden
> age: the period of the Muslim Conquest, and especially the politics of the
> Umayyads.[111]

G. Khodr does not expatiate on the irrelevance of the Arab nationalist thesis, but he starts from a conviction that Arab identity is synonymous with cultural openness and spiritual energy. Sadly, these distinctive and promising traits eventually became dilapidated and disfigured due to various ideological manipulations.

G. Khodr, as a true theologian of conviviality, has worked with diligence and perspicacity to pick out the most salient and distinctive features of this cultural Arab identity:

---

111 G. Khodr, 'Le christianisme, l'islam et l'arabité', op. cit. p. 93.

Unity on monotheism, continuity with Arab tradition, universality thanks to humanism, initially literary and then also scientific. These seem to me to be the elements of Arab identity since its inception.[112]

These are indeed traits that belong both to the religious experience of Semitic people and to Arab cultural tradition itself. Here, his interpretation of Arab identity in terms of both religion and culture clearly betrays a major concern not to fuse Islam and Arab identity, but rather to dissociate them. The vicissitudes of history clearly show that Arab identity is indissolubly linked to Islam, but also that Arab identity always has been, and still is, far greater than Islam. If we limit Arab identity to its religious Muslim element, we might give undue value to a narrow logic that then claims the right to justify everything. G. Khodr's approach, on the other hand, enables a wide scope for assimilation and synthesis:

Arab identity only makes sense when it synthesises, when it is unconditionally open to pre-Arab history as a prefiguration and symbol of contemporary openness to modernity. In other words, Arab identity can only claim to be a spiritual and intellectual vessel for new values if it also sees itself as encompassing the Semitic Middle East and Hellenism. It will then offer a peaceful space for the development of Hebrew culture. When people look at the lives of Arabs, they should be able to observe: these people are true Semites.[113]

To a modern reader, this is so clearly true and natural that it would be idle to argue the point. Modern Arabs should therefore seek to revive the rich potential that is so deeply ingrained within them. They would then enjoy a culture wonderfully open to diversity, rather than a monolithic one. Arab thinkers therefore now need to address and rethink the nature of the initial encounter between Semitic identity and Hellenism – one concrete result having been that their own identity underwent change, and a new perception of Arab identity developed. However distasteful the task, it must be carried out at some point in order to safeguard the opportunities for Arab culture to achieve its long-awaited impact.

---

112 *Ibid.*, p. 96. G. Khodr frequently vilifies what he terms 'mummified cultural Arabism (ourba)', the reason for the decadence of the Arab nation (G. Khodr, *Law hakaitu masrât-tufûlah, op. cit.*, p. 76).

113 G. Khodr, 'Le christianisme, l'islam et l'arabité', op. cit. p. 96–97. Offering further explanation for his thinking, he states that Arab identity has proved itself 'especially in the period of the Abbasids, capable of assimilating non-native populations.' It is therefore 'a fusion of all the ancient Middle Eastern heritages' (*Ibid*, p. 102).

And similarly, the reinterpretation of Arab identity will lead to its being assigned a new cultural mission. What was achieved at the original synthesis should offer inspiration to what can now be achieved to meet the expectations of an Arab world keen to become fully and authentically open to modernity. The paradigm at the first synthesis was focused on the person: 'To be Arab meant at that time to welcome and to create humanness.'[114] This humanism should as it were define the heart of Arab cultural identity. From the point of view of cultural humanism, what is most important is to enable the development of an ambition among Arabs to foster human dignity, a fundamental attribute that reveals the different spiritual allegiances that have shaped the whole of Arab civilisation. This profound challenge both satisfies the longing for diversity, and yet also increases thirst for its dual dimension, both human and divine. Simply put, in G. Khodr's vision of the future, Arab identity would become the ideal locus for the emergence of the authentic human. Arab identity, thus defined, is the very antithesis of all the ideological efforts to contain and manipulate suffered by Islam throughout the sociopolitical history of the first Muslim dynasties. [115]

Rehabilitating the Arab identity of Arab Christians

In G. Khodr's mind, truly Arab humanism is due in part to the active presence of Arab Christian communities. Arab diversity thus arguably in itself guarantees

---

114 G. Khodr, 'Le christianisme, l'islam et l'arabité', op. cit. p. 94. Among the values characteristic of Arab cultural identity, G. Khodr highlights especially tolerance, gentleness, and the spiritual riches of the Arab soul (G. Khodr, *Law hakaitu masrâ-t-tufûlah, op. cit.*, p. 76–77).

115 G. Khodr considers that some political theories, such as the supremacy of the Muslim nation and of *jihâd*, were developed as a containment strategy in order to legitimate political power: 'Dialogue with Islam, however, encounters the difficulty of a sociological reality, the notion of *umma*, and the equally sociological difficulty that the Middle East still operates under the system of communitarian organisation, *millet*, defined by the Ottomans, and which creates a structure inimical to dialogue. Some of the great Arab Muslim thinkers are abandoning the political interpretation of the *umma*, favouring instead an understanding of citizenship, so that Islam in its turn is called to become a kind of Ecclesia.' (G. Khodr, 'Les chrétiens d'Orient dans un contexte pluraliste', op. cit.). *Jihâd*, which is a relic of the ancient ideology of Islamic political power, is best identified as a purely canonic requirement in a war situation: 'The Arab empire called itself the dwelling of Islam – the name derives from *salâm*, peace. Peace depends on the Muslims. Absent this peace and the Koranic revelation, humans are relegated to a war situation. *Jihâd* remains a canonic reality that grants to sacred warriors, who are potential martyrs, a sword and a desire for purification, and to Islamised defeated warriors the salvation of their souls. This is why the Muslim space is not really geographically permanent. (G. Khodr, 'Le christianisme oriental et l'homme moderne', op. cit.).

such humanism. The role of Arab Christians is therefore best examined in the light of cultural diversity. The Orthodox Bishop of Mount Lebanon, without wishing to set himself up as prophet, nevertheless suggests that Arab Christianity redeems the Arab instinct to withdraw. Thanks to the voice of Arab Christianity, which still rings out in the societies of the Arab world, Arab identity enjoys a different human and religious sensitivity:

> By refusing to be assimilated into Islam, Christians such as the Taghlib and the Ghanssanids made a powerful contribution to establishing a creative distinction between Islam and Arab identity. Thanks to John of Damascus, their refusal of religious assimilation gave rise to the first theological thinking in Islamic territories.[116]

Arab Christians and Arab Muslims may share the same Middle Eastern Semitic heritage, but their religious sensitivities and world visions diverge. There are major doctrinal differences between Christian and Muslim theologies, but their common ground of Semitism influences and shapes their mental attitudes. Arab Christians were Semitic and Arab before they were Christian. This organic link roots them viscerally in Arab identity. G. Khodr has eloquent examples to illustrate this sociocultural grounding. The issue of repelling violence appears to fit within this analysis:[117]

> Is Orthodoxy somehow Muslim, or are Middle Eastern Christianity and Islam born of the same Semitic identity, a cultural version of the immutable Word of God? Surely we find in the Middle East a similar kind of fundamentalism, which among Christians is admittedly a gentle form and not – or perhaps not entirely – political, but which is violent among Muslims? Is our gentle spirit the inevitable result of being an oppressed people?[118]

This statement by G. Khodr highlights the incoherence of the attitude of Christians in an Arab world inclined to discount the influence of Christian faith. Interactions between Christians and Muslims do indeed tend to be marked by tense

---

116 G. Khodr, 'Le christianisme, l'islam et l'arabité', op. cit. p. 97.

117 'The poor of the Middle East would rather be ruled by the poor of the Arabian Peninsula than stay under the yoke of the Byzantines. Seen in this light, the conquest represents a revolt by all Semites, driven by the last wave of Semites to surge out of the peninsula.' (G. Khodr, 'Le christianisme, l'islam et l'arabité', op. cit. p. 102–103.)

118 G. Khodr, 'Le christianisme oriental et l'homme moderne', op. cit.

and negative expectations, by outbursts of aggression, and by exclusion. Semitic identity, however, which is understood to be the shared core of the three mono-theistic religions, enables other similarities, in terms of patterns of thought, or behavioural models and instincts.

But beyond these, there is a clear distinctiveness to Christians living in an Arab context, which in turn highlights the difference between Arab identity and Islam. Arab Christianity thus contributes to identifying not only the distinct nature of Christian faith, but also, indirectly, the deep-seated distinctiveness of Islam. So there is a dialectical relationship of recognition between these two major Arab identities:

> Any reflection on the relationship between Christianity and the Arabs can only be dialectical, in the sense that it has a bearing on the situation of Christianity and the situation of the Arabs in the ways they move, interact, and evolve. Both parties have a long history and live in hope of fulfilment. Both are currently living under tension and are drawn to the future. We must constantly bear this in mind; for in such circumstances, it will block any progress in understanding if we stick to a static perception of the Church and Arab identity as being immutable, given once and for all. In reality, the Church is on a path to resurrection. The same is true in the Arab world. They will meet at the end of time in a universal transfiguration.[119]

So it turns out that Christianity and Arab identity are both experiencing the same metamorphosis. It signals their deep embeddedness in human history, and brings them together in a relationship of mutual support. Neither can evolve in a healthy way in isolation or unilaterality. The fates of Christianity and Arab identity are therefore in some way entwined with each other. Hence the existential worry afflicting some Middle Eastern Christians when they realise that the recognition of Arab Christianity implies that they must unconditionally and unavoidably share in a much jeopardised Arab reality.

G. Khodr hopes, through theological lucidity, to exorcise these anxieties. Dar-ingly, he goes so far as to integrate Arab identity into the very heart of the Chris-tian faith.

> Arab identity is the expression of their evangelical identity, a welcoming and free spirit in the midst of their Muslim context. Their current patriarch has

---

119 G. Khodr, 'Le christianisme, l'islam et l'arabité', op. cit. p. 100.

even said, in a moment of indignation: 'The Muslims are our hosts.' Everyone knows that this is no longer true, but let's forget history for the moment.[120]

And indeed, if we look for Eastern Christianity without reference to Arab identity, there is every chance that we shall only ever see counterfeit versions. Arab identity predated both Christianity and Islam, but has been deeply influenced by these two monotheistic views of the universe. There is also an undeniable trace of Jewish influence. The greatest influence on Arab identity, however, has been the encounter between Islam and Christianity on Arab soil. It is true that Arab identity can never be fully appreciated without reference to Islam, but without Christianity and Muslim–Christian conviviality it might seem completely rootless and incoherent. This is because Christian faith, in the context of the Arab world, can only become incarnate in Arab life itself, and can only find expression in the specific idioms of Arab culture.

Despite differences that sometimes affect the attitude of Arab Christians towards Arab identity,[121] on the whole Christians in the Arab world remain open-minded. They do need, however, to remain focused on understanding their faith in an intelligent and contextualised way, and on realistic ways to bear witness within Arab societies.[122] Thanks to the evolutionary distinctiveness of Arab identity, and because of the living and dialectical relationship between Arab identity and Christianity, Arab Christians are now called to formulate a new Arab Christian

---

120 G. Khodr, 'Le Liban religieux', Article written for *Version Originale*, Le trimestriel de réflexion, no. 5, *Proche-Orient*, 6 September 1994, and published on the website of the Greek Orthodox Archdiocese of Mount Lebanon, www.ortmtlb.org.lb.

121 'Christianity in our countries is still strongly marked by the conflict between Orthodox and Catholic, but also by a desire for conviviality in our witness and in our Arab future. Not all our countries have the same level of sensitivity on the matter of Arab identity. It is the Antioch Church and Palestinian Christians who are most strongly committed to this route' (G. Khodr, 'Renouveau interne, œcuménisme et dialogue.', op. cit., p. 28).

122 While focusing his interest on the urgency of this kind of authentic witness, G. Khodr also pays attention to the impact of the ecclesiological diversity that has always typified the Christian presence in the Arab world. 'The mutual understanding between the Churches cannot hide their different understandings of history, and of the presence, the sensitivities, and the political commitment of the others. The mindset of the Copts, the Syriacs, the Greek Catholics, the Maronites, the Armenians and the Orthodox has clearly been shaped not only by theology, but also by history. Every event of both distant and recent history has been carried down through history and has marked the deeply religious and deeply wounded soul of the Middle East. Each [community] rationalises its own historical position with the same energy as it keeps faith with its beliefs and liturgy. The interaction between Christians is still dominated, if somewhat less than in the past, by an emotion that, although raw, nevertheless conceals true piety.' (G. Khodr, 'Les chrétiens d'Orient dans un contexte pluraliste', op. cit.).

theology. It will be able to describe itself as intimately bound to Arab soil, and rely on what G. Khodr calls 'the expression of the evangelical nature' of the baptised in Arab lands. This kind of Christian witness is extremely sensitive and requires a very creative approach.

> The key importance of Arab identity for Middle Eastern Christianity is that the Arab element could truly ferment ecumenism in the region. If Christians can draw on their Syrian or Copt heritage and seek to express it in intelligible ways, they will find inspiration that brings them closer to Muslim sensitivities. They will have helped to recreate a Christianity that is neither Greek nor Latin, but is a Middle Eastern Christianity which, having freed itself of any alien dependency, can seek out its own identity and so enrich the Christian world, establish creative organisational structures on the ground, and engage in dialogue with the various religions of the Arab continent.[123]

G. Khodr recognises the reality that the Christian communities have to start from a point of ecclesial allegiance, but he exhorts them to tune their theology to Arab sensitivities. This interpretative work will add to the initial adaptation of the *kerygma* to fit Greek, Syriac and Copt moulds.[124] In other words, Arab Christians are now called to recreate an authentically Arab Christianity.[125] Following the example of Arab theologians, who had to engage with courage and creativity in their first contacts with Islam, they will need to undertake a reinterpretation of the *kerygma*. This will have a major impact on how they can influence contemporary Arab culture. The Orthodox Bishop of Mount Lebanon is quick to point out how much Christian faith has affected modern Arabic: 'The written language now used in the Arab Muslim world is incomprehensible without reference to the nineteenth-century Arabic version of the Bible.'[126] It seems clear that Christian

---

123 G. Khodr, 'Le christianisme, l'islam et l'arabité', op. cit. p. 98–99.

124 On this, G. Khodr himself makes a start on this task of reinterpretation in that he redefines the exact way in which Arab Orthodoxy relates to Byzantine theology: 'For us, Byzantium was never any more than the Gospel told in the Greek-Syriac language.' (G. Khodr, 'Renouveau interne, œcuménisme et dialogue', op. cit., p. 28).

125 G. Khodr is firmly convinced that Arabic is capable of conveying the content of Christian faith, which is constantly reinterpreted, without in any way altering its substance: 'To say that Arabic is resistant to Christianity is pure fantasy. It lent itself admirably to the translation of Greek philosophy, it has communicated abstract research, especially mathematics, and has proved that it can be used to convey the intelligence and the needs of mankind, and to satisfy the demands of reason.' (G. Khodr, 'Le christianisme, l'islam et l'arabité', op. cit., p. 101).

126 G. Khodr, 'La responsabilité et le témoignage prophétique du chrétien dans la cité',

faith has succeeded in penetrating the interstices of contemporary Arab idiom. This linguistic impact hints at the reality of a slow and progressive encroachment into the Arab soul, which is struggling with a strong challenge from Christianity. We are witnessing here a deep interaction between two strong forces: on the one hand, the linguistic and cultural force of Arab identity, and on the other, the religious and theological force of Christianity. This exchange has been happening throughout Arab history, yet there is nothing to prevent Arab Christians from reshaping their adventure to meet other challenges, in other contexts. Arab Christians may seem just now to be in an almost hopelessly precarious situation, but they need to embrace a bold spirit of evangelism and believe strongly in their fundamental ability to witness.

In support of this, G. Khodr presents a historical review of the achievements of Christians who, since Islam burst onto the scene, had been considered as condemned to the humble fate of *dhimmitude*:

> The powers of the world and their strength and riches have not obscured their
> tremendous witness, given with constant faithfulness for generation after
> generation. They have not been seduced by the real or apparent magnificence
> of the other. They have certainly sinned, until recent decades, by their sense
> of cultural superiority. They may have taken strength from human knowledge.
> Responding to the demands of the Abbasid Caliphate, they have thus
> been able to translate Greek philosophy into Arabic. It was thanks to them
> that Europe, via Arabic translated into Latin, gained knowledge of Greek
> philosophy. At the time of the Umayyads, they were the organisers of the
> Muslim state. For a long time, they were the only doctors and pharmacologists
> of Islam. During the nineteenth and twentieth centuries they rescued the
> Arabic language from its deterioration and created a new style. It was they
> who introduced the major contemporary political ideas. They are unrivalled
> poets. They are present throughout the world of art, not to mention their

---

op. cit. According to G. Khodr, this Christian influence is older still than the earliest interactions between Muslims and Christians. 'The Church of Antioch, which dominates in our country, has welcomed under its roof a number of itinerant monks who had neither house nor home. It is as if, through these nomadic worshippers, God had adopted the wanderers in the wastes, and had made life in the desert, in its shape and its significance, one of the paths to salvation. There are other hints of encounters between Christ and Arabs. We cannot overlook the works of Arab Christian writers down the generations. [...] The Koran itself, as shown by the Islamologist Tor Andrae, is the best witness to the organic link between Syriac Christianity and Islam.' (G. Khodr, 'Le christianisme, l'islam et l'arabité', op. cit., p. 104).

current contribution to the worlds of juridical science, medicine, and other disciplines both in the mother country and in the diaspora.[127]

Any Arab Christian can be proud of these achievements, which have changed, and in some cases transfigured, Arab culture. This major challenge has been delegated to the leading lights of Arab intelligentsia, both Christian and Muslim. A major rehabilitation of Arab identity and of the Arab vocation of Christians is called for to safeguard the continuity and rich creativity of Christian witness.

The nature of Christian witness in the Arab world

G. Khodr concludes a careful and thorough analysis of the identity of Arab Christians by reviewing all his thoughts and condensing them into a most evocative formula:

Christians are a community of love, not a confessional community. For us who follow Christ, the only thing that binds us together is His promise to remain among us, and that has nothing to do with the tyranny of time. A testament of love is our binding force, and it is our only chance to help Muslims to taste fully the beauty of being human. We are the ones called to wash feet.[128]

This approach is clearly linked to a bold ecclesiology that describes the Christian community in both spiritual and eschatological terms.[129] As a community of love seeking to bring about the Kingdom of God in the heart of the Arab world, Arab Christians are called to behave as those who are in communion. Their only desire is to live full and authentic lives in the societies of this world, which are the natural setting for their historical existence. And in fact this is the direction taken by G. Khodr when he firmly and critically addresses all those who believe that they can preserve Christian truth by shutting themselves up in a homogenous

---

127 G. Khodr, 'Les chrétiens d'Orient dans un contexte pluraliste', op. cit.

128 G. Khodr, L'espérance en temps de guerre (in Arabic), Beirut, Éditions An-Nahar, 1987, pp. 242–243.

129 G. Khodr criticises the empty ecumenism practised in the Middle East and deplores the lack of theological lucidity in studies of the deep identity of the Church: 'I strongly suggest that we should not engage on a technical level with ecumenism. The word does not have any real application in the Middle East. No rapprochement is possible if the Church is reduced to a sociological identity, if historical issues are seen as more important than spiritual, or even if, ultimately, we accept the risk of losing the faith provided the notion of ethnicity survives, together with the myths we have woven around it.' (G. Khodr, 'Renouveau interne, œcuménisme et dialogue', op. cit., p. 31).

and defended ghetto.[130] The task is to reinterpret the political struggle of Arab Christians by redirecting it to greater openness towards the Muslim Other. For Arab Christians, their commitment to fight for an egalitarian and equitable society would signal a clear commitment in the heart of Arab life.[131] It is in sharing their life with Arab Muslims that Arab Christians will best witness to their Christian faith.

It is not a question, however, of imposing Christian truth on the whole of the Arab world, as if Christ should imperiously reveal Himself as the absolute ruler of the universe, the omnipotent divine master and vanquisher of the power of sin and evil. Any plan to bear witness relying on the strength of Christ's victorious presence in human history is a brutal contradiction of the spirituality of the Cross. There is therefore an urgent need for catharsis deep within Arab Christians: 'Those who have not experienced catharsis, the first stage of spiritual development in the Christian Middle East, are capable only of polemics, of triumphalism, and of shallow and vain speech.'[132] A purified Arab Christian soul should gain a new understanding of the Christian faith and spirituality. If love, in G. Khodr's theological vision, is the only requirement of the Gospel, then Christian witness in the contemporary Arab world is surely a genuine act of embracing all that is Arab. By taking on board all that is truly Arab in the widest sense in society, Arab Christians in their witness must adopt an attitude of humility and gratitude for the seeds divinely sown that emphasise the splendour of creation:

This view, based on the love of Arab peoples, of past Arab history and of

---

130 According to the Orthodox Bishop of Mount Lebanon, withdrawing into ethnic and confessional redoubts represents a serious impasse; those who choose this option under the mistaken impression that it will help them survive are simply choosing to be trapped. Middle Eastern Christians who choose to live protected from danger, in an isolated area (Harat Al-Nasâra) are exhibiting a phobia inherited from their distant past. An eschatological ecclesiology should enable hope for conversion to overcome the fear of the Other. The mentality of the enclosed community must be resisted, and the promise of diversity welcomed, in spite of the demons lying in wait for both Christians and Muslims in an Arab world riven by trauma: 'Today, Jesus came to abolish the Christian quarter, and to pull down the walls, after he had abolished the Jewish quarter. Historically, of course, Christians were not the ones responsible for having built their quarter.' (G. Khodr, *L'espérance en temps de guerre*, p. 80) The conversion of Arab Christians, on the other hand, elicits a second conversion on the part of their Muslim partners, who must at all costs rethink the notion of citizenship in the societies of the Arab world.
131 'The aim of the Christians' national struggle was that they should no longer be the Christian quarter in the Arab world.' (G. Khodr, *L'espérance en temps de guerre*, p. 32.)
132 G. Khodr, 'Renouveau interne, œcuménisme et dialogue', op. cit., p. 31.

future Arab tensions, this vision that accepts the Arab world as a framework,
as the starting point in a struggle to open up to the world and its values, is
linked to a spiritual experience and is part of a witness to faith. First, however,
we need to close down any disdain towards desert dwellers.[133]

If G. Khodr speaks of purifying Christians, it is because he sees that Christian
witness in the modern Arab world is reminiscent of a birth, a breaking apart. Arab
Christians are called to cut themselves off from their former instincts and anxieties. Only through deep acceptance of the Arab people will they be able to love
them. Once the Arab people are accepted and loved, they will be ready to open
themselves up spontaneously and freely to the essential truths of Christianity. Any
other approach would be fruitless, and might lead to hostility.

If Arab Christians are to witness effectively, they will need to feel truly at home
in their world,[134] which is a *sine qua non* for them to be fully in tune with Arab
spirit and culture. The *kerygma* cannot easily infuse a society of anonymous and
confused people. The first duty of Arab Christians is therefore to study carefully
the distinctive nature of Arab identity, the privileged place where the love of God
can be revealed in the context of Arab life:

How can we convey the mad message of Christ in a world dominated by
the recited word? What is the future of witness in a society which is under
the spell of the word? In the desert, the landscape is uncluttered by objects;
we can therefore see with extraordinary clarity the immense spaces. On arid
soil under a clear sky, each individual object is distinct from the others and
easily seen for what it is. The mind thus learns to see a thing as a whole, and
not as its parts, learns that lived experience can bypass discursive knowledge
and receive faith as an experience, a call from the divinity that gains nothing
from any body of doctrine: 'God alone is God'. If a prophet should stand up

---

133 G. Khodr, 'Le christianisme, l'islam et l'arabité', op. cit. p. 103–104. According to G.
Khodr, Arab Christians have always done their best to keep their faith alive and to preserve
their spiritual heritage in the Arab world (see G. Khodr, *Law hakaitu masrâ-t-tufûlah, op. cit.*,
p. 103).
134 'First and foremost, Christians living in Arab lands must feel completely at home. It is
their duty to become an indispensable presence, and to bear witness to their faith in Arabic. It
was after all Arabs who were the hearers when the first Christian sermon burst upon the world
after Pentecost. [...] The Church under a tent could be used as an expression symbolising the
presence of Christ to the Arab world.' (G. Khodr, 'Le christianisme, l'islam et l'arabité',
op. cit., p. 98.)

and rant, he says little else. If thinking is organised, it is not focused on the invisible *ruah* that only God knows, but on earthly things.[135]

In order to avoid narrow or simplistic interpretations of evangelical preaching in Arab lands, we must fully understand the background that shapes the Islamic vision of the world. Before engaging in any witnessing, Arab Christians must spend a long time meditating on the distinctiveness of Koranic theology. We can only learn to love Islam by contemplating its splendours. Once that love is born, Islam can become the privileged beneficiary of the message. The task is one of communion and solidarity, not proselytism and appropriation.

In order to engage in Christian witness, Arab Christians should prepare to speak the truth of God by patiently and honestly exploring the Arab landscape and the receptivity of the Arab population. This mark of honour and commitment ensures that the whole person is engaged. By way of a concrete proposal, G. Khodr suggests that his fellow Christians should live out the love of God through actions before they say anything. Their lived commitment will trace out another way of seeing God as Arabs scan the horizon in their religious quest:

> Shown to us through his divine mercy, He is yet greater still than the biblical Word that identifies Him as the God of Sabaoth. He does not lead an army. He does not conquer peoples. He does not bless any country or devolve it to tribes of Bedouins, He does not share booty among the victors, He neither enthrones nor casts down kings, He does not confuse His cause with a conquest, He does not spread His religion by the sword, He does not undertake or bless any crusade, nor maintain one through administrative structures, He never sets Himself up in our temporal world. He does not burn heretics, He does not violate consciences, He does not scour the paths of the Earth to gain a proselyte. He tolerates the right to make mistakes, and the freedom of the sinner.[136]

The God of Jesus Christ, as portrayed by G. Khodr, is seen as a God who fully defends the freedom of mankind. He is therefore a God who constantly transcends any images and words attempting to paint a true portrait of Him. This kind of witness perfectly suits the historic condition of the Christian communities living in the Arab world. It is a word of truth that longs to liberate the Arab mindset from

---

135 G. Khodr, 'La communication du message en terre d'islam', op. cit., pp. 373–374.
136 G. Khodr, 'Grandeur et humilité de Dieu', op. cit., p. 18.

idolatry and to emancipate Arab life from servitude. These two requirements are based in an apophatic theology that respects diversity. Arab Christians, engaged in a pilgrimage for freedom, need only one unique message of witness to their Christian faith, which is the freedom of both God and mankind. For in the final analysis, no act of love could be truly authentic if it does not actively commit to acknowledging the initial free gift of liberty.

The modern witness of Arab Christians is grounded in freedom and will be highly attuned to the changes and challenges of the contemporary Arab world. In a spirit of wise discernment, Christians will be able to meet the challenges faced by the societies of the Arab world. According to G. Khodr, two major causes need defending: Arab identity and Palestine. The first, a cultural issue, should incite Arab Christians to partner with their Arab neighbours in a review and critical reshaping of their Arab cultural heritage. Their ultimate aim is to help birth an Arab renaissance, a context within which the various sensitivities that adorn Arab life can flourish. The second cause is more political, and will encourage these same Christians to fight all the injustices inflicted on the Palestinian people and their land. This dual commitment, both cultural and political, can claim to be an explicit theology of incarnation:

> Since the time of His incarnation and ascension, Christ is firmly situated in history until the end of time, when He will have gathered up all of humanity and returned them to the Father. In His travels through the centuries, Christ meets Arabs as much as He does other peoples, He talks to them, He walks alongside them, and will continue to do so until human time flows into eternal time.[137]

G. Khodr's profoundly held religious conviction leads him to see Christ as truly present in the lives and in the history of Arab humanity. It is a presence bringing love and companionship. Unless it is aided by Christian witness, however, this presence will become quietly marginalised. Only a deep commitment to Arab humanity can transform this presence into an astonishing force for conversion and transfiguration. A crucial element is the willing open-mindedness of the Muslim interlocutors themselves. If they are not on board, then the Christian witness will fall on stony ground and vanish into obscurity and irrelevance.[138] Hence the courageous call from G. Khodr to the whole Arab world, encouraging renewal and

---

137 G. Khodr, 'Le christianisme, l'islam et l'arabité', op. cit. p. 100.

138 Taking up this point, G. Khodr is often tempted to repeat: 'We are the inheritors of the dead.' (G. Khodr, *Law hakaitu masrâ-t-tufûlah, op. cit.*, p. 8).

regeneration. Arab Christians have a key part to play in this renewal, by offering their lives as a witness:

> For in the Arab world they are not Muslim converts, but they are those who came before, they are rooted in the land and continue to live with courage. They are not afraid of martyrdom and retain the hope that Islamism will adopt modernity. They see, however, that this process is slow to come. For Christians, culture seems to be a privileged place for encounter, in part because it is the place in which some secularity exists; it also enables the development of an analytical spirit and rationality, which often defeats Fideism. They can only see true progress in the Muslim world when it breaks the link between Islamism and politics by embracing the national cause of each country.[139]

Despite the hope held by Christians, their witness must take account of the existential realities for Arab peoples. In other words, it must respect the pace of change within the Arab cultural mindset – albeit without yielding to it altogether – for it is the only soil within which to seed Christian truth. Where the cultural mindset has not yet absorbed certain aspects of modernity, such as the separation of religion and politics, then Arab Christians must be prepared to engage on two fronts. First, they must take the risk of trying to accelerate change, even if this leads to some undesirable consequences. Second, they must adopt an attitude of understanding and sympathetic patience. And here our Christian communities will face an agonising dilemma. On the one hand, they will not themselves want – or be able – to drive the adoption of modernity by the Arab world.[140] On the other hand, they will not want either to endorse a now pathological Arab reticence to engage with the demands and imperatives universally acknowledged as integral

---

139 G. Khodr, 'Les chrétiens d'Orient dans un contexte pluraliste', op. cit.

140 G. Khodr repeatedly insists on the reality of otherness, and feels bound to present it as a hermeneutical example of a just and fruitful way to understand one's interlocutor. Because of Muslim otherness, which is a synonym of diversity, there should be no unilateral activity here: 'Middle Eastern Christianity has for fourteen centuries been living out its fate alongside Islamism, which is the term by which I propose to indicate the integration between civil life and culture that derives from Koranic revelation. The notion of diversity is all the more relevant because the message of the Gospel is received in a variety of Churches, and Islamism too is very varied.' (G. Khodr, 'Les chrétiens d'Orient dans un contexte pluraliste', op. cit.). He even suggests that otherness in the Arab world must necessarily include the Jewish people: 'Diversity will only be fully consummated when Jewishness is included in this discourse.' (G. Khodr, 'Les chrétiens d'Orient dans un contexte pluraliste', op. cit.).

to modernity.[141] However, they are well aware that if they rush Arab society this will give rise to incomprehension and even rebuttals. They must therefore adopt a careful approach of deep solidarity.

By insisting on the acknowledgement of human freedom,[142] both individual and collective, G. Khodr hopes to establish a secure theological foundation for plurality in the Arab world. This would safeguard conviviality and confer on it the status of foundational truth for the Arab people. Given the long-standing ordeal of Muslim–Christian relationships, the atavistic challenges and traumatic reactions, deception is dangerous and cannot simply be remedied by temporary curative solutions or provisional precautionary measures. Freedom must be explicitly and irrevocably acknowledged in order to enable success for conviviality between Arab Christians and Arab Muslims. Only those who are free can expose themselves to the challenges of the Other:

> And yet there are many Arabs, both Muslims and Christians, who desire
> real conviviality, a creative osmosis. The texts and history have led to a
> Christian anthropology and a Muslim anthropology. The two different kinds
> of behaviour and mindset often live well together and nourish each other. So
> we sometimes find Byzantine icons in Muslim homes. We often meet Muslim
> pilgrims in our monasteries. And when Christians move from the Muslim
> context in which they grew up they miss some aspects of Islamic presence,
> such as the calling of the muezzin. We experience the absence of the Other
> as a lack, though we do not wish for an overpowering presence. Maybe it is

---

141 'When today we study [...] Middle Eastern Christians in a pluralist context, we see them in their historical context and can reflect sympathetically on their great achievements and on their deficiencies. The key issue is to find out how we can live within Islamism, for even in countries where there is a certain measure of secular rule, as in Lebanon where the structure of the nation is as yet unclear, collective memory is dominated by the omnipresence of Islam and the anxiety that it may seek to overrule events and freedoms.' (G. Khodr, 'Les chrétiens d'Orient dans un contexte pluraliste', op. cit.)

142 'We can moreover hardly speak of diversity unless we allow the Other their own spiritual autonomy, their doctrinal integrity and their freedom.' (G. Khodr, 'Les chrétiens d'Orient dans un contexte pluraliste', op. cit.) By referring to Gregory of Nyssa, G. Khodr establishes a theological basis for the freedom of the Other: 'The right to life, he states, is based on the conviction that the image of God in us is freedom. This image, when it is understood as freedom, excludes any form of slavery, and thus any infringement of freedom.' (G. Khodr, 'La liberté religieuse. Vision orthodoxe', op. cit., p. 58). Because the Other is free, they become a key part of communion among people: 'His individuality is an essential part of my being. I can only welcome him by listening to his self-revelation.' (*Ibid.*, p. 61.)

the case that Middle Eastern Christians can only be imagined in a Muslim context. Islamism is the object of their love and yet also of their pain.[143]

A respectful distance seems therefore to present the best conditions for inter-action. The sincere desire of both parties to engage is best supported by a space that accommodates free expression by all. A desire for conviviality alone is not enough to banish the fear that the exchange might be stale or awkward. What is needed is the security of a well-regulated framework ensuring that both Christians and Muslims can enjoy convivial communion and interaction.

Those Muslims taking part may be surprised – or even indignant – at the demanding tone of the Orthodox Bishop of Mount Lebanon in a recent outburst. A realistic assessment of decades of dialogue, however, suggests that his demand was a realistic one. In this connection, it is significant that G. Khodr has recently favoured speaking of 'pre-dialogue' between Christians and Muslims.[144] His realis-tic and critical understanding justifies this modest approach. Muslim interlocutors have made real and sincere efforts at theological dialogue, but encounters between Muslims and Christians still, in G. Khodr's view, fall short of expectations. Hence his recommendation of a pre-dialogue to enable mutual appreciation that faith-fully respects how each interlocutor understands themselves. However, he also acknowledges that Muslims have already made a genuine theological effort to try to understand Christianity by studying foundational Christian documents. There is still a dilemma, though. Middle Eastern Christians are constantly torn between love for Islam and their suffering at the hands of Islam, either directly or indirectly. The greatest suffering is not the physical pain of persecution, in a latent form of provo-cation that is unfortunately all too common in the societies of the Arab world. Their real suffering is because Arab Muslims have not yet shown any true willingness to understand Christian truth or to open themselves up to the mystery of Christ. In other words, it is not only Christ who slumbers in the shadows of Islam. G. Khodr is also distressed by another form of slumber. For Muslims too are heavily lost in deep theological sleep. At the dawn of Christian truth, it is Islam that slumbers.

Lebanon, the land of challenge and distinctiveness

G. Khodr is thinking especially of Lebanon when he speaks of the institutional and legal framework for Muslim–Christian conviviality. His deep-seated beliefs

---

143 G. Khodr, 'Les chrétiens d'Orient dans un contexte pluraliste', op. cit.
144 See G. Khodr, 'La nature de l'islam', op. cit., p. 49.

have given him a different geopolitical understanding of the region. His view is that 'historic Syria',[145] the inheritor of the glory of Antioch, is the leading force. In a spirit of realistic compromise, however, he acknowledges the emergence of the Lebanese state as the proving ground for Muslim–Christian conviviality in the Arab world. If Byzantium is still the model,[146] Lebanon is liable to offer an important proving ground for conviviality to evolve in constructive freedom. G. Khodr thus places the issue of Lebanese identity in the wider setting of Middle Eastern history and theology.[147] This acknowledges the dual outlook of the Lebanese Orthodox. On the one hand, they cherish their Antiochian identity, which marks their affiliation to a mystical theology resistant to being limited by national identity. On the other hand, they are irrevocably committed to the challenge of Lebanese conviviality, while yet being unable to establish within wider Orthodoxy a substantive or idealised notion of Lebanese identity:

> The Orthodox concluded a marriage of convenience with Lebanon, which subsequently evolved into an intelligent affection. To be an ethnic Arab Christian (as some claim) or to have a Middle Eastern cultural affiliation is eminently reconciled with a strong and unwavering loyalty to Lebanon.[148]

It turns out, therefore, that Lebanese identity is not incompatible with either Arab identity or Orthodoxy. However, those who are Lebanese Orthodox are marked in their very core by facing in these two directions, one cultural and one religious. And, *mutatis mutandis*, the same applies to the other communities within Lebanon. The convergence within Lebanon of the confessional distinctions

---

145 G. Khodr, *Hadha-l-'âlam lâ yakfî*, Beirut, 2006, p. 115.

146 'Byzantium remains for us a utopia forever calling to be reconquered or restored to be the framework that will always regulate the relationship between the political 'city' and the kingdom of God, which is already established in sacramental life and in the Orthodox understanding of spiritual life.' (G. Khodr, 'La liberté religieuse. Vision orthodoxe', op. cit., p. 48). This assertion may be weakened by a remarkably surprising statement that Byzantium is the heiress of Antioch, G. Khodr's favourite nation (*Law hakaitu masrâ-t-tufûlah, op. cit.*, p. 9).

147 In an article published in the Lebanese daily *An-Nahar* (18 March 2006), G. Khodr awards primacy to the affiliation to Antioch, as the principal locus in which the global identity of the Antiochian Orthodoxy originated and is preserved. On the other hand, the Orthodox presence in Lebanon is due not only to a decision to affiliate, but also to a steadfast loyalty to the only Arab country whose constitution advocates a benign neutrality vis-à-vis religious faith.

148 G. Khodr, 'Le Liban religieux', op. cit.

towards a focal point of shared Lebanese identity is still of key importance, in that it conveys democratic acceptance of freedom and diversity.[149]

Clearly, then, G. Khodr's political vision is indissolubly linked to his mystical theology. A theologian, however, deals in ideas, whereas the political thinker deals with reality. And the reality to which the Orthodox Bishop of Mount Lebanon is responding is none other than the experience of Muslim–Christian conviviality. This is a highly distinctive challenge, and one that offers to the Arab world the possibility of salvation. And yet the Lebanese reality is one of trauma, disappointment and grievous suffering. G. Khodr has attempted an idealised portrayal that describes in fine detail the reasons for its structural fragility:

> Paradoxically, Lebanon is both multiconfessional and secular, in accordance with its own unique formula that means it gives support to all the religions as a group, yet is independent of them all in its political structures.[150]

That it should be both confessional and secular seems to defy logic. The challenge it sets is a difficult one, and the weight of history has in the end revealed its lack of realism.[151] At all events, the Orthodox Bishop of Mount Lebanon remains aware of the enormous value of Lebanese distinctiveness. He denounces its distortions and failures, yet still treasures the possibilities it offers. He judges that Lebanon could yet develop a flourishing cultural life that would far exceed the significance of the historic figures linked with the recent history of this minute country. As a dialectician of the mind, he suggests that the best that Lebanon offers is its striving always to surpass itself. And indeed the idea of Lebanon always

---

149 G. Khodr, *Du dialogue islamo-chrétien et de la convivialité*, Jounieh, Éditions Saint-Paul, 2000, p. 63.

150 G. Khodr, 'Le Liban religieux', op. cit.

151 G. Khodr, in a spirit of clarity and practicality, has identified the true impact of the different factors destabilising and possibly exacerbating the fragility of Lebanese conviviality: 'The current direction of travel of the state is not towards deconfessionalisation as prescribed in the Taif Agreement. Will the country be able to maintain its pluralism and tolerance, acknowledged as a manifestation of conviviality, in the face of Islamic advances? The answer to this question depends strongly on the future of the Iranian regime. Will the country look different in the light of the increasing importance of Israel in the region? Economics will play a major part here. Will Lebanon play a significant part in the reshaping of the Middle East? Becoming a satellite after the signature of the peace treaty might lead to a new wave of migration, principally among Christians. For the "rest who will be saved", maybe they will enable an authentic religious revival. The Middle East will be able to cope with technological progress and apparent modernisation, but religious life will remain deeply embedded in its soul.' (G. Khodr, 'Le Liban religieux', op. cit.).

exceeds the reality of Lebanon.[152] And there's the rub. The Lebanese are in agony about the fragility of their failing conviviality.[153] They are aware that they are condemned to freedom, and they know that this has terrible consequences for their state, which is weakened by conflict and division.

So G. Khodr's aim is to defend the spiritual heart of Lebanon rather than some other purely technical system for managing the country's social and political life. The management of politics, he says, is for politics to do.[154] Human life is complex, and requires proper technical competence. For him, though, the important thing is the divine energy that stirs deep within the Lebanese communities.[155] The communities will flourish in a life of authentic religious faith and bring about the kingdom of fundamental goodness that secretly animates human history, if they can trace back to the original source of this gift; it is the noble mission of the Christians to facilitate the tracing. Their spiritual being is neither formally nor materially bound to their national historical or political situation; it is rooted in the vital relationship of love that binds them to the generous love of God. Given the frailty of human life in general, and of Arab life in particular, the turbulent political crises that trouble their national existence are a reminder of the fundamental inability of the Lebanese to eradicate evil and sin and to hasten the coming of

---

152 This dialectical approach necessarily evokes the attitude of Hamîd Mourânî, a Lebanese philosopher and follower of Hegel, who considers that the salvation of Lebanon lies in the evolutionary dynamic of its internal tensions (see his essay in political philosophy, written in Arabic, *La conscience historique maronite entre l'ancien et le nouveau,* Essais herméneutiques, Beirut, 1981).

153 Despite the scars of the Lebanese war, G. Khodr persists in believing that the reasons for Christian apathy lie elsewhere than in a fear of Islamic hegemony: 'In Lebanon, emigration affects all religious communities. There is no religious explanation for it. In southern Turkey, the Christians are leaving. In Iraq too. But there is every indication that in this country they are not deprived of their freedom to worship. For the last few years, the Copts have been emigrating for the first time. As a general rule, it is not obvious that the decisive reason for all this emigration is a fear of increasing fundamentalism. My aim here is not to analyse this emigration phenomenon. It does not appear to me to be linked to the fact that Christians are becoming disenchanted with cultural diversity.' (G. Khodr, 'Les chrétiens d'Orient dans un contexte pluraliste', op. cit.).

154 When G. Khodr openly declares that 'politics is developed and transformed by politics' (G. Khodr, 'La responsabilité et le témoignage prophétique du chrétien dans la cité', op. cit.), he is soberly positing the principle that politics is automous. His intention is to distinguish Christian political theology from any suggestion that it might be involved with some Islamic vision of the theological/political configuration of the human city: 'Politics is to a certain extent autonomous. This is why various Christians can take up various positions, and live with their right to be different. But they are united in fighting flagrant injustice, which leaves no room for diverging political analysis.' (*Ibid.*)

155 G. Khodr, *Du dialogue islamo-chrétien et de la convivialité, op. cit.*, p. 68.

the Kingdom. For G. Khodr, the experience of withdrawing is more radical even than the existential anxiety of the Lebanese, and especially of the Christians, and leads him to the conclusion that any purely political action, any purely human enterprise, is doomed to be imperfect and ineffectual:

> For us, Christian witness acts like an epiphany. I mean that it shines like a Byzantine liturgy but without making a lasting mark in the events or the intellectual life of our peoples. The marginal elements of society do not shape the historical narrative, and their thinking does not register in the discourse of the Arab intelligentsia. Their discourse is Marxist, nationalist or Islamist. The meek are only noticed when they adopt secular language. Muslims can retain their own vocabulary and impose it on public discourse. […] The fact is that for a long time, here and there and in various places, Christians have been deprived of any real influence on public life and have been marginalised in political discourse. Are they to be wanderers for ever, like the Syro-Jordanian Church in the fourth century that wandered in the deserts and was labelled 'The Church in tents'? The flock and their pastors were in effect Bedouins. Perhaps we will long remain spiritual pilgrims, or a kind of Stylites perched in the middle of the Arab lands, mad witnesses to the love of Christ, immersed in, and emerging from, the waters of Arabia, hoping for eternal theophanies like the one at the Jordan when Christ was baptised.[156]

Torn between the traumas of their history and the theophanies of the promised Kingdom, Lebanese Christians remain tormented by their apparent powerlessness in the present moment. They long with all their hearts to see the Lebanese model succeed. Crushed and ambushed by history, however, they constantly find that they are diverted from their noble aim. So we need to establish whether the Lebanese Christians are now in a position to take up their fragile political Cross. G. Khodr, however, calls on them to show how creative they can be in their evangelical witnessing. It seems that the label of pilgrims or Stylites suits them well, since it implies an extreme form of salutary kenosis.

G. Khodr describes Christians as impulsively generous in the solicitude they long to show to others. Seen in this light, their Lebanese identity will only be

---

156 G. Khodr, 'Les chrétiens d'Orient dans un contexte pluraliste', op. cit. The principal problem for Christianity, according to G. Khodr, is that the Christian faith transcends all political systems and can, paradoxically, exist alongside any system within the limits of the ephemeral conditions of history (G. Khodr, *Law hakaitu masrâ-t-tufûlah, op. cit.*, p. 46).

effective if it facilitates the generous open-heartedness of Christian witness, in an unprecedented outpouring in the crucible of prosaic day-to-day conviviality. At this point, what the Spirit can achieve thanks to their evangelical witness is far more important than anything that Christians might achieve in social or political terms. So here, in Arab territory, a whole new opportunity opens up for Christians for communion: 'When speaking of history in the Middle East one necessarily assumes that Islam is the universal orthodoxy.'[157] If this is true, then Lebanon is a privileged space in the heart of the Arab world in which Christians can join in responding to the calls for human dignity that are normally the preserve of their Muslim neighbours. The distinctiveness of the Lebanese state will be defined by the challenge of diversity to Islam, and this distinctiveness results from a free gift. For, as G. Khodr puts it so eloquently, Islam has become the unique fate of Arab Christianity. In Lebanon, that fate will need to meet its ultimate destiny.

The opportunities and limitations of a re-examined inclusivist theology

How can we fully understand a theological mind as rich and as extensive as that of Georges Khodr? His published works do not present us with a systematic and complete body.[158] He explores ideas and approaches them from a wide range of points of view, and the reader might think his thoughts scattered or even indecisive. One might even be led to think he is somehow suspending judgement, failing to reach conclusions, or even being incoherent. We need only look at the multitude of vistas that the Orthodox Bishop of Mount Lebanon has opened up and from which he has reinterpreted human life in the Arab world to see the richness of his enquiries and of the challenges he has identified. His sources are as diverse as his approaches. His basic frame of reference has remained Eastern patrology. The system offers a coherent understanding of the *kerygma* in the spirit of an ortho-dox faith called to meet the challenges of the time and of the current situation in Arab lands. The richness and depth of his perceptions should encourage an excep-tional growth in renewed understanding of the Christian faith in the context of the

---

157 G. Khodr, 'Le christianisme oriental et l'homme moderne', op. cit.

158 In theological hermeneutics, for example, G. Khodr appears not to have formulated his own system: 'Georges Khodr hat keine hermeneutisches System entwickelt' [Georges Khodr has not developed a system of hermeneutics], A. E. Kattan, 'Wort und Leib. Zur Hermeneutik Georges Khodr in ihrem islamischen Kontext'. On several occasions, however, he invites Christians and Muslims in the Arab world to engage with sacred texts using a new hermeneutics in order to open up religious faith to the legitimate promises of modernity (see G. Khodr, *Law hakaitu masrâ-t-tufûlah, op. cit.*, p. 74).

contemporary Arab world. Arab Christians should note here that they are dealing not with someone who is wedded to dogma, nor a simple practitioner of biblical exegesis or of theoretical moral or political theology, but with an interesting hybrid, a doctrinaire scholar in whom clear thinking and mystical intuition work together. G. Khodr conveys the patristic tradition faithfully and in an original way, and offers contemporary Arab theology a wealth of new ideas that he hopes will renew and energise the evangelistic witness of the Christian communities in the Arab world. Being neither dilettante nor eclectic, nor indeed relativist in his theological research, he focuses instead on the urgency of preaching and pastoral care, and builds his thinking around the one, supreme person of Christ. This Christ is the one worshipped in the Antiochian Orthodox Church, which longs to reveal to the Arab world the glory of God's gentleness.

I do not pretend to be an infallible interpreter of G. Khodr's thinking, but it is clear that his contribution to instigating conviviality comes from a Christocentric perspective. His is a median and nuanced approach that avoids on the one hand the theological exclusivism he condemns and on the other the relativist pluralism he rejects. Contemporary Arab theology rejoices in benefiting from his intelligent theological thinking, even though its Christocentric presuppositions are subordinated to the supremacy of Christian truth as formulated in the ecumenical councils of the first millennium of the Christian era. By situating his theological contribution within a search for authenticity that aims to go beyond not only the legalism that petrifies revelation in the written word, but also the illuminism that sees truth evaporate wordlessly, G. Khodr energetically formulates a theology of conviviality that acknowledges diversity as a space tolerated in the vastness of divine love. So in his case we can speak of a baseless pluralism shaped by an implicit inclusivism. This form of pluralism is characterised by its spiritual and mystical origins and is not based on theological foundations. In other words, for Khodr, Christ remains the way towards God. He is the only path that leads God to mankind and mankind to God. However, the wide range of other paths reflects the immense work of the Spirit of God at the heart of creation. This diversity signals God's active and multifaceted presence in the world. The same Christ is thus received and experienced in many different ways in the various religions of the world. The place of Islam is unique, in the sense that it offers an elucidation of Christ's mystery with a level of authenticity that comes close to the Bible itself.

The major challenge in the case of such tempered inclusivism lies in the appropriation of the other. G. Khodr does not anywhere concede to Islam that it might constitute an autonomous path to God, independent of any reference to Christ. The Christian theology of Islam, as he outlines it in his many articles and lectures, simply highlights its possible affinities with the core of Christian truth.[159] And where Islam is clearly beyond any Christological redemption, he honestly and courageously states that the human mind is not capable of finding the Christian and Muslim perceptions of the divine mystery compatible. Alongside its theologically radical nature, G. Khodr's thinking remains unconditionally open-hearted and imbued with the love and gentleness of kenotic spirituality. Assaad Elias Kattan has made a study of Khodr's theological vocabulary,[160] and notes that his desire to imitate the style of the Koran does not in any way obscure the theological lucidity and faithfulness to the Christian faith in the writings of the Orthodox Bishop of Mount Lebanon. One of the best examples of this mechanism of proximity and distancing in relation to Koranic thought is the way in which G. Khodr reproduces the Koranic verse that glorifies the status of the best nation.[161] Instead of adopting the same theological exclusivism, G. Khodr attenuates the expression and adapts it: the Christian community is among the best nations of the world. He is thus acknowledging the vast extent of the goodness that the Word of God constantly nourishes through His spirit of holiness.

G. Khodr's theological work consists entirely in interpreting the diversity among religions in the light of Christian Christology. His hermeneutics have a dual purpose. On the one hand, other religions are perceived in terms of their intrinsic richness; on the other, they are brought into the mysterious wisdom of the unique divine plan carried out in Jesus Christ for the salvation of the whole world. This leaves many issues to be explored. For if it is legitimate for the Christian theology advocated by G. Khodr to interpret Islam according to its own understanding and within the framework of its own categories, then this can work the other way around too. G. Khodr's interpretation, however, does not accept that Christian faith can be integrated into Islam. He maintains that Islam would never be able to accept the central and unique aspect of Christian faith, the divine drama played out on the Cross. This conflict of interpretation should nevertheless lead both sides to reject the hermeneutics of exclusion. There is therefore much discernment work to be done to ensure that inclusivist interpretations do not disrespect the integrity of faith

---

159 G. Khodr's understanding is that Christians can only draw close to reality through the spirit of Christ (G. Khodr, *Law hakaitu masrâ-t-tufûlah, op. cit.*, p. 35). This makes it essential to interpret the reality of Islam from a resolutely Christological perspective.

160 A. E. Kattan, 'Le nouvel apport langagier de Georges Khodr', in Collectif, *Vers une terminologie théologique chrétienne arabe unifiée*, Ghazir, Éditions du Séminaire Patriarcal Maronite, 2005, p. 129.

161 'You are the best community ever raised for humanity – you encourage good, forbid evil, and believe in Allah' (Koran 3, 110).

and sensitivity of the Other. And there's the rub. Theological inclusivism is difficult to reconcile with the autonomous diversity that is inherent in God's own plan.

If the Christian interpretation of Islam as established and developed by G.
Khodr does not adopt an exclusive stance towards Koranic revelation, it does
nevertheless adopt an integrative theological approach. The theology of religions
that best fits with G. Khodr's beliefs is, it seems to me, one that grants Islam the
freedom of a space within Christian truth itself. He considers the Christian truth of
incarnation to be immense and inexhaustible, so that it allows variety and diversity within the polymorphic expanse of its historical development. In other words,
G. Khodr's theology can accommodate a certain level of pluralism, provided it
is understood within a Christological approach that expands to match the extent
of the universe. Instead of granting that interfaith diversity is *sui generis* real,
autonomous and generative of the human condition, Khodr prefers to draw it into
the vast enveloping freedom provided by the divine wisdom. That wisdom was
above all made visible in the self-revelation of God through Jesus Christ. So it is
a deductive diversity, not original, autonomous or self-generating.

My observations align with a currently lively vein of theological thought in the
debate between inclusivists and pluralists within contemporary Western Christian
theology. The debate with G. Khodr's theology is justified by the magnitude of his
ambition and his explicit theological commitment. For now, I shall limit myself to
one conclusion. I express it with a caution that derives neither from scepticism nor
from a fear of jeopardy. I would express it as follows: G. Khodr claims affiliation
to an Orthodox theology that is not only concerned with the unicity of salvation
but also respectful of the intrinsic diversity of the human condition.[162] In his mind,
the Orthodox path followed by the Church of the Middle East is well capable
of rescuing Eastern theological understanding from the exclusivist traps inherited from a juridical and rational philosophical tradition. His deepest conviction,
however, is that theology, whether Eastern or Western, is naturally subordinated to
the glory of the truth. The value of Orthodox theology could be its mystical optimism that draws the transfigured universe into the abundant, free and unmerited
love of the Trinity. That such apocatastasis is not justified in Orthodoxy contrasts
with the requirement in Western theology for intelligibility.

All in all, it seem to me that G. Khodr's endeavour is to establish conviviality

---

162 It is important here to repeat G. Khodr's statement, quoted above, on his ecclesiological
approach: 'There is a sense in which Christianity is not exclusive. It is depth, but it is not
everything. I wrote a few years ago that it is anathema to equate the one with the whole.' (G.
Khodr, 'La liberté religieuse. Vision orthodoxe', op. cit., p. 60).

on the basis of this absence of theological justification. His mystical attitude does not mean that the orthodoxy he advocates explicitly rejects the principle of divine unicity. So in spite of the impact of his Eastern theological affiliation, G. Khodr considers it almost impossible to conceive of plurality integral to the very order of divine revelation. He is prepared to tolerate, or rather acknowledge, the need for natural and legitimate diversity in the pathways of spiritual experience that correspond to the different cultural sensitivities among humanity, but he objects to attempts to jeopardise the unicity of divine will, declaring them incoherent and futile. His harmonious vision of the divine plan does not admit of multiple parallel manifestations. So in conclusion, the best guarantee of human conviviality is not so much the recognition of multiple initiatives independent of Christ, but rather a diversity of receptions of the same Christic mystery in the heart of the one plan of salvation.

4

Liberation: the site of fraternity (Grégoire Haddad)

The work of Grégoire Haddad (1924–2015) was first and foremost a lifetime commitment. His theological writing springs from a mature reflection on the practice of commitment. His principal focus is the urgency of the Kingdom, which foreshadows the liberation of mankind. His approach belongs in an epistemological and existential framework that is markedly different from previous models. This secular and humanist champion considers that theology should not be stifled within a narrow field arbitrarily defined as religious. Real human life is the privileged site for this Christian theology. His one and only aim is to enable all people, wherever they are, to develop over time in response to the fundamental instincts that shape us as people. As this development occurs, people are drawn together and a fundamental pattern of solidarity emerges between them, thus demonstrating that conviviality is the result of a focus on the liberation of humanity. A Christian theology of conviviality should be set up not as a theoretical construct with its own internal logic and epistemological coherence, but rather in terms of the historical challenges faced by people every time they attempt to free themselves of any kind of injustice, oppression, exploitation, enslavement, alienation or levelling down.

This chapter is in three sections, which correspond to the three key elements in Grégoire Haddad's work. The first section treats of the evangelical radicalism that is a fundamental characteristic of his commitment. This is an attitude that lies at the root of his life and his work, infusing and guiding both. The second section, closely linked to the first, explores the theme of liberation that is crucial to the aim of the whole of his output. Radicalism is meaningless if it does not lead to the liberation of mankind. And this liberation claims also to apply to the liberation of God Himself. The third section, therefore, gives a broad-brush outline of the dual liberation of both Christ and humanity. Viewed in terms of this triple perspective, conviviality is revealed as the site in which liberation is deployed and realised.

The preferential option of Christian radicalism

Commitment as prophetic path

In contemporary Christian communities in the Arab world, the word 'liberation' is not widely used. The watchword is more likely to be 'survival'. There is a huge and damaging level of expectation weighing down the Christian faith. It is required to retreat into a defensive position in order to protect the physical existence of individuals and groups who, in Lebanon and in a few countries of the Arab world, continue to claim allegiance to the message of Jesus Christ. Christian witness within the societies of the current Arab world is at risk of floundering, paralysed by the tell-tale line that divides liberation from survival.

Grégoire Haddad's theological originality is that he has refocused Christian witness on demands for the liberation so deeply desired by contemporary Arabs. For them, liberation is the best guarantee of survival and conviviality. Physical survival without commitment to the liberation of the Arab peoples is indeed a kind of spiritual death, whereas to survive as a true Christian in the Arab world is a mark of evangelistic courage. Christians are thus called to work energetically in defence of the lives of others. This is at any rate one of the fundamental intuitions guiding Grégoire Haddad's work.

As a figurehead in the Lebanese struggle against injustice, poverty and oppression, Haddad sees his Christian faith as driven by a radical impulse towards liberation. He was born in the Lebanese mountains (Souk El Gharb, 1924), at a time when Lebanon was becoming emancipated, albeit in painfully limited and divided form, from its former stifling occupation by the Ottomans. His Orthodox family was highly sensitive to the demands of Protestant reform, and Grégoire Haddad deliberately opted to join and flourish in Eastern Catholicism.

He was ordained priest in 1949 in the Melkite Greek Catholic Church, and devoted himself to social work in which his daily contact with the working classes made him keenly aware of the misery and suffering in the Beirut suburban areas. He immediately focused the energy of his faith on the needs of this disinherited and disoriented population, and in 1957 he founded the Mouvement Social, a nonconfessional space that drew together the social and political forces prioritising the defence of the humanity of all people and the development of better social justice for the whole Lebanese population. In 1965 the synod of the Melkite Greek

Catholic Church appointed him bishop of the Lebanese capital, a position of key importance in the social landscape of Lebanese Christianity.

His evangelical spirituality and analytical humanity led him to promote a theological vision based on the key notions of Christ and mankind. From the start, he declared his commitment to the poor and the young. In 1974, in collaboration with Jérôme Chahine, he therefore set up an avant-garde cultural magazine, *Âfâq*, dedicated to widening perspectives among Christian believers, to freeing them from the dominant Eastern confessionalism, and to enabling them to conform, as far as possible, to the requirements of democratic and egalitarian secularism. He hoped that his cultural magazine would play an instrumental role in spreading among Lebanese society, and thence on into the rest of the Arab world, new humanitarian ideas coming from the West. It seemed to him that it was essential, in theological terms, to foster within the Arab world a familiarity with the profound intuitions of the authentic evangelism that seeks fully to embody the relevance of the Good News of Jesus Christ.

In a Lebanese society ruled by the imperatives of Arab culture, Grégoire Haddad's commitment could not avoid the political space and its inevitable clashes with the underground activities of the Lebanese political class. The few articles he published in his new magazine quickly led to an outpouring of protest. Grégoire Haddad was keen to defend the cause of all Lebanese confessions, and to adapt his theological language to the desires of young Lebanese students who were alive to the promises of international and Arab socialism. He also sought to defend the claims of the Palestinian people whose increasing presence as an armed force in Lebanon was threatening the stability of the country. His own behaviour and style of life was ruled by simplicity of expression and material asceticism. These factors combined to draw the ire of the excessively confessionalised sociopolitical class in Lebanon, itself tragically tense with sociocultural divisions of political and religious origin. He was dubbed the 'red bishop' and forces combined to oust him and snuff out the critical drive behind his mission. An unhealthy coalition between extreme-right groups of both Christians and Muslims succeeded in removing him from office. In 1975, as the major disruption of civil war loomed, threatening to dislocate Lebanon – as sadly foreseen by our rebel Lebanese bishop – the synod of the Greek Catholic Church asked Grégoire Haddad to offer his resignation.

Bravely accepting the incomprehension, the disappointment and the bitterness, Grégoire Haddad resolved to spend the rest of his life dedicated to the cause of the Arab people. His dismay was redeemed by his incisive joy in the Good News of Christ. Wounded, he nevertheless faced up to the ordeal and threw himself with renewed vigour into his social and humanitarian struggle. He became increasingly alive to the challenges, in salutary, social and political terms, faced by Christian believers in Lebanon who sought to heal a Middle Eastern Arab society that had long suffered the bruising consequences of conflict between confessions, and was mercilessly eroded by structural paralysis.

Grégoire Haddad's life was focused on pastoral ministry, and he had no ambitions to develop a formal academic career. Occasional publications did however voice his theological thinking. Around one hundred articles, lectures and panel discussions reveal the profound motivations of his Christian commitment. He also wrote a few books, including the title that provides the background reference material for this study, *Libérer le Christ et l'homme*, which was first published in 1974. It collates the articles published in the magazine *Âfâq*, and constitutes the essence of Grégoire Haddad's theological vision. His incisive style contrasts sharply with the conformist spirit of other local theological writers. The former Bishop of Beirut would however prefer practice to theory. Had he not felt obliged to explain his Christian and humanitarian convictions, he would frankly have preferred not to engage in writing. One fact is beyond dispute: the shining example of his life only intensifies the authenticity of his writing. There is an exceptional and enlightening coherence and harmony between his thinking and his way of life.[1]

Love as the ultimate foundation of the theology of commitment

In his extensive pastoral work on humanitarian, social, cultural, religious and political liberation, Grégoire Haddad constantly claimed allegiance to a spirituality

---

1 Other titles make it clear that Grégoire Haddad was interested in different aspects of the reality of a life of Christian witness. *Le christianisme et la femme* (1975) is a fervent work of advocacy for the liberation of Lebanese and Arab women. *Le pape et le Liban* (1997) recalls the most significant moments of John Paul II's visit to Lebanon and offers an interpretation of the messages of solidarity and support sent by the universal Church to the Churches of Lebanon. *Méditations spirituelles* (1997) is an anthology of the editorial articles Haddad regularly wrote for the theological journal (*Échanges, Al-Râbita*) of a small Lebanese association called la Fraternité des Malades du Liban. He used them to write spiritual reflections on suffering, the spiritual life and Christian love, three topics that nourished his life and his commitment to the most destitute of society. His last work, *La laïcité totale* (2001), was conceived as a project for radical change in Lebanese mentality and society. The change was based on the principle of the separation of religious and political power, and aimed to usher in a democratic Lebanese society. Having received a literary education, Grégoire Haddad wrote poetry, and works on grammar and literature. He also prepared for publication two works on simplifying Arab grammar, renewal in art, and the process of writing poetry.

founded on the initial gift of divine love. We should therefore start this chapter by taking a global view of his vision. The subsequent descriptions will illustrate the features we explore here. Rather than limit the concept of liberation to random philosophical or political categories, Haddad is keen to link it to God's loving plan conceived in Jesus Christ for the whole of humanity. All human work towards liberation is given meaning, realised and completed through Jesus Christ, who is the incarnation of God's unconditional love. In his *Méditations spirituelles*, Grégoire Haddad states:

> I am only fully myself, and therefore free, in that extension of the thinking and acting self of Christ; I am only free when I am freed from the narrow-minded and selfish 'small me', so that Christ is given free rein in me, and is no longer hampered or handicapped by my narrow-mindedness.[2]

This 'me' of Christ is thus invested with a value that transcends all selfishness and all the narrow-mindedness of modern subjectivity. To be liberated is to remodel one's ego on the pattern of the Christlike ego that is fully infused with a spirit of welcome, of presence, of giving. Grégoire Haddad remains devoted to Christ precisely because, as an exceptional person in human history, He fully incarnates unwavering openness to being in relationship with mankind, to unconditional giving, and to fraternal service. The author of the *Méditations* sees no need to engage in a critical theological deprecating human nature, but instead highlights that Jesus Christ embodies the true link between the hopes of mankind and what God offers: 'Christ did not come to destroy nature, but to fulfil it. He did not come to cancel suffering, but to show its true worth.'[3] If this is true, then all Christian theological discourse should be able to defend the principle of this link. Similarly, Christianity should continue to embody spiritual and moral standards that do not fit with mainstream individualist complacency.

The real issue here is the meaning of the Christian message in the modern world. Humanity these days seems to be adopting a very tortuous path. People are searching for salvation and joy while suffering through weakness, solitude and incomprehension. Grégoire Haddad calls this the birth of a new world: 'The whole universe is working and preparing to give birth, to recreate [ ] Any birth necessarily involves pain.' It is therefore important to give meaning to the whole of human experience, including the searching, the suffering and the birthing. And

---

2 Grégoire Haddad, *Méditations spirituelles*, Beirut, 1997, p. 54 (hereafter MS).
3 MS, p. 19.

in truth, this meaning is revealed in the communion between people, the highest achievement of the work of Christ.[4]

The human condition is nevertheless often prey to painful ruptures. On the one hand, people aspire to a sense of communion. On the other, they hold on to the narrow sphere of their own egoism. Only Christ can heal the ruptures by offering each one of us a sense of 'me' that is reconciled with 'myself' and with the Other: 'Communion is a keenly felt need for each of us, to achieve fulfilment and joy, so it cannot result from natural relationships. Suffering has shown that it is impossible, but Christ has shown that it is possible.'[5] Clearly, he uses 'natural' here in the sense of the negative forces that are destructive towards communion. Anything opposed to our impulse towards openness and our desire for communion is thus due to our selfish, inward-looking tendency to inflexibility. If Christ suffers with and for us, it is because we are seeking to liberate ourselves from this existential tension in order to find our deeper authentic selves. Christ meets us in the very crucible of our suffering. As humans, we are thus motivated by our search for authenticity and this culminates in our quest for communion.

Grégoire Haddad similarly defines life as being a site of action and participation. The dynamics of relationship imbue all the connections within human existence:

> Life is not a mechanical or material repetition of the same actions. It is the participation in action of the personal, of that which is my most profound being. It is the development of this action, of this being. It is the radiance and replication of this being. And this life is spiritual.[6]

Communion among people, joy and the spiritual dimension of life are thus strongly linked. In Grégoire Haddad's terminology, spiritual matters are those that belong to a life of true and authentic communion between people who are seeking to respond to their calling to be in relationship in this world. Over the years, Christian spirituality has tended to become a conceptual flight of fancy not properly grounded in reality. An enclosed and self-centred universe of joy is not sanctioned in Christian faith, however. Our world recreates itself endlessly in search of joy. Any spirituality worthy of the name must have concrete consequences on the daily lives of human beings. Relationships are the crucible in which true evangelical commitment is tested and crystallised.

---

4 MS, p. 14.
5 MS, p. 32.
6 MS, p. 44.

The requirements of authentic evangelism are a strong challenge to the faith of Christians, who are called to find their joy in pursuing active fraternal communion. If, as Grégoire Haddad maintains, people evolve towards sharing mutually edifying company, energising life and creative openness,[7] then the joy they seek will become incompatible with anodyne suffocating quietism:

> The Lord does not wish us to enjoy a lazy kind of joy, a false joy that would result from moral indolence or lack of courage and that we would gain without any effort or spiritual progress.[8]

The magnitude of the joy draws faith to the pinnacle of action. It would be absurd to think of faith as inactive, not working or incarnate. For Grégoire Haddad, true joy is putting his Christian faith to work in the service of humanity here and now, in the local context of the historic existence of the Christian communities of contemporary Lebanon. Lebanese Christians can only find true joy in making a real contribution to building up their own humanity and that of their neighbours, in the historic context that is truly theirs. Joy cannot be outside time and history. As everyone knows, Islam, Arab culture and modernity are an integral part of the historical challenges faced by Christians living in the Arab world.

If this is true, then people must be able to rely on their natural predisposition to help enable for them and for those around them the joy promised by Jesus Christ. For in the last analysis, if Christianity does not preach joy for mankind, then it will quickly disappear in a sterile and enclosed institutional system. This joy is within the reach of those who are willing to release their deep-seated and enriching potential to be present in the moment. Grégoire Haddad calls this potential 'attention': 'Attention is the principal means given to us by God so that we can attain fulfilment in our own lives and for the universe, so that we can accept who we are and our lives, and so develop and flourish in the truth of eternal reality.'[9] Since we as humans mould ourselves and our integrity through contact

---

7 'All beings evolve towards a warmer welcome, a greater generosity, and more union.' (MS, p. 72.)

8 MS, p. 28. By focusing his thoughts on action, he eventually developed a concept of eternity as a site of intense activity rather than a passive immersion in worship: 'In eternity we will not engage in boring worship, but finally attain the perfect tenderness through the generosity of all, the welcome of all, the communion shared between all and with the Trinity.' (MS, p. 72.) His words describe the active aspect of communion as conceived in Christian faith in perfect symbiosis with the requirements of relational joy.

9 MS, p. 23.

with others, it turns out that attention is the very best way to forge authentic relationships. To be attentive to the Other is to take in the whole of that person, and
willingly to offer a positive response to their deepest needs, those that are truest
to their human nature. This approach also implies a deep engagement with the
unalterable distinctiveness of that Other, an engagement that is a *sine qua non* for
true mutual communion and relational joy.

The Arab world as a testing ground for evangelical authenticity

Grégoire Haddad therefore seeks to express his Christian faith in terms of authentic presence. The presence of God in mankind then becomes for any fruitful relationship its *raison d'être* and the guarantee of its durability. It is in our nature as
humans to converge towards the presence of love which, within the limitations
of the historical experience of contemporary humanity, makes available to us the
nature of God. The heart of that presence is the infinitely tender love of God:
'Presence that saves me from my solitude. Presence that gives meaning to my life,
that is to say, significance and direction, and thus saves me from the temptation of
the present time, of absurdity, of nausea… and of despair.'[10] God's presence can
manifest in a multiplicity of ways according to context and local tradition. In the
perspective of a theology of liberation, Grégoire Haddad conceives of that presence as a gradual unveiling of the love of God in the crucible of human poverty.
A comprehensive vocabulary of inner therapy can be deployed to describe the
specific consequences of such a presence in a person's life.

Relationship, communion, presence – these are the key words used by Grégoire Haddad. His theological journey is most closely associated with a vision of
the liberating love of God. Any love that does not set mankind free negates the
primary dignity seeded deep into the very nature of creation. Christianity, in historical terms, thus reflects the experience of a presence that is constantly fortified
by the gift to the world of an inexhaustible life-giving love, one that transcends all
obstacles to relationship. So it is no longer surprising that the author of the *Méditations* expresses his faith thus: 'The most important aspect of Christianity in my
life is to believe in love, the love that is God in Himself, and the love that He is
vis-à-vis mankind.'[11] Love becomes the hearth in which glows the Christian faith.
Without the regenerating force of love, the very fact of Christianity is unthinkable.
Without the creative energy and analytical lucidity of discernment, Christianity is

---

10 MS, p. 81.
11 MS, p. 82.

in danger of succumbing to the temptations of the dark ages: to revert to a system of intolerance and tyranny that favours power at the cost of charity.

In order to preserve Lebanese and Arab Christianity from the rigidity of canons and scholasticism, from compromising the freshness of its first passion, and from becoming ossified in repetitive stereotypical ideas and endlessly rehearsed commentaries, Grégoire Haddad offers a theology of liberating love. It is a love that is proved only in the daily struggle of the Arab people. Every pastoral project undertaken by the former Bishop of Beirut is focused on the categorical imperative of Gospel love. A historical and analytical interpretation of this fundamental principle is more important than ever to the lives of the Christian communities. The concrete implications of this interpretation, as they develop, begin to outline the limits and distinctive features of the different theological sensitivities within the universal Church.

In other words, Grégoire Haddad is well aware that the Christian message can be delivered in a variety of accents. The theoretical and practical difficulties presented to Christian communities by the situation in Arab countries hardly need highlighting. The only remedy that can possibly be offered by Christianity is liberation: 'To live in love is not a matter of intelligence or reasoning, of sentiment or affection. It is a matter of will and action.'[12] The principal motivation for Christian spirituality must be loving through action, in order to defeat the death dealt by injustice and oppression, and this active form of love must not be allowed to disregard real people in their historical condition, those who suffer daily. This is a very serious undertaking, and risks 'missing depth if we dissociate God from mankind; or seek to love only God; or forget that since the time of Christ, God and mankind are one and the same reality; or want to love God in humanity but not in specific individuals, as if the individual were to be ignored and God were at the core of mankind but somehow independent of real individuals.'[13] To restore mankind to God's plan is a course so obvious as not to need justifying, since mankind is at the very heart of God's plan. A love devoid of partners would be fundamentally absurd and inconsistent.

The former Bishop of Beirut is seeking out nothing less than the historical fulfilment of the Kingdom of God. This fulfilment cannot however simply disregard the sociocultural issues of the Arab world. Christian communities of the Middle East promote the humanity of mankind, but surely not simply so they can resort to convenient humanist assertions that are unwelcome in Arab culture.

---

12 MS, p. 88.
13 MS, p. 107.

That culture is by its very nature unable to contemplate any reductive suggestions of intimacy involving either mankind or God. Their disregard, however,
could prevent Arab theologians, both Muslim and Christian, from formulating a
relevant critique of daily reality for the Arab peoples. Grégoire Haddad does not
feel obliged to uphold the intransigence of a culture that imposes its own ways
of thinking on anyone wishing to understand it, but he does appeal for the true
liberation of all those who claim to belong to that culture. The love that sets us
free is offering to help Arabs who long to explore a new way of relating to their
identity and their culture:

> To love someone else as a free individual is to take account of their freedom,
> to accept that they are different and accept them with their differences; it is to
> accept that they may have ways of thinking, of judging, of acting, of reacting
> that are different from mine; it is not to impose on that person my way of
> seeing things; if they need education, it is to help that education, that is to
> say their self-education, their gaining of increasing freedom, their maturity,
> their personality – and not force them into moulds of my own or others'
> making; it is to accept that their freedom may spring surprises on me and their
> personality may develop in their own authentic direction; it is to approach
> this free person in their space, not force them into my own; it is to accept that
> I may seem weak while I am waiting for their personality to evolve, but also
> know when to be strong with them – to the extent of being heroic or saintly –
> when I am able to enter into dialogue with their truly free self.[14]

This freedom offered by Jesus Christ to the Arab peoples is a huge project of
human conversion. Christians would therefore do very well to discuss the notion
of freedom itself. Before undertaking such a major task, Grégoire Haddad did
indeed devote much thought to the conditions that might make it possible. His
pastoral ministry had taught him to evaluate the soul of Lebanese society, which
was resistant to innovation and constantly petrified by ancestral fears.

Towards an Arab theology of liberation

Three fields of liberation

As Christians respond to their calling to be authentic witnesses of the Good News,

---

14 MS, p. 112.

they will not be able to ignore the deep-seated aspirations of the Arab societies in which they live. If, however, Arab culture makes it hard for individuals to overcome traditional instincts of fear and deadlock, then Christians – who genuinely believe in and expect the best in each individual – should offer pathways to liberation. The liberating energy of Christian faith can lurk half-hidden in the different ways in which Christians engage with daily reality. Crucially, their efforts must be focused where they will affect issues accessible to the Arab mindset. Any Christian discourse in an Arab context should therefore avoid expatiating on theological speculation. Far better to interact with the daily concerns of our Arab neighbours. Arab culture in its current sociopolitical configuration appears to be ignoring a significant key aspect of Arab identity, that is, the gradual emancipation of the depths of the Arab soul. So what is needed is a reinterpretation of the deepest aspirations of contemporary Arab people, in order to integrate them into the universal yearnings of mankind. We might then see bursts of authentic and universal joy arising from the abyss of the human ordeal suffered by the Arab people. An Arab Christian theology of liberation should ensure that its searching should respond to those deepest aspirations. The Arab heart will only hear the heart of the Gospel if the Christian message is in tune with Arab cultural sensitivities. Christians, in order successfully to integrate into Arab culture, must be able accurately to identify the places in the Arab world where there is great need, and offer concrete solutions.

A first opportunity for liberation is the one in the very heart of the human personality. Grégoire Haddad constantly strove to encourage individuals towards freedom and maturity within Lebanese society. Individuals need to be enabled to free themselves from influences that hold them hostage by infantilising them. Education should be designed to meet the needs of each person, and to fit with the reality of their life. In the case of Christian mission, a person's awakening to faith should also be in tune with the individual's personality. Only when someone is released from external influences will they be able to listen to their own inner voice and hear in it the quiet loving voice of God, and foster a closer relationship with Christ and with others. As is sadly well known, passing on the Christian faith in Lebanon and in the other societies of the Arab world has always been a matter of fierce conflict between two opposing forces. The traditional model has forced inherited and ancient patterns of thought on those who have been made to assimilate them; the more sensitive modern approach advocates presenting and explaining the substance and the values in ways that will speak to the contemporary challenges faced by the Arab peoples. Grégoire Haddad is a strong champion of the second approach.

A second opportunity for liberation is found in the ways Christians speak about God. This is the topic in Grégoire Haddad's major work, *Libérer le Christ et l'homme*. While some Christians in Lebanon continue to think it important to throw up a defensive wall around Christianity in order to protect it from history and the salutary jolts it delivers, the former Bishop of Beirut reaches a conclusion that is diametrically opposed. His pastoral ministry suggests that it is far more important to show the urgent need in the Bible to liberate God from human attempts to control Him. In the final analysis, the Bible tells us about the liberation of both God and mankind. The theologian's vocation is to highlight the revolutionary essence of the teachings transmitted by the life and preaching of Jesus Christ. Clearly, there was a difficult contrast between the official interpretation of Scripture and Grégoire Haddad's own interpretation, and he paid for his theological audacity by suffering a number of personal difficulties.

A third opportunity for liberation is in the implied openness to the Other. In the context of a secular sociocultural society, those who welcome otherness are those who have experienced inner liberation and been emancipated from an overpowering ego. The value of hospitality can then operate as the key vector for conviviality, which is based on mutual acceptance and respect. Any person who is different is someone who should challenge the Christian heart. Whole human lives can be frittered away at a sub-human level; to prevent this, Christians should practice evangelical hospitality. Practical measures may be needed to enable otherness to flourish in liberty:

> It may be that individual hospitality is inadequate to solving the problems
> faced by refugees and displaced persons, and that collective solutions are
> needed, sometimes on a national or even international level. These are
> economic measures, but alongside them there must also be human measures.
> Each stranger must feel welcomed, adopted, and accepted with joy by a
> person: something that can only come from loving hospitality.[15]

In this reflection, Haddad is emphasising the urgent need to establish a connection between the two acts of evangelical love, the individual gesture and the measures offered by the collective structure. These two complementary acts need to combine and amplify each other in order to overcome and remedy historical failures. Individual action can bear fruit in heart conversion, while collective

---

15 MS, p. 131.

actions can lead to the removal of structural and systemic injustice. Someone with experienced pastoral lucidity is called for if the delicate synergy between these two actions is to be successfully conjugated.

Witnessing flaws and the requirements of the present circumstances

Anyone reading Grégoire Haddad's writing more widely and deeply will gain an idea of his theological background, and will realise that liberation is the force that drives evangelical witness among committed Christians. So we must now focus in greater detail on the three major themes of his work: the radical nature of theological research, the liberation of Christ, and the liberation of mankind. The key point here is to show the implications for salvation of working towards liberation in the lives of Lebanese Christian communities. Each of these three themes can be linked to sketching out revolutionary beliefs, to formulating novel proposals, and to refining and realising bold concepts. This first section of this study will examine the assumptions and implications linked to the notion of radicalism in Grégoire Haddad's theology.

In his exploration of radicalism, Grégoire Haddad aims to question the well-entrenched marks of Christian faith that have become mired in the surrounding confusion of Lebanese confessionalism. We shall look to find evidence to prove that asking questions can be beneficial and promote regeneration. As well as sincere doubt and vigorous interrogation, we shall argue for pious questioning and a calm approach to radical revision. Prudently and circumspectly, we shall identify the crisis in the Church in Lebanon and examine its causes.

> Is the Church sick in Lebanon and in all the Arab Middle East? Is it in its final throes? Or is it experiencing revival? Is it because of the clergy that things are going so badly for the Churches in these countries? Were they all to be replaced, would this bring renewal or reform? Or maybe it is because of the structures inherited from the Middle Ages, so that renewing and reforming these would bring new life? Or is it that the Churches are misunderstanding the Gospel and the words of Christ on the essential nature of the Church? If this is so, would renewal be the answer? Or will it be necessary to destroy all the structures that make the Church an institution?[16]

---

16 Grégoire Haddad, *Libérer le Christ et l'homme*, Beirut, n.d, n.p, rev. and updated edn., p. 9 (henceforth LCH).

Haddad's string of questions is in danger of irritating committed readers, but he is careful to avoid the kind of trivial and naïve queries that one might find in more general and less well-considered complaints. His points pick out with care the particular difficulties facing Lebanese Christianity. Later in his text, he refers to confessionalism and indirectly identifies it as the cause of the sterility of Christian faith.

With a consistently analytical eye he enumerates and examines one by one the imperfections and failings of the Church in Lebanon. He looks at ritual and wonders how it might best be made relevant to the modern era. He finishes his inquiry by asking three fundamental questions on the vitality of the Christian presence in Lebanon and in the Arab world.

Who is Christ? What can be said of Him today, in contemporary language? Can the language of God be meaningful in our current age? Is the language mysterious, metaphysical, inconsistent? When people believe in God, is this necessarily a form of enslavement or alienation?[17]

Three theological issues are of huge import, as they entail a major revision of the deposit of the Christian faith: the significance of Christ for Arab people, the pertinence of Christian theological language in an Arab Muslim environment, and the relevance of the Christian faith. In order for this faith to continue to gain status as foundational and normative in the lives of Arab people, new and different ways to express and proclaim it need to be developed so as to speak to the way contemporary Arabs meet the challenges in their lives.

A number of factors have contributed to the prevailing rise of fatigue, dejection and withdrawal. Christians who hope to revive the flame of faith must avoid retreating into passivity. Grégoire Haddad pays particular attention to the effect of fear among Christians. Christian communities in Lebanon seem to be sinking into indifference and inaction, but this is probably because of their spirit of witness is paralysed by fear. We need no further proof of this than the timorous attitude of Christians who are nervous of the consequences of radical theological questioning and research; we see that Christian power is diminishing in the midst of a society ruled by confessionalism, that the faith of the less educated is being weakened, and the ecclesiastical authorities are making use of disciplinary measures to condemn and excommunicate.

These fears, however, are driven by a vision that is diametrically opposed to the

---

17 LCH, pp. 9–10.

vision of Christ. The final fear is the one that most clearly reveals the infirm condition of the Christian communities: 'What remains is the final fear: that Christian society should dwindle and disappear, and consequently then also all Christianity and Christian faith itself in the Arab Middle East.'[18] This fear clearly shows that Christians in Lebanon persist in confusing Christianity with Christ[19] and the Church, and faith with the cultural expression of dogma. There is therefore an urgent need to learn true theological discernment. Christian truth can be expressed through many different cultural expressions. The faith itself can only be strengthened when one of these forms of expression is subjected to criticism.

If local theological reflections are at risk of being dominated by apocalyptic fears, then any radical reassessment will benefit from a renewed focus on the authentic heart of the Christian faith. Christ alone is able to liberate Middle Eastern Christians from their anxieties. So they will need to rediscover the boldness that stirred the early believers who lived alongside Christ, and inspired the spiritual and theological energies of the band of apostles. It is also urgent to ensure that Christ once more becomes the principal focus:

> Paul's radicalism focuses the entire Christian religion on Christ, and this is what liberated Christianity and the Christian community from all fear and all dependence on any things other than Christ Himself, however much those things may still to us today seem holy, and however much we might trust in such things.[20]

It appears, however, that this kind of theological boldness is linked to the receptivity of Christian communities. And this is where faith in Lebanon is in danger of straying. There are many who are not well able to exercise subtle discernment in the matter of Christ's identity.

For they fail to work at distinguishing Christianity, as it is imperfectly represented in Lebanese society, from Christ, as He longs to reveal Himself in all the riches of His core being:

> Christianity is Christ, faith in Christ, and life hidden in Christ, life that comes from Christ. Christianity is also witness to Christ, public life in and for Christ.

---

18 LCH, p. 15.
19 Grégoire Haddad is clear that he intends his critical remarks to apply only to the historical existence of Christianity: 'Criticism of Christianity and of Christians should never extend to Christ.' (LCH, p. 15).
20 LCH, p. 16.

We should always distinguish clearly between on the one hand Christ, the only absolute, and on the other hand – and these things can be highly relative – our faith in Him, and the ways in which we express this faith and bear witness to Him.[21]

This distinction enables us to see the need for radicality more clearly. We are not talking about radicalising Christianity in the sense of petrifying it as a monolithic sociocultural request. Rather, the radicalisation must be expressed as a refocusing on Christ. For Christians, 'radical' means Christ Himself, as he appears to the community of believers struggling with everyday challenges. And if anything is relative, it is that this form of radicalism liberates Christ from the historical manipulations so often practised on him. To be radical in a Christian sense is to allow every last golden strand of Good News to be generously woven into the living weft of daily Christian commitment.

Discernment criteria

To Grégoire Haddad, this is so clearly true and natural that it would be idle to argue the point. In spite of this clarity, however, he is careful to make explicit the criteria that should govern the deployment of radicalism. Hence the question about the criterion of radical adherence to Christ, which should train Christians to live according to what Haddad names the radicalism of life and of truth. From the start, he rules out certain false criteria, among which he includes tradition, the Magisterium of the Church, the Gospel as a text that can only be interpreted with the aid of external criteria, and even the believer's intelligence, enlightened by the Holy Spirit. One might well find the range of these exclusions surprising. However, a closer look at the background of his approach can help us see how radical it was. Grégoire Haddad rules out even the Gospel, because as a fundamental text it also requires hermeneutical guidance, so that it cannot be of itself an absolute criterion. So instead of taking it as an absolute criterion, he prefers to designate it as the supreme guidance itself.[22] Other sources of guidance, such as the teaching of the Church, Church tradition, the human sciences, the enlightened intelligence of the believer, all make their contribution: 'They are best described as the means of enlightenment serving the two absolute criteria.'[23] They are not

---

21 LCH, p. 18.
22 LCH, pp. 39–40.
23 LCH, p. 53.

absolute criteria, but sources of guidance, and the distinction is an important one. The first absolute criterion is Christ:[24]

> The first criterion is Christ as He is Himself, in the perfection of His being
> […] a being who is unique and said of Himself what no other had dared to say,
> revealing that His nature is deeper and more infinite than any other being.[25]

As an absolute criterion, Christ cannot be apprehended other than through the ways He has been mediated historically, our primary sources. We must however be very careful never to confuse absolute criterion with explicatory source.

Theological lucidity of this kind will soon be an identifying mark of true renewal for the Christian faith.

The other criterion, paradoxically also absolute, is mankind itself. The paradox at the heart of this approach is that Grégoire Haddad's liberating theology requires us to sustain the bipolarity of the two absolutes. And this in turn means that the absolute is no longer unique and exclusive, but rather dual and interactive. Viewed like this, mankind becomes the centre, the criterion and the absolute.[26] It is the unique status of humans, their place in God's economy, that justifies assigning such dignity to mankind:

> People are of greater value than the Sabbath. They are the masters of the
> Sabbath, which was nevertheless an institution seen as founded by God and
> one of the most sacred elements of the Jewish religion. They are the ultimate
> ground of all institutions, of the universe, of life and death, of the present
> and the future – in short, of everything. They are the purpose of Christ, and
> worthy to be served by the one considered in Christianity as the man-God, the
> absolute. They are the purpose of faith and of knowing the Son of Man. They
> are the fully mature version of mankind, perfect in Christ.[27]

This anthropological explanation does not call for excessive mystical over-tones, but is fairly consonant with the purposes of the Incarnation. The privileged position of humans has never before been so boldly explained. Only someone who has carried out an intense examination of the riches of the mystery of Christ could

---

24 LCH, p. 20.
25 LCH, pp. 21–22.
26 LCH, p. 23.
27 LCH, p. 24.

dare to present humans as the ultimate aim and fulfilment of Christ Himself. But we are not speaking here of just any human. The human who can be described as absolute is the perfect human as conceived within God's plan. Historical humans only conform to such a description when their lives align with that ultimate plan and move towards their own distant future. Grégoire Haddad explains further: 'The person who serves as reference and criterion is the whole person and every person.'[28] This new human identity is linked to that of the fully mature version of mankind. Step by step we thus come to appreciate the fuller picture of the nature of the new, perfected human, the one who is the core and the ultimate purpose of the whole divine economy. The key point of this anthropological understanding is the initial notion of 'reference' that draws the humans of history, the real humans worn down in their mortal fragility, those addressed by God in and through Christ, into a reality that promises a rewarding sense of fulfilment.

In order to spare Arab Christianity a process of spiritual necrosis, Haddad advocates a radical form of evangelism that takes inspiration only from Christ and mankind: 'We must conclude that the radical strategy is guided exclusively by Christ and mankind in a continuous and complementary intertwining development.'[29] It is thanks to the complementarity between these two foundations that Christians find meaning and fulfilment. In interpreting Matthew 22:35–39, the former Bishop of Beirut is establishing a dialectical relationship between the divine absolute and the human absolute. The chiasmus thus outlined draws together in harmonious synergy the actions of God and of mankind. He explains further that 'the absolute in existence is God, and the absolute in the actions of mankind is the love of God', adding subsequently that 'the absolute in being is mankind, and the absolute in action is the love of mankind.'[30] The very fact that these theological points have to be made at the start shows how carefully both words and subject matter need to be judged. The balance between the divine and the human is extremely delicate. To err to one side or to the other could lead the whole enterprise astray into either theologism or humanism. As faithful Christians we must reject both these extremes. Maintaining the two poles in balance enables us to gain a clearer understanding of the ultimate meaning of human life, which only reaches true fulfilment in each of us when the potential for love that comes from God's free gift of Himself through Jesus Christ is allowed to blossom fully. Here we see exactly how to understand the central role of Christ

---

28 LCH, p. 24.
29 LCH, p. 26.
30 LCH, p. 42.

vis-à-vis the many other issues that have gained historical pre-eminence in religious institutions.[31]

Assign meaning, or identify a common requirement?

In more concrete terms, we can see that a radical attitude is the way to approach understanding the mystery of God and of mankind. But radicalism itself cannot serve as an absolute yardstick: 'Radicalism, any kind of radicalism, is not an end in itself but a means to serve both Christ and mankind.'[32] For Christians to be radical, therefore, could mean that they are freed of the prejudices and misunderstandings that are still frequently found among convinced Christians; that they have rediscovered a serious approach to evangelism that punctures the religious conventions and the dated, superannuated practices in their communities; that they are ready to embrace the rising sap of new forms of Christian commitment. In short, we are talking here of a fresh dynamism in the power of evangelism. To illustrate this, Grégoire Haddad quotes the need in Lebanon to re-examine the nature of the confessional Christian institutions that have a surreptitious upper hand in the mind of Christians:

> It is not contrary to the Gospel that Christian society is immersed in civil society; rather, we are reminded of these words of Christ's: 'unless a grain of wheat falls into the earth and dies, it remains just a single grain; but if it dies, it bears much fruit' (John 12, 24). Its immersion does not imply that Christian faith disappears; indeed, it could lead to renewal.[33]

It is only radicalism of this kind that can eradicate such prejudice from the mind of Lebanese Christians. For this prejudice is rooted deep within the collective subconscious. As is well known, the key reason for its strong hold on the imagination of many Christians is their fear of Islam. The *leitmotif* of this theology of liberation is the need for death to lead to renewal. Here, death implies turning one's back on the sociopolitical privileges granted to the community as such.[34]

---

31 According to Grégoire Haddad, all theological research must focus jointly on Christ and on mankind: 'Research work, however important and risky it might be, is possible and should be encouraged, provided that it concentrates on Christ and on witnessing to him, and that it serves the cause of mankind.' (LCH, pp. 54–55).

32 LCH, p. 35.

33 LCH, p. 16.

34 Most of Grégoire Haddad's experiences and of his theological reflection took place before

A radical theological assessment of Lebanese reality clearly shows that there is opportunity available to the Christian community to spread the message of the Gospel, and bear witness to it – in other words, a space for living out liberation. If we believe that the message has universal relevance, then we must exercise diligence in adapting it to the particular sociocultural context. In this sense, faithful adherence to the deposit of the Christian faith means on the one hand representing the truth faithfully (without diluting it, even in part, for the sake of ease or adaptation), and on the other hand making accommodation to the intelligence and ability of one's hearers, especially if, as in our generation, they have a better level of knowledge and understanding of life than did the generations before them.[35]

This dual work of adaptation calls for both intellectual and spiritual lucidity. For theological truth is dependent on the way it is expressed within the local cultural idiom; moreover, our understanding of the reality of human life is determined by the presuppositions and cognitive means that are integral to our overall concept of mankind, the world and history. It is therefore salutary to remember that there is no such thing as a culturally neutral approach to human reality. In every generation, Christians deploy their own cultural ability and defend their own particular understanding of Christian truth. Sensitivity and preferences play a far greater part than does any systematic or rigorous control over the essential reality of Christian truth. Christians therefore urgently need to be intellectually humble and display sober and ethical behaviour.

In a reflection that is as close-grained as it is profound, Grégoire Haddad outlines a theoretical and conceptual framework for the application of this kind of radicalism:

> If a radical position on Christian religious problems is to require knowledge
> of the truth that sets us free, and of life that brings constant renewal and
> progress; if the criteria for authentic radicalism in Christianity are Christ and
> human beings, in an interactive relationship; and if the dynamic synergy of
> knowledge and interactive experience together establish us firmly not only

---

the Lebanese war. It was a time when Lebanese Christians still enjoyed a privileged status compared to other Lebanese citizens. The situation was much changed by disappointments arising from fifteen years of war and fifteen years of foreign occupation. Now, many Christians in Lebanon are calling for greater justice and a rebalancing of the Lebanese political system. Grégoire Haddad's call is in any case still topical, as he maintains that the greatest danger to Lebanese Christianity is fear of the Other: 'The real danger to Christian faith is not radical research but rather a multiplicity of fears and taboos.' (LCH, p. 53).
35 LCH, p. 45.

within, rather than outside, truth and life, but also on the path towards the whole truth and abundant life, then the door stands open to plurality in our ways of thinking and of living, without any need to deny religion, to reject faith, or to succumb to atheism or heresy [...] This is because the plurality of ways of thinking are many, and are within one single faith, the faith in Christ and in mankind, a faith that is open to constant evolution.[36]

This theological boldness opens the gates wide to theological pluralism, a notion that requires the greatest discernment in terms of how theological radicalism is lived out in practice. It must be based above all on how the truth of Christ is revealed in the lives of people in particular historical contexts. Human lives are in a constant state of change, so any rigidity in official forms of expression and institutional practice can only hinder revelation. If our lives are a progress towards the truth of Christ, then we must create favourable conditions for progress towards that goal by confidently engaging with our evolving historical context. The reality of our experience will thus play a key role in clarifying and nurturing evangelical truth.

A liberated and liberating Christology

Liberating Christ

According to Grégoire Haddad, to start by liberating Christ means to prioritise the theological perception that encompasses the whole of the anthropological vision. The liberation of Christ involves a reassessment of the whole edifice of Christian theology. This edifice includes a proper perception of the human person. Logically, if a person has a religious affiliation, this means that their anthropological nature derives from their theological nature, and thus that anthropology is derived from theology. If, therefore, we can review the way in which Christians and Christianity think about and express the nature of Christ, it will be easier to engage in a radical review of the Christian understanding of mankind.

One of the things on which the former Bishop of Beirut takes issue with Christians and historical Christianity is that they have monopolised Christ.[37] Historically, Christianity is entitled to develop a Christology that fits with its experience of faith and its sociocultural context, but it does not have the right to call this

---

36 LCH, p. 28.
37 LCH, p. 61.

the absolute truth. The way that Christianity has been experienced historically has necessarily been conditioned by its historical context, both sociocultural and sociopolitical. Christianity has been seen as 'the sum of the sociocultural expressions of the Gospel',[38] a specific way to conceive and express the mystery of Christ. If Christ is the image of an absolute God revealed at the core of human history, then in their theological expression Christian Churches can only offer one historical form of it, conditioned by many aspects of cultural and political context and social practice.

We are not talking here of depriving Christians of Christ, nor of rejecting any religious experience of Christ. Rather, we are encouraging Christians to approach the mystery of Christ in different ways. 'To liberate Christ from Christian culture'[39] can, according to Grégoire Haddad, mean opening the door to other religious approaches to Christ outside the Christian tradition, and even outside Christian cultural references. His is an indirect call for diversity in religious pathways. Whether or not we are happy with it, the content of Christian truth, and Christian religious practice, have left their mark in societies and cultures. This has fostered an interactive dialectic between Church and society. If this is true, then liberating Christ means releasing Him from two different forms of limitation. On the one hand, He is limited when Christian dogma insists it is the only way to encounter the mystery of God. On the other hand, He is limited when human life within society is regulated only in terms of the dominant cultural norms.

In other words, it is necessary boldly to dissociate the truth of Christ from Christian truth. Grégoire Haddad recommends achieving this by means of another dissociation. He means the way in which the identity of Christ is confused with the identity of Christian institutions:

> Because Christ, as an absolute value, is fully identified with the Christian
> religion and the Church as an institution – a contextual expression of Christ
> in His incarnation and the ongoing historical perception of Him – those who
> look to Christ are unable fully to perceive His true nature. If He is the absolute
> truth for all, and all need Him more than anything else, and if this misleading
> identification prevents us from recognising Him, then the identification must
> be rejected, however difficult that may be and whatever the consequences.[40]

38 LCH, p. 63.
39 LCH, p. 64.
40 LCH, pp. 60–61.

Clearly, the liberation that we seek is driven mainly by a desire for open-mindedness between people and for ecumenical and interfaith ministry. Above all, Grégoire Haddad seeks to offer Christ to the whole of humanity. In order to do this, he aims to free Him from the confines of Christianity. There is in both Catholic and Orthodox traditions, however, a very close association between the notion of Christ and that of the Church. In order to justify the dissociation on theological grounds, the concept of 'Church' needs to be expanded:

> We are speaking here of distinction, not dissociation. It is unthinkable to divide the one from the other if we truly believe that Christ is in His members and His members are in Him. [...] We therefore have to look at other consequences. Christ is the only true absolute value. The Church, however, only has a part in this absolute value if by 'Church' we mean humanity, every person and the whole person. If by 'Church' we only mean some people, those who partake in the life of the visible Church, or even only those who have a particular part to play in serving the whole Church, then the Church loses its absolute value. Ecclesial authority cannot replace Christ. Nor should it even replace its members who share the same faith. It is a core part of Christ's teaching that all are on an equal footing in responsibility and service. [41]

Taking a prudent theological approach, Grégoire Haddad thus prefers the word 'distinction'. It preserves the real relationship that develops between Christ and Christians. Without Christ, the Church has no intrinsic value. But if it identifies itself, in anticipation, with the whole of mankind, then its vocation will become universal and it will be able to host the gathering of all peoples and all cultures, accommodating diversity and solidarity. In this way, it will be Christ Himself, not the institutional Church, that becomes the focus of history. Christian communities are entitled to imagine an appropriate framework for welcome and sharing, but they are not entitled to make such an institutional framework the only place where communion with Christ is possible.

This theological distinction may be dangerous, but in Grégoire Haddad's view it is the only way of salvation for Christianity, which will be salvaged only if the mystery of Christ is safeguarded. If Christ is monopolised and deprived of his universality, this will be fatal to Christianity:

> In the eyes of many, the mystical body of Christ has become a social body,

---

41 LCH, pp. 59–60.

duplicating civil society, and the Bride of Christ has become an ecclesial
authority that has centralised under its own control the missionary activities
of teaching, explicating and leading. Once again, in theological, spiritual,
ministry and social terms, Christ has been displaced and removed from his
crucial absolute position.[42]

Any human organisation is necessarily marked by human relativity. Christ aims
to be the absolute crux of the love of God. No human institution, however sublime,
could possibly claim to identify with the magnitude of the being of Christ. The
various theological characteristics that have marked Christianity throughout its
history have contributed to the partial and incomplete revelation of the mystery
of Christ. Logically, however, evolution and maturity must also involve constant
reassessment and recalibration. Christians should therefore have no anxiety about
their theological duty to liberate the absolute Christ from the Christian Christ:

> Imaginary, mental and sentimental representations, whether they resemble
> reality or are based on it, are more difficult to relativise. On the one hand, they
> are necessary because the mind is structured to imagine and to experience
> emotion. On the other hand, they are insufficient because they cannot fully
> match the true face of Christ. So we have baby Jesus, crucified Jesus, Jesus
> the king, almighty Jesus, Jesus the doctor, the heart of Jesus, Jesus in the
> communion host, Jesus the Saviour, Jesus the head of the Church [...] What
> we can say is that these representations are only partial, and marked by
> history; that is to say, marked by a civilisation that is alien to most of those
> now living. If today's living Christ and today's living humans are the measure
> of everything, and if the representations no longer fulfil their function – which
> is to convey the living Christ to living humans – then the true Christ, today's
> Christ, must be liberated from the Christ who appeared as He did in history:
> yesterday's Christ, and the historical representations of Christ. Today's Christ
> must now walk alongside human beings in all their shapes and with all their
> aspirations.[43]

The centre of gravity of traditional Christian understanding needs to be moved
aside in order to bring this liberation about. Instead of aligning theological thinking to the Christological learnings inherited from the past, we must rethink the

---

42 LCH, p. 59.
43 LCH, p. 65.

mystery of Christ in terms of the paradigms and schemas that fit with the contemporary experience of the divine. Our discernment criteria no longer derive from a calcified deposit of faith, but from the existential challenge of a lived history that speaks to people and societies in their day-to-day experiences and their struggle to maintain the fundamental values of humanity.

So the liberation of Christ will enable Christians not only to have a different experience of His being and His presence, but also to live in a different way their faith and their commitment:

> When we say that Christ is the absolute centre of the Christian's faith and life, then this should lead to a fundamental change in that person's devotional practices [...] It is only in relation to the saints that Christ is central – He is the absolute centre. To say that Christ is the absolute centre necessarily entails a fundamental change in our theology, in the way we understand God, in His relationship with mankind, and in mankind's relationship with Him.[44]

Christians who are willing to engage with this jeopardy are therefore called to a full personal conversion. When Christian theology is able to free itself from old Christological understandings that no longer correspond to the current experience, ways of thinking or of speaking, of people today, then the whole system of Christian thinking will undergo a major mutation. Christian faith will then be able to offer a new way of understanding the presence of God in Jesus Christ. Christological mediation will still be the only mediation for salvation. How people understand and receive that mediation will change according to contemporary modes of reception.

To liberate Christ, therefore, is to set in train a process of profound change that will affect all of Christian life and thought. This change will restore Christian faith to the centre of human existence.

Far from diminishing the strength of faith in Jesus Christ, this liberation should make Christians even more strongly attached to Christ and to his work of love. This will be the cost of restoring relevance and radiance to Christian discourse. Grégoire Haddad calls for all of life and thinking to be refocused onto the Christ event and the person of Christ. He insists, however, that this refocusing should happen only after the work of conversion, which implies a permanent process of liberation and renewal. It will be beneficial for Christian theological reason to revisit where Christ has been revealed in order for Christ to be presented under a new light.

---

44 LCH, p. 56.

Liberating mankind

Liberating Christ, it seems, is both extremely simple and also infinitely complex. In order to avoid all the possible misunderstandings, Grégoire Haddad explains that the liberation of Christ does not in any way damage His status as the absolute centre of the universe. Rather, it effectively reinforces the fact that He holds this unique status:

> According to the Christian faith, Christ has within Himself all the fulness of liberty. More than that, He is the liberator and Saviour of mankind. There is therefore clearly no need for humans to liberate the person of Christ; they do however need to liberate Him from the historical incarnations and collusions that prevent His being recognised as the absolute value, and His being the absolute criterion for truth and life.[45]

This very clear theological assertion ably deflects any accusations of aberration or heresy. In a society alienated from God and metaphysical considerations, it is fundamentally important to Grégoire Haddad to present to the world a Christ capable of freeing humans from their fears and servitude. This Christ must once more be seen as the ultimate meaning of life, and it is our foremost duty as humans to allow Him to be revealed in His full glory. Human aspirations are so great in our present day that a flawed or incoherent Christ could not possibly fulfil all legitimate expectations:

> People these days are more aware than in earlier times of wholeness and relativity, we are more conscious that the universe and the world of humans is all one, and we have gained awareness of how it changes and evolves. We are able to gaze towards cosmic, uniting and evolving horizons. If the true Christ does not measure up to these dimensions and horizons, then human beings will not see that they need Him.[46]

If the dogmatic affirmations of Christian theology need to be reviewed and reformulated, this is because the modern human mind is driven by a need for change and evolution. On the one hand, the riches of Christ are inexhaustible. On the other hand, the drive to search is limitless for the human mind. We therefore need Christological approaches that can take account of these two imperatives.

---

45 LCH, p. 75.
46 LCH, p. 65.

A progressive Christian theology could serve as a royal road towards a renewed perception of the mystery of Christ. To be progressive, it will take account of the existential link between Christ and those who commit to working for the good of all people. Theologically, we are not wanting at all costs to shake off the yoke of tradition and build up from scratch. Rather, Grégoire Haddad's theological vision places the highest importance on the bond of love between mankind and Christ. The bond is deeply etched into the struggle of daily life and the battle against injustice and poverty. The former Bishop of Beirut is not seeking to rewrite the theological basis for the Christ event, but rather to transform Christological ortho-doxy into Christological orthopraxis. Christians are called at all times to be guided by that highest of sciences, love.[47] In preparing the new theological theory, we are called to commit to faith and to love in order to defend the values defended by Christ. Through love for Christ and for all those to whom Christ has devoted His strength and His life, Christians will be given the right words to speak of Christ to the modern world.

Responding to criticism levelled at him when as bishop he took up the cause of the poor and the oppressed, Grégoire Haddad clarifies his position by focusing the debate on the 'cause of mankind'. Instead of speaking of the 'Grégoire Haddad affair' or the '*Âfâq* affair', or even of the 'avant-gardist theology affair', he prefers to focus the attention of the protagonists on people:

There is a unique 'cause' that deserves the attention and sacrificial devotion of everyone, both their life and their time. It is the reality that wears down both individuals and groups in Lebanon and in other Arab countries: the reality of under-development, injustice, exploitation and servitude of all kinds. We all need to wake up to this, to reject it, and to work together to fight it and promote development, justice and liberty. We need to see the fruits of this promotion as they affect minds, souls and bodies. Other matters are secondary; they and other questions and problems are worth attending to only if they further the fundamental cause.[48]

For mankind, then, the most important cause is mankind. This truth is endorsed

---

47 Grégoire Haddad reckons that 'those who wish to live out a radical Christian faith have no need of new forms of knowledge, of philosophy, of theology, of biblical exegesis or other religious sciences' (LCH, p. 66). Believers who are loyal to Christ and open-hearted to the world and its suffering 'are not exempted from rediscovering the most noble form of knowledge, which Paul calls love' (LCH, p. 67).
48 LCH, p. 148.

by Christ, to whom Grégoire Haddad is open and loyal, and who desires the joy
of all people. If God's principal concern is mankind, then the struggle to liberate
mankind should become the one central object of interest and commitment for all
true Christians. Christianity is not an abstract metaphysical theological construct,
nor a structural and canonical organisational system to organise human life, but
rather a universal form of humanism. It offers each person the opportunity to
realise their vocation as a human being in accordance with the principles of personal dignity and conviviality.

Christianity, however, should not claim to be the only deposit for humanity's
values. In seeking out authentic humanity, Christ has placed His trust in mankind.
According to Grégoire Haddad, Christianity is not entitled to claim exclusive
rights to having generated human values such as liberty, justice, peace, equality,
democracy, solidarity, participation, unity, etc. Scholars will in due course examine
and determine the origin of these values.[49] An authentic conversion process should
lead Christians to liberate human values from the clutches of Christianity. Even
if all that is authentically human fits seamlessly within the logic of the Kingdom
of God, evangelical radicalism requires us to prefer those things that nations and
cultures uphold as the best of human values. Only open-mindedness and solidarity
will unlock this kind of cross-cultural collaboration in the search for mankind's
unique humanity. The paths, through their diversity, will reveal the key points of
collaboration.

In order to reach their full potential as humans, Christians should do all they
can to liberate themselves as people from all that prevents them from fulfilling
their calling. They are called to be people of dignity, fraternity, authenticity and
solidarity, creative and sharing. This liberation, however, is not the prerogative of
Christians. It affects all human beings. As human beings, and in response to their
calling through the Gospel, Christians must play their part here. The liberation of
mankind is a process that derives from the very nature of human beings. Since
they are called to liberty, any form of servitude is in direct contradiction to their
nature:

> [...] because servitude makes one person subject to another, and negates
> their absolute value, whether the servitude is imposed by an object, a system,
> an institution, a group, or even a part of the person themselves, and even if
> the other is an absolute other: Christ the Man, or God the Father. For a true
> absolute cannot impose subjection on other absolutes, since their relationship

---

49 LCH, pp. 67–68.

is as one liberty to other liberties. If it turns out that a person is the slave of what they call 'God' then that God is not the true God, but an idol, the fruit of their imagination.[50]

This passage helps us to situate the principal points of liberation. Grégoire Haddad sees two options. External liberation, and internal liberation. Any situation could be considered to be servitude where a person is required to be and to think in ways that are alien to their deepest and most authentic human aspirations. Their social habits, their relationship to God and to other people, their involvement in a religious system, all these are testing situations in which they might experience either drift and failure, or authenticity and fulfilment.

The principal difficulty, as so often, is linked to the defining criteria. There is undoubtedly a serious epistemological fracture when we postulate 'liberation'. This difficulty is becoming increasingly serious. All religions and spiritual traditions, and nearly all philosophical systems, set the notion of liberation as a fundamental aspect of their world vision. Grégoire Haddad's thinking does not adopt this difficult and dangerous path. For that which some see as liberation and flourishing can appear to others to be enslavement and alienation. This makes it difficult judiciously to pinpoint what feels like joy or rewarding achievement. Grégoire Haddad prefers to focus on the values advocated in the Gospel: fraternal love, authentic sharing, healing forgiveness, spiritual creativity, and so on. In this way he hopes to promote a spirituality of radical mildness, setting down markers and signs of progress. It is then incumbent on each one of us, in debate and in sharing, to set out how we feel most comfortable and what actions are appropriate.

To summarise, then, we can say that Grégoire Haddad's theology establishes that the liberation of Christ is the precursor to the liberation of mankind. Christ, badly understood and poorly received, can only result in the enslavement of mankind. If we are called to liberate Christ, then it is surely in order better to liberate mankind. These two liberations coexist, and indeed mutually support each other. The ultimate goal is nevertheless the liberation of mankind. The challenges of history are realised in and through the humans who live it. At the risk of oversimplification, one might say that a single ultimate goal – consolidating human conviviality – shapes the whole of Grégoire Haddad's theological thinking. Liberating mankind from the structures of injustice and oppression only makes sense if it leads to greater fraternisation between people.

---

50 LCH, p. 76.

The challenges of a liberating radicalism

At first sight, Grégoire Haddad's theology appears to operate on a purely theoretical level. The practical conclusions that he reaches through his bold reflections on the notion of theological radicalism, however, show how his approach can be translated into reality through suggestions and advice carefully attuned to the questions and the needs of the Christian communities in Lebanon and in the wider Arab world. Haddad's hope is that his recommendations will be applied to the different ways in which people engage in sociopolitical life in Lebanon. He therefore not only shows his disapproval of excommunication,[51] but also loudly calls for a reassessment of the social, political and even cultural choices made by Lebanese Christians.[52] For example, he questions the Christian justification for a socialist or liberal vision for the economy. He also asks whether permanent revolution can fit with the most profound aspects of common life. These questions bear witness to the theological lucidity of all of his spiritual, intellectual and practical witness.

As to radicalism, it appears that by its very nature it too is intimately linked to the message of the Gospel, to the extent that its creative energy is essential to fully understanding the truth of Christianity. We need therefore to ask whether Christian truth is not better perceived by the human mind in terms of mildness and kenosis. Those who support this theological objection are overlooking the subversive effect of evangelical mildness. Even if the terms change, the real impact of healing and of salvation is the same. Any evangelical mildness that does not shake up routine life or overturn patterns of resignation and stagnation can quickly degenerate into fatal lethargy. In order to liberate humans and enable them to fully flourish as people, nothing will be more effective than a tireless search for authenticity carried out with patient, lucid and yet meek radicalism. This gentle radicalism works in tandem with a true conviviality founded on respect for the Other.

Another possible objection might be to fear a negative impact of radicalism on the acceptance of diversity in Lebanon. A radical approach that 'innocently' or 'unrealistically' rushed to shake off the yoke of history and build afresh runs the risk of overlooking the benefits of the socioreligious diversity that currently dominates in the Lebanese nation. If a theological plan for radicalism were to pledge a shared secular ideal for Lebanese society, then one might legitimately

---

51 'The age of excommunications is definitely over, even in the institution that used them most extensively. Criticism, analysis and reassessment need also to fit with the objectivity of the scientific approach and with charity.' (LCH, p. 28.)
52 The two concluding chapters, entitled 'Les opérations de libération' and 'Déductions et conclusions' respectively (LCH, pp. 82–144) aim to identify how evangelical commitment can be carried out in practice in Lebanese society.

worry that a whole tradition of conviviality among religious groups could be lost. But to make this objection is to disregard Grégoire Haddad's judicious distinction in defining radicalism between the allocation of new theological content and clearly establishing minimum standards and authenticity. According to this second definition, radicalism is likely to apply to a wide range of situations in Lebanon. Those who will be closely involved need to be consulted in identifying and defining them. In matters of faith, the work of regeneration is necessarily teamwork. If the plural nature of Lebanon is to be preserved, a radical approach to Christian faith will supply the justifications and means best suited to plurality and to all that it promises.

It is in any case impossible to evaluate the whole of Grégoire Haddad's theological thinking within the narrow confines of this one chapter. It of course lacks the necessary historical distance, the wide-angle lens on his work, and the synthesis of his various approaches and evaluations. In the hope, however, that a suitable analysis will be forthcoming, we can for now pay tribute to the magnitude of his struggle and his original thinking. No previous Lebanese Catholic bishop had dared such boldness in terms of faith and political commitment, in seeking out evangelical radicalism and human liberation. Some of those obsessed with the need to submit strictly to the tradition of Catholic teaching continue to view with suspicion the 'red' former Bishop of Beirut's new theological writing, but for countless Lebanese people Haddad remains a model of commitment, worthy of their profound admiration and pious gratitude. Conditions in modern Lebanon have made Christians anxious, and desperately withdrawn in the face of the uncertain future of Middle Eastern Christianity. However, Christians in Lebanon will one day be able to move beyond this uncomfortable moment in history and they will then find in Haddad's revolutionary theological thinking a signpost to the potential of new salvation and life.

5

The vocation of an Arab theology of conviviality

In this final chapter, I shall re-examine the issue of conviviality that has been so vigorously debated in local Lebanese theology. I shall attempt here to suggest new areas for reflection that I believe might offer a better understanding of the theological, cultural and political issues underlying Muslim–Christian convivial-ity. Lebanese society, and societies in the parts of the Arab world where there is still a significant Christian presence, will need to face up to these. The advantage of this kind of approach is that we shall take account of what has been learned in the theological models that we have examined, and will be able to formulate our theological reflections around the relevant political and cultural issues. Given how very closely linked political and religious issues are within Arab society, it is important to examine these three spheres in terms of the way they mutually interact. We shall then need to address some serious issues that have led to inter-minable discussions on the impact of culture and politics on religion, and on the prospects for a purely theoretical speculation on the urgent need for, and ultimate justification of, a radical theological reform.

This chapter, therefore, will consider the problem of conviviality in its widest sense. To focus these remarks on the most important basis of conviviality, I shall approach the theological issue via its most sensitive point, at which convivial-ity can either flourish or decline. The focus of Christian theological discussion needs to be shifted from the deep-seated and instinctual pull of the duty to preach directly and immediately. We are learning that Christian truth can be experienced, and can spread, in ways other than by ensuring the survival of confessional bodies and institutional powers.[1] Promoting Arab conviviality is a symbolic form of

---

1 Throughout the final decades of last century, the theology of secularisation was attempting to

Christian witness in the Arab world. Now, this kind of conviviality is far from being simply the passive coexistence of two communities. Rather, it requires the Christian faith constantly to come up against the harsh realities of Arab life. One of the most urgent of these harsh realities is to restore the human dignity of the Arab peoples who have been so downtrodden by the alienating power of political and religious ideologies.

It may be true that the resurrection of the Arab peoples is at the heart of both Christian and Islamic faith, but the paths that lead to it are substantially different. Islamic and Christian scholars, given their respective theological sensitivities, may offer diametrically opposed approaches. Anyone advancing this idea will therefore need all the lucidity and creativity available in the subversive energy of religious faith. For if we make uniform and indiscriminate use of the theological methods and intellectual approaches dictated by a specific period, we will end up with a wrong understanding of history and a dangerous understanding of faith. In other words, if we determine that there is only one way to approach reality, via one inherited past theological paradigm, we risk holding back the energy of our faith, making it as immutable as the stars fixed in the heavens, and thus suffocating the irrepressible dynamism of human life. A courageous reassessment of the Christian faith could enable Arab Christians energetically and dauntlessly to work on restoring the dignity of the Arab peoples. Above all, they need to be willing to risk taking on the challenge and run with the twists and turns of living history.

Their long-term mission will need them to be ready to adapt to change. It requires a trio of tasks. The first task is to tackle the root difficulties inherent in conviviality by seeking to formulate its defence in theological terms. The notion of conviviality will be best served if it is underpinned by a new theological

---

emancipate Christian truth from institutional influence. This echoed Western cultural changes following the Enlightenment. Postmodern philosophy, however, is now re-examining the status of cultural identity and its impact on redefining the convictions and truths that shape the configuration of peoples and human communities. The Canadian philosopher Charles Taylor is a leading thinker on this issue (see J. Pélabay, *Charles Taylor penseur de la pluralité*, Laval-Paris, Les Presses de l'Université Laval-L'Harmattan, 2001). We need also to remember that contemporary philosophers, when they tackle the issue of identity, fall into two opposing groups. In the first are the true inheritors of the Enlightenment who defend the idea of individual liberty and the autonomy of the individual vis-à-vis the community, whereas the second comprises those who inherit the spirit of Romanticism, and are keen to revive the notion of the community and the cultural identity of different human groups. Modern Christian theology would therefore do well to make intelligent and creative use of the fruits of this confrontation. Theologians should reap the benefits of the new anthropological approach which constantly emphasises the synergy that can develop between the individual impulse to faith and its impact on reception in the community.

understanding of the beliefs of the Christian faith. The second task is to attempt to identify the particular features of the conviviality challenge in Lebanon and the ways in which it might reveal opportunities for Muslims and Christians to share in the challenge of building a genuine shared life. The third, the least theoretical and the most daunting task, addresses the dangerous issue of the promised land, a stumbling block for these three Semitic monotheistic religions. The notion of conviviality is so obviously closely bound to the earth that we do not need to labour the point. The major difficulty, however, is the underlying exclusivist theology. We therefore need to formulate a new theological approach to the idea of the promised land. It will need to reassess the unjustifiable claims to possession and exclusivity. This kind of critical reflection illustrates the way in which the new theology of conviviality will need to be seen as a tool for discernment and as offering the potential for reform and change in the Arab world.

Developing a new foundation for conviviality

The context for witness by Arab Christians

Arab Christians are seeking today to understand the meaning of the deep changes affecting the Arab world. Their efforts follow two intersecting lines of investigation. The first examines the fate they share with the other human populations living in the Arab world, and the second explores how their specific identity and historic vocation opens particular ways of seeing that world. Taken together, these two lines of investigation give rise to two complementary forms of witness. The shared fate enables them to witness to a spirit of solidarity; their specific identity stimulates faithful witness under examination. Both forms of witness require constant vigilance and an unwavering openness to criticism and readiness to adjust and amend. For Christians to promote their vocation within the Arab world increasingly means that they must willingly embrace their shared communal fate in such a way as to meet the deepest aspirations of all the people who share their world. Most Lebanese theologians have paid particular attention to this notion of shared fate. Their words of witness have expressed the urgent need to demonstrate solidarity with their Arab neighbours and compatriots.

Clearly, then, Arab Christians need to engage in a truthful dialogue with their Muslim interlocutors. It is becoming day by day more obvious that they cannot continue to reflect, decide and act on their own. As they accumulate experiences, and on occasion embarrassments, they are realising that Muslim–Christian dialogue is now the historic destiny of their Arab Christianity. Some Arab Christians, however, consider any such partnership disastrous. They are led to this conclusion by their observation that the Arab world is in a parlous state, dislocated, disillusioned, confused, reactionary and vindictive.[2] They therefore assume that any possible Muslim interlocutors will want to reject outright any approaches or attempts at dialogue. They believe they have spotted in the Koran itself the germs of the fundamentalism and intolerance that both sustain and exacerbate the inflexibility of Islam. Whenever dialogue between Muslims and Christians is unfruitful, this negative attitude is likely to be a hindering factor.

Because of the many ambiguities that surround and jeopardise reality in the Arab world, Arab Christian communities live in constant fear for their future. Looking at the various attitudes of Christians, we shall try here to describe the three major groups. The first group is large and encompasses people with a spirit of general deep-seated weariness, disappointed with all those who are losing confidence in the meaning of their life and witness in the confusing and dangerous context of the modern Arab world. Those in the second group, far smaller, remain optimistic about the reality of Arab life and doggedly promote the ideas of integration, enculturation and of active Christian presence in solidarity with their compatriots. A third, medium-sized group, includes those who remain expectant and watch for signs that might suggest future changes in Arab life, either towards possible salutary conversion or to irreversible decline.

Those who engage reflectively with the first of these groups – without either judging or condemning – will want to examine more thoroughly the challenges faced by Muslim–Christian conviviality in the context of Arab societies. The situation in Lebanon is in many ways emblematic, or at least symptomatic. The analysis here therefore implicitly refers to the problems encountered in dialogue in Lebanon. The second part of this final chapter will aim to confirm the truth

---

2 This somewhat pessimistic viewpoint seems to overlook the fact that some Arab countries, especially Saudi Arabia and Jordan, have a more open attitude and are willing to engage in dialogue – indeed they have organised some major interfaith meetings. The latest initiative by the Saudi king (the International Conference on Dialogue, in Madrid, 16–18 July 2008; the visit by the Saudi king to the Vatican on 6 November 2007 [these were recent when the book was first published – transl.]) were unanimously welcomed by the international community, for all that the initiatives still lack a solid theological basis and a real determination to engage in a joint reassessment of the whole legal and political system underpinning the governments of Arab societies. The significance of the visit by the Saudi king to the Vatican extended further than a simple personal initiative, in that it signalled an openness to the world on the part of Sunni Islam. A similar openness has also been indicated in Iran, another Islamic country that officially claims to be regulated by Islamic sharia. The hermeneutic freedom generally characteristic of Shiite theology is likely to be favourable to interfaith pluralism, and in particular to Christianity.

of this statement. Given that the hopes of Lebanese Christians and other Arab Christians are to a large extent very similar, it would be legitimate to think of Lebanon as the point of focus for conviviality between Muslims and Christians. Lebanon presents an unusual concatenation of sociopolitical features, so that it contains within itself, both in practice and in theory, all the possible permutations for Muslim–Christian encounter in the Arab world. The experience so far in Lebanon, certainly over the last twenty years and probably in the future also, could have been and might yet become the experience of Arab societies prepared to allow religious communities, both Christian and Muslim, to explore together a life of truly interactive and flourishing conviviality.

More specifically, we should add, dialogue between Muslims and Christians has always served as the symbolic crucible for such conviviality. The dialogue has so far mostly taken place among academics and specialists. Any such dialogue must of course follow the dictates of the relevant religious faith, and must constantly interrogate how individuals and communities experience the lived reality of a life of conviviality. As an exchange develops, it will enable the theoretical principles and the existential reality to nourish each other dialectically. We shall therefore now examine the issue of conviviality through the prism of exchange and dialogue.

This reflection does not aim to provide a theoretical justification; it situates the dialogue between Muslims and Christians in three areas of human experience: politics, culture and theology. Three critical explorations will engage in turn with each of these areas. First, a synopsis of the positive benefits specific to the Arab experience of any dialogue between Muslims and Christians. Next, a critical evaluation of the difficulties and obstacles that hinder the best possible outcomes for Muslim–Christian conviviality. And last, a look ahead to the potential for authenticity and enrichment that a thriving Arab experience of dialogue and conviviality might promise. These three investigations seem at first sight to overlap considerably, so a key interrogation central to them all should lend clarity and coherence. We are aiming here to enable Arab Christians to gain a lucid understanding of the implications of these three explorations. In other words, these Christians are invited to witness to the fundamental values of their Christian faith in a spirit of critical and constructive lucidity: they will need to ask audacious questions, to speak with transparency, and with authentic commitment.

Conviviality tested out in the political sphere

That we look first here at the issue of politics does not in any way signify that a

Christian theology of Muslim–Christian conviviality should inevitably be read through a purely sociological lens. The tensions between Islam and Christianity that have a bearing on Muslim–Christian conviviality in the societies of the Arab world are not only political; in these societies, however, political experience is such that Christian theologians need to proceed boldly, and take on the challenges of politics in the Arab world. The message of the Koran has been infused with politics, so there is a need to pay careful attention to the difficulties that can arise in an Islamic society anxious to reinforce the historical evidence for its religious conviction. Politics and theology are closely woven into the thinking and behaviour of Arab societies, so any dialogue between Muslims and Christians must be approached in a spirit of vigilance and critical evaluation.

At the crux of this difficulty three dramas are interwoven and have created trauma for those who care about Arab conviviality. The first of these dramas is the history of totalitarianism attached to some Muslim dynasties that, in some historical periods, did not hesitate to use their despotic power to persecute and martyr both Christian and Muslim Arab minorities. The second drama is linked to the indefensible aggression of the medieval Crusades that bloodied the Middle East and shattered its unity. The third drama, which is more recent and has generated deep and widespread collective trauma, is the apocalyptic grief that swathes the land of Palestine. The war in Lebanon is closely linked to this third drama. Lebanese conviviality has been weakened, betrayed in two ways: first, by the regional powers who wanted to shrink down the Arab–Israeli conflict by locating it on Lebanese soil, and second, by the decline of the communities in Lebanon, which revealed themselves unworthy of their human and spiritual vocation. The three dramatic and violent episodes they have experienced have made a deep impression on the relationships between Muslims and Christians in the Arab world. They are a negative point of reference, constantly inciting each side to adopt a critical attitude and to develop a strategy of self-purification.

These dramas may have been harmful, but they can also act as warnings indirectly addressed to Muslims and Christians. They give each of the two communities opportunity to strip out of their political relationship the stench of intolerance and hegemony that has poisoned their past experiences. One of the current benefits of the theology of dialogue, both Christian and Muslim, is that it rejects the validity of any political model that might, either symbolically or in reality, inspire it to deny the otherness of the Other. Any dialogue between Muslims and Christians must always be ready to emphasise the importance of critical clarity on the issue of political governance of the human city.

Muslim–Christian conviviality, however, has been indirectly affected by

Western interferences in the Arab world. The interferences are governed by three sets of interests: the unilateral and partisan exploitation of oil reserves in Arab countries, the defence of Israeli interests – at the expense of the the peace so long desired by the Palestinian and Israeli peoples – and the progressive democratisation of Arab societies. Some Western powers, such as the United States, are especially keen to promote the first two of these, whereas the European Union is increasingly wanting to promote a gradual democratisation that they see as linked to a cautious and realistic dialectic between Arab Muslim tradition and the demands of Western – mostly European – post-modernity. Those involved in the dialogue between Muslims and Christians need therefore to denounce any form of interference that might result in Arab peoples becoming subservient. Openness to the values of globalisation should not come at the expense of cultural distinctiveness. Arab Christians must therefore make a major contribution to building up a true sense of partnership between the Arab Middle East and the West. We should applaud Muslims wanting to remain faithful to their commitment to the key principles of the vision of mankind in the Koran, while yet showing that it is always possible to negotiate specific conditions for worldwide human conviviality. It should be possible for humanity to develop constructive ways to interact between the different cultural entities that harbour long traditions of human wisdom.

This same Arab dialogue must also be equipped to avoid the two dangerous tendencies – demonisation on the one hand, and beatification on the other – that can ensnare the experience of cultural interaction. Neither civilisation, Muslim or Western, should be either excessively glorified or abominated. A careful and critical examination is what is required to identify the strengths and the failings of each civilisation. In terms of political analysis, the societies of the Arab world would do well to be reminded of the values inherent in managing communitarian pluralism. Explicit reference to the Muslim faith should not be used to stifle individual or collective freedom. It is even possible to reinterpret Muslim tradition towards a better acknowledgement of social and political diversity. In parallel, Western societies need to acknowledge that respect for human rights involves a proper recognition of the specificity of religious experience. The Western focus on its own concerns must give way to focus on the concerns of the whole world. Western democracy, currently exercised within the 'walls' of the West (*intra muros*) must be fairly and honestly applied outside those walls (*extra muros*).

The preservation of Christian witnessing in the Arab world may be closely linked to the survival of the Arab Christian communities, but it is also true that their survival will depend on the way in which Arab Christians work out in practice the true nature of their political commitment. Any dialogue between Muslims and Christians will fail to result in a work of conversion of both hearts and structures unless it encourages Christians to throw themselves heart and soul into defending and promoting the three major political issues that will be crucial to the future of the Arab world: first, an effort to convert, or better still to defuse the Israeli strategy that has robbed the Palestinian people of their most basic rights and is paralysing the peace process between the two peoples; second, the democratisation of the Arab political regimes, i.e. the establishment of a fair and creative synergy between the Islamic and Western traditions of human rights;[3] and third, the promotion of prosperity for all Arab citizens, thanks to a better use, and fairer distribution, of natural resources and wealth within Arab societies.

If Arab Christians can show through engaging in dialogue between Muslims and Christians that they have the political acuity to engage with these three issues, their Muslim interlocutors will realise that by their presence and their witness the Arab Christian communities remain key to the very survival of the Arab world. It would therefore be good to remember that in the terms of evangelical radicalism, the need to survive comes second in importance to serving one's sisters and brothers. Arab Christians do indeed need to dare to believe that Islam is aware of and sympathetic to their troubles and that at the core of their troubles lies the seed of their evangelical fruitfulness. Arab Muslims, on the other hand, will benefit in dialogue from the different and positive contribution of their Christian interlocutors, and will learn to resist the temptation to see them as undifferentiated and view them through a disparaging political lens. The analytical contribution of the Arab Christian mindset will then earn respect for itself, and not through any association with the theological distinctiveness of the Christian faith. When, in dialogue, Arab Christians propose ways in which political life could be improved, their ideas will be assessed – whether positively or negatively – not because they are identified with the Christian faith, but according to their own intrinsic value.

It will be as they live a life of shared challenge and destiny that Arab Christians will be able to look forward to greater fulfilment through promoting Arab

---

3 The Arab world is currently experiencing a democratic insurgency [*the so-called Arab Spring of 2010–2012 – transl.*] that has mobilised the whole of the Arab population, both Muslim and Christian. Certain Christian religious leaders, driven by an atavistic inclination to submit to Muslim political power, are too fearful to denounce openly the unjust behaviour of Arab political regimes; some Arab Christians, however, are taking the initiative themselves and are deciding to take an active part in these peaceful democratic revolutions. By disassociating themselves from the official stance of their Churches, they are drawing closer to the demands of their Christian faith and are working to make Christ present by taking concrete action in the heart of the modern Arab world, while not affiliating their political engagement to any specific confessional group.

conviviality. Whatever affects the Arab world affects them even more viscerally, for in the heart of that world they are a delicate link, a sensitive element, perhaps even the evanescent yeast that is destined to ferment the authenticity of Arab life. If they are hoping for some form of conversion in political Islam, they should at all costs avoid imposing this conversion from outside. They need to prove their full solidarity with modern Islam which, paradoxically, is currently experiencing crises that are not only their most painful but also their most promising. Only Islam itself can take responsibility for its own transformation, which needs to arise out of the development of its own history. External factors should only act as powerful positive stimuli. It is the dialogue between Muslim and Christian interlocutors that will demonstrate how they might seriously envisage possible ways in which Arab peoples living in the pluralist context of a shared Arab political life could thrive as fulfilled human beings.

Arab Christianity therefore needs now to abandon any illusions of extravagant metamorphoses. The Arab world will only experience true renaissance if three fundamental political conditions are all met: the reconciliation of worldwide Islam with Western civilisations; a peaceful and equitable solution to the Arab–Israeli conflict; and innovative ways to exploit the resources within Islamic sociopolitical thinking on the subjects of reconciliation, adaptation and evolution. Clearly, these three conditions will need to be met simultaneously, both internally and externally. Their mutually reinforcing impact will be at its most effective if their interplay and interaction coincide in terms of timing and content. The dialogue between Muslims and Christians, once committed to bringing clarity to political life, will enable both sides to see the need for collaboration in tackling these three political issues. It is Arab Christians who should take full ownership of the implications of their natural position within the societies of the Arab world. Thanks to this natural position, they should be able to display authentic confidence in Islam. Their vocation of prophetic discernment calls them to ensure the best possible, the most fruitful and salutary, encounter between Islam and its Western counterpart. Through gentle witness to the Gospel, they will be able to remind their Arab Muslim interlocutors that the sociopolitical values of the Muslim nation will be secured only if they are willing to embrace the inevitability of the reciprocal relationship of influence. Arab Christians are better placed to condemn, without fear of the consequences, the extreme positions on the two sides.

Arab Christians should then be able explicitly to stand against two polarising tendencies: the excessive legalism of Islamic fundamentalism, and the excesses of lax Western ethics. If they will only accept that the Arab world will never, and should never, become a second – but Arab – West, they will be open to rediscovering the family likenesses between the sociopolitical visions of Arab Christianity on the one hand and of Arab Islam on the other. In the light of this affinity they will be able to attenuate and thus restrain the excesses that distort each side – Muslim and Western – in their vision of mankind and of the human city. We need to pay particular attention to any analysis of Western hegemony. It is this hegemony that worries Muslim societies and exacerbates their sense of distrust and suspicion. And at the same time, we should give due respect to Muslim demands for Islam to be given full and fair recognition in multiconfessional and pluralist societies. By insisting on the legitimacy of their demands, Muslims risk feeding tensions with the West. Clear-eyed analysis is essential in any dialogue between Muslims and Christians in order to save each side from resorting to damaging stubbornness and violence.

Conviviality tested out in the cultural sphere

Lucidity in politics requires an underlying lucidity on cultural issues. Urgency can however mean that political action takes precedence over any purely cultural considerations. Arab Christian communities are now fewer, and this is a loud wake-up call. In current conditions in the Arab world, only political commitment can offer any guarantee of safety. In this context, political commitment involves a work of conversion both in minds and in structures, in order more strongly to establish the space within which Muslim–Christian conviviality can operate in the Arab world. The nature of this commitment will be dictated by the global cultural visions defended by Christianity and Islam respectively. The encounter between these two global cultural visions will mean that when the dialogue between Muslims and Christians is conducted within the context of the Arab world, it will be inevitably distinctive and particularly normative.

No one would think to deny that Islam was born within Arab culture, or that Arab identity is fundamentally suffused with Islam. But it is also acknowledged that Islam arose within Arab Judaism, Arab Christianity, and Arab polytheism, the archaic form of modern secular religiosity. In fostering their courageous dialogue, Arab Christians and Arab Muslims are encountering the exceptional challenge they face, in which Islam and Christianity both confront their shared Arab heritage. Only an Arab dialogue can deliver the most stringent of challenges to Islam, since Muslims might disdain engaging with any other form of religiosity as being a radical and alien Other. Only in Arab Christianity can Islam acknowledge the force of the double affinity: a monotheistic faith, with shared Arab roots.

Non-Muslim Arab identity thus remains a touchstone that challenges and under-mines any claim to superiority on the part of Muslims.

Regrettably, however, Arab Christians have often preferred to alienate them-selves culturally, for fear of having to alienate themselves on religious grounds. Many Arab Christians are keen to distance themselves from the Arab roots from which they were born. Their insistence on wrongly associating Arab identity with Islam means that they end up denying the first and mistrusting the second. Any dialogue between Muslims and Christians should help Arab Christians to become better aware of their Arab cultural identity. Although some academic works may be disseminated in foreign languages, the fact remains that Middle Eastern Chris-tianity belongs firmly in the Arab cultural sphere. The popularity of some Syriac, Greek or Copt communities, often only superficial and temporary, cannot under-mine the fact that the Christian communities are fully integrated into Arab culture. There are inherent difficulties in making Western knowledge available in Arab culture, but Arab Christians should not be discouraged from acknowledging both in theory and in practice that the one Arab culture they share is both coherent and normative. Following the example of Christian pioneers in the Arab renais-sance, they should participate wholeheartedly in reviving and regenerating Arab thinking. The dialogue between Muslims and Christians should involve encourag-ing both Muslim and Christian interlocutors to interact more fully on a cultural level. Jointly, they should work to promote the benefits of the Arab perception of the world, which should lend its specific insights to define the ways in which Arab societies meet the challenge of modernity and post-modernity. Individuals, whether Christian or Muslim, may develop their own enthusiasm for a particular Western culture, but it is important to establish whether Christianity can fully flourish in Arab soil, and whether Islam can set the Arab identity free from any particular theological hegemony. This is a serious enquiry, and it will require a serious attempt to establish a shared cultural responsibility. Only an honest and fruitful dialogue between Muslims and Christians will ensure that the implications of the enquiry are fully explored. So far, the dialogue has been limited to well-worn clichés. In the wake of the radical demands of globalisation, we are now well beyond pathological repetition. In the context of the Arab world, we now need to liberate those who are stuck in shared ideas that lack theoretical legitimacy and existential relevance. As long as Arab Christians persist in believing that it is not possible for them to live out the distinctive nature of their Christian faith in a genuinely Arab cultural context, and Arab Muslims persist in thinking that it is not possible for Arab identity to be receptive to Christian wisdom, the fundamental antipathy between Arab Muslim and Christian communities will continue.

So the most fundamental task for any dialogue between Muslims and Christians is to dissipate cultural ambiguity and overcome assumed antipathy. A reassessment of the basic cultural problem in the Arab world is called for. Three fundamental notions must be methodically and rigorously analysed: Arab identity, the cultural dimension of Christianity, and the cultural dimension of Islam. If Arab identity can be defined as belonging essentially to Semitic Middle Eastern culture, then it no doubt shares some of the major features of that culture, and among them a sense of the sacred and of religion, obvious markers of metaphysical dependence on the physical world. Beyond paying more attention to reality and to the proper identification of objects, this acknowledgement of a transcendence that gives shape and direction to the human world can infuse the Arab cultural experience and make it distinctive. Seen under this light, Arab identity can become not only the nursery soil for Arab Christianity and Arab Islam but also their frame of reference. Careful and lucid analysis should help the interlocutors in the dialogue between Muslims and Christians to claim Arab identity as their shared cultural framework.

So if Christianity and Islam each include to a different extent cultural aspects appropriate to their visible history, consideration should be given to setting up a monitoring process that might identify the similarities and differences between Christian and Muslim cultures. Arab Christians risk deluding themselves if they persist in maintaining that the Christian faith is better suited to a visible history suffused with Western culture. In fact, such an unsubstantiated statement could threaten Muslim–Christian conviviality, for it might lead Muslim interlocutors to consider that Christianity does not properly belong within the Arab cultural sphere. They might even be led to disregard – in theory at least – Christian difference, and even eventually to work at directly or indirectly removing the physical presence of Christians. It is therefore not absurd to detect, in the context of the religious tensions inherent in Arab societies, an unhealthy collusion between Arab Christians seeing themselves as provoked to expatriation and Arab Muslims contemplating ideological fratricide.

Should this be true, then Arabs engaging in dialogue between Muslims and Christians are called to promote an attitude towards cultural entente that will help widen the scope of Arab identity, so that Islam, Christianity and cultural modernity can each find ways of expressing their truth and their energy. The effect of history, and in particular of the trauma of Western colonialism inflicted on Arab societies, may mean that Islam enjoys greater opportunities for legitimacy and affirmation than Christianity and – to an even greater extent – cultural modernity. In self-defence, Arabs may have lost a sense of reason and clarity, and have become more obdurate. The original Arab nature of Christianity, since it predates the emergence of Islam, should give Arab Christians an option to offer their Muslim interlocutors a form of deep therapy based on their collective memory.

For Arab Muslims, this cultural therapy will serve as catharsis, and for Arab Christians as reminiscence. Through dialogue in Arabic, Arab Muslims should be able gradually to shake off the impediments born of successive defeats and affronts endured since the emergence of Western political modernity and the stifling of the Ottoman empire; Arab Christians should be able to remind themselves of the status and value of their massive contribution to shaping Arab culture before, during and after the political establishment of the faithful Arab Muslim community. Sharing their commitment to this project to promote an Arab cultural renaissance should enable the dialogue between Muslims and Christians to re-establish its practical validity.

What is needed just now is to coordinate efforts to modernise contemporary Arab thinking. Arab Christian sensitivities should not remain on the sidelines, where they have been until now, quite possibly because of Christian reticence. The complete absence of any significant efforts towards joint Muslim–Christian collaboration may be due in part to the categorical refusal by certain fundamentalist Islamists to contemplate it. Their refusal is due to a total rejection of any intrusion by or even grafting of anything alien that might compromise the purity of the Muslim vision. The humanities have shown us that cultural perception is neither monolithically transparent nor completely homogeneous. We therefore have to recognise the mutual interference of perceptions and of horizons. Dialogue between Muslims and Christians should prove that the riches of Arab culture are due specifically to the confluence and interaction of those three notions mentioned above: Arab identity, the cultural dimension of Christianity, and the cultural dimension of Islam.

Once Christian and Muslim Arabs start feeling that together they belong to the same cultural horizon and that they truly share the same preoccupations on modernisation, they will learn better to share the same social space. A shared understanding of the social problems facing the Arab world will enable them, in a spirit of harmonious agreement, to contemplate suitable solutions and to design specific ways to engage with them. Cultural agreement shapes social agreement. This is why dialogue between Muslims and Christians should never, for the sake of focusing on urgent and important matters, neglect or underestimate the influence of culture. Any number of social conflicts causing conflict among Arab societies are due to cultural failures. Whatever other sociopolitical priorities there may be, any dialogue between Muslims and Christians must defend the importance of viewing cultural issues with the kind of clarity of vision that is also linked with a theological understanding of mankind.

Conviviality tested out in the theological sphere

The status of the third test of lucidity brings to light a hidden ambiguity. The threefold dimensions of politics, culture and theology in truth do not fit with the way that the Arab religious mind works. Rather, they fit with Arab nature and the particular hierarchy of priorities dictated by its history. Undeniably, however, religious perception is the main driving force for both individual and collective behaviour in the societies of the Arab world. Caught up in the snare of the third world, it has not yet been able to dispatch its false gods. Theological lucidity therefore dictates that any dialogue between Muslims and Christians should be tackled with particular boldness. Religious experience suggests a taboo resistant to all blows. In the Arab world, the huge influence of the divine will penetrates every aspect of life. Any freedom in theological thinking is limited to exploring variety in external expressions. The core content of divine revelation always remains unaltered and unalterable.

As long as Arabs, both Christian and Muslim, are too nervous to examine anew their respective faiths, they will not be able to meet on shared ground looking at the key aspects of their religious experience. There is absolutely no point in reviving old Muslim–Christian theological controversies. The historical distance between medieval and modern controversies is such that new formulations need to be explored for the two faiths that have arisen in the interval. This is why any new theological enquiry, to be effective and fruitful, should be carried out in constant reference to the challenges of difference. Just as Arab Christians are invited to rework the way they express their faith, taking account of the different theology of Koranic revelation, Arab Muslims are also invited to revise the theological expression of their religious experience, taking account of the cultural impact of Christian theology of the Word made flesh on their religious thinking. An open-minded theological attitude should enable both sides to avoid any ambiguous compromises, and instead to respect two principles valued in our postmodern period: a proper respect of difference as a challenge and an enriching aspect of identity, and intercultural solidarity leading to a better understanding of the mystery of human life.

Three theological notions need urgently to be defined: God, mankind, and the hermeneutics of plurality. Each of these notions will benefit from therapeutic clarity as they are explored within the dialogue between Muslims and Christians.

Once misunderstandings are set aside, it will become clearer where there is agreement and where there is divergence. The last section of this reflection will not aim to elucidate all the different aspects of each issue, but simply to pick out the theological priorities that need to be urgently addressed in any dialogue between Arab Muslims and Christians. Muslim reticence to engage in theological dialogue may prove a barrier, so it is important that Arab interlocutors should highlight from the start the potential benefits of theological conversation, and that they will not in any way compromise the faithfulness of believers, nor the coherence of their vision.

Preserving the otherness of God

When looking at their theological perception of God, both Christians and Muslims are invited to focus above all on His divine transcendence. Since Arab culture is fundamentally suffused with the omnipresent and active presence of the divine will in different sectors of human life, there is an ever-present risk that both Christian and Muslim theological thinking might slide towards anthropomorphism. In order to avoid any temptation to theological manipulation, the dialogue between Arab Muslims and Christians must categorically defend the principle that there is no overlap whatever between the Word of God and the words of mankind. An Arab theology of dissociation may help avoid the risk that both Christian and Muslim communities might misunderstand or misrepresent the plan of the divine economy.

A theology of dissociation that respects the transcendence of God does not negate the principle of revelation held in both Christian and Islamic faith. On the contrary, it will help both Christians and Muslims to avoid confusing their human words with the divine Word. This should enable the Word of God to be more clearly and freely revealed to contemporary Arabs so that it can find proper expression in the reality of the Arab world. Ultimately, this theology will mean no longer using the Word of God as a device to block and forbid any open-minded interaction between people, or to undermine positive attempts at communication between Arab Christians and Arab Muslims primarily designed to foster a better shared life and destiny.

The dialectic between 'God wholly Other' and 'God close to us' will serve to correct any trenchant or inflexible theological assertions that might stifle theological reflection. Muslims insist that God is transcendent, whereas Christians emphasise the historicity of mediation between humans and the divine, but both offer a clear justification for exploring this dialectic. If God is *par excellence* beyond the power of humans to conceive of Him, then any human understanding of Him will by definition be inappropriate. In Islam, no human approach to the will of God, however closely inspired by Koranic revelation, will be able to fully grasp the divine mystery. In Christianity, no human reception of the face of God, however closely inspired by the theology of incarnation, will do justice to the splendour of the light of God. Both these approaches acknowledge that human life is finite, which will be helpful to promoting good understanding between Muslims and Christians. Viewed positively, human finiteness will always be better understood by those who remain open-minded towards divine transcendence, which in terms of an epistemological verification of theological knowledge will serve as a key tool for authentication and correction.

Complicity between the son and the vicar

Christianity and Islam enable the development of two different yet complementary approaches to how the status of mankind is perceived in theological terms within a global vision of creation. Any dialogue between Muslims and Christians should aim to highlight the complementarity of these two perceptions as a source of enrichment. A number of disagreements between Islam and Christianity are due to the different approaches to mankind in the Bible and the Koran. These disagreements can affect legal, political and socioeconomic debates aiming to reach a universal consensus on the way we regulate sharing life on our planet and of the use of mineral resources and global wealth.

It was a basic intuition revealed through exploring the images in the Bible and the Koran that lay at the root of this anthropological investigation.[4] The Christian revelation sees humans as the beloved children of God, whereas the Islamic revelation sees humans as managing agents whose dignity derives from their voluntary submission to God and the way that God entrusts to them the management of created life. We can thus see that there is from the start a distinction between the two theological perceptions. In the biblical corpus, God, driven by his immense love, creates human beings in His image to be like Him (Genesis 1.27), and establishes him as His partner, His associate and His heir; in the Koranic corpus, God, by pure decree out of His immeasurable power, creates human beings out of clay, without any reference to His divine nature or any possible ontological affinity, and establishes him as a lieutenant and manager of the Earth (Koran 24,55)

---

4 See my volume on comparative Islamic and Christian anthropology (M. Aoun, *Fils et vicaire. Pour une anthropologie islamo-chrétienne comparée*, Paris, L'Harmattan, 2015).

The biblical concept of creation emphasises that human beings have their place at the heart of creation to the extent that, through pure divine grace, they are able to share in the very nature of God (Psalm 8.6–7; 2 Peter 3.4); the Koranic concept, on the other hand, emphasises the submissive nature of human beings (Koran 3,83; 2,131; 4,125) and fixes an unbridgeable chasm between the Creator and the creation. Islam thus places mankind in creation as a servant who adores God, a creature who by grace is enabled in every way to receive the Word of God and to live according to its demands. Mankind may even be granted the privilege of serving as viceroy of the universe, before whom angels prostrate themselves, but for ever in a position of ontological difference that definitely separates the created being from the divine transcendence.

There may be overlaps between these two anthropological visions, but it is nevertheless clear that in Christianity mankind is granted a radically different destiny from the one granted in Islam. This fundamental divergence does not negate the affinities we identified arising from the shared monotheistic theology of creation underlying the three related religions, Judaism, Christianity and Islam; it does however give rise to significant theological consequences and thus to two very different anthropological visions in terms of the status and role of mankind in society. The Christian theology of adoptive children and partner heirs grants humans full liberty, in the spirit of their adoptive status, to create and elaborate the principles of cosmic legislation to regulate both individual and collective life; the Muslim theology of submissive lieutenants and obedient servants reduces the scope of any such liberty and restricts it within the bounds of revealed Koranic law, which either implicitly or explicitly includes all the moral, social and political ordinances of the divine will.

In spite of the divergence between these two perceptions, any dialogue between Muslims and Christians must nevertheless make every effort to show that they are compatible and complementary. Many Arab Muslims are truly keen to show their Christian interlocutors the value of an anthropological understanding that takes careful account of complexities in the sociopolitical life of the community of believers. Muslim tradition has evolved a careful legal structure principally inspired by the theology of freedom in the management of creation,[5] and it provides people with the norms and regulations best suited to helping them live out

---

5 'The Koran allows the legal initiative of the believer, or at least of the lawyer, wide room for manoeuvre. The proper response to this call should only be initiative, freedom, or in fact categorical effort (*ijtihâd*), renewal (*tajdîd*).' (J. Berque, *Relire le Coran*, Paris, Albin Michel, 1993, p. 88.)

in daily life their faithfulness to the Word of God. The religious anthropological complementarity between Islam and Christianity should therefore be expressed through combining the key aspects of these two approaches. The Christian category of liberty, derived from the biblical concept of the heir, would map well onto the Muslim category of faithfulness, derived from the Koranic concept of the lieutenant. The Koran's theology of faithfulness enables concrete, detailed normativity to emerge, while the theology of the Bible allows the freedom to establish fundamental principles for criticism and rectification. This mutually supportive pattern means that the content of Islamic legislation can constantly be adjusted by the formal requirements for analytical amendment in the theology of adoption. The presence of a rich and varied body of law in Islam can therefore compensate for the absence of practical legislation within Christianity. Whether the issue is the faithful lieutenant's legal activity or the analytical work carried out in liberty by the child and heir, the one and only point of reference will remain the absolute transcendence of God.

The fostering of hermeneutical pluralism

The hermeneutics of diversity will need to be privileged in any dialogue between Arab Muslims and Christians. It can be understood in two ways: either as a plural hermeneutics of the foundational texts, or as a hermeneutics acknowledging the variety in religious experience pathways. Whichever sense is taken, any dialogue between Muslims and Christians will need to demonstrate that an Arab theology keen to safeguard the full potential meaning of the revealed text is useful for salvation. One of the basic tasks for any dialogue between Muslims and Christians is to restore the value of all the interpretive traditions within Christianity and Islam that have supported the principle of having the religious text fully open to review.

The theology of dialogue between Muslims and Christians will need to become a hermeneutical theology; for to the extent that it revives the old paradigms of free interpretation of foundational texts, it will enable the interlocutors not only to revisit their own ancient theological texts, but also, and especially, to draft a new form of Muslim–Christian theological agreement. This should enable better emphasis on the legitimacy of the different theological perceptions of God's plan for salvation. In other words, the draft will be able to show that the different interpretations may sometimes reach beyond the normally understood limits of religious affiliation. If tradition allows varied interpretations within the same community, that justifies variety outside the religious system of that community.

Once it is clear that the hermeneutics of plurality does not affect the creation as devised by the divine plan, then theological divergence can be perceived as distinctive steps along the way. They pull together an irreducible body of religious truth that no attempts at harmonisation will be able to dismiss. It is therefore necessary to devise an ethics of plurality capable of preserving distinctiveness without damaging interpersonal harmony. So Arab interlocutors in the dialogue between Muslims and Christians are invited to lay the foundations of an ethical charter. There is no lack of references from the Bible and the Koran authorising a solid theological foundation of fundamental difference. A whole dialectic of unity and diversity can be found throughout both the Bible and the Koran. By empha-sising this dialectic, the hermeneutics of diversity will not only acknowledge the *de facto* existence of the religious Other but also – and especially – will show the positive value of otherness in the process by which both Christian and Muslim religious growth and maturity develop.

Both the Bible and the Koran include more or less explicit exhortations to discern and acknowledge otherness. In Christianity, the part played by the Spirit of God extends beyond the limits of visible historical mediation by ecclesiasti-cal institutions. It is the Spirit of God that will lead mankind into all truth (John 16.13). In keeping with the conciliary intuitions at Vatican II, one can think that the same Spirit can inspire different faith experiences and different ways of receiv-ing the biblical message. As long as the Muslim experience of faith bears witness to divine transcendence, it can surely be accepted as an aspect of the work of the Spirit. The Koran, meanwhile, insists that God is absolutely free in terms of who He guides and who strays from Him (Koran 42,8). It is God, and not the Prophet, who inspires mankind to follow the path of salvation (Koran 10,99; 39,41; 88,21–22). God's original plan seems to allow that humans will follow different paths in their religious experience (Koran 5,48). The original Koranic vision appears to be less monistic (Koran 11,118) since diversity is written into God's plan. The exist-ing plurality of religious traditions is designed so that human beings can become mutually acquainted, acknowledge each other's legitimacy and help each other to work well together at constructing their world (Koran 49,13). This insight should help in the development of a shared Muslim–Christian hermeneutics of diversity. In other words, we are looking at the birth of a new hermeneutical approach that might bring renewal to the Muslim–Christian perception of revealed truth by seeking to identify within the energy of Muslim–Christian faith possible adjust-ments and reformulations; these might enable the two communities thoughtfully to revisit their own distinctive theological assets and to use them with intelligence in order to strengthen their spiritual solidarity as they pursue a shared human future of maturity and fulfilment.

The future of Muslim–Christian conviviality in the Arab world is closely dependent on the way in which Christians and Muslims approach their dialogue. If, as they set out their stall for the dialogue, they boldly present this threefold witness to clarity (in the fields of politics, culture and theology), they will be able to overcome the impact of the regional political tragedy. If the Arab elite, especially the religious elite, can sincerely commit to encouraging authentic two-way reflection in which the two communities can express themselves while remaining true to their deepest aspirations, then the Arab world will be able to present itself as a reconciled, mature and responsible society. Only this kind of dialogue – a successful dialogue with the Other embodied by Arab Christians – will enable Arab Muslims to repair the image they carry of the Western Other. And for Arab Christians, only this kind of dialogue will enable them to cut free from hereditary paralysis, having gained the courage to witness to truth as they face those whom they have always considered might ultimately cause their disappearance, the Arab Muslim Other. The meeting of these two Others offers a glimpse of the distant future of Arab identity.

Lebanese conviviality: distinctiveness, challenges and promises

This albeit brief threefold strategy for openness, theologically bold, may seem presumptuous, and certainly idealistic. We have been attempting to describe an abstract paradigm that might well prove to be impossible. It is therefore urgent to give concrete expression to a historical experience of conviviality. In the terms of the discussion in this current volume, the logical example is that of Lebanon, where modern Islam is particularly to be found. Modern Islam is seeking to offer a new interpretation of its religious, cultural and political vocation. Lebanon also has useful experience to offer in terms of its cultural experience focused on Muslim–Christian conviviality.

Two intuitions provide us with guidance here. Given that Lebanon as a nation leads a secular shared life, it needs here, first, to revive a calm and objective joint reflection; it was threatened by the dramatic consequences of the Lebanese war (1975–1990), which could have imperilled the distinctive founding vision of Lebanese identity. Second, Lebanon urgently needs to present to the cultural debate among the international community its model of pluralist society, which the catharsis of its crisis will have rendered highly relevant as a paradigm. These two intuitions, taken together, guide the theme of this exploration and its development. We shall adopt here a structural analysis in the hope of highlighting the ways in which a fruitful and constructive exchange might develop between the two Lebanese communities. We shall also hope to discover the constellation of religious, cultural and political factors that might – and should – ensure that any dialogue between Muslims and Christians is truly original and makes a fundamental impact.

We should straight away acknowledge a methodological caveat. We are after all attempting to justify two labels which, in the Lebanese context, might provoke disapproval or at least surprise. My hope is that Lebanese Christianity and Lebanese Islam are two concepts which can be extended to embrace the cultural diversity of the fundamental characteristics of each; my desire to demonstrate this is driven by my conviction that Lebanon has been, and I sincerely hope will remain, a crucible of civilisations in which both rootedness and fusion can make a deep impression on even the most intransigent and culturally disparate ethnic groups. This would mean that there truly is a Lebanese form of Christianity that may be an integral part of Eastern, Antiochian and Arab Christianity but is also distinctive specifically because it is Lebanese. And similarly there is a Lebanese form of Islam that, although definably Arab, is also, thanks to its being rooted in Lebanese soil, somewhat removed from the temptation to uniformity that mercilessly hounds Muslims worldwide. In actual fact, even Arab Islam presents an enticing mosaic of surprising contrasts and disparities, from Egyptian Islam outraged by social misery to Saudi Islam muffled by technological intrusion, via Palestinian Islam locked into a battle for national liberation.

The picture needs nuance, however, because the Lebanese war and the vicissitudes of the Arab political situation have led to a double rapprochement. The Islam described as Lebanese has somewhat magically joined forces with Arab – Iranian, even – Islam, whereas the Christianity described as Lebanese has been drawn to Arab Christianity. There are different explanations for these rapprochements in the two communities. Lebanese Islam is increasingly tending to align itself to the identitarian claims of Arab and even worldwide Islam. Lebanese Christianity, on the other hand, is being forced to review its position in society, and by constantly questioning and reviewing synodical theology it is attempting to revive the fortunes of Arab Christianity. The presence of Lebanese Christians is marked by genuinely spiritual witnessing, humble identification with the cause of the Arab people, and profound involvement in the human and cultural life of the Arab world.

The truly Lebanese identity of these two religious communities is highly likely to be called into question in the new sociopolitical situation in the Arab world. Their shared secular history and their moving experience of coexistence will nevertheless provide constant ringing reminders of the crucial need for future solidarity that might bring benefits and salvation for all. The truth of this is easily proved. We need only look at the positive dedication that, despite the current political difficulties, continues to affect daily life in Lebanon and to sow seeds of hope for the development of a harmonious future. If there is a risk that the alignment of Lebanese Muslims to Arab or Iranian Islam might compromise its particular Lebanese distinctiveness, the adoption by Lebanese Christians of the values of authentic Christian presence in the Arab world might help in the emergence of a better Muslim–Christian conviviality in Lebanon.

Before we look in greater detail at these factors, we should highlight that they are inevitably synchronous. This is because opportunities that might favour a constructive contribution to the dialogue between Muslims and Christians on a worldwide scale are assembled in a unique way in Lebanon. Taken separately, these same factors can of course also affect the status of the dialogue that is surely also happening in countries where Islam and Christianity, in different ways, live side by side.

Arab affiliation

The first distinctive characteristic of Lebanese conviviality is clearly the fact that both the Christian and the Muslim communities would instinctively and unhesitatingly claim affiliation to the Arab identity of the society around them. This welcoming Arab identity is agreed by all to be the cultural reference *par excellence* for all Arabic speakers born in the Arab Middle East. It is strictly speaking cultural in origin, but is not easily distinguished from its Islamic *Weltanschauung*, which explains the tensions among Lebanese Muslims in search of their identity. Some think it increasingly dangerous to continue celebrating a cultural and secular Arab identity at a time when the whole Arab world is engaging in regrettable strategies designed to foster partisan assimilation and an ideological conflation of Arab identity with Islam.

If this is truly happening, the aberration will force a huge challenge on Lebanese conviviality. In spite of the political failures of the current cultural approach to Arab identity, clearly the very fact of reducing Arab culture to its later Islamic accretion is a fallacious simplification and an unacceptable alteration of reality. The lessons of Antiquity clearly do not allow this damaging misrepresentation. Twenty-first century statistics should not affect our assessment of responsibilities and plaudits in the development and growth of Arab civilisation. Prior to the domination by political Islam of the Middle East, Judaism and Christianity, together with Arab nomad paganism, were the original influences on Arab identity. Over the centuries, and right up to the modern renaissance, the different Christian com-munities made a massive contribution to the revival of Arab culture by resisting Ottoman obscurantism. If Lebanese Christians are looking for a way to validate their Arab identity, it is precisely because they see being Arab not as a religious or even an ethnic label, but rather as a cultural reference that collates the various Semitic influences originating from the ancient Middle East. They are keen to be authentic in their evangelism, and this goes hand in hand with wanting to acknowledge their cultural validation.

To be more precise, Lebanese Christianity is a thoroughly Arab Christianity, and its distinctive characteristic is that this is true both on cultural and evangelical grounds. Lebanese Christianity needs first and foremost to renew the link between Arab identity and its authentic cultural roots by rejecting outright not only the unacceptable claims of Arab pan-Islamism, but also – by fostering and respecting the legitimate specificity of the different Arab nationalities – the excitable extrem-ism of pan-Arab nationalism. Because of its particular status, it is only Lebanese Christianity that can take on and defend this cause, which is the cause of all Arab Christians. And it is because Lebanese Christianity is culturally embedded in the Arab identity that it is able to initiate a more fruitful dialogue with Lebanese Islam.

In their dialogue with Christians, Arabs might be tempted by Islamist thought patterns to bring in a difficult confusion of value judgements and assorted incoher-ent prejudices. To prevent this, Lebanese Christianity is able, first, to share with Islam its full understanding of the fundamental patterns in Islamic thinking, which emerged and flourished in the midst of (more or less peaceful) Judeo-Christian history. Second, it is able to offer that same Islam a better and more culturally grounded presentation of Christian truth, since it is often presented through cul-tural idioms drawn from the twin Greek and Latin heritage, which are alien to Arab Semitic sensitivities. So in any dialogue conducted with Islam by Lebanese Christians, they will be aware of their Arab cultural identity, and thus far better able to foster a future that might hold promise for a population that longs to marry the salvation potential of these two great religions.

Diversity within reciprocity

A second characteristic of Lebanese conviviality is that its citizens share a politi-cal and social life that is an intense web of relationships rich in religious diver-sity. Any Lebanese dialogue between Muslims and Christians might therefore, uniquely, enable it to exceed expectations as a consistent and effective instrument.

It is only in Lebanon that Islam, thanks to its Lebanese connections, is aware and properly appreciative of the various Christian doctrinal differences and the particular features of the three Lebanese Churches: Catholic, Orthodox and Protestant. These three theological strands offer complementary contributions that can enable Islam to grasp the ultimate truth of Christianity, while providing ways to compensate for any difficulties or insufficiencies that they might encounter in their dialogue from the different theoretical approaches. It is only in Lebanon that Christianity, through its Lebanese witnesses, can gain better knowledge of Islam by collating the theological, philosophical and political thinking of the three Muslim communities: Sunni, Shiite and Druze. And clearly, the same pattern of complementarity is applicable to Christian attempts to understand the intimate link in Islam between truth and reality. The people of Lebanon have every interest in making this potential for openness and exchange a very real part of their relationships. The potential will only become reality if and when the Lebanese interlocutors in conviviality are willing to accept not only the principle that they have absolute freedom of conscience but also the ontologically foundational status of cultural diversity.

So it seems clear that any such Lebanese dialogue, if conducted under the best possible conditions, might turn out to be very fruitful. If the Lebanese people can gain a new, 'converted' perspective, they will find that they have a new and decisive message for the world about the future for interfaith relationships. The variety of religions within Lebanon, moreover, instead of enabling confrontation and mutual exclusion, could ensure the dialogue is realistic. Islam and Christianity, especially on Lebanese soil, both know and feel the sobering truth that they are on fragile ground. In the crucible of pain that Lebanese society is experiencing, a conversion to humanist values shared by both these religious traditions might emerge. Both Christians and Muslims are deeply aware of the bitter hurts and divisions tearing at their communities; both need to show the Lebanese people that the overriding interests of mankind should come before the dogmatic demands of their respective religious systems. Careful management of alienness and difference might enable both sides to adopt a fresh cultural outlook that resolutely values humanity. A renewed pluralistic cultural outlook would bear witness to the fact that the Lebanese people carry a true existential concern for each other that will enable them to seek a better understanding of their shared future. And a further thought. By introducing their Muslim fellow citizens to the concept of ecumenical open-mindedness – an ethical approach to relationships that is not yet fully honoured in relationships among Christians – Lebanese Christians might hope to see Lebanese Muslim communities develop a real hunger for theological dialogue. Such dialogue clearly demonstrates openness to the Other and should in its turn initiate constructive developments in the Lebanese dialogue between Muslims and Christians.

Sharing power

And here we encounter the third characteristic of Lebanese conviviality. Various factors have led Lebanese Christians and Muslims to create and adapt a political regime designed to ensure that representatives from the diverse population groups participate in government: a state structured along confessional lines; the pervasive communitarian mentality so prone to dysfunction and dislocation; and the particular status of the Lebanese mountains. Nowhere else has power distributed in such a debatable way led to such a profound human experience of difference. In this, Lebanon provides a groundbreaking model, as we shall easily show. True dialogue, taking account of all its serious implications, has not been possible either in the supposedly Christian West, where Muslims are in the minority, nor in the Muslim Middle East, where Christians are in the minority. Do we need to remind ourselves, in this connection, that only those who are free and equal are in a position to enter dialogue and exchange? The particular nature of the political regime in Lebanon in effect makes it possible to go beyond either of these models in the West or the Middle East, in which the interlocutors often feel constrained for cultural, legal or social reasons, and all the more so because of numerical imbalance. Leaving aside any misplaced chauvinism, the dialogue between Muslims and Christians in Lebanon is crucially important because it takes place on an egalitarian footing between communities that see themselves and each other as responsible for a shared duty.

This theoretical perspective, however, has never found true practical expression in the context of Lebanese society. Why, we might ask ourselves, has this failed, and where should the blame lie? Is it with the confessional model itself, which suffers from serious structural defects, or with the frailty of humans, who succumb so easily to the temptation of corruption? For whatever reason, the Lebanese model has not been able to deliver on its promises. Should it then serve as a model? This is an extremely complex question. The value of a model depends not only on its objective relevance but also on its historical feasibility. In the case of Lebanon, these two factors have never been treated with the seriousness they merit. The Lebanese people have been overwhelmed by regional instability and violence, and have therefore, unforgivably, failed properly to reassess their own model of conviviality.

One consequence of this approach, however, has been generally increased awareness worldwide of the importance of communitarian and religious thinking. Western societies are reconsidering the importance of communitarian and religious identity, while Arab societies have been hoping for emancipation from the strict hegemonic control of extreme confessionalism. The comparison is highly significant. The two worlds, in solidarity, are in search of the same unique solution. The Western world has been suffering from an excess of individualism, and is seeking to revive the spirit of community affiliation, whereas the Arab world, suffering from an excess of confessionalism, longs for greater individual rights and freedoms. Lebanon, it appears, sits at the intersection between these two aspirations, and it should honour its privileged position. In order to achieve this, the Lebanese people need to acknowledge the importance of their own particular experience of conviviality.

In other words, in Lebanon conviviality can rely on the support of the legal system and the government executive. It is a fundamental constitutional reality. Sadly, there is no secular input in the promotion of conviviality. There are different views on this. Some suggest that it is due to the innately confessional structure of the Middle Eastern Arab mindset. Others prefer to consider that the secular section of Lebanese society should not be labelled as yet another – albeit isolated – confession. It would nevertheless be both highly beneficial and humbly realistic to bring secularists into the conversation to provide background and serve as a yardstick for those engaging in Lebanese conviviality to reassess their openness and interaction.

Lebanese conviviality has after all never been only of interest to those involved in academic and scholarly debate. It has repeatedly been seen as a *sine qua non* for Lebanon's survival. Even at a worldwide level, intercultural plurality is now no longer simply an intellectual luxury. The indifference in modern Western societies towards religion is in clear contrast to the involvement of postmodern politics in promoting and defending plurality. In the case of Lebanon, political power is under the grip of religious confessionalism. What is needed now is for that grip to be loosened, not in order to relegate communitarian identity to the background, but in order better to integrate it into a pattern of relationships that conform with the requirements of the Charter of Human Rights.

There are good practical reasons for this, related to the issue of power sharing. Power is shared in a balanced way, decided pro rata on the basis of the size of the communities in Lebanon and their importance in political and strategic terms, both within and beyond Lebanon itself. This process is more significant among Lebanese Islamic communities, which are by no means monolithic. Before hostilities broke out in 1975 they had been in a slight numeric minority (40 percent), second largest after the Christian population, yet they enjoyed the prerogatives due to an equal partner; today, it is the duty of the Muslim population to promote a fair share of power for their Christian neighbours, who are now the second largest population group. If the three Lebanese Muslim communities, Sunni, Shiite and Druze, can be persuaded of the positive value of sharing power in this way, then Lebanese Islam, regardless of its numerical growth, should be able to display not only cultural flexibility but also a determination to share and promote complementarity.

The purifying challenges of history

The fourth characteristic of Lebanese conviviality is linked to its almost providential association with the many and rich vicissitudes of the nation's history. The dialogue is therefore burdened with a plethora of painful confrontations. Although tragically exacerbated, they bore within them the certain seeds of salvation and renewal. That is why the application of *tabula rasa* would in fact hinder any progress. It would deprive the dialogue of one of its fundamental characteristics, its permanent conflictual nature, which paradoxically secures its immunity and establishes its distinctiveness. Since the first emergence of diversity in today's Lebanon, alternating periods of friction and of reconciliation have weakened Lebanese conviviality. In the last resort, however, the belligerents have invariably turned to dialogue, which has increasingly been seen as an essential tool. It offers a path to a relative – and as yet incomplete – peace, and each new resolution to keep interconfessional peace yields a rich harvest of preventative measures and learned wisdom.

At every difficult turn in Lebanese history, it has therefore been possible to present the process of dialogue as the unique and sovereign remedy. And indeed, reconciliation and renewed dialogue have invariably been the only truly worthwhile outcomes to the most acute political crises. The history of Lebanon, complex and deeply significant, could be used to enrich the deployment of various forms of pluralist conviviality, but anyone wishing to do this will need to acknowledge that the conviviality itself is closely linked to an ongoing spirit of antagonism. Its intrinsic value has never been obscured by any dramatic manifestation. In other words, relationships between Lebanese Muslims and Christians, although usually polemical in character, have always taken the risk of being radical: their distinctiveness derives from the mutual synergy between rival interlocutors. It is however no longer surprising that the important notion of *legitimate conflict*, sadly abused – and thus debased – now often features prominently in communitarian interactions in Lebanese political life.

Rooted in the everyday

Rather than a debate between academics, the dialogue between Muslims and Christians, the bedrock for Lebanese conviviality, has emerged as essentially an existential exchange dictated less by notional preconditions than by the reality of shared life. People engage in it not as the logical outcome of abstract reasoning, but rather as a spontaneous and repeated phenomenon arising from daily encounters. It is, to be precise, a dialogue that invites those involved to bear in mind the interests and concerns of all the interlocutors. It focuses not only on the theoretical suppositions lurking in the respective theological background discourse of each side, but also, and especially, on the real-life implications of the shared daily struggle as they cope with the vagaries of daily life.

In this sense, it is the practical commitment of the Lebanese people to conviviality that motivates, nourishes and shapes what they are doing, not the reverse. This explains the extraordinary vitality of this mode of communication, which is a skill passed on down the generations thanks to the experience of the initiated. There is a growing perception that the cultural education of Lebanese youth should be focused on the art of conviviality and on exercising the art of dialogue, so it is increasingly urgent to pass the skill on. This kind of training can claim to respond to the fundamental predisposition of Lebanese society. Openness to diversity can enable Lebanese young people to overcome pathological distrust and tense apprehension.

Here again, the comparison is especially significant. The experience of daily life in Lebanon certainly highlights the challenges that lie ahead in the practice of conviviality. Because the Lebanese communities live in close proximity to each other, both tensions and radicalism are attenuated. At a time when Western Islam is concerned that excessive freedom might undermine the external marks of Islamic faith, Arab Christianity is still concerned about the lack of freedom in the societies of the Arab world. The same suffering arises from two different causes. On the one hand, too much freedom, and on the other, too little. This paradox is the very place where Lebanese conviviality may have a useful contribution to make.

Unlike the Muslim minority in the West who fear the hegemony of the majority, and the Christian minority in Muslim countries who fear they might gradually lose their liberty, both Christian and Muslim Lebanese are able to regroup purposefully and thus better appreciate the wisdom they derive from sharing their living space. Having long experienced confrontation, and learned from their wide experience to discern both objectively and fairly a range of identities and differences, they will be able to seize opportunities for genuine interaction and open themselves up to intimate and profound self-examination. Their existence in the midst of Lebanese daily life naturally lends greater credibility to all their efforts at mutual openness. In this kind of dialogue, a privileged space opens up in which different people can lay themselves open to each other while respecting the frailties of each and nourishing the dialectic of difference. This kind of openness makes any secular involvement in Lebanon hugely valuable. The neutrality of secularism is better able to interrogate both Christian and Muslim visions about the root of their claims to be absolute. Logically, this kind of enquiry should foster a salutary reassessment of the presuppositions of religious faith, and hence a more appropriate description of religious identity and how it has been perceived in historical, social, and especially political terms.

The deleterious effects of the war have left the Lebanese experience of Muslim–Christian conviviality mired in dismissive slurs and harsh value judgements; however, the lessons learned and the promises of Lebanese history suggest that it might rise again, renewed and restored. What we suggest here is obviously simply notional. By outlining the distinctiveness of Lebanese conviviality, I am not attempting a detailed manifesto or a militant speech, but rather a critical reflection on how well the current Lebanese ordeal might challenge, enable and indeed stimulate convivial dialogue. In the context of this volume's overall approach, the methodological signposts are more important than adopting specific ideas. Even exploring the three fields mentioned above (politics, culture and theology) will serve only to guide local theological reflection and practice. The analysis and evaluation of the Lebanese ordeal must look forward. In truth, once identified, the intrinsic value of this distinctiveness is that it calls upon all those who long to see, at the start of this third millennium, a true and lasting harmony between the two great monotheistic religions of mankind. Lebanon stands ready to serve as one of the privileged places able to exercise this kind of conviviality in order to prove its historical worth.

The authentic human, the promised land of conviviality

The experience of Lebanese conviviality clearly shows that home soil is the best place to share meetings and exploration. An Arab theology of conviviality should rethink the concept of home soil in terms of the ethics of relationships. This is all the more important since Semitic thinking seems to focus on the symbolism of soil as the place where identity is created and made secure. Arab Christians, because of their exacerbated kenotic mysticism, appear to have shaken off – albeit painfully – the temptation to define their identity in terms of geography and geopolitics; Jews and Muslims, however, have persisted in their dramatic confrontations, inspired by the identitarian notion of the promised land. If fellow Semites have to live with this kind of tension among them, they will find it impossible to practise openness to others or hospitality. The notion of the promised land must be revisited; and the unjustified notion rejected that (all too) human claims to possess and dominate a particular space might equate to a divine design to grant justification and blessing.

The interpretation that I am offering here suggests that in terms of the theology of the universal divine economy, the land is necessarily linked to salvation. For the land, election and salvation are the three narrative categories that relate to a far larger symbolism that encompasses the whole of the human person. Christ is understood in Christian hermeneutics to be the key to interpreting the Old Testament, so the promised land will no longer be a geographical place of salvation, but the symbol of any human person called to redefine themselves in the light of the promise of divine presence. As soon as a person is fully enveloped by the notion of salvation, then it is not an ethnic entity, or even a people invested with a divine mission, that is most important in terms of the rediscovery of Christian faith, but rather a notion of humanity fully reconciled to self, and open to encountering personal salvation by faithfully responding to the call from the Kingdom to be a new creation. It is in any case the very nature of the salvation offered by God in Jesus Christ that it transcends all frontiers and affiliations, and overturns any attempts at recovery strategies. Even seen as a model, the idea of a promised land and a chosen people would fail to translate the universal nature of the salvation offered by God to the whole of humanity. Viewed through the lens of conviviality, salvation can be described as thoroughly human, entirely and definitively free, and unconditionally universal. It is human because it reaches to the deepest parts of a person's heart as they freely develop their full potential through relationship. It is free, because it is offered expecting no return and without restriction. It is universal, because no part of the whole world is excluded from the diversity of cultural or spiritual experiences. Because of these three characteristics, the restrictive regulations in the Old Testament no longer serve as controlling paradigms. The exegetical work required by this new hermeneutical approach will therefore be to re-read the teachings in the Old Testament and to reinterpret them using semantic substitution: person instead of land; reconciled and open-minded humanity instead of chosen people; and liberation and sanctification for all the peoples of Earth instead of, for one particular population, the status of chosen people, wooed into a sacred union.

An awkward question

The 'promised land' is an ambiguous expression, tainted by old ideology and suspected of conveying traditions of theological exclusivism. Contrary to an extremely common misunderstanding in certain Christian circles, the biblical notion of the 'promised land' in fact refers to the birth of a new humanity. The new hermeneutics of conviviality must therefore be able to show that this notion encompasses anthropological implications rather than purely geographical, spatial or temporal ones. In order to clarify these implications, we need to deconstruct the different models that have accreted around it in Christian theology. And here we encounter a specific difficulty. We need to venture beyond the usual bounds of hermeneutics and critique what is traditionally accepted in Christian faith. In truth, this is an idea that constantly evades any bold innovative approach, because of its ideological complexity.

I would like to be able to justify this better than is possible here, but my starting point is that God would not promise mankind a land, but rather a place of genuine encounter. To promise a geographical land would limit theology to absolute immobility. This is unthinkable, a kind of martyrdom of reason. On the other hand, their faith enables Christians to understand the notion that God gives Himself, so that they can work towards the advent of His complete humanity, as already mystically prefigured in the perfect man, Jesus Christ. If God is the *raison d'être* of humans, then the promise must be related to the possibility that humans can achieve perfect humanity.

This is not an obvious reinterpretation. It will require courage to cleanse away the burden and accretions of different biblical traditions. So I offer here only the rough outlines of a new theological interpretation of the idea of the promised land, being extremely economical and simplifying the very complex textual subtleties of Scripture. I shall use three critical approaches in support of this reinterpretation. The first two are purposely taken from biblical hermeneutics, and the third is a deliberately critical theological reflection. The common denominator is my desire to reach a better understanding of how the Christian faith is set alight by the power of reason.

Disavowing the Old Testament

In the critical approach suggested by the texts of the Old Testament, three passages are bound together in one. The first shows the close link between humans and the soil of the ground. But rather than mankind treating the ground as sacred and submitting to it, it is the soil that is subject to mankind as its point of reference.

Genesis establishes[6] that humanity was born of that *'adamah* who was God's handiwork, and Isaiah and Hosea remind us that the 'Earth' serves to indicate mankind. For if God calls Himself the Bridegroom of the Earth, it is not for the sake of the soil, but for the sake of mankind.[7] We humans, therefore, are the bearers of the ultimate meaning of the Earth.

The second statement bears this idea out. It reveals the central place mankind occupies in God's economy. In Psalm 115 (v.16) we learn that the heavens belong to Yahweh, but that the Earth was given to the children of Abraham. The land therefore belongs to mankind, and mankind does not belong to the land. More-over, the land stands as a symbol of the faithful covenant with God. The land is no longer a geographical entity, but rather a state of communion. Infidelity could lead to Israel losing the land – that is to say, the covenant with God – as stated in Deuteronomy 28.63: 'you shall be plucked off the land that you are entering to possess.' This is why the prophets constantly insisted that idolatry towards a land should be openly denounced. Isaiah (5.8) castigates those who 'join house to house, who add field to field.'

The third and last statement refers to an emphatically eschatological perspec-tive on the ultimate meaning of land. In Psalms 25 (v.13) and 37 (v.3) the Earth represents the eschatological reality of the reward for the just, who put their whole faith in God. From the point of view of the coming Kingdom, a new Earth will arise and will effect reconciliation between all people. So in the 'new heavens and a new Earth' (Isaiah 65.17) that God will create, humans will experience the key characteristics of the Kingdom. Humanity's Earth, therefore, will be full of promise in that all of humanity, reconciled, will share fraternal harmony.

These three statements all point towards acknowledging the fundamental dignity of human beings and of their crucial status in relation to a land. They establish the dignity of humans and ensure that they stand above any intimations that land might be sacred. To limit God's promise to one geographical location is to reify the relationship between mankind and God, and relationships between humans. God's promise is greater than one land, than one people and than one

---

6 'Then the Lord God formed man from the dust of the ground, and breathed into his nostrils the breath of life; and the man became a living being.' (Genesis 2.7). The note in the Jerusalem Bible explains that mankind came from the soil (*'adamah*) and that this collective noun became the name of the first human. In another passage in the same book, humans will return to the ground: 'By the sweat of your face you shall eat bread until you return to the ground, for out of it you were taken; you are dust, and to dust you shall return.' (Genesis 3.19). There is thus a very clear link between the land of mankind and the humanity of mankind.
7 Hosea 2.5; Isaiah 45.8; 62.4; Song of Songs 4.12; 5.1; 6.2; 2 Maccabees 5.19.

civilisation. It is to be found in the welcome given to the truth of each person, wherever and whenever they live or have lived on Earth and in history.

A wider perspective in the New Testament

The texts of the New Testament confirm the aspects of autonomy that we have been looking at, but bring them into the new perspective that arises from the Christ event. In the Christian faith, the Kingdom announced by Christ is seen as an inexhaustible dynamic process whose promise to mankind will be fulfilled perpetually, throughout eternity. No one can therefore claim that redeemed humans have reached their full potential. So in the spirit of the Beatitudes, the notion of the Earth is a new and serious defining concept: 'Blessed are the meek, for they shall inherit the Earth' (Matthew 5.5). Here, 'the Earth' implies that the meek will possess spiritual gifts. It is gentleness among humans that fashions the genuine Earth of humanity. This can help us to understand why the letter to the Colossians urges Christians to 'set your minds on things that are above, not on things that are on Earth' (Colossians 3.2). The reality of the things that are on the Earth is gauged according to the fundamental values promulgated in the spiritual charter of the Beatitudes. And as a charter, it prefigures the condition of a humanity that is perpetually being redeemed.

The texts of the New Testament also emphasise the obsolescence of the Earth, not only in eschatological terms, but also in terms of the consistent historical experience of humans living on the Earth. As Matthew puts it,[8] the Earth will 'pass away' and will be replaced by a 'new Earth' (Revelation 21.1). That is the new Earth we are awaiting: 'in accordance with his promise, we wait for new heavens and a new Earth, where righteousness is at home' (2 Peter 3.13). When the second letter of Peter speaks of righteousness, it is referring to the gentleness of the Kingdom that is prefigured in the Beatitudes. And according to the letter to the Romans,[9] only those who are free will be able to live in the new Earth that has been transfigured to reflect that Kingdom.

The obsolescence of the Earth makes genuine freedom possible. This kind of

---

8 'Truly I tell you, this generation will not pass away until all these things have taken place. Heaven and earth will pass away, but my words will not pass away.' (Matthew 24.34–35).
9 'I consider that the sufferings of this present time are not worth comparing with the glory about to be revealed to us. For the creation waits with eager longing for the revealing of the children of God; for the creation was subjected to futility [...] in hope that the creation itself will be set free from its bondage to decay and will obtain the freedom of the glory of the children of God.' (Romans 8.18–21).

freedom will enable mankind to reach ever further beyond all its previous historical struggles. To be free, therefore, is constantly to transcend our previous self in
order to perfect within us the image of Christ, which belongs to a future of inexhaustible potential. Without this freedom, any human experience can degenerate
into a shrunken life of limitation and servitude. It is not therefore a collective ownership of land that God promises, but rather progressive emancipation for each
human from earthly possessions or historical confinement, so that the Kingdom
of liberty and gentleness can come about in the very heart of every person's daily
life. The standard criterion for all life on Earth then becomes 'the freedom of the
glory of the children of God' (Romans 8.21). In order to honour that freedom,
humans must cast aside any selfish desire for possessions. Unlike those who think
that by possessing the Earth they possess God, the Christian faith invites us to
transfigure the way in which we seek to inhabit the land. We shall not view the
land we inhabit as a collective possession, but instead, liberated and free of pos-
sessiveness, we shall view it with detachment.

A new understanding of the promise

These reinterpretations may be modest, but they now enable me to present my own
understanding of the promised land in terms of the radical innovation born of the
Christ event. If the radical nature of the Gospel is relevant to the salvation of the
world, it is because it celebrates mankind as the 'land' favoured by God in a unique
way. The salvation offered by God in Jesus Christ redeems human beings by
leading them to attain their full and authentic potential. What God promises people,
therefore, is certainly not a land ('*adamah*) but an Adam redeemed in the image of
his future humanity. We need to say 'future', because no human being is able fully
to attain their full human potential. To do so would be fatal, as it would enclose
the person in a sclerotic performative role. To possess a land would then indeed be
merely an embellished form of such limitation. In the opposite case, neither God
nor humanity is tied down to a specific land or ideology. Those who are tethered
to a promised land will limit their perception of the divine mystery to tending their
own small field and vine. Rendered prisoners of that same land, they will enclose
their human identity within the narrow bounds of their material possessions. Christ
invites us, rather than risk having God as our possession by wishing at all costs to
possess the 'promised land', to dispossess ourselves of ourselves in order to regain
a self who is freely open to diversity and to the gentle joy of sharing.

   This is why Christian salvation is not tethered to a geographical location, but
is anchored in the heart of mankind. So now the figure of Abraham is emerging

more clearly: he is the father and brother of all people who have no land or religion. He is an emblematic figure, the prototype itinerant human, free of any institutional control and bravely open to the disconcerting experience of religious faith. Secular before the term was coined, not tied in any way to the land, his only promise is to be willing in himself to incarnate humanity open to the mystery of faith, to worldwide diversity and fraternity. His humanity is a perpetual promise, always on the road, as he is. He therefore remains the symbol of the itinerant, forever open to the potentiality of future authenticity.

The boldness of a new theological openness

This three-pronged approach, although rudimentary, may I hope have some truth, and it leads me to the conclusion that the promised land is none other than human beings transfigured in the image of a humanity constantly being challenged and never complete. This overview has been a rapid sketch, and therefore, I freely confess, inevitably incomplete,[10] but it offers a way into what could be a useful reassessment of this challenging new interpretation. I am nonetheless aware that this outline sets in stone a matter that is in truth made up of nuance, well documented, and not necessarily explicit in all its affirmations. And there lies beyond this current volume a whole field of biblical and theological hermeneutics to explore. The texts we have examined belong to different contexts and present a variety of divergent yet reconcilable elements. They may not always relate directly to each other, but neither do they exclude each other.

---

10 I am especially aware of the complex and ambivalent nature of relying first and foremost on the novel nature of the Christ event, that is to say, on its unprecedented and unexpected potential for subversion. For everyone is well aware that the Christ event is by definition incarnationist. This could be taken to mean that human authenticity, when defined in historical terms, requires that it be geographically fixed, since human beings are not pure spirit but located bodies that exist only in a space (Descartes would have preferred the word term *étendue expanse*). In truth, however, we can only experience authenticity, and seek its fulfilment, in the dual context of time and space. This is why Judaism believes it can only reach complete fulfilment in the promised land, and Islam in an Islamic state. These spaces are necessarily within territorial bounds, even if the expectations of the faithful extend across the whole world. The same is true of historical and institutional Christianity, or at least since the time of Constantine. We need only recall the medieval experience of Christianity acting in concert with political powers, and seeking unlimited extension to its territory (by establishing Christian mission worldwide and Christian states that might prefigure the coming of the Kingdom). The description of the human condition in terms of geopolitical and sociocultural context should not in any way prevent the Christ event, in its universality, from enabling liberation and openness to diversity.

Throughout this reflection we have seen a dichotomy between the promise of land and the promise of authentic being. So in closing I would like to remove any suspicion that my theological reassessment might have been based on hostility towards the spiritual experience of the Jewish people; towards the notion of belonging and tradition invested in the concept of a land; or towards any possible similarity between the restoration of the earthly Jerusalem and the Second Coming of Christ. If in this reassessment I have sought to minimise textual references to the 'promised land' and the 'chosen people', this has been only in order to emphasise the astonishingly radical nature of the Christ event, which brings in liberation and a decentring of the self, gentleness, and welcome to otherness ('to belong to a land is to rise above it'). At the heart of these Gospel values there is a long path towards a truly human Earth, a place where the humans of history will be fulfilled and transfigured. It will also be a place of conviviality and authenticity in sharing. In this place, communion between humans will become the very place where God appears. Authentic human conviviality itself will become the land promised by God. Beyond geographical boundaries and the limits of identity, people will meet and share and thus be able to transcend their nature and move towards a horizon where they will encounter their greatest hopes.

Conclusion

The theoretical and practical difficulties endured by the Christian communities in the Arab world are so evident that they barely need pointing out. This work has attempted to redefine the theoretical framework within which the Christian faith could and must engage with the challenges of Arab conviviality. It is extremely worrying that theological and prophetic pronouncements in the Arab world are becoming increasingly timid and rare. The sociocultural and sociopolitical situation in the Arab world is currently forcing Christians to turn in on themselves in stubborn isolation. They need urgently to engage in a radical reassessment of their position, since it seems unlikely that the current merciless pattern will reverse.

Because of the existential tensions that constantly assault Arab Christians, their contemporary theology, originally an organised if divided structure, is now being pulled still further apart as identities are threatened: their few shared intuitions are now a splay of different sensitivities. Their theology is now the polar opposite of a converging structure. It cannot in any way be described as a unified body that is growing and becoming more focused; instead, it feels its way hesitatingly forward, focusing only on that which will help physical survival. This Arab theology, however, has its own content, its own principles; had it not, had it been spineless, had it lacked a fundamental coherence and original and focused intuitions, it would never have blossomed and been able to nourish the commitment and hope of the Arab Christian communities that quietly subscribe to it. Through examining the theological models presented in this volume, I have hoped to show the vital relevance of contextual theological reflection; arguably, for the purposes of a contemporary understanding of the Christian faith, the presentations would have needed to be better adapted to rational discourse.

This is because contemporary Arab Christian theology leans less towards internal rational legitimation (due to a lack of scientific paradigm) than towards existential duties (due to their deep intensity of life commitment). It is their commitment, rather than their thirst for scholarship, that supports the efforts

of Lebanese theologians to engage in conviviality. The developments in Christian theological discourse, both within the Christian Churches and within the
university and research communities, show that these various efforts are often
inadequate. The context that gave rise to these theological models has in truth
undergone fundamental change. A two-pronged effort is now required: first, to
analyse the efforts at conviviality, and second, to formulate a new local theology
that can take account of not only the changes that have affected the Arab world
but also the many ways in which, in these postmodern times, Christian theology
has moved on. Christians need to abandon the minority mindset that focuses on
survival, and instead join forces to fight against the obscurantism of the dominant
Arab ideologies; and above all, to play their part in developing a new Arab solidarity of positive citizenship, in which the rights of Arab people are promoted, while
safeguarding their Arab context and natural environment.

Our leading theme of conviviality will benefit from a proper respect for the
whole of Arab humanity. It is only through solidarity with Arab humanity that the
Christian notion of conviviality can be rescued from withdrawing into its tacti-
cal survival mode. The Arab people will best be able to appreciate the benefits of
Christian theology when they see its responsiveness to different approaches and
sensitivities. And in turning to a new way of explaining theology, religious faith
among Arabs – both Christian and Muslim – will discover an understanding sufficiently wide and fruitful to encompass the whole of Arab history.

Future developments in Arab Christian theology on conviviality must therefore surely willingly accept that the Christian faith should find its place in a
religiously pluralist worldwide landscape. This is the mission that the different
Christian communities in the Arab world must take on in their religious discourse.
Any success they encounter will very much depend on how well the message is
received among Muslims in the Arab world. If Arab Christians are able to modernise not only the conceptual framework but also the language they use, their
reflections are sure to resonate with both the thought processes and the practices
of Muslim theology.

In truth, it is only the language of love that will be able to express the distinctive yet universal characteristics of the Christ event in the context of contemporary
Arab societies, so Arab Christian theology will need to adapt the language of love
in order to speak credibly of their commitment and witness. They will then be
speaking to both emotion and reason in their Arab hearers. Having thus adapted
the language they use, contemporary Arab theologians will be armed with the
power to spread the message of salvation effectively to all Arab people. The work
we have started in this book aims to encourage this work of adaptation. It is at

this stage only an attempt. I am keen to underline the word 'attempt', as its scope is deliberately limited. It would however be pointless to foster a methodological approach for its own sake only, as an end in itself, or to abandon the calling to adapt because of a strong need to survive. In conclusion, therefore, I offer a twofold reflection on the theological background that should guide the new accessibility of the Christian message of witness in the societies of the Arab world.

As the first part of this reflection, we shall look at the new approach to interfaith plurality. I would like to defend the legitimacy of a threefold distinction within religious systems themselves. In other words, to identify three levels at which we see the truth of religious faith. The first level is the inevitable acknowledgement of a universal charter for human rights. Religions around the world are more or less unanimous in acknowledging this. Their acknowledgement enables the different religious systems to agree on the ultimate purpose of human life. And here they can agree with secularists who earnestly promote the value and dignity of human beings, their freedom and their inalienable distictiveness. The second level is that of the spiritual values preached by all religions: mercy, compassion, forgiveness, sacrifice and self-giving love, the mysticism of the interior life and of communion. Being spiritual, every religious faith is supposed to preach values such as these as part of human life. They enrich and deepen the humanity of each person. It is tremendously valuable that religions are all in full agreement about them.

These two levels, of course, guarantee that people will experience justice, peace, and the opportunity to flourish fully. Conviviality between people should therefore join in promoting them in order to bring about better solidarity between people of faith. It is only the third requirement for distinctiveness that might be problematic. It concerns an area which focuses on the deliberately different metaphysical understandings of the different religious systems. Here, dogma asserts that it faithfully represents the divine nature, or at least the divine will and the divine economy of salvation. And it is here that we need to adopt a seriously different approach. Instead of asserting that the metaphysical understandings are equivalent to the very being of God and that they include the divine will itself, I would like to defend the mystical link between the believer and their deep-seated experience, while acknowledging the absolute liberty of God to choose how He reveals Himself. In other words, I would like to suggest that religions keep this third level in its own distinct sphere which I would call the sphere of culturally located theological sensitivity. There would be two advantages to this approach. First, preserving the relevance of salvation by faith for those who adhere to the theological formulations of a specific cultural context, and second, to legitimise the diverse other faith experiences expressed in other cultural contexts.

Rather than load onto any specific religion's dogma an artificial metaphysical exclusivity that might be both inappropriate and dangerous, I suggest thinking of it as a theological sensitivity, thus granting their own legitimacy to each of many different experiences of communion with the divine. These experiences of communion underlie all the dogmatic formulations that preserve and nourish the faith of a community. It may be unthinkable, as well as extremely dangerous, to cultivate disagreement on the subject of the human and spiritual values that belong in the first two categories of truth that we identified above; it is quite legitimate, and even advisable, however, to promote different theological perceptions of the divine mystery. Legitimate, because of both the inexhaustible riches of the divine being and the hermeneutical dignity of human reason. Each theological world or system has its own distinctive sensitivities, its own particular ways not only to seek the absolute, but also and especially to receive the ways in which the absolute relates to humans in the immense diversity of their historical experiences.

The second part of my reflection is closely linked to the first, and it offers an ecumenical reflection on the mystery of Christ. We find here the key symbol of the Christian faith and the particular channel that reveals the love of God. In specific terms, we need to re-examine the question of the universality of Christ, based on a reassessment of the Christian faith in the light of the current claims of worldwide intercultural diversity. Ultimately, this line of thought aims to elucidate whether we should see Christ as the exclusive property of the Christian system of religion, or whether it would not be better to see Him as a universal truth, one that speaks to the worldwide human spirit outside, or alongside, the culturally Christian under-standing of His mystery.

At the dawn of the third millennium, Christianity longs to show that its message of love is relevant to all. It travels along different channels of ecclesial allegiance, of theological sensitivities, and of cultural rootedness. Yet all Christians are able to agree and together proclaim that Jesus Christ is the ultimate incarnation of the love of God. If Christ is revealed in this way as the symbol of an absolute love, limitless and open to all the inhabitants of the universe, then we might wonder why Christianity still finds it so hard to witness to the relevance of this fundamen-tal truth. My sense is that, beyond human weakness and the basic incoherence of institutions, Christians fail to achieve their intended goal to witness because of the ambiguity that hobbles their approach to the mystery of Christ.

It is more than ever necessary that theology (discourse about God) should be brought closer to anthropology (discourse about mankind). In other words, Chris-tians and the different Christian Churches must now proclaim Christ as a symbol of the love that humans long to discover, to experience, and to bring about in the reality of their daily lives. If Christ is the historical channel that shows forth the love of God, and if this love does not lay down any historical conditions for it to become real, other than that which derives from its own nature – to love and be loved – I see no reason why Christ should not be able to reveal Himself outside the institutions that explain and protect His mystery. If love is the universal value of humanity, and Christians clearly state that in Christ all is love, then we must surely agree that any human being can know Christ and live in Him if they know and live in love.

So before we agree on who Christ is – a dangerous and near impossible task – men and women in the twenty-first century would do better to agree on the meaning of love. And here, it seems to me that love is not likely to be under-stood in contradictory terms that might defeat its own purpose. In proclaiming Christ, Christians are in effect proclaiming love, and vice versa. All those who believe that love is the ultimate meaning of any human life should not be able any longer to resist opening their hearts to the mystery of Christ. How their faith might translate in terms of affiliation, expression or practical outcome – these all become subsidiary matters, mere add-ons to the fundamental allegiance that brings life to the whole person. It is admittedly not new, in Christian theological discourse, to reinterpret Christ as the manifestation of the love of God. But to free Christ from all the cultural, historical and legal bonds of the Christian religious system is a bold contemporary attempt that requires all baptised Christians to exhibit great courage, sincere solidarity, and especially a deep-seated sense of communion of both heart and mind. And these very laudable attitudes need also to be supported by a genuine attempt to address in intelligible terms the ambient cultural modernity. It could, after all, be a stumbling block to all contemporary theological discourse.

Clearly, then, contemporary Arab Christian theology needs to refresh its con-ceptual and procedural approach. I have in this book recalled reflections that could, if we linger over them, mask the vital importance of a profound theologi-cal conversion among Arab Christians. The whole of this book, indeed, argues for such a conversion. So if I may voice a final wish at the end of this analysis, it would be as follows. Channelling their traditional fears for their own survival, Arab Christians now have the agonising task of bringing together the intercultur-ality and the universality of Christ into a fresh theological formulation; it needs to be one that might speak to the modern Arab mind in such a way that mature, responsible and respectful Arabs might want to engage with it in the hope of reaching abundant fulfilment. The task is becoming ever more pressing. The tasks of conversion and adaptation need to be far more than noisy empty slogans, and they must come to fruition as effective action. Christian faith must no longer be stifled in narrow-minded, collective phobias arbitrarily described as essential to survival. It is high time: the Christian communities of the Arab world must shake off the yoke of inertia and start to build on new ground. The Spirit of God will lead them into the full truth, the one best suited to their Arab world and to their ambition to work for the good of all Arab people. It is only amid such hopes that the 'Arab Christ' can come into being.